Praise for *The New Jim Crow*

"An instant classic."

—Cornel West, from the foreword

"[An] extraordinary book. . . . Michelle Alexander has placed a critical spotlight on a reality our nation can't afford to deny. We ignore her careful research and stay silent about mass incarceration's devastating effects at our own and our nation's peril."

—Marian Wright Edelman

"Striking. . . . Alexander deserves to be compared to Du Bois in her ability to distill and lay out as mighty human drama a complex argument and history."

—Darryl Pinckney, *The New York Review of Books*

"The Bible of a social movement."

—*San Francisco Chronicle*

"A devastating account of a legal system doing its job perfectly well. Alexander looks in detail at what economists usually miss, namely the entire legal structure [and] . . . does a fine job of truth-telling, pointing a finger where it rightly should be pointed: at all of us, liberal and conservative, white and black."

—*Forbes*

"Alexander is absolutely right to fight for what she describes as a 'much needed conversation' about the wide-ranging social costs and divisive racial impact of our criminal-justice policies."

—Ellis Cose, *Newsweek*

"Invaluable . . . a timely and stunning guide to the labyrinth of propaganda, discrimination, and racist policies masquerading under other names that comprises what we call justice in America."

—*Daily Kos*

"A troubling and profoundly *necessary* book."

—*The Miami Herald*

"[An] important book."

—The Baltimore Sun

"A stunning debut."

—Journal of Blacks in Higher Education

"Many critics have cast doubt on the proclamations of racism's erasure in the Obama era, but few have presented a case as powerful as Alexander's."

—In These Times

"[Written] with rare clarity, depth, and candor."

—Counterpunch

"A call to action for everyone concerned with racial justice and an important tool for anyone concerned with understanding and dismantling this oppressive system."

—Sojourners

"Undoubtedly the most important book published in this century about the U.S."

—Birmingham News

"[A] searing indictment of the War on Drugs. . . . If you care even a little about racial justice, *The New Jim Crow* should be on your bookshelf. It is the most important book you will read this year."

—Seattle Post-Intelligencer

"A well-researched book."

—Clarence Page, Chicago Tribune

"Carefully researched, deeply engaging, and thoroughly readable."

—Publishers Weekly (starred review)

"An explosive debut."

—Kirkus Reviews

"[Alexander's] analysis reflects the passion of an advocate and the intellect of a scholar."

—Marc Mauer, executive director of The Sentencing Project and the author of *Race to Incarcerate*

"Michelle Alexander argues convincingly that the huge racial disparity of punishment in America is not the mere result of neutral state action. She sees the rise of mass incarceration as opening up a new front in the historic struggle for racial justice. And she's right. If you care about justice in America, you need to read this book!"

—Glenn C. Loury, professor of economics at Brown University and author of *Race, Incarceration, and American Values*

Michelle Alexander is a highly acclaimed civil rights lawyer, advocate, and legal scholar. As an associate professor of law at Stanford Law School, she directed the Civil Rights Clinic and pursued a research agenda focused on the intersection of race and criminal justice. In 2005, Alexander won a Soros Justice Fellowship that supported the writing of *The New Jim Crow* and accepted a joint appointment at the Kirwan Institute for the Study of Race and Ethnicity and the Moritz College of Law at The Ohio State University, where she currently serves as an associate professor of law. Prior to joining academia, Alexander engaged in civil rights litigation in both the private and nonprofit sector, ultimately serving as the director of the Racial Justice Project for the ACLU of Northern California, where she helped to launch a national campaign against racial profiling. Currently she devotes much of her time to freelance writing, public speaking, supporting groups and organizations engaged in movement-building to end mass incarceration, and caring for her three young children.

Alexander is a graduate of Stanford Law School and Vanderbilt University. She has clerked for Justice Harry A. Blackmun on the U.S. Supreme Court and for Chief Judge Abner Mikva on the D.C. Circuit of the U.S. Court of Appeals, and has appeared as a commentator on CNN and MSNBC, among other media outlets. *The New Jim Crow* is her first book. For more information, visit www.newjimcrow.com. (Photo courtesy of Zócalo Public Square, zocalopublicsquare.org.)

The New Jim Crow

The New Jim Crow

Mass Incarceration in the
Age of Colorblindness

Revised Edition

MICHELLE ALEXANDER

20 YEARS

THE NEW PRESS

Request for permission to reproduce selections from this book should be mailed to:
Permissions Department, The New Press, 38 Greene Street, New York, NY 10013.

Published in the United States by The New Press, New York, 2012
Distributed by Perseus Distribution

LIBRARY OF CONGRESS CATALOGING-IN-PUBLICATION DATA

Alexander, Michelle.
The new Jim Crow : mass incarceration in the age of colorblindness / Michelle Alexander.
p.   cm.
Includes bibliographical references and index.
ISBN 978-1-59558-103-7 (hc. : alk. paper)
1. Criminal justice, Administration of—United States.
2. African American prisoners—United States.   3. Race discrimination—
United States.   4. United States—Race relations.   I. Title.
HV9950.A437 2010
364.973—dc22   2009022519

The New Press publishes books that promote and enrich public discussion and understanding of
the issues vital to our democracy and to a more equitable world. These books are made possible by
the enthusiasm of our readers; the support of a committed group of donors, large and small; the
collaboration of our many partners in the independent media and the not-for-profit sector;
booksellers, who often hand-sell New Press books; librarians; and above all by our authors.

www.thenewpress.com

Composition by NK Graphics
This book was set in Fairfield LH Light

Printed in the United States of America

18   20   19   17

For Nicole, Jonathan, and Corinne

Contents

Foreword

CORNEL WEST

Michelle Alexander's *The New Jim Crow* is the secular bible for a new social movement in early twenty-first-century America. Like C. Vann Woodward's *The Strange Career of Jim Crow*—a book Martin Luther King Jr. called "the historical bible of the Civil Rights Movement"—we are witnessing the unique union of a powerful and poignant text with a democratic awakening focused on the poor and vulnerable in American society. *The New Jim Crow* is an instant classic because it captures the emerging spirit of our age. For too long, there has been no mass fight back against the multileveled assault on poor and vulnerable people, despite the heroic work of intellectual freedom fighters including Marian Wright Edelman, Angela Davis, Loïc Wacquant, Glenn Loury, Marc Mauer, and others. Yet the sleepwalking is slowly but surely coming to a close as more and more fellow citizens realize that the iron cage they inhabit—maybe even a golden cage for the affluent—is still a form of bondage. *The New Jim Crow* is a grand wake-up call in the midst of a long slumber of indifference to the poor and vulnerable. This indifference promotes a superficial ethic of success—money, fame, and pleasure—that leaves too many well-adjusted to injustice. In short, this book is a genuine resurrection of the spirit of Martin Luther King Jr. amid the confusion of the Age of Obama.

While the Age of Obama is a time of historic breakthroughs at the level of racial symbols and political surfaces, Michelle Alexander's magisterial work takes us beyond these breakthroughs to the systemic breakdown of black and poor communities devastated by mass unemployment, social neglect, economic abandonment, and intense police surveillance. Her subtle analysis shifts our attention from the racial symbol of America's achievement to the actual substance of America's shame: the massive use of state power to incarcerate hundreds of thousands of precious poor, black, male (and, increasingly, female) young people in the name of a bogus "War on Drugs." And her nuanced historical narrative tracing the unconscionable treatment and brutal control of black people—slavery, Jim Crow, mass incarceration—takes us beneath the political surfaces and lays bare the structures of a racial caste system alive and well in the age of colorblindness. In fact, the very discourse of colorblindness—created by neoconservatives and neoliberals in order to trivialize and disguise the depths of black suffering in the 1980s and '90s has left America blind to the New Jim Crow. How sad it is that this blindness has persisted under both Republican and Democratic administrations and remains to this day hardly acknowledged or examined in our nation's public discourse.

The New Jim Crow shatters this silence. Once you read it, you have crossed the Rubicon and there is no return to sleepwalking. You are now awakened to a dark and ugly reality that has been in place for decades and that is continuous with the racist underside of American history from the advent of slavery onward. There is no doubt that if young white people were incarcerated at the same rates as young black people, the issue would be a national emergency. But it is also true that if young black middle- and upper-class people were incarcerated at the same rates as young black poor people, black leaders would focus much more on the prison-industrial complex. Again, Michelle Alexander has exposed the class bias of much of black leadership as well as the racial bias of American leadership, for whom the poor and vulnerable of all colors are a low priority. As Alexander puts it in her fiery and bold last chapter, "The Fire This Time" (with echoes from the great James Baldwin!), "It is this failure to care, really care across color lines, that lies at the core of this system of control and every racial caste system that has existed in the United States or anywhere else in the world."

Martin Luther King Jr. called for us to be lovestruck with each other, not colorblind toward each other. To be lovestruck is to care, to have deep compassion, and to be concerned for each and every individual, including the poor and vulnerable. The social movement fanned and fueled by this historic book is a democratic awakening that says we do care, that the racial caste system must be dismantled, that we need a revolution in our warped priorities, a transfer of power from oligarchs to the people—and that we are willing to live and die to make it so!

Preface

This book is not for everyone. I have a specific audience in mind—people who care deeply about racial justice but who, for any number of reasons, do not yet appreciate the magnitude of the crisis faced by communities of color as a result of mass incarceration. In other words, I am writing this book for people like me—the person I was ten years ago. I am also writing it for another audience—those who have been struggling to persuade their friends, neighbors, relatives, teachers, co-workers, or political representatives that something is eerily familiar about the way our criminal justice system operates, something that looks and feels a lot like an era we supposedly left behind, but who have lacked the facts and data to back up their claims. It is my hope and prayer that this book empowers you and allows you to speak your truth with greater conviction, credibility, and courage. Last, but definitely not least, I am writing this book for all those trapped within America's latest caste system. You may be locked up or locked out of mainstream society, but you are not forgotten.

Acknowledgments

It is often said, "It takes a village to raise a child." In my case, it has taken a village to write this book. I gave birth to three children in four years, and in the middle of this burst of joyous activity in our home, I decided to write this book. It was written while feeding babies and during nap times. It was written at odd hours and often when I (and everyone else in the household) had little sleep. Quitting the endeavor was tempting, as writing the book proved far more challenging than I expected. But just when I felt it was too much or too hard, someone I loved would surprise me with generosity and unconditional support; and just when I started to believe the book was not worth the effort, I would receive—out of the blue—a letter from someone behind bars who would remind me of all the reasons that I could not possibly quit, and how fortunate I was to be sitting in the comfort of my home or my office, rather than in a prison cell. My colleagues and publisher supported this effort, too, in ways that far exceeded the call of duty. I want to begin, then, by acknowledging those people who made sure I did not give up—the people who made sure this important story got told.

First on this list is Nancy Rogers, who was dean of the Moritz College of Law at Ohio State University until 2008. Nancy exemplifies outstanding leadership. I will always remember her steadfast encouragement, support, and flexibility, as I labored to juggle my commitments to work and family. Thank you, Nancy, for your faith in me. In this regard, I also want to thank john powell, director of the Kirwan Institute for the Study of Race and

Ethnicity. He immediately understood what I hoped to accomplish with this book and provided critical institutional support.

My husband, Carter Stewart, has been my rock. Without ever once uttering a word of complaint, he has read and reread drafts and rearranged his schedule countless times to care for our children, so that I could make progress with my writing. As a federal prosecutor, he does not share my views about the criminal justice system, but his different worldview has not, even for a moment, compromised his ability to support me, lovingly, at every turn in my efforts to share my truth. I made the best decision of my life when I married him.

My mother and sister, too, have been blessings in my life. Determined to ensure that I actually finished this book, they have exhausted themselves chasing after the little people in my home, who are bundles of joy (and more than a little tiring). Their love and good humor have been food for my soul. Special thanks is also owed Nicole Hanft, whose loving kindness in caring for our children will forever be appreciated.

I deeply regret that I may never be able to thank, in person, Timothy Demetrius Johnson, Tawan Childs, Jacob McNary, Timothy Anderson, and Larry Brown-Austin, who are currently incarcerated. Their kind letters and expressions of gratitude for my work motivated me more than they could possibly know, reminding me that I could not rest until this book was done.

I am also grateful for the support of the Open Society Institute of the Soros Foundation, as well as for the generosity of the many people who have reviewed and commented on portions of the manuscript or contributed to it in some way, including Sharon Davies, Andrew Grant-Thomas, Eavon Mobley, Marc Mauer, Elaine Elinson, Johanna Wu, Steve Menendian, Hiram José Irizarry Osorio, Ruth Peterson, Hasan Jeffries, Shauna Marshall, and Tobias Wolff. My dear friend Maya Harris is owed special thanks for reading multiple drafts of various chapters, never tiring of the revision process. Lucky for me, my sister, Leslie Alexander, is an African American history scholar, so I benefited from her knowledge and critical perspective regarding our nation's racial history. Any errors in fact or judgment are entirely my own, of course. I also want to express my appreciation to my outstanding editor and publisher, Diane Wachtell of The New Press, who believed in this book before I had even written a word (and waited very patiently for the final word to be written).

A number of my former students have made important contributions to this book, including Guylando Moreno, Monica Ramirez, Stephanie Beckstrom, Lacy Sales, Yolanda Miller, Rashida Edmonson, Tanisha Wilburn, Ryan King, Allison Lammers, Danny Goldman, Stephen Kane, Anu Menon, and Lenza McElrath. Many of them worked without pay, simply wanting to contribute to this effort in some way.

I cannot close without acknowledging the invaluable gifts I received from my parents, who ultimately made this book possible by raising me. I inherited determination from my mother, Sandy Alexander, who astounds me with her ability to overcome extraordinary obstacles and meet each day with fresh optimism. I owe my vision for social justice to my father, John Alexander, who was a dreamer and never ceased to challenge me to probe deeper, for greater truth. I wish he were still alive to see this book; though I suspect he knows something of it still. This book is for you, too, Dad. May you rest in peace.

Introduction

Jarvious Cotton cannot vote. Like his father, grandfather, great-grandfather, and great-great-grandfather, he has been denied the right to participate in our electoral democracy. Cotton's family tree tells the story of several generations of black men who were born in the United States but who were denied the most basic freedom that democracy promises—the freedom to vote for those who will make the rules and laws that govern one's life. Cotton's great-great-grandfather could not vote as a slave. His great-grandfather was beaten to death by the Ku Klux Klan for attempting to vote. His grandfather was prevented from voting by Klan intimidation. His father was barred from voting by poll taxes and literacy tests. Today, Jarvious Cotton cannot vote because he, like many black men in the United States, has been labeled a felon and is currently on parole.[1]

Cotton's story illustrates, in many respects, the old adage "The more things change, the more they remain the same." In each generation, new tactics have been used for achieving the same goals—goals shared by the Founding Fathers. Denying African Americans citizenship was deemed essential to the formation of the original union. Hundreds of years later, America is still not an egalitarian democracy. The arguments and rationalizations that have been trotted out in support of racial exclusion and discrimination in its various forms have changed and evolved, but the outcome has remained largely the same. An extraordinary percentage of black men in the United States are legally barred from voting today, just as they have been throughout most of American history. They are also subject to legalized discrimination in employment, housing, education, public benefits, and jury service, just as their parents, grandparents, and great-grandparents once were.

What has changed since the collapse of Jim Crow has less to do with the basic structure of our society than with the language we use to justify it. In the era of colorblindness, it is no longer socially permissible to use race, explicitly, as a justification for discrimination, exclusion, and social contempt. So we don't. Rather than rely on race, we use our criminal justice system to label people of color "criminals" and then engage in all the practices we supposedly left behind. Today it is perfectly legal to discriminate against criminals in nearly all the ways that it was once legal to discriminate against African Americans. Once you're labeled a felon, the old forms of discrimination—employment discrimination, housing discrimination, denial of the right to vote, denial of educational opportunity, denial of food stamps and other public benefits, and exclusion from jury service—are suddenly legal. As a criminal, you have scarcely more rights, and arguably less respect, than a black man living in Alabama at the height of Jim Crow. We have not ended racial caste in America; we have merely redesigned it.

I reached the conclusions presented in this book reluctantly. Ten years ago, I would have argued strenuously against the central claim made here—namely, that something akin to a racial caste system currently exists in the United States. Indeed, if Barack Obama had been elected president back then, I would have argued that his election marked the nation's triumph over racial caste—the final nail in the coffin of Jim Crow. My elation would have been tempered by the distance yet to be traveled to reach the promised land of racial justice in America, but my conviction that nothing remotely similar to Jim Crow exists in this country would have been steadfast.

Today my elation over Obama's election is tempered by a far more sobering awareness. As an African American woman, with three young children who will never know a world in which a black man could not be president of the United States, I was beyond thrilled on election night. Yet when I walked out of the election night party, full of hope and enthusiasm, I was immediately reminded of the harsh realities of the New Jim Crow. A black man was on his knees in the gutter, hands cuffed behind his back, as several police officers stood around him talking, joking, and ignoring his human existence. People poured out of the building; many stared for a moment at the black man cowering in the street, and then averted their gaze. What did the election of Barack Obama mean for him?

Like many civil rights lawyers, I was inspired to attend law school by the civil rights victories of the 1950s and 1960s. Even in the face of growing social and political opposition to remedial policies such as affirmative action, I clung to the notion that the evils of Jim Crow are behind us and that, while we have a long way to go to fulfill the dream of an egalitarian, multiracial democracy, we have made real progress and are now struggling to hold on to the gains of the past. I thought my job as a civil rights lawyer was to join with the allies of racial progress to resist attacks on affirmative action and to eliminate the vestiges of Jim Crow segregation, including our still separate and unequal system of education. I understood the problems plaguing poor communities of color, including problems associated with crime and rising incarceration rates, to be a function of poverty and lack of access to quality education—the continuing legacy of slavery and Jim Crow. Never did I seriously consider the possibility that a new racial caste system was operating in this country. The new system had been developed and implemented swiftly, and it was largely invisible, even to people, like me, who spent most of their waking hours fighting for justice.

I first encountered the idea of a new racial caste system more than a decade ago, when a bright orange poster caught my eye. I was rushing to catch the bus, and I noticed a sign stapled to a telephone pole that screamed in large bold print: THE DRUG WAR IS THE NEW JIM CROW. I paused for a moment and skimmed the text of the flyer. Some radical group was holding a community meeting about police brutality, the new three-strikes law in California, and the expansion of America's prison system. The meeting was being held at a small community church a few blocks away; it had seating capacity for no more than fifty people. I sighed, and muttered to myself something like, "Yeah, the criminal justice system is racist in many ways, but it really doesn't help to make such an absurd comparison. People will just think you're crazy." I then crossed the street and hopped on the bus. I was headed to my new job, director of the Racial Justice Project of the American Civil Liberties Union (ACLU) in Northern California.

When I began my work at the ACLU, I assumed that the criminal justice system had problems of racial bias, much in the same way that all major institutions in our society are plagued with problems associated with conscious and unconscious bias. As a lawyer who had litigated numerous class-action employment-discrimination cases, I understood well the many ways in which racial stereotyping can permeate subjective decision-making processes at all levels of an organization, with devastating consequences. I was familiar with the challenges associated with reforming institutions in which racial stratification is thought to be normal—the natural consequence of differences in education, culture, motivation, and, some still believe, innate ability. While at the ACLU, I shifted my focus from employment discrimination to criminal justice reform and dedicated myself to the task of working with others to identify and eliminate racial bias whenever and wherever it reared its ugly head.

By the time I left the ACLU, I had come to suspect that I was wrong about the criminal justice system. It was not just another institution infected with racial bias but rather a different beast entirely. The activists who posted the sign on the telephone pole were not crazy; nor were the smattering of lawyers and advocates around the country who were beginning to connect the dots between our current system of mass incarceration and earlier forms of social control. Quite belatedly, I came to see that mass incarceration in the United States had, in fact, emerged as a stunningly comprehensive and well-disguised system of racialized social control that functions in a manner strikingly similar to Jim Crow.

In my experience, people who have been incarcerated rarely have difficulty identifying the parallels between these systems of social control. Once they are released, they are often denied the right to vote, excluded from juries, and relegated to a racially segregated and subordinated existence. Through a web of laws, regulations, and informal rules, all of which are powerfully reinforced by social stigma, they are confined to the margins of mainstream society and denied access to the mainstream economy. They are legally denied the ability to obtain employment, housing, and public benefits—much as African Americans were once forced into a segregated, second-class citizenship in the Jim Crow era.

Those of us who have viewed that world from a comfortable distance—yet sympathize with the plight of the so-called underclass—tend to interpret the experience of those caught up in the criminal justice system primarily through the lens of popularized social science, attributing the staggering increase in incarceration rates in communities of color to the predictable, though unfortunate, consequences of poverty, racial segregation, unequal educational opportunities, and the presumed realities of the drug market, including the mistaken belief that most drug dealers are black or brown. Occasionally, in the course of my work, someone would make a remark suggesting that perhaps the War on Drugs is a racist conspiracy to put blacks back in their place. This type of remark was invariably accompanied by nervous laughter, intended to convey the impression that although the idea had crossed their minds, it was not an idea a reasonable person would take seriously.

Most people assume the War on Drugs was launched in response to the crisis caused by crack cocaine in inner-city neighborhoods. This view holds that the racial disparities in drug convictions and sentences, as well as the rapid explosion of the prison population, reflect nothing more than the government's zealous—but benign—efforts to address rampant drug crime in poor, minority neighborhoods. This view, while understandable, given the sensational media coverage of crack in the 1980s and 1990s, is simply wrong.

While it is true that the publicity surrounding crack cocaine led to a dramatic increase in funding for the drug war (as well as to sentencing policies that greatly exacerbated racial disparities in incarceration rates), there is no truth to the notion that the War on Drugs was launched in response to crack cocaine. President Ronald Reagan officially announced the current drug war in 1982, before crack became an issue in the media or a crisis in poor black neighborhoods. A few years after the drug war was declared, crack began to spread rapidly in the poor black neighborhoods of Los Angeles and later emerged in cities across the country.[2] The Reagan administration hired staff to publicize the emergence of crack cocaine in 1985 as part of a strategic effort to build public and legislative support for the war.[3] The media campaign was an extraordinary success. Almost overnight, the media was saturated with images of black "crack whores," "crack dealers," and "crack babies"— images that seemed to confirm the worst negative racial stereotypes about impoverished inner-city residents. The media bonanza surrounding the "new demon drug" helped to catapult the War on Drugs from an ambitious federal policy to an actual war.

The timing of the crack crisis helped to fuel conspiracy theories and general speculation in poor black communities that the War on Drugs was part of a genocidal plan by the government to destroy black people in the United States. From the outset, stories circulated on the street that crack and other drugs were being brought into black neighborhoods by the CIA. Eventually, even the Urban League came to take the claims of genocide seriously. In its 1990 report "The State of Black America," it stated: "There is at least one concept that must be recognized if one is to see the pervasive and insidious nature of the drug problem for the African American community. Though difficult to accept, that is the concept of genocide."[4] While the conspiracy theories were initially dismissed as far-fetched, if not downright loony, the word on the street turned out to be right, at least to a point. The CIA admitted in 1998 that guerrilla armies it actively supported in Nicaragua were smuggling illegal drugs into the United States—drugs that were making their way onto the streets of inner-city black neighborhoods in the form of crack cocaine. The CIA also admitted that, in the midst of the War on Drugs, it blocked law enforcement efforts to investigate illegal drug networks that were helping to fund its covert war in Nicaragua.[5]

It bears emphasis that the CIA never admitted (nor has any evidence been revealed to support the claim) that it intentionally sought the destruction of the black community by allowing illegal drugs to be smuggled into the United States. Nonetheless, conspiracy theorists surely must be forgiven for their bold accusation of genocide, in light of the devastation wrought by crack cocaine and the drug war, and the odd coincidence that an illegal drug crisis suddenly appeared in the black community after—not before—a drug war had been declared. In fact, the War on Drugs began at a time when illegal drug use was on the decline.[6] During this same time period, however, a war was declared, causing arrests and convictions for drug offenses to skyrocket, especially among people of color.

The impact of the drug war has been astounding. In less than thirty years, the U.S penal population exploded from around 300,000 to more than 2 million, with drug convictions accounting for the majority of the increase.[7] The United States now has the highest rate of incarceration in the world, dwarfing the rates of nearly every developed country, even surpassing those in highly repressive regimes like Russia, China, and Iran. In Germany, 93 people are in prison for every 100,000 adults and children. In the United States, the rate is roughly eight times that, or 750 per 100,000.[8]

The racial dimension of mass incarceration is its most striking feature. No other country in the world imprisons so many of its racial or ethnic minorities. The United States imprisons a larger percentage of its black population than South Africa did at the height of apartheid. In Washington, D.C., our nation's capitol, it is estimated that three out of four young black men (and nearly all those in the poorest neighborhoods) can expect to serve time in prison.[9] Similar rates of incarceration can be found in black communities across America.

These stark racial disparities cannot be explained by rates of drug crime. Studies show that people of all colors *use and sell* illegal drugs at remarkably similar rates.[10] If there are significant differences in the surveys to be found, they frequently suggest that whites, particularly white youth, are more likely to engage in drug crime than people of color.[11] That is not what one would guess, however, when entering our nation's prisons and jails, which are overflowing with black and brown drug offenders. In some states, black men have been admitted to prison on drug charges at rates twenty to fifty times greater than those of white men.[12] And in major cities wracked by the drug war, as many as 80 percent of young African American men now have criminal records and are thus subject to legalized discrimination for the rest of their lives.[13] These young men are part of a growing undercaste, permanently locked up and locked out of mainstream society.

It may be surprising to some that drug crime was declining, not rising, when a drug war was declared. From a historical perspective, however, the lack of correlation between crime and punishment is nothing new. Sociologists have frequently observed that governments use punishment primarily as a tool of social control, and thus the extent or severity of punishment is often unrelated to actual crime patterns. Michael Tonry explains in *Thinking About Crime*: "Governments decide how much punishment they want, and these decisions are in no simple way related to crime rates."[14] This fact, he points out, can be seen most clearly by putting crime and punishment in comparative perspective. Although crime rates in the United States have not been markedly higher than those of other Western countries, the rate of incarceration has soared in the United States while it has remained stable or declined in other countries. Between 1960 and 1990, for example, official crime rates in Finland, Germany, and the United States were close to identical. Yet the U.S. incarceration rate quadrupled, the Finnish rate fell by 60 percent, and the German rate was stable in that period.[15] Despite similar crime rates, each government chose to impose different levels of punishment.

Today, due to recent declines, U.S. crime rates have dipped below the international norm. Nevertheless, the United States now boasts an incarceration

rate that is six to ten times greater than that of other industrialized nations[16]—
a development directly traceable to the drug war. The only country in the
world that even comes close to the American rate of incarceration is Russia,
and no other country in the world incarcerates such an astonishing percentage of its racial or ethnic minorities.

The stark and sobering reality is that, for reasons largely unrelated to actual crime trends, the American penal system has emerged as a system of
social control unparalleled in world history. And while the size of the system
alone might suggest that it would touch the lives of most Americans, the primary targets of its control can be defined largely by race. This is an astonishing development, especially given that as recently as the mid-1970s, the
most well-respected criminologists were predicting that the prison system
would soon fade away. Prison did not deter crime significantly, many experts
concluded. Those who had meaningful economic and social opportunities
were unlikely to commit crimes regardless of the penalty, while those who
went to prison were far more likely to commit crimes again in the future.
The growing consensus among experts was perhaps best reflected by the
National Advisory Commission on Criminal Justice Standards and Goals,
which issued a recommendation in 1973 that "no new institutions for adults
should be built and existing institutions for juveniles should be closed."[17]
This recommendation was based on their finding that "the prison, the refor-
matory and the jail have achieved only a shocking record of failure. There is
overwhelming evidence that these institutions create crime rather than prevent it."[18]

These days, activists who advocate "a world without prisons" are often
dismissed as quacks, but only a few decades ago, the notion that our society
would be much better off without prisons—and that the end of prisons was
more or less inevitable—not only dominated mainstream academic discourse in the field of criminology but also inspired a national campaign by
reformers demanding a moratorium on prison construction. Marc Mauer,
the executive director of the Sentencing Project, notes that what is most remarkable about the moratorium campaign in retrospect is the context of imprisonment at the time. In 1972, fewer than 350,000 people were being
held in prisons and jails nationwide, compared with more than 2 million
people today. The rate of incarceration in 1972 was at a level so low that it
no longer seems in the realm of possibility, but for moratorium supporters,

that magnitude of imprisonment was egregiously high. "Supporters of the moratorium effort can be forgiven for being so naïve," Mauer suggests, "since the prison expansion that was about to take place was unprecedented in human history."[19] No one imagined that the prison population would more than quintuple in their lifetime. It seemed far more likely that prisons would fade away.

Far from fading away, it appears that prisons are here to stay. And despite the unprecedented levels of incarceration in the African American community, the civil rights community is oddly quiet. One in three young African American men will serve time in prison if current trends continue, and in some cities more than half of all young adult black men are currently under correctional control—in prison or jail, on probation or parole.[20] Yet mass incarceration tends to be categorized as a criminal justice issue as opposed to a racial justice or civil rights issue (or crisis).

The attention of civil rights advocates has been largely devoted to other issues, such as affirmative action. During the past twenty years, virtually every progressive, national civil rights organization in the country has mobilized and rallied in defense of affirmative action. The struggle to preserve affirmative action in higher education, and thus maintain diversity in the nation's most elite colleges and universities, has consumed much of the attention and resources of the civil rights community and dominated racial justice discourse in the mainstream media, leading the general public to believe that affirmative action is the main battlefront in U.S. race relations—even as our prisons fill with black and brown men.

My own experience reflects this dynamic. When I first joined the ACLU, no one imagined that the Racial Justice Project would focus its attention on criminal justice reform. The ACLU was engaged in important criminal justice reform work, but no one suspected that work would eventually become central to the agenda of the Racial Justice Project. The assumption was that the project would concentrate its efforts on defending affirmative action. Shortly after leaving the ACLU, I joined the board of directors of the Lawyers' Committee for Civil Rights of the San Francisco Bay Area. Although the organization included racial justice among its core priorities, reform of the criminal justice system was not a major part of its racial justice work. It was not alone.

In January 2008, the Leadership Conference on Civil Rights—an organiza-

tion composed of the leadership of more than 180 civil rights organizations—
sent a letter to its allies and supporters informing them of a major initiative
to document the voting record of members of Congress. The letter explained
that its forthcoming report would show "how each representative and senator cast his or her vote on some of the most important civil rights issues of
2007, including voting rights, affirmative action, immigration, nominations,
education, hate crimes, employment, health, housing, and poverty." Criminal justice issues did not make the list. That same broad-based coalition
organized a major conference in October 2007, entitled Why We Can't Wait:
Reversing the Retreat on Civil Rights, which included panels discussing
school integration, employment discrimination, housing and lending discrimination, economic justice, environmental justice, disability rights, age
discrimination, and immigrants' rights. Not a single panel was devoted to
criminal justice reform.

The elected leaders of the African American community have a much
broader mandate than civil rights groups, but they, too, frequently overlook
criminal justice. In January 2009, for example, the Congressional Black
Caucus sent a letter to hundreds of community and organization leaders
who have worked with the caucus over the years, soliciting general information about them and requesting that they identify their priorities. More than
thirty-five topics were listed as areas of potential special interest, including
taxes, defense, immigration, agriculture, housing, banking, higher education, multimedia, transportation and infrastructure, women, seniors, nutri-
tion, faith initiatives, civil rights, census, economic security, and emerging
leaders. No mention was made of criminal justice. "Re-entry" was listed, but
a community leader who was interested in criminal justice reform had to
check the box labeled "other."

This is not to say that important criminal justice reform work has not been
done. Civil rights advocates have organized vigorous challenges to specific
aspects of the new caste system. One notable example is the successful
challenge led by the NAACP Legal Defense Fund to a racist drug sting operation in Tulia, Texas. The 1999 drug bust incarcerated almost 15 percent
of the black population of the town, based on the uncorroborated false
testimony of a single informant hired by the sheriff of Tulia. More recently,
civil rights groups around the country have helped to launch legal attacks
and vibrant grassroots campaigns against felon disenfranchisement laws and

have strenuously opposed discriminatory crack sentencing laws and guide-lines, as well as "zero tolerance" policies that effectively funnel youth of color from schools to jails. The national ACLU recently developed a racial justice program that includes criminal justice issues among its core priori-ties and has created a promising Drug Law Reform Project. And thanks to the aggressive advocacy of the ACLU, NAACP, and other civil rights organi-zations around the country, racial profiling is widely condemned, even by members of law enforcement who once openly embraced the practice.

Still, despite these significant developments, there seems to be a lack of appreciation for the enormity of the crisis at hand. There is no broad-based movement brewing to end mass incarceration and no advocacy effort that approaches in scale the fight to preserve affirmative action. There also re-mains a persistent tendency in the civil rights community to treat the crimi-nal justice system as just another institution infected with lingering racial bias. The NAACP's website offers one example. As recently as May 2008, one could find a brief introduction to the organization's criminal justice work in the section entitled Legal Department. The introduction explained that "despite the civil rights victories of our past, racial prejudice still pervades the criminal justice system." Visitors to the website were urged to join the NAACP in order to "protect the hard-earned civil rights gains of the past three decades." No one visiting the website would learn that the mass in-carceration of African Americans had already eviscerated many of the hard-earned gains it urged its members to protect.

Imagine if civil rights organizations and African American leaders in the 1940s had not placed Jim Crow segregation at the forefront of their racial justice agenda. It would have seemed absurd, given that racial segregation was the primary vehicle of racialized social control in the United States during that period. This book argues that mass incarceration is, metaphori-cally, the New Jim Crow and that all those who care about social justice should fully commit themselves to dismantling this new racial caste system. Mass incarceration—not attacks on affirmative action or lax civil rights enforcement—is the most damaging manifestation of the backlash against the Civil Rights Movement. The popular narrative that emphasizes the death of slavery and Jim Crow and celebrates the nation's "triumph over race" with the election of Barack Obama, is dangerously misguided. The colorblind pub-lic consensus that prevails in America today—i.e., the widespread belief that race no longer matters—has blinded us to the realities of race in our society and facilitated the emergence of a new caste system.

Clearly, much has changed in my thinking about the criminal justice system since I passed that bright orange poster stapled to a telephone pole ten years ago. For me, the new caste system is now as obvious as my own face in the mirror. Like an optical illusion—one in which the embedded image is impossible to see until its outline is identified—the new caste system lurks invisibly within the maze of rationalizations we have developed for persistent racial inequality. It is possible—quite easy, in fact—never to see the embedded reality. Only after years of working on criminal justice reform did my own focus finally shift, and then the rigid caste system slowly came into view. Eventually it became obvious. Now it seems odd that I could not see it before.

Knowing as I do the difficulty of seeing what most everyone insists does not exist, I anticipate that this book will be met with skepticism or something worse. For some, the characterization of mass incarceration as a "racial caste system" may seem like a gross exaggeration, if not hyperbole. Yes, we may have "classes" in the United States—vaguely defined upper, middle, and lower classes—and we may even have an "underclass" (a group so estranged from mainstream society that it is no longer in reach of the mythical ladder of opportunity), but we do not, many will insist, have anything in this country that resembles a "caste."

The aim of this book is not to venture into the long-running, vigorous debate in the scholarly literature regarding what does and does not constitute a caste system. I use the term *racial caste* in this book the way it is used in common parlance to denote a stigmatized racial group locked into an inferior position by law and custom. Jim Crow and slavery were caste systems. So is our current system of mass incarceration.

It may be helpful, in attempting to understand the basic nature of the new caste system, to think of the criminal justice system—the entire collection of institutions and practices that comprise it—not as an independent system but rather as a *gateway* into a much larger system of racial stigmatization and permanent marginalization. This larger system, referred to here as mass incarceration, is a system that locks people not only behind actual bars in actual prisons, but also behind virtual bars and virtual walls—walls that are invisible to the naked eye but function nearly as effectively as Jim Crow laws once did at locking people of color into a permanent second-class citizenship. The term *mass incarceration* refers not only to the criminal justice system but also to the larger web of laws, rules, policies, and customs that control those labeled criminals both in and out of prison. Once released, former prisoners enter a hidden underworld of legalized discrimination and permanent social exclusion. They are members of America's new undercaste.

The language of caste may well seem foreign or unfamiliar to some. Public discussions about racial caste in America are relatively rare. We avoid talking about caste in our society because we are ashamed of our racial history. We also avoid talking about race. We even avoid talking about class. Conversations about class are resisted in part because there is a tendency to imagine that one's class reflects upon one's character. What is key to America's understanding of class is the persistent belief—despite all evidence to the contrary—that anyone, with the proper discipline and drive, can move from a lower class to a higher class. We recognize that mobility may be difficult, but the key to our collective self-image is the assumption that mobility is always possible, so failure to move up reflects on one's character. By extension, the failure of a race or ethnic group to move up reflects very poorly on the group as a whole.

What is completely missed in the rare public debates today about the plight of African Americans is that a huge percentage of them are not free to move up at all. It is not just that they lack opportunity, attend poor schools, or are plagued by poverty. They are barred by law from doing so. And the major institutions with which they come into contact are designed to prevent their mobility. To put the matter starkly: The current system of control permanently locks a huge percentage of the African American community out of the mainstream society and economy. The system operates through our criminal justice institutions, but it functions more like a caste system than a system of crime control. Viewed from this perspective, the so-called underclass is better understood as an *undercaste*—a lower caste of individuals who are permanently barred by law and custom from mainstream society. Although this new system of racialized social control purports to be colorblind, it creates and maintains racial hierarchy much as earlier systems of control did. Like Jim Crow (and slavery), mass incarceration operates as a tightly networked system of laws, policies, customs, and institutions that operate collectively to ensure the subordinate status of a group defined largely by race.

This argument may be particularly hard to swallow given the election of Barack Obama. Many will wonder how a nation that just elected its first black president could possibly have a racial caste system. It's a fair question. But as discussed in chapter 6, there is no inconsistency whatsoever between the election of Barack Obama to the highest office in the land and the existence of a racial caste system in the era of colorblindness. The current system of control depends on black exceptionalism; it is not disproved or undermined by it. Others may wonder how a racial caste system could exist when most Americans—of all colors—oppose race discrimination and endorse colorblindness. Yet as we shall see in the pages that follow, racial caste systems do not require racial hostility or overt bigotry to thrive. They need only racial indifference, as Martin Luther King Jr. warned more than forty-five years ago.

The recent decisions by some state legislatures, most notably New York's, to repeal or reduce mandatory drug sentencing laws have led some to believe that the system of racial control described in this book is already fading away. Such a conclusion, I believe, is a serious mistake. Many of the states that have reconsidered their harsh sentencing schemes have done so not out of concern for the lives and families that have been destroyed by these laws or the racial dimensions of the drug war, but out of concern for bursting state budgets in a time of economic recession. In other words, the racial ideology that gave rise to these laws remains largely undisturbed. Changing economic conditions or rising crime rates could easily result in a reversal of fortunes for those who commit drug crimes, particularly if the drug criminals are perceived to be black and brown. Equally important to understand is this: Merely reducing sentence length, by itself, does not disturb the basic architecture of the New Jim Crow. So long as large numbers of African Americans continue to be arrested and labeled drug criminals, they will continue to be relegated to a permanent second-class status upon their release, no matter how much (or how little) time they spend behind bars. The system of mass incarceration is based on the prison label, not prison time.

Skepticism about the claims made here is warranted. There are important differences, to be sure, among mass incarceration, Jim Crow, and slavery—the three major racialized systems of control adopted in the United States to date. Failure to acknowledge the relevant differences, as well as their implications, would be a disservice to racial justice discourse. Many of the differences are not as dramatic as they initially appear, however; others serve to illustrate the ways in which systems of racialized social control have managed to morph, evolve, and adapt to changes in the political, social, and legal context over time. Ultimately, I believe that the similarities between these systems of control overwhelm the differences and that mass incarceration, like its predecessors, has been largely immunized from legal challenge. If this claim is substantially correct, the implications for racial justice advocacy are profound.

With the benefit of hindsight, surely we can see that piecemeal policy reform or litigation alone would have been a futile approach to dismantling Jim Crow segregation. While those strategies certainly had their place, the Civil Rights Act of 1964 and the concomitant cultural shift would never have occurred without the cultivation of a critical political consciousness in the African American community and the widespread, strategic activism that flowed from it. Likewise, the notion that the *New* Jim Crow can ever be dismantled through traditional litigation and policy-reform strategies that are wholly disconnected from a major social movement seems fundamentally misguided.

Such a movement is impossible, though, if those most committed to abolishing racial hierarchy continue to talk and behave as if a state-sponsored racial caste system no longer exists. If we continue to tell ourselves the popular myths about racial progress or, worse yet, if we say to ourselves that the problem of mass incarceration is just too big, too daunting for us to do anything about and that we should instead direct our energies to battles that might be more easily won, history will judge us harshly. A human rights nightmare is occurring on our watch.

A new social consensus must be forged about race and the role of race in defining the basic structure of our society, if we hope ever to abolish the New Jim Crow. This new consensus must begin with dialogue, a conversation that fosters a critical consciousness, a key prerequisite to effective social action. This book is an attempt to ensure that the conversation does not end with nervous laughter.

It is not possible to write a relatively short book that explores all aspects of the phenomenon of mass incarceration and its implications for racial justice. No attempt has been made to do so here. This book paints with a broad brush, and as a result, many important issues have not received the attention they deserve. For example, relatively little is said here about the unique experience of women, Latinos, and immigrants in the criminal justice system, though these groups are particularly vulnerable to the worst abuses and suffer in ways that are important and distinct. This book focuses on the experience of African American men in the new caste system. I hope other scholars and advocates will pick up where the book leaves off and develop the critique more fully or apply the themes sketched here to other groups and other contexts.

What this book is intended to do—the only thing it is intended to do—is to stimulate a much-needed conversation about the role of the criminal justice system in creating and perpetuating racial hierarchy in the United States. The fate of millions of people—indeed the future of the black community itself—may depend on the willingness of those who care about racial justice to re-examine their basic assumptions about the role of the criminal justice system in our society. The fact that more than half of the young black men in many large American cities are currently under the control of the criminal justice system (or saddled with criminal records) is not—as many argue—just a symptom of poverty or poor choices, but rather evidence of a new racial caste system at work.

Chapter 1 begins our journey. It briefly reviews the history of racialized social control in the United States, answering the basic question: How did we get here? The chapter describes the control of African Americans through racial caste systems, such as slavery and Jim Crow, which appear to die but then are reborn in new form, tailored to the needs and constraints of the time. As we shall see, there is a certain pattern to the births and deaths of racial caste in America. Time and again, the most ardent proponents of racial hierarchy have succeeded in creating new caste systems by triggering a collapse of resistance across the political spectrum. This feat has been achieved largely by appealing to the racism and vulnerability of lower-class whites, a group of people who are understandably eager to ensure that they never find themselves trapped at the bottom of the American totem pole. This pattern, dating back to slavery, has birthed yet another racial caste system in the United States: mass incarceration.

The structure of mass incarceration is described in some detail in chapter 2, with a focus on the War on Drugs. Few legal rules meaningfully constrain the police in the drug war, and enormous financial incentives have been granted to law enforcement to engage in mass drug arrests through military-style tactics. Once swept into the system, one's chances of ever being truly free are slim, often to the vanishing point. Defendants are typically denied meaningful legal representation, pressured by the threat of lengthy sentences into a plea bargain, and then placed under formal control—in prison or jail, on probation or parole. Upon release, ex-offenders are discriminated against, legally, for the rest of their lives, and most will eventually return to prison. They are members of America's new undercaste.

Chapter 3 turns our attention to the role of race in the U.S. criminal justice system. It describes the method to the madness—how a formally race-neutral criminal justice system can manage to round up, arrest, and imprison an extraordinary number of black and brown men, when people of color are actually no more likely to be guilty of drug crimes and many other offenses than whites. This chapter debunks the notion that rates of black imprisonment can be explained by crime rates and identifies the huge racial disparities at every stage of the criminal justice process—from the initial stop, search, and arrest to the plea bargaining and sentencing phases. In short, the chapter explains how the legal rules that structure the system guarantee discriminatory results. These legal rules ensure that the undercaste is overwhelmingly black and brown.

Chapter 4 considers how the caste system operates once people are released from prison. In many respects, release from prison does not represent the beginning of freedom but instead a cruel new phase of stigmatization and control. Myriad laws, rules, and regulations discriminate against ex-offenders and effectively prevent their meaningful re-integration into the mainstream economy and society. I argue that the shame and stigma of the "prison label" is, in many respects, more damaging to the African American community than the shame and stigma associated with Jim Crow. The criminalization and demonization of black men has turned the black community against itself, unraveling community and family relationships, decimating networks of mutual support, and intensifying the shame and self-hate experienced by the current pariah caste.

The many parallels between mass incarceration and Jim Crow are explored in chapter 5. The most obvious parallel is legalized discrimination. Like Jim Crow, mass incarceration marginalizes large segments of the African American community, segregates them physically (in prisons, jails, and ghettos), and then authorizes discrimination against them in voting, employment, housing, education, public benefits, and jury service. The federal court system has effectively immunized the current system from challenges on the grounds of racial bias, much as earlier systems of control were protected and endorsed by the U.S. Supreme Court. The parallels do not end there, however. Mass incarceration, like Jim Crow, helps to define the meaning and significance of race in America. Indeed, the stigma of criminality functions in much the same way that the stigma of race once did. It justifies a legal, social, and economic boundary between "us" and "them." Chapter 5 also explores some of the differences among slavery, Jim Crow, and mass incarceration, most significantly the fact that mass incarceration is designed to warehouse a population deemed disposable—unnecessary to the functioning of the new global economy—while earlier systems of control were designed to exploit and control black labor. In addition, the chapter discusses the experience of white people in this new caste system; although they have not been the primary targets of the drug war, they have been harmed by it—a powerful illustration of how a racial state can harm people of all colors. Finally, this chapter responds to skeptics who claim that mass incarceration cannot be understood as a racial caste system because many "get tough on crime" policies are supported by African Americans. Many of these claims, I note, are no more persuasive today than arguments made a hundred years ago by blacks and whites who claimed that racial segregation simply reflected "reality," not racial animus, and that African Americans would be better off not challenging the Jim Crow system but should focus instead on improving themselves within it. Throughout our history, there have been African Americans who, for a variety of reasons, have defended or been complicit with the prevailing system of control.

Chapter 6 reflects on what acknowledging the presence of the New Jim Crow means for the future of civil rights advocacy. I argue that nothing short of a major social movement can successfully dismantle the new caste system. Meaningful reforms can be achieved without such a movement, but unless the public consensus supporting the current system is completely overturned, the basic structure of the new caste system will remain intact. Building a broad-based social movement, however, is not enough. It is not nearly enough to persuade mainstream voters that we have relied too heavily on incarceration or that drug abuse is a public health problem, not a crime. If the movement that emerges to challenge mass incarceration fails to confront squarely the critical role of race in the basic structure of our society, and if it fails to cultivate an ethic of genuine care, compassion, and concern for every human being—of every class, race, and nationality—within our nation's borders (including poor whites, who are often pitted against poor people of color), the collapse of mass incarceration will not mean the death of racial caste in America. Inevitably a new system of racialized social control will emerge—one that we cannot foresee, just as the current system of mass incarceration was not predicted by anyone thirty years ago. No task is more urgent for racial justice advocates today than ensuring that America's current racial caste system is its last.

1

The Rebirth of Caste

[T]he slave went free; stood a brief moment in the sun; then moved back again toward slavery.

—W.E.B Du Bois, *Black Reconstruction in America*

For more than one hundred years, scholars have written about the illusory nature of the Emancipation Proclamation. President Abraham Lincoln issued a declaration purporting to free slaves held in Southern Confederate states, but not a single black slave was actually free to walk away from a master in those states as a result. A civil war had to be won first, hundreds of thousands of lives lost, and then—only then—were slaves across the South set free. Even that freedom proved illusory, though. As W.E.B. Du Bois eloquently reminds us, former slaves had "a brief moment in the sun" before they were returned to a status akin to slavery. Constitutional amendments guaranteeing African Americans "equal protection of the laws" and the right to vote proved as impotent as the Emancipation Proclamation once a white backlash against Reconstruction gained steam. Black people found themselves yet again powerless and relegated to convict leasing camps that were, in many ways, worse than slavery. Sunshine gave way to darkness, and the Jim Crow system of segregation emerged—a system that put black people nearly back where they began, in a subordinate racial caste.

Few find it surprising that Jim Crow arose following the collapse of slavery. The development is described in history books as regrettable but predictable, given the virulent racism that gripped the South and the political dynamics of the time. What is remarkable is that hardly anyone seems to imagine that similar political dynamics may have produced another caste system in the years following the collapse of Jim Crow—one that exists today. The story that is told during Black History Month is one of triumph; the system of racial caste is officially dead and buried. Suggestions to the contrary are frequently met with shocked disbelief. The standard reply is: "How can you say that a racial caste system exists today? Just look at Barack Obama! Just look at Oprah Winfrey!"

The fact that some African Americans have experienced great success in recent years does not mean that something akin to a racial caste system no longer exists. No caste system in the United States has ever governed all black people; there have always been "free blacks" and black success stories, even during slavery and Jim Crow. The superlative nature of individual black achievement today in formerly white domains is a good indicator that the old Jim Crow is dead, but it does not necessarily mean the end of racial caste. If history is any guide, it may have simply taken a different form.

Any candid observer of American racial history must acknowledge that racism is highly adaptable. The rules and reasons the political system employs to enforce status relations of any kind, including racial hierarchy, evolve and change as they are challenged. The valiant efforts to abolish slavery and Jim Crow and to achieve greater racial equality have brought about significant changes in the legal framework of American society—new "rules of the game," so to speak. These new rules have been justified by new rhetoric, new language, and a new social consensus, while producing many of the same results. This dynamic, which legal scholar Reva Siegel has dubbed "preservation through transformation," is the process through which white privilege is maintained, though the rules and rhetoric change.[1]

This process, though difficult to recognize at any given moment, is easier to see in retrospect. Since the nation's founding, African Americans repeatedly have been controlled through institutions such as slavery and Jim Crow, which appear to die, but then are reborn in new form, tailored to the needs and constraints of the time. As described in the pages that follow, there is a certain pattern to this cycle. Following the collapse of each system of control, there has been a period of confusion—transition—in which those who are most committed to racial hierarchy search for new means to achieve their goals within the rules of the game as currently defined. It is during this period of uncertainty that the backlash intensifies and a new form of racialized social control begins to take hold. The adoption of the new system of control is never inevitable, but to date it has never been avoided. The most ardent proponents of racial hierarchy have consistently succeeded in implementing new racial caste systems by triggering a collapse of resistance across the political spectrum. This feat has been achieved largely by appealing to the racism and vulnerability of lower-class whites, a group of people who are understandably eager to ensure that they never find themselves trapped at the bottom of the American hierarchy.

The emergence of each new system of control may seem sudden, but history shows that the seeds are planted long before each new institution begins to grow. For example, although it is common to think of the Jim Crow regime following immediately on the heels of Reconstruction, the truth is more complicated. And while it is generally believed that the backlash against the Civil Rights Movement is defined primarily by the rollback of affirmative action and the undermining of federal civil rights legislation by a hostile judiciary, the seeds of the new system of control—mass incarceration—were planted during the Civil Rights Movement itself, when it became clear that the old caste system was crumbling and a new one would have to take its place.

With each reincarnation of racial caste, the new system, as sociologist Loïc Wacquant puts it, "is less total, less capable of encompassing and controlling the entire race."[2] However, any notion that this evolution reflects some kind of linear progress would be misguided, for it is not at all obvious that it would be better to be incarcerated for life for a minor drug offense than to live with one's family, earning an honest wage under the Jim Crow regime—notwithstanding the ever-present threat of the Klan. Moreover, as the systems of control have evolved, they have become perfected, arguably more resilient to challenge, and thus capable of enduring for generations to come. The story of the political and economic underpinnings of the nation's founding sheds some light on these recurring themes in our history and the reasons new racial caste systems continue to be born.

The Birth of Slavery

Back there, before Jim Crow, before the invention of the Negro or the white man or the words and concepts to describe them, the Colonial population consisted largely of a great mass of white and black bondsmen, who occupied roughly the same economic category and were treated with equal contempt by the lords of the plantations and legislatures. Curiously unconcerned about their color, these people worked together and relaxed together.[3]

—Lerone Bennett Jr.

The concept of race is a relatively recent development. Only in the past few centuries, owing largely to European imperialism, have the world's people been classified along racial lines.[4] Here, in America, the idea of race emerged as a means of reconciling chattel slavery—as well as the extermination of American Indians—with the ideals of freedom preached by whites in the new colonies.

In the early colonial period, when settlements remained relatively small, indentured servitude was the dominant means of securing cheap labor. Under this system, whites and blacks struggled to survive against a common enemy, what historian Lerone Bennett Jr. describes as "the big planter apparatus and a social system that legalized terror against black and white bondsmen."[5] Initially, blacks brought to this country were not all enslaved; many were treated as indentured servants. As plantation farming expanded, particularly tobacco and cotton farming, demand increased greatly for both labor and land.

The demand for land was met by invading and conquering larger and larger swaths of territory. American Indians became a growing impediment to white European "progress," and during this period, the images of American Indians promoted in books, newspapers, and magazines became increasingly negative. As sociologists Keith Kilty and Eric Swank have observed, eliminating "savages" is less of a moral problem than eliminating human beings, and therefore American Indians came to be understood as a lesser race—uncivilized savages— thus providing a justification for the extermination of the native peoples.[6]

The growing demand for labor on plantations was met through slavery. American Indians were considered unsuitable as slaves, largely because native tribes were clearly in a position to fight back. The fear of raids by Indian tribes led plantation owners to grasp for an alternative source of free labor. European immigrants were also deemed poor candidates for slavery, not because of their race, but rather because they were in short supply and enslavement would, quite naturally, interfere with voluntary immigration to the new colonies. Plantation owners thus viewed Africans, who were relatively powerless, as the ideal slaves. The systematic enslavement of Africans, and the rearing of their children under bondage, emerged with all deliberate speed—quickened by events such as Bacon's Rebellion.

Nathaniel Bacon was a white property owner in Jamestown, Virginia, who managed to unite slaves, indentured servants, and poor whites in a revolutionary effort to overthrow the planter elite. Although slaves clearly occupied the lowest position in the social hierarchy and suffered the most under the plantation system, the condition of indentured whites was barely better, and the majority of free whites lived in extreme poverty. As explained by historian Edmund Morgan, in colonies like Virginia, the planter elite, with huge land grants, occupied a vastly superior position to workers of all colors.[7] Southern colonies did not hesitate to invent ways to extend the terms of servitude, and the planter class accumulated uncultivated lands to restrict the options of free workers. The simmering resentment against the planter class created conditions that were ripe for revolt.

Varying accounts of Bacon's rebellion abound, but the basic facts are these: Bacon developed plans in 1675 to seize Native American lands in order to acquire more property for himself and others and nullify the threat of Indian raids. When the planter elite in Virginia refused to provide militia support for his scheme, Bacon retaliated, leading an attack on the elite, their homes, and their property. He openly condemned the rich for their oppression of the poor and inspired an alliance of white and black bond laborers, as well as slaves, who demanded an end to their servitude. The attempted revolution was ended by force and false promises of amnesty. A number of the people who participated in the revolt were hanged. The events in Jamestown were alarming to the planter elite, who were deeply fearful of the multiracial alliance of bond workers and slaves. Word of Bacon's Rebellion spread far and wide, and several more uprisings of a similar type followed.

In an effort to protect their superior status and economic position, the planters shifted their strategy for maintaining dominance. They abandoned their heavy reliance on indentured servants in favor of the importation of more black slaves. Instead of importing English-speaking slaves from the West Indies, who were more likely to be familiar with European language and culture, many more slaves were shipped directly from Africa. These slaves would be far easier to control and far less likely to form alliances with poor whites.

Fearful that such measures might not be sufficient to protect their interests, the planter class took an additional precautionary step, a step that would later come to be known as a "racial bribe." Deliberately and strategically, the planter class extended special privileges to poor whites in an effort to drive a wedge between them and black slaves. White settlers were allowed greater access to Native American lands, white servants were allowed to police slaves through slave patrols and militias, and barriers were created so that free labor would not be placed in competition with slave labor. These measures effectively eliminated the risk of future alliances between black slaves and poor whites. Poor whites suddenly had a direct, personal stake in the existence of a race-based system of slavery. Their own plight had not improved by much, but at least they were not slaves. Once the planter elite split the labor force, poor whites responded to the logic of their situation and sought ways to expand their racially privileged position.[8]

By the mid-1770s, the system of bond labor had been thoroughly transformed into a racial caste system predicated on slavery. The degraded status of Africans was justified on the ground that Negros, like the Indians, were an uncivilized lesser race, perhaps even more lacking in intelligence and laudable human qualities than the red-skinned natives. The notion of white supremacy rationalized the enslavement of Africans, even as whites endeavored to form a new nation based on the ideals of equality, liberty, and justice for all. Before democracy, chattel slavery in America was born.

It may be impossible to overstate the significance of race in defining the basic structure of American society. The structure and content of the original Constitution was based largely on the effort to preserve a racial caste system—slavery—while at the same time affording political and economic rights to whites, especially propertied whites. The Southern slaveholding colonies would agree to form a union only on the condition that the federal government would not be able to interfere with the right to own slaves. Northern white elites were sympathetic to the demand for their "property rights" to be respected, as they, too, wanted the Constitution to protect their property interests. As James Madison put it, the nation ought to be constituted "to protect the minority of the opulent against the majority."[9] Consequently, the Constitution was designed so the federal government would be weak, not only in its relationship to private property, but also in relationship to the rights of states to conduct their own affairs. The language of the Constitution itself was deliberately colorblind (the words *slave* or *Negro* were never used), but the document was built upon a compromise regarding the prevailing racial caste system. Federalism—the division of power between the states and the federal government—was the device employed to protect the institution of slavery and the political power of slaveholding states. Even the method for determining proportional representation in Congress and identifying the winner of a presidential election (the electoral college) were specifically developed with the interest of slaveholders in mind. Under the terms of our country's founding document, slaves were defined as three-fifths of a man, not a real, whole human being. Upon this racist fiction rests the entire structure of American democracy.

The Death of Slavery

The history of racial caste in the United States would end with the Civil War if the idea of race and racial difference had died when the institution of slavery was put to rest. But during the four centuries in which slavery flourished, the idea of race flourished as well. Indeed, the notion of racial difference—specifically the notion of white supremacy—proved far more durable than the institution that gave birth to it.

White supremacy, over time, became a religion of sorts. Faith in the idea that people of the African race were bestial, that whites were inherently superior, and that slavery was, in fact, for blacks' own good, served to alleviate the white conscience and reconcile the tension between slavery and the democratic ideals espoused by whites in the so-called New World. There was no contradiction in the bold claim made by Thomas Jefferson in the Declaration of Independence that "all men are created equal" if Africans were not really people. Racism operated as a deeply held belief system based on "truths" beyond question or doubt. This deep faith in white supremacy not only justified an economic and political system in which plantation owners acquired land and great wealth through the brutality, torture, and coercion of other human beings; it also endured, like most articles of faith, long after the historical circumstances that gave rise to the religion passed away. In Wacquant's words: "Racial division was a consequence, not a precondition of slavery, but once it was instituted it became detached from its initial function and acquired a social potency all its own."[10] After the death of slavery, the idea of race lived on.

One of the most compelling accounts of the postemancipation period is *The Strange Career of Jim Crow*, written by C. Vann Woodward in 1955.[11] The book continues to be the focal point of study and debate by scholars and was once described by Martin Luther King Jr. as the "historical bible of the Civil Rights Movement." As Woodward tells the story, the end of slavery created an extraordinary dilemma for Southern white society. Without the labor of former slaves, the region's economy would surely collapse, and without the institution of slavery, there was no longer a formal mechanism for maintaining racial hierarchy and preventing "amalgamation" with a group of people considered intrinsically inferior and vile. This state of affairs produced a temporary anarchy and a state of mind bordering on hysteria, particularly among the planter elite. But even among poor whites, the collapse of slavery was a bitter pill. In the antebellum South, the lowliest white person at least possessed his or her white skin—a badge of superiority over even the most skilled slave or prosperous free African American.

While Southern whites—poor and rich alike—were utterly outraged by emancipation, there was no obvious solution to the dilemma they faced. Following the Civil War, the economic and political infrastructure of the South was in shambles. Plantation owners were suddenly destitute, and state governments, shackled by war debt, were penniless. Large amounts of real estate and other property had been destroyed in the war, industry was disorganized, and hundreds of thousands of men had been killed or maimed. With all of this went the demoralizing effect of an unsuccessful war and the extraordinary challenges associated with rebuilding new state and local governments. Add to all this the sudden presence of 4 million newly freed slaves, and the picture becomes even more complicated. Southern whites, Woodward explains, strongly believed that a new system of racial control was clearly required, but it was not immediately obvious what form it should take.

Under slavery, the racial order was most effectively maintained by a large degree of contact between slave owners and slaves, thus maximizing opportunities for supervision and discipline, and minimizing the potential for active resistance or rebellion. Strict separation of the races would have threatened slaveholders' immediate interests and was, in any event, wholly unnecessary as a means of creating social distance or establishing the inferior status of slaves.

Following the Civil War, it was unclear what institutions, laws, or customs would be necessary to maintain white control now that slavery was gone.

Nonetheless, as numerous historians have shown, the development of a new racial order became the consuming passion for most white Southerners. Rumors of a great insurrection terrified whites, and blacks increasingly came to be viewed as menacing and dangerous. In fact, the current stereotypes of black men as aggressive, unruly predators can be traced to this period, when whites feared that an angry mass of black men might rise up and attack them or rape their women.

Equally worrisome was the state of the economy. Former slaves literally walked away from their plantations, causing panic and outrage among plantation owners. Large numbers of former slaves roamed the highways in the early years after the war. Some converged on towns and cities; others joined the federal militia. Most white people believed African Americans lacked the proper motivation to work, prompting the provisional Southern legislatures to adopt the notorious black codes. As expressed by one Alabama planter: "We have the power to pass stringent police laws to govern the Negroes— this is a blessing—for they must be controlled in some way or white people cannot live among them."[12] While some of these codes were intended to establish systems of peonage resembling slavery, others foreshadowed Jim Crow laws by prohibiting, among other things, interracial seating in the first-class sections of railroad cars and by segregating schools.

Although the convict laws enacted during this period are rarely seen as part of the black codes, that is a mistake. As explained by historian William Cohen, "the main purpose of the codes was to control the freedmen, and the question of how to handle convicted black law breakers was very much at the center of the control issue."[13] Nine Southern states adopted vagrancy laws—which essentially made it a criminal offense not to work and were applied selectively to blacks—and eight of those states enacted convict laws allowing for the hiring-out of county prisoners to plantation owners and private companies. Prisoners were forced to work for little or no pay. One vagrancy act specifically provided that "all free negroes and mulattoes over the age of eighteen" must have written proof of a job at the beginning of every year. Those found with no lawful employment were deemed vagrants and convicted. Clearly, the purpose of the black codes in general and the vagrancy laws in particular was to establish another system of forced labor. In W.E.B. Du Bois's words: "The Codes spoke for themselves. . . . No open-minded student can read them without being convinced they meant nothing more nor less than slavery in daily toil."[14]

Ultimately, the black codes were overturned, and a slew of federal civil rights legislation protecting the newly freed slaves was passed during the relatively brief but extraordinary period of black advancement known as the Reconstruction Era. The impressive legislative achievements of this period include the Thirteenth Amendment, abolishing slavery; the Civil Rights Act of 1866, bestowing full citizenship upon African Americans; the Fourteenth Amendment, prohibiting states from denying citizens due process and "equal protection of the laws"; the Fifteenth Amendment, providing that the right to vote should not be denied on account of race; and the Ku Klux Klan Acts, which, among other things, declared interference with voting a federal offense and the violent infringement of civil rights a crime. The new legislation also provided for federal supervision of voting and authorized the president to send the army and suspend the writ of habeas corpus in districts declared to be in a state of insurrection against the federal government.

In addition to federal civil rights legislation, the Reconstruction Era brought the expansion of the Freedmen's Bureau, the agency charged with the responsibility of providing food, clothing, fuel, and other forms of assistance to destitute former slaves. A public education system emerged in the South, which afforded many blacks (and poor whites) their first opportunity to learn to read and write.

While the Reconstruction Era was fraught with corruption and arguably doomed by the lack of land reform, the sweeping economic and political developments in that period did appear, at least for a time, to have the potential to seriously undermine, if not completely eradicate, the racial caste system in the South. With the protection of federal troops, African Americans began to vote in large numbers and seize control, in some areas, of the local political apparatus. Literacy rates climbed, and educated blacks began to populate legislatures, open schools, and initiate successful businesses. In 1867, at the dawn of the Reconstruction Era, no black man held political office in the South, yet three years later, at least 15 percent of all Southern elected officials were black. This is particularly extraordinary in light of the fact that fifteen years after the passage of the Voting Rights Act of 1965—the high water mark of the Civil Rights Movement—fewer than 8 percent of all Southern elected officials were black.[15]

At the same time, however, many of the new civil rights laws were proving largely symbolic.[16] Notably absent from the Fifteenth Amendment, for example, was language prohibiting the states from imposing educational, residential, or other qualifications for voting, thus leaving the door open to the states to impose poll taxes, literacy tests, and other devices to prevent blacks from voting. Other laws revealed themselves as more an assertion of principle than direct federal intervention into Southern affairs, because enforcement required African Americans to take their cases to federal courts, a costly and time-consuming procedure that was a practical impossibility for the vast majority of those who had claims. Most blacks were too poor to sue to enforce their civil rights, and no organization like the NAACP yet existed to spread the risks and costs of litigation. Moreover, the threat of violence often deterred blacks from pressing legitimate claims, making the "civil rights" of former slaves largely illusory—existing on paper but rarely to be found in real life.

Meanwhile, the separation of the races had begun to emerge as a comprehensive pattern throughout the South, driven in large part by the rhetoric of the planter elite, who hoped to reestablish a system of control that would ensure a low-paid, submissive labor force. Racial segregation had actually begun years earlier in the North, as an effort to prevent race-mixing and preserve racial hierarchy following the abolition of Northern slavery. It had never developed, however, into a comprehensive system—operating instead largely as a matter of custom, enforced with varying degrees of consistency. Even among those most hostile to Reconstruction, few would have predicted that racial segregation would soon evolve into a new racial caste system as stunningly comprehensive and repressive as the one that came to be known simply as Jim Crow.

The Birth of Jim Crow

The backlash against the gains of African Americans in the Reconstruction Era was swift and severe. As African Americans obtained political power and began the long march toward greater social and economic equality, whites reacted with panic and outrage. Southern conservatives vowed to reverse Reconstruction and sought the "abolition of the Freedmen's Bureau and all political instrumentalities designed to secure Negro supremacy."[17] Their campaign to "redeem" the South was reinforced by a resurgent Ku Klux Klan, which fought a terrorist campaign against Reconstruction governments and local leaders, complete with bombings, lynchings, and mob violence.

The terrorist campaign proved highly successful. "Redemption" resulted in the withdrawal of federal troops from the South and the effective abandonment of African Americans and all those who had fought for or supported an egalitarian racial order. The federal government no longer made any effort to enforce federal civil rights legislation, and funding for the Freedmen's Bureau was slashed to such a degree that the agency became virtually defunct.

Once again, vagrancy laws and other laws defining activities such as "mischief" and "insulting gestures" as crimes were enforced vigorously against blacks. The aggressive enforcement of these criminal offenses opened up an enormous market for convict leasing, in which prisoners were contracted out as laborers to the highest private bidder. Douglas Blackmon, in *Slavery by Another Name*, describes how tens of thousands of African Americans were arbitrarily arrested during this period, many of them hit with court costs and fines, which had to be worked off in order to secure their release.[18] With no means to pay off their "debts," prisoners were sold as forced laborers to lumber camps, brickyards, railroads, farms, plantations, and dozens of corporations throughout the South. Death rates were shockingly high, for the private contractors had no interest in the health and well-being of their laborers, unlike the earlier slave-owners who needed their slaves, at a minimum, to be healthy enough to survive hard labor. Laborers were subject to almost continual lashing by long horse whips, and those who collapsed due to injuries or exhaustion were often left to die.

Convicts had no meaningful legal rights at this time and no effective redress. They were understood, quite literally, to be slaves of the state. The Thirteenth Amendment to the U.S. Constitution had abolished slavery but allowed one major exception: slavery remained appropriate as punishment for a crime. In a landmark decision by the Virginia Supreme Court, *Ruffin v. Commonwealth*, issued at the height of Southern Redemption, the court put to rest any notion that convicts were legally distinguishable from slaves:

> For a time, during his service in the penitentiary, he is in a state of penal servitude to the State. He has, as a consequence of his crime, not only forfeited his liberty, but all his personal rights except those which the law in its humanity accords to him. He is for the time being a slave of the State. He is civiliter mortus; and his estate, if he has any, is administered like that of a dead man.[19]

The state of Mississippi eventually moved from hiring convict labor to organizing its own convict labor camp, known as Parchman Farm. It was not alone. During the decade following Redemption, the convict population grew ten times faster than the general population: "Prisoners became younger and blacker, and the length of their sentences soared."[20] It was the nation's first prison boom and, as they are today, the prisoners were disproportionately black. After a brief period of progress during Reconstruction, African Americans found themselves, once again, virtually defenseless. The criminal justice system was strategically employed to force African Americans back into a system of extreme repression and control, a tactic that would continue to prove successful for generations to come. Even as convict leasing faded away, strategic forms of exploitation and repression emerged anew. As Blackmon notes: "The apparent demise . . . of leasing prisoners seemed a harbinger of a new day. But the harsher reality of the South was that the new post–Civil War neoslavery was evolving—not disappearing."[21]

Redemption marked a turning point in the quest by dominant whites for a new racial equilibrium, a racial order that would protect their economic, political, and social interests in a world without slavery. Yet a clear consensus among whites about what the new racial order should be was still lacking. The Redeemers who overthrew Reconstruction were inclined to retain such segregation practices as had already emerged, but they displayed no apparent disposition to expand or universalize the system.

Three alternative philosophies of race relations were put forward to compete for the region's support, all of which rejected the doctrines of extreme racism espoused by some Redeemers: liberalism, conservatism, and radicalism.[22] The liberal philosophy of race relations emphasized the stigma of segregation and the hypocrisy of a government that celebrates freedom and equality yet denies both on account of race. This philosophy, born in the North, never gained much traction among Southern whites or blacks.

The conservative philosophy, by contrast, attracted wide support and was implemented in various contexts over a considerable period of time. Conservatives blamed liberals for pushing blacks ahead of their proper station in life and placing blacks in positions they were unprepared to fill, a circumstance that had allegedly contributed to their downfall. They warned blacks that some Redeemers were not satisfied with having decimated Reconstruction, and were prepared to wage an aggressive war against blacks throughout the South. With some success, the conservatives reached out to African American voters, reminding them that they had something to lose as well as gain and that the liberals' preoccupation with political and economic equality presented the danger of losing all that blacks had so far gained.

The radical philosophy offered, for many African Americans, the most promise. It was predicated on a searing critique of large corporations, particularly railroads, and the wealthy elite in the North and South. The radicals of the late nineteenth century, who later formed the Populist Party, viewed the privileged classes as conspiring to keep poor whites and blacks locked into a subordinate political and economic position. For many African American voters, the Populist approach was preferable to the paternalism of liberals. Populists preached an "equalitarianism of want and poverty, the kinship of a common grievance, and a common oppressor."[23] As described by Tom Watson, a prominent Populist leader, in a speech advocating a union between black and white farmers: "You are kept apart that you may be separately fleeced of your earnings. You are made to hate each other because upon that hatred is rested the keystone of the arch of financial despotism that enslaves you both. You are deceived and blinded that you may not see how this race antagonism perpetuates a monetary system which beggars both."[24]

In an effort to demonstrate their commitment to a genuinely multiracial, working-class movement against white elites, the Populists made strides toward racial integration, a symbol of their commitment to class-based unity. African Americans throughout the South responded with great hope and enthusiasm, eager to be true partners in a struggle for social justice. According to Woodward, "It is altogether probable that during the brief Populist upheaval in the nineties Negroes and native whites achieved a greater comity of mind and harmony of political purpose than ever before or since in the South."[25]

The challenges inherent in creating the alliance sought by the Populists were formidable, as race prejudice ran the highest among the very white populations to which the Populist appeal was specifically addressed—the depressed lower economic classes. Nevertheless, the Populist movement initially enjoyed remarkable success in the South, fueled by a wave of discontent aroused by the severe agrarian depression of the 1880s and 1890s. The Populists took direct aim at the conservatives, who were known as comprising a party of privilege, and they achieved a stunning series of political

victories throughout the region. Alarmed by the success of the Populists and
the apparent potency of the alliance between poor and working-class whites
and African Americans, the conservatives raised the cry of white supremacy
and resorted to the tactics they had employed in their quest for Redemption,
including fraud, intimidation, bribery, and terror.

Segregation laws were proposed as part of a deliberate effort to drive a
wedge between poor whites and African Americans. These discriminatory
barriers were designed to encourage lower-class whites to retain a sense of
superiority over blacks, making it far less likely that they would sustain interracial political alliances aimed at toppling the white elite. The laws were, in
effect, another racial bribe. As William Julius Wilson has noted, "As long as
poor whites directed their hatred and frustration against the black competi-
tor, the planters were relieved of class hostility directed against them."[26] Indeed, in order to overcome the well-founded suspicions of poor and illiterate
whites that they, as well as blacks, were in danger of losing the right to vote,
the leaders of the movement pursued an aggressive campaign of white supremacy in every state prior to black disenfranchisement.

Ultimately, the Populists caved to the pressure and abandoned their former allies. "While the [Populist] movement was at the peak of zeal," Woodward observed, "the two races had surprised each other and astonished their
opponents by the harmony they achieved and the good will with which they
co-operated."[27] But when it became clear that the conservatives would stop
at nothing to decimate their alliance, the biracial partnership dissolved, and
Populist leaders re-aligned themselves with conservatives. Even Tom Watson, who had been among the most forceful advocates for an interracial alliance of farmers, concluded that Populist principles could never be fully
embraced by the South until blacks were eliminated from politics.

The agricultural depression, taken together with a series of failed reforms
and broken political promises, had pyramided to a climax of social tensions.
Dominant whites concluded that it was in their political and economic interest to scapegoat blacks, and "permission to hate" came from sources that
had formerly denied it, including Northern liberals eager to reconcile with
the South, Southern conservatives who had once promised blacks protection from racial extremism, and Populists, who cast aside their dark-skinned
allies when the partnership fell under siege.[28]

History seemed to repeat itself. Just as the white elite had successfully
driven a wedge between poor whites and blacks following Bacon's Rebellion

by creating the institution of black slavery, another racial caste system was emerging nearly two centuries later, in part due to efforts by white elites to decimate a multiracial alliance of poor people. By the turn of the twentieth century, every state in the South had laws on the books that disenfranchised blacks and discriminated against them in virtually every sphere of life, lending sanction to a racial ostracism that extended to schools, churches, housing, jobs, restrooms, hotels, restaurants, hospitals, orphanages, prisons, funeral homes, morgues, and cemeteries. Politicians competed with each other by proposing and passing ever more stringent, oppressive, and downright ridiculous legislation (such as laws specifically prohibiting blacks and whites from playing chess together). The public symbols and constant reminders of black subjugation were supported by whites across the political spectrum, though the plight of poor whites remained largely unchanged. For them, the racial bribe was primarily psychological.

The new racial order, known as Jim Crow—a term apparently derived from a minstrel show character—was regarded as the "final settlement," the "return to sanity," and "the permanent system."[29] Of course, the earlier system of racialized social control—slavery—had also been regarded as final, sane, and permanent by its supporters. Like the earlier system, Jim Crow seemed "natural," and it became difficult to remember that alternative paths were not only available at one time, but nearly embraced.

The Death of Jim Crow

Scholars have long debated the beginning and end of Reconstruction, as well as exactly when Jim Crow ended and the Civil Rights Movement or "Second Reconstruction" began. Reconstruction is most typically described as stretching from 1863 when the North freed the slaves to 1877, when it abandoned them and withdrew federal troops from the South. There is much less certainty regarding the beginning of the end of Jim Crow.

The general public typically traces the death of Jim Crow to *Brown v. Board of Education*, although the institution was showing signs of weakness years before. By 1945, a growing number of whites in the North had concluded that the Jim Crow system would have to be modified, if not entirely overthrown. This consensus was due to a number of factors, including the increased political power of blacks due to migration to the North and the growing membership and influence of the NAACP, particularly its highly successful legal campaign challenging Jim Crow laws in federal courts. Far more important in the view of many scholars, however, is the influence of World War II. The blatant contradiction between the country's opposition to the crimes of the Third Reich against European Jews and the continued existence of a racial caste system in the United States was proving embarrassing, severely damaging the nation's credibility as leader of the "free world." There was also increased concern that, without greater equality for African Americans, blacks would become susceptible to communist influence, given Russia's commitment to both racial and economic equality. In Gunnar Myrdal's highly influential book *The American Dilemma*, published in 1944, Myrdal made a passionate plea for integration based on the theory that the inherent contradiction between the "American Creed" of freedom and equality and the treatment of African Americans was not only immoral and profoundly unjust, but was also against the economic and foreign-policy interests of the United States.[30]

The Supreme Court seemed to agree. In 1944, in *Smith v. Allwright*, the Supreme Court ended the use of the all-white primary election; and in 1946, the Court ruled that state laws requiring segregation on interstate buses were unconstitutional. Two years later, the Court voided any real estate agreements that racially discriminated against purchasers, and in 1949 the Court ruled that Texas's segregated law school for blacks was inherently unequal and inferior in every respect to its law school for whites. In 1950, in *McLaurin v. Oklahoma*, it declared that Oklahoma had to desegregate its law school. Thus, even before *Brown*, the Supreme Court had already begun to set in motion a striking pattern of desegregation.

Brown v. Board of Education was unique, however. It signaled the end of "home rule" in the South with respect to racial affairs. Earlier decisions had chipped away at the "separate but equal" doctrine, yet Jim Crow had managed to adapt to the changing legal environment, and most Southerners had remained confident that the institution would survive. *Brown* threatened not only to abolish segregation in public schools, but also, by implication, the entire system of legalized discrimination in the South. After more than fifty years of nearly complete deference to Southern states and noninterference in their racial affairs, *Brown* suggested a reversal in course.

A mood of outrage and defiance swept the South, not unlike the reaction to emancipation and Reconstruction following the Civil War. Again, racial equality was being forced upon the South by the federal government, and by 1956 Southern white opposition to desegregation mushroomed into a vicious backlash. In Congress, North Carolina senator Sam Ervin Jr. drafted a racist polemic, "the Southern Manifesto," which vowed to fight to maintain Jim Crow by all legal means. Erwin succeeded in obtaining the support of 101 out of 128 members of Congress from the eleven original Confederate states.

A fresh wave of white terror was hurled at those who supported the dismantling of Jim Crow. White Citizens' Councils were formed in almost every Southern city and backwater town, comprised primarily of middle- to upper-middle-class whites in business and the clergy. Just as Southern legislatures had passed the black codes in response to the early steps of Reconstruction, in the years immediately following *Brown v. Board*, five Southern legislatures passed nearly fifty new Jim Crow laws. In the streets, resistance turned violent. The Ku Klux Klan reasserted itself as a powerful terrorist organization, committing castrations, killings, and the bombing of black homes and churches. NAACP leaders were beaten, pistol-whipped, and shot. As quickly as it began, desegregation across the South ground to a halt. In 1958, thirteen school systems were desegregated; in 1960, only seventeen.[31]

In the absence of a massive, grassroots movement directly challenging the racial caste system, Jim Crow might be alive and well today. Yet in the 1950s, a civil rights movement was brewing, emboldened by the Supreme Court's decisions and a shifting domestic and international political environment. With extraordinary bravery, civil rights leaders, activists, and progressive clergy launched boycotts, marches, and sit-ins protesting the Jim Crow system. They endured fire hoses, police dogs, bombings, and beatings by white mobs, as well as by the police. Once again, federal troops were sent to the South to provide protection for blacks attempting to exercise their civil rights, and the violent reaction of white racists was met with horror in the North.

The dramatic high point of the Civil Rights Movement occurred in 1963. The Southern struggle had grown from a modest group of black students demonstrating peacefully at one lunch counter to the largest mass movement for racial reform and civil rights in the twentieth century. Between autumn 1961 and the spring of 1963, twenty thousand men, women, and children had been arrested. In 1963 alone, another fifteen thousand were imprisoned, and one thousand desegregation protests occurred across the region, in more than one hundred cities.[32]

On June 12, 1963, President Kennedy announced that he would deliver to Congress a strong civil rights bill, a declaration that transformed him into a widely recognized ally of the Civil Rights Movement. Following Kennedy's assassination, President Johnson professed his commitment to the goal of "the full assimilation of more than twenty million Negroes into American life," and ensured the passage of comprehensive civil rights legislation. The Civil Rights Act of 1964 formally dismantled the Jim Crow system of discrimination in public accommodations, employment, voting, education, and federally financed activities. The Voting Rights Act of 1965 arguably had even greater scope, as it rendered illegal numerous discriminatory barriers to effective political participation by African Americans and mandated federal review of all new voting regulations so that it would be possible to determine whether their use would perpetuate voting discrimination.

Within five years, the effects of the civil rights revolution were undeniable. Between 1964 and 1969, the percentage of African American adults registered to vote in the South soared. In Alabama the rate leaped from 19.3 percent to 61.3 percent; in Georgia, 27.4 percent to 60.4 percent; in Louisiana, 31.6 percent to 60.8 percent; and in Mississippi, 6.7 percent to 66.5 percent.[33] Suddenly black children could shop in department stores, eat at restaurants, drink from water fountains, and go to amusement parks that were once off-limits. Miscegenation laws were declared unconstitutional, and the rate of interracial marriage climbed.

While dramatic progress was apparent in the political and social realms, civil rights activists became increasingly concerned that, without major economic reforms, the vast majority of blacks would remain locked in poverty. Thus at the peak of the Civil Rights Movement, activists and others began to turn their attention to economic problems, arguing that socioeconomic inequality interacted with racism to produce crippling poverty and related social problems. Economic issues emerged as a major focus of discontent. As political scientists Frances Fox Piven and Richard Cloward have described, "blacks became more indignant over their condition—not only as an oppressed racial minority in a white society but as poor people in an affluent one."[34] Activists organized boycotts, picket lines, and demonstrations to attack discrimination in access to jobs and the denial of economic opportunity.

Perhaps the most famous demonstration in support of economic justice is the March on Washington for Jobs and Economic Freedom in August 1963. The wave of activism associated with economic justice helped to focus President Kennedy's attention on poverty and black unemployment. In the summer of 1963, he initiated a series of staff studies on those subjects. By the end of the summer, he declared his intention to make the eradication of poverty a key legislative objective in 1964.[35] Following Kennedy's assassination, President Lyndon Johnson embraced the antipoverty rhetoric with great passion, calling for an "unconditional war on poverty," in his State of the Union Address in January 1964. Weeks later he proposed to Congress the Economic Opportunities Bill of 1964.

The shift in focus served to align the goals of the Civil Rights Movement with key political goals of poor and working-class whites, who were also demanding economic reforms. As the Civil Rights Movement began to evolve into a "Poor People's Movement," it promised to address not only black poverty, but white poverty as well—thus raising the specter of a poor and working-class movement that cut across racial lines. Martin Luther King Jr. and other civil rights leaders made it clear that they viewed the eradication of economic inequality as the next front in the "human rights movement" and made great efforts to build multiracial coalitions that sought economic justice for all. Genuine equality for black people, King reasoned, demanded a radical restructuring of society, one that would address the needs of the black and white poor throughout the country. Shortly before his assassination, he envisioned bringing to Washington, D.C., thousands of the nation's disadvantaged in an interracial alliance that embraced rural and ghetto blacks, Appalachian whites, Mexican Americans, Puerto Ricans, and Native Americans to demand jobs and income—the right to live. In a speech delivered in 1968, King acknowledged there had been some progress for blacks since the passage of the Civil Rights Act of 1964, but insisted that the current challenges required even greater resolve and that the entire nation must be transformed for economic justice to be more than a dream for poor people of all colors. As historian Gerald McKnight observes, "King was proposing nothing less than a radical transformation of the Civil Rights Movement into a populist crusade calling for redistribution of economic and political power. America's only civil rights leader was now focusing on class issues and was planning to descend on Washington with an army of poor to shake the foundations of the power structure and force the government to respond to the needs of the ignored underclass."[36]

With the success of the Civil Rights Movement and the launching of the Poor People's Movement, it was apparent to all that a major disruption in the nation's racial equilibrium had occurred. Yet as we shall see below, Negroes stood only a "brief moment in the sun." Conservative whites began, once again, to search for a new racial order that would conform to the needs and constraints of the time. This process took place with the understanding that whatever the new order would be, it would have to be formally race-neutral—it could not involve explicit or clearly intentional race discrimination. A similar phenomenon had followed slavery and Reconstruction, as white elites struggled to define a new racial order with the understanding that whatever the new order would be, it could not include slavery. Jim Crow eventually replaced slavery, but now it too had died, and it was unclear what might take its place. Barred by law from invoking race explicitly, those committed to racial hierarchy were forced to search for new means of achieving their goals according to the new rules of American democracy.

History reveals that the seeds of the new system of control were planted well before the end of the Civil Rights Movement. A new race-neutral language was developed for appealing to old racist sentiments, a language accompanied by a political movement that succeeded in putting the vast majority of blacks back in their place. Proponents of racial hierarchy found they could install a new racial caste system without violating the law or the new limits of acceptable political discourse, by demanding "law and order" rather than "segregation forever."

The Birth of Mass Incarceration

The rhetoric of "law and order" was first mobilized in the late 1950s as Southern governors and law enforcement officials attempted to generate and mobilize white opposition to the Civil Rights Movement. In the years following *Brown v. Board of Education*, civil rights activists used direct-action tactics in an effort to force reluctant Southern states to desegregate public facilities. Southern governors and law enforcement officials often characterized these tactics as criminal and argued that the rise of the Civil Rights Movement was indicative of a breakdown of law and order. Support of civil rights legislation was derided by Southern conservatives as merely "rewarding lawbreakers."

For more than a decade—from the mid-1950s until the late 1960s—conservatives systematically and strategically linked opposition to civil rights legislation to calls for law and order, arguing that Martin Luther King Jr.'s philosophy of civil disobedience was a leading cause of crime. Civil rights protests were frequently depicted as criminal rather than political in nature, and federal courts were accused of excessive "lenience" toward lawlessness, thereby contributing to the spread of crime. In the words of then–vice president Richard Nixon, the increasing crime rate "can be traced directly to the spread of the corrosive doctrine that every citizen possesses an inherent right to decide for himself which laws to obey and when to disobey them."[37] Some segregationists went further, insisting that integration causes crime, citing lower crime rates in Southern states as evidence that segregation was necessary. In the words of Representative John Bell Williams, "This exodus of Negroes from the South, and their influx into the great metropolitan centers of other areas of the Nation, has been accompanied by a wave of crime. . . . What has civil rights accomplished for these areas? . . . Segregation is the only answer as most Americans—not the politicians— have realized for hundreds of years."[38]

Unfortunately, at the same time that civil rights were being identified as a threat to law and order, the FBI was reporting fairly dramatic increases in the national crime rate. Beginning in the 1960s, crime rates rose in the United States for a period of about ten years. Reported street crime quadrupled, and homicide rates nearly doubled. Despite significant controversy over the accuracy of crime statistics during this period (the FBI's method of tracking crime was changing), sociologists and criminologists agree that crime did rise, in some categories quite sharply. The reasons for the crime wave are complex but can be explained in large part by the rise of the "baby boom" generation—the spike in the number of young men in the fifteen-to-twenty-four age group, which historically has been responsible for most crimes. The surge of young men in the population was occurring at precisely the same time that unemployment rates for black men were rising sharply, but the economic and demographic factors contributing to rising crime were not explored in the media. Instead, crime reports were sensationalized and offered as further evidence of the breakdown in lawfulness, morality, and social stability in the wake of the Civil Rights Movement.[39]

To make matters worse, riots erupted in the summer of 1964 in Harlem and Rochester, followed by a series of uprisings that swept the nation following the assassination of Martin Luther King Jr. in 1968. The racial imagery associated with the riots gave fuel to the argument that civil rights for blacks led to rampant crime. Cities like Philadelphia and Rochester were described as being victims of their own generosity. Conservatives argued that, having welcomed blacks migrating from the South, these cities "were repaid with crime-ridden slums and black discontent."[40]

Barry Goldwater, in his 1964 presidential campaign, aggressively exploited the riots and fears of black crime, laying the foundation for the "get tough on crime" movement that would emerge years later. In a widely quoted speech, Goldwater warned voters, "Choose the way of [the Johnson] Administration and you have the way of mobs in the street."[41] Civil rights activists who argued that the uprisings were directly related to widespread police harassment and abuse were dismissed by conservatives out of hand. "If [blacks] conduct themselves in an orderly way, they will not have to worry about police brutality," argued West Virginia senator Robert Byrd.[42]

While many civil rights advocates in this period actively resisted the attempt by conservatives to use rising crime as an excuse to crack down on impoverished black communities, some black activists began to join the calls for "law and order" and expressed support for harsh responses to lawbreakers. As Vanessa Barker describes in *The Politics of Imprisonment,* black activists in Harlem, alarmed by rising crime rates, actively campaigned for what would become the notorious Rockefeller drug laws as well as other harsh sentencing measures.[43] Wittingly or unwittingly, they found themselves complicit in the emergence of a penal system unprecedented in world history. Black support for harsh responses to urban crime—support born of desperation and legitimate concern over the unraveling of basic security in inner-city communities—helped provide political cover for conservative politicians who saw an opening to turn back the clock on racial progress in the United States. Conservatives could point to black support for highly punitive approaches to dealing with the problems of the urban poor as "proof" that race had nothing to do with their "law and order" agenda.

Early on, little effort was made to disguise the racial motivations behind the law and order rhetoric and the harsh criminal justice legislation proposed in Congress. The most ardent opponents of civil rights legislation and desegregation were the most active on the emerging crime issue. Well-known segregationist George Wallace, for example, argued that "the same Supreme Court that ordered integration and encouraged civil rights legislation" was now "bending over backwards to help criminals."[44] Three other prominent segregationists—Senators McClellan, Erwin, and Thurmond—led the legislative battle to curb the rights of criminal defendants.[45]

As the rules of acceptable discourse changed, however, segregationists distanced themselves from an explicitly racist agenda. They developed instead the racially sanitized rhetoric of "cracking down on crime"—rhetoric that is now used freely by politicians of every stripe. Conservative politicians who embraced this rhetoric purposefully failed to distinguish between the direct action tactics of civil rights activists, violent rebellions in inner cities, and traditional crimes of an economic or violent nature. Instead, as Marc Mauer of the Sentencing Project has noted, "all of these phenomenon were subsumed under the heading of 'crime in the streets.'"[46]

After the passage of the Civil Rights Act, the public debate shifted focus from segregation to crime. The battle lines, however, remained largely the same. Positions taken on crime policies typically cohered along lines of racial ideology. Political scientist Vesla Weaver explains: "Votes cast in opposition to open housing, busing, the Civil Rights Act, and other measures time and again showed the same divisions as votes for amendments to crime bills. . . . Members of Congress who voted against civil rights measures proactively designed crime legislation and actively fought for their proposals."[47]

Although law and order rhetoric ultimately failed to prevent the formal dismantling of the Jim Crow system, it proved highly effective in appealing to poor and working-class whites, particularly in the South, who were opposed to integration and frustrated by the Democratic Party's apparent support for the Civil Rights Movement. As Weaver notes, "rather than fading, the segregationists' crime-race argument was reframed, with a slightly different veneer," and eventually became the foundation of the conservative agenda on crime.[48] In fact, law and order rhetoric—first employed by segregationists—would eventually contribute to a major realignment of political parties in the United States.

Following the Civil War, party alignment was almost entirely regional. The South was solidly Democratic, embittered by the war, firmly committed to the maintenance of a racial caste system, and extremely hostile to federal intervention on behalf of African Americans. The North was overwhelming Republican and, while Republicans were ambivalent about equality for African Americans, they were far more inclined to adopt and implement racial justice reforms than their Democratic counterparts below the Mason-Dixon line.

The Great Depression effectuated a sea change in American race relations and party alignment. The New Deal—spearheaded by the Democratic
Party of President Franklin D. Roosevelt—was designed to alleviate the suffering of poor people in the midst of the Depression, and blacks, the poorest
of the poor, benefited disproportionately. While New Deal programs were
rife with discrimination in their administration, they at least included blacks
within the pool of beneficiaries—a development, historian Michael Klarman
has noted, that was "sufficient to raise black hopes and expectations after
decades of malign neglect from Washington."[49] Poor and working-class whites
in both the North and South, no less than African Americans, responded
positively to the New Deal, anxious for meaningful economic relief. As a result, the Democratic New Deal coalition evolved into an alliance of urban
ethnic groups and the white South that dominated electoral politics from
1932 to the early 1960s.

That dominance came to an abrupt end with the creation and implementation of what has come to be known as the Southern Strategy. The
success of law and order rhetoric among working-class whites and the intense
resentment of racial reforms, particularly in the South, led conservative
Republican analysts to believe that a "new majority" could be created by
the Republican Party, one that included the traditional Republican base, the
white South, and half the Catholic, blue-collar vote of the big cities.[50] Some
conservative political strategists admitted that appealing to racial fears and
antagonisms was central to this strategy, though it had to be done surrepti-
tiously. H.R. Haldeman, one of Nixon's key advisers, recalls that Nixon himself deliberately pursued a Southern, racial strategy: "He [President Nixon]
emphasized that you have to face the fact that the whole problem is really
the blacks. The key is to devise a system that recognizes this while not appearing to."[51] Similarly, John Ehrlichman, special counsel to the president,
explained the Nixon administration's campaign strategy of 1968 in this way:
"We'll go after the racists."[52] In Ehrlichman's view, "that subliminal appeal to
the anti-black voter was always present in Nixon's statements and speeches."[53]

Republican strategist Kevin Phillips is often credited for offering the most
influential argument in favor of a race-based strategy for Republican political
dominance in the South. He argued in *The Emerging Republican Majority*,
published in 1969, that Nixon's successful presidential election campaign
could point the way toward long-term political realignment and the building
of a new Republican majority, if Republicans continued to campaign primar-

ily on the basis of racial issues, using coded antiblack rhetoric.[54] He argued that Southern white Democrats had become so angered and alienated by the Democratic Party's support for civil rights reforms, such as desegregation and busing, that those voters could be easily persuaded to switch parties if those racial resentments could be maintained. Warren Weaver, a *New York Times* journalist who reviewed the book upon its release, observed that Phillips's strategy largely depended upon creating and maintaining a racially polarized political environment. "Full racial polarization is an essential ingredient of Phillips's political pragmatism. He wants to see a black Democratic party, particularly in the South, because this will drive into the Republican party precisely the kind of anti-Negro whites who will help constitute the emerging majority. This even leads him to support some civil rights efforts."[55] Appealing to the racism and vulnerability of working-class whites had worked to defeat the Populists at the turn of the century, and a growing number of conservatives believed the tactic should be employed again, albeit in a more subtle fashion.

Thus in the late 1960s and early 1970s, two schools of thought were offered to the general public regarding race, poverty, and the social order. Conservatives argued that poverty was caused not by structural factors related to race and class but rather by culture—particularly black culture. This view received support from Daniel Patrick Moynihan's now infamous report on the black family, which attributed black poverty to a black "subculture" and the "tangle of pathology" that characterized it. As described by sociologist Katherine Beckett, "The (alleged) misbehaviors of the poor were transformed from adaptations to poverty that had the unfortunate effect of reproducing it into character failings that accounted for poverty in the first place."[56] The "social pathologies" of the poor, particularly street crime, illegal drug use, and delinquency, were redefined by conservatives as having their cause in overly generous relief arrangements. Black "welfare cheats" and their dangerous offspring emerged, for the first time, in the political discourse and media imagery.

Liberals, by contrast, insisted that social reforms such as the War on Poverty and civil rights legislation would get at the "root causes" of criminal behavior and stressed the social conditions that predictably generate crime. Lyndon Johnson, for example, argued during his 1964 presidential campaign against Barry Goldwater that antipoverty programs were, in effect, anticrime programs: "There is something mighty wrong when a candidate for the highest office bemoans violence in the streets but votes against the War on Poverty, votes against the Civil Rights Act and votes against major educational bills that come before him as a legislator."[57]

Competing images of the poor as "deserving" and "undeserving" became central components of the debate. Ultimately, the racialized nature of this imagery became a crucial resource for conservatives, who succeeded in using law and order rhetoric in their effort to mobilize the resentment of white working-class voters, many of whom felt threatened by the sudden progress of African Americans. As explained by Thomas and Mary Edsall in their insightful book *Chain Reaction*, a disproportionate share of the costs of integration and racial equality had been borne by lower- and lower-middle-class whites, who were suddenly forced to compete on equal terms with blacks for jobs and status and who lived in neighborhoods adjoining black ghettos. Their children—not the children of wealthy whites—attended schools most likely to fall under busing orders. The affluent white liberals who were pressing the legal claims of blacks and other minorities "were often sheltered, in their private lives, and largely immune to the costs of implementing minority claims."[58] This reality made it possible for conservatives to characterize the "liberal Democratic establishment" as being out of touch with ordinary working people—thus resolving one of the central problems facing conservatives: how to persuade poor and working-class voters to join in alliance with corporate interests and the conservative elite. By 1968, 81 percent of those responding to the Gallup Poll agreed with the statement that "law and order has broken down in this country," and the majority blamed "Negroes who start riots" and "Communists."[59]

During the presidential election that year, both the Republican candidate, Richard Nixon, and the independent segregationist candidate, George Wallace, made "law and order" a central theme of their campaigns, and together they collected 57 percent of the vote.[60] Nixon dedicated seventeen speeches solely to the topic of law and order, and one of his television ads explicitly called on voters to reject the lawlessness of civil rights activists and embrace "order" in the United States.[61] The advertisement began with frightening music accompanied by flashing images of protestors, bloodied victims, and violence. A deep voice then said:

> It is time for an honest look at the problem of order in the United States. Dissent is a necessary ingredient of change, but in a system of government that provides for peaceful change, there is no cause that

justifies resort to violence. Let us recognize that the first right of every American is to be free from domestic violence. So I pledge to you, we shall have order in the United States.

At the end of the ad, a caption declared: "This time . . . vote like your whole world depended on it . . . NIXON." Viewing his own campaign ad, Nixon reportedly remarked with glee that the ad "hits it right on the nose. It's all about those damn Negro–Puerto Rican groups out there."[62]

Race had become, yet again, a powerful wedge, breaking up what had been a solid liberal coalition based on economic interests of the poor and the working and lower-middle classes. In the 1968 election, race eclipsed class as the organizing principle of American politics, and by 1972, attitudes on racial issues rather than socioeconomic status were the primary determinant of voters' political self-identification. The late 1960s and early 1970s marked the dramatic erosion in the belief among working-class whites that the condition of the poor, or those who fail to prosper, was the result of a faulty economic system that needed to be challenged. As the Edsalls explain, "the pitting of whites and blacks at the low end of the income distribution against each other intensified the view among many whites that the condition of life for the disadvantaged—particularly for disadvantaged blacks—is the responsibility of those afflicted, and not the responsibility of the larger society."[63] Just as race had been used at the turn of the century by Southern elites to rupture class solidarity at the bottom of the income ladder, race as a national issue had broken up the Democratic New Deal "bottom-up" coalition—a coalition dependent on substantial support from all voters, white and black, at or below the median income.

The conservative revolution that took root within the Republican Party in the 1960s did not reach its full development until the election of 1980. The decade preceding Ronald Reagan's ascent to the presidency was characterized by political and social crises, as the Civil Rights Movement was promptly followed by intense controversy over the implementation of the equality principle—especially busing and affirmative action—as well as dramatic political clashes over the Vietnam War and Watergate. During this period, conservatives gave lip service to the goal of racial equality but actively resisted desegregation, busing, and civil rights enforcement. They repeatedly raised the issue of welfare, subtly framing it as a contest between hardworking, blue-collar whites and poor blacks who refused to work. The not-so-subtle message to working-class whites was that their tax dollars were going to support special programs for blacks who most certainly did not deserve them. During this period, Nixon called for a "war on drugs"—an announcement that proved largely rhetorical as he declared illegal drugs "public enemy number one" without proposing dramatic shifts in drug policy. A backlash against blacks was clearly in force, but no consensus had yet been reached regarding what racial and social order would ultimately emerge from these turbulent times.

In his campaign for the presidency, Reagan mastered the "excision of the language of race from conservative public discourse" and thus built on the success of earlier conservatives who developed a strategy of exploiting racial hostility or resentment for political gain without making explicit reference to race.[64] Condemning "welfare queens" and criminal "predators," he rode into office with the strong support of disaffected whites—poor and working-class whites who felt betrayed by the Democratic Party's embrace of the civil rights agenda. As one political insider explained, Reagan's appeal derived primarily from the ideological fervor of the right wing of the Republican Party and "the emotional distress of those who fear or resent the Negro, and who expect Reagan somehow to keep him 'in his place' or at least echo their own anger and frustration."[65] To great effect, Reagan echoed white frustration in race-neutral terms through implicit racial appeals. His "color-blind" rhetoric on crime, welfare, taxes, and states' rights was clearly understood by white (and black) voters as having a racial dimension, though claims to that effect were impossible to prove. The absence of explicitly racist rhetoric afforded the racial nature of his coded appeals a certain plausible deniability. For example, when Reagan kicked off his presidential campaign at the annual Neshoba County Fair near Philadelphia, Mississippi—the town where three civil rights activists were murdered in 1964—he assured the crowd "I believe in states' rights," and promised to restore to states and local governments the power that properly belonged to them.[66] His critics promptly alleged that he was signaling a racial message to his audience, suggesting allegiance with those who resisted desegregation, but Reagan firmly denied it, forcing liberals into a position that would soon become familiar—arguing that something is racist but finding it impossible to prove in the absence of explicitly racist language.

Crime and welfare were the major themes of Reagan's campaign rhetoric. According to the Edsalls, one of Reagan's favorite and most-often-repeated anecdotes was the story of a Chicago "welfare queen" with "80 names, 30 addresses, 12 Social Security cards," whose "tax-free income alone is over $150,000."[67] The term "welfare queen" became a not-so-subtle code for "lazy, greedy, black ghetto mother." The food stamp program, in turn, was a vehicle to let "some fellow ahead of you buy a T-bone steak," while "you were standing in a checkout line with your package of hamburger."[68] These highly racialized appeals, targeted to poor and working-class whites, were nearly always accompanied by vehement promises to be tougher on crime and to enhance the federal government's role in combating it. Reagan portrayed the criminal as "a staring face—a face that belongs to a frightening reality of our time: the face of the human predator."[69] Reagan's racially coded rhetoric and strategy proved extraordinarily effective, as 22 percent of all Democrats defected from the party to vote for Reagan. The defection rate shot up to 34 percent among those Democrats who believed civil rights leaders were pushing "too fast."[70]

Once elected, Reagan's promise to enhance the federal government's role in fighting crime was complicated by the fact that fighting street crime has traditionally been the responsibility of state and local law enforcement. After a period of initial confusion and controversy regarding whether the FBI and the federal government should be involved in street crime, the Justice Department announced its intention to cut in half the number of specialists assigned to identify and prosecute white-collar criminals and to shift its attention to street crime, especially drug-law enforcement.[71] In October 1982, President Reagan officially announced his administration's War on Drugs. At the time he declared this new war, less than 2 percent of the American public viewed drugs as the most important issue facing the nation.[72] This fact was no deterrent to Reagan, for the drug war from the outset had little to do with public concern about drugs and much to do with public concern about race. By waging a war on drug users and dealers, Reagan made good on his promise to crack down on the racially defined "others"—the undeserving.

Practically overnight the budgets of federal law enforcement agencies soared. Between 1980 and 1984, FBI antidrug funding increased from $8 million to $95 million.[73] Department of Defense antidrug allocations increased from $33 million in 1981 to $1,042 million in 1991. During that same period, DEA antidrug spending grew from $86 to $1,026 million, and FBI antidrug allocations grew from $38 to $181 million.[74] By contrast, funding for agencies responsible for drug treatment, prevention, and education was dramatically reduced. The budget of the National Institute on Drug Abuse, for example, was reduced from $274 million to $57 million from 1981 to 1984, and antidrug funds allocated to the Department of Education were cut from $14 million to $3 million.[75]

Determined to ensure that the "new Republican majority" would continue to support the extraordinary expansion of the federal government's law enforcement activities and that Congress would continue to fund it, the Reagan administration launched a media offensive to justify the War on Drugs.[76] Central to the media campaign was an effort to sensationalize the emergence of crack cocaine in inner-city neighborhoods—communities devastated by deindustrialization and skyrocketing unemployment. The media frenzy the campaign inspired simply could not have come at a worse time for African Americans.

In the early 1980s, just as the drug war was kicking off, inner-city communities were suffering from economic collapse. The blue-collar factory jobs that had been plentiful in urban areas in the 1950s and 1960s had suddenly disappeared.[77] Prior to 1970, inner-city workers with relatively little formal education could find industrial employment close to home. Globalization, however, helped to change that. Manufacturing jobs were transferred by multinational corporations away from American cities to countries that lacked unions, where workers earn a small fraction of what is considered a fair wage in the United States. To make matters worse, dramatic technological changes revolutionized the workplace—changes that eliminated many of the jobs that less skilled workers once relied upon for their survival. Highly educated workers benefited from the pace of technological change and the increased use of computer-based technologies, but blue-collar workers often found themselves displaced in the sudden transition from an industrial to a service economy.

The impact of globalization and deindustrialization was felt most strongly in black inner-city communities. As described by William Julius Wilson, in his book *When Work Disappears*, the overwhelming majority of African Americans in the 1970s lacked college educations and had attended racially segregated, underfunded schools lacking basic resources. Those residing in ghetto communities were particularly ill equipped to adapt to the seismic changes taking place in the U.S. economy; they were left isolated and jobless. One study indicates that as late as 1970, more than 70 percent of all blacks working in metropolitan areas held blue-collar jobs.[78] Yet by 1987, when the drug war hit high gear, the industrial employment of black men had plummeted to 28 percent.[79]

The new manufacturing jobs that opened during this time period were generally located in the suburbs. The growing spatial mismatch of jobs had a profound impact on African Americans trapped in ghettos. A study of urban black fathers found that only 28 percent had access to an automobile. The rate fell to 18 percent for those living in ghetto areas.[80]

Women fared somewhat better during this period because the social-service sector in urban areas—which employs primarily women—was expanding at the same time manufacturing jobs were evaporating. The fraction of black men who moved into so called pink-collar jobs like nursing or clerical work was negligible.[81]

The decline in legitimate employment opportunities among inner-city residents increased incentives to sell drugs—most notably crack cocaine. Crack is pharmacologically almost identical to powder cocaine, but it has been converted into a form that can be vaporized and inhaled for a faster, more intense (though shorter) high using less of the drug—making it possible to sell small doses at more affordable prices. Crack hit the streets in 1985, a few years after Reagan's drug war was announced, leading to a spike in violence as drug markets struggled to stabilize, and the anger and frustration associated with joblessness boiled. Joblessness and crack swept inner cities precisely at the moment that a fierce backlash against the Civil Rights Movement was manifesting itself through the War on Drugs.

No one should ever attempt to minimize the harm caused by crack cocaine and the related violence. As David Kennedy correctly observes, "[c]rack blew through America's poor black neighborhoods like the Four Horsemen of the Apocalypse," leaving behind unspeakable devastation and suffering.[82] As a nation, though, we had a choice about how to respond. Some countries faced with rising drug crime or seemingly intractable rates of drug abuse and drug addiction chose the path of drug treatment, prevention, and education or economic investment in crime-ridden communities. Portugal, for example, responded to persistent problems of drug addiction and abuse by decriminalizing the possession of all drugs and redirecting the money that would have been spent putting drug users in cages into drug treatment and prevention. Ten years later, Portugal reported that rates of drug abuse and addiction had plummeted, and drug-related crime was on the decline as well.[83]

Numerous paths were available to us, as a nation, in the wake of the crack crisis, yet for reasons traceable largely to racial politics and fear mongering we chose war. Conservatives found they could finally justify an all-out war on an "enemy" that had been racially defined years before.

Almost immediately after crack appeared, the Reagan administration leaped at the opportunity to publicize crack cocaine in an effort to build support for its drug war. In October 1985, the DEA sent Robert Stutman to serve as director of its New York City office and charged him with the responsibility of shoring up public support for the administration's new war. Stutman developed a strategy for improving relations with the news media and sought to draw journalists' attention to the spread of crack cocaine in inner-city communities. As Stutman recounted years later:

> The agents would hear me give hundreds of presentations to the media as I attempted to call attention to the drug scourge. I wasted no time in pointing out its [the DEA's] new accomplishments against the drug traffickers. . . . In order to convince Washington, I needed to make it [drugs] a national issue and quickly. I began a lobbying effort and I used the media. The media were only too willing to cooperate, because as far the New York media was concerned, crack was the hottest combat reporting story to come along since the end of the Vietnam War.[84]

The strategy bore fruit. In June 1986, *Newsweek* declared crack to be the biggest story since Vietnam/Watergate, and in August of that year, *Time* magazine termed crack "the issue of the year." Thousands of stories about the crack crisis flooded the airwaves and newsstands, and the stories had a clear racial subtext. The articles typically featured black "crack whores," "crack babies," and "gangbangers," reinforcing already prevalent racial stereotypes of black women as irresponsible, selfish "welfare queens," and black men as "predators"—part of an inferior and criminal subculture.[85] When two popular sports figures, Len Bias and Don Rogers, died of cocaine overdoses in June 1986, the media erroneously reported their deaths as caused by crack, contributing to the media firestorm and groundswell of political activity and public concern relating to the new "demon drug," crack cocaine. The bonanza continued into 1989, as the media continued to disseminate claims that crack was an "epidemic," a "plague," "instantly addictive," and extraordinarily dangerous—claims that have now been proven false or highly misleading. Between October 1988 and October 1989, the *Washington Post* alone ran 1,565 stories about the "drug scourge." Richard Harwood, the *Post*'s ombudsmen, eventually admitted the paper had lost "a proper sense of perspective" due to such a "hyperbole epidemic." He said that "politicians are doing a number on people's heads."[86] Sociologists Craig Reinarman and Harry Levine later made a similar point: "Crack was a godsend to the Right. . . . It could not have appeared at a more politically opportune moment."[87]

In September 1986, with the media frenzy at full throttle, the House passed legislation that allocated $2 billion to the antidrug crusade, required the participation of the military in narcotics control efforts, allowed the death penalty for some drug-related crimes, and authorized the admission of some illegally obtained evidence in drug trials. Later that month, the Senate proposed even tougher antidrug legislation, and shortly thereafter, the president signed the Anti-Drug Abuse Act of 1986 into law. Among other harsh penalties, the legislation included mandatory minimum sentences for the distribution of cocaine, including far more severe punishment for distribution of crack—associated with blacks—than powder cocaine, associated with whites.

Few criticisms of the legislation could be heard en route to enactment. One senator insisted that crack had become a scapegoat distracting the public's attention from the true causes of our social ills, arguing: "If we blame crime on crack, our politicians are off the hook. Forgotten are the failed schools, the malign welfare programs, the desolate neighborhoods, the wasted years. Only crack is to blame. One is tempted to think that if crack did not exist, someone somewhere would have received a Federal grant to develop it."[88] Critical voices, however, were lonely ones.

Congress revisited drug policy in 1988. The resulting legislation was once again extraordinarily punitive, this time extending far beyond traditional criminal punishments and including new "civil penalties" for drug offenders. The new Anti-Drug Abuse Act authorized public housing authorities to evict any tenant who allows any form of drug-related criminal activity to occur on or near public housing premises and eliminated many federal benefits, including student loans, for anyone convicted of a drug offense. The act also expanded use of the death penalty for serious drug-related offenses and imposed new mandatory minimums for drug offenses, including a five-year mandatory minimum for simple possession of cocaine base—with no evidence of intent to sell. Remarkably, the penalty would apply to first-time offenders. The severity of this punishment was unprecedented in the federal system. Until 1988, one year of imprisonment had been the maximum for possession of any amount of any drug. Members of the Congressional Black Caucus (CBC) were mixed in their assessment of the new legislation—some believed the harsh penalties were necessary, others convinced that the laws were biased and harmful to African Americans. Ultimately the legislation passed by an overwhelming margin—346 to 11. Six of the negative votes came from the CBC.[89]

The War on Drugs proved popular among key white voters, particularly whites who remained resentful of black progress, civil rights enforcement, and affirmative action. Beginning in the 1970s, researchers found that racial attitudes—not crime rates or likelihood of victimization—are an important determinant of white support for "get tough on crime" and antiwelfare measures.[90] Among whites, those expressing the highest degree of concern about crime also tend to oppose racial reform, and their punitive attitudes toward crime are largely unrelated to their likelihood of victimization.[91] Whites, on average, are more punitive than blacks, despite the fact that blacks are far more likely to be victims of crime. Rural whites are often the most punitive, even though they are least likely to be crime victims.[92] The War on Drugs, cloaked in race-neutral language, offered whites opposed to racial reform a unique opportunity to express their hostility toward blacks and black progress, without being exposed to the charge of racism.

Reagan's successor, President George Bush Sr., did not hesitate to employ implicit racial appeals, having learned from the success of other conservative politicians that subtle negative references to race could mobilize poor and working-class whites who once were loyal to the Democratic Party. Bush's most famous racial appeal, the Willie Horton ad, featured a dark-skinned black man, a convicted murderer who escaped while on a work furlough and then raped and murdered a white woman in her home. The ad blamed Bush's opponent, Massachusetts governor Michael Dukakis, for the death of the white woman, because he approved the furlough program. For months, the ad played repeatedly on network news stations and was the subject of incessant political commentary. Though controversial, the ad was stunningly effective; it destroyed Dukakis's chances of ever becoming president.

Once in the Oval Office, Bush stayed on message, opposing affirmative action and aggressive civil rights enforcement, and embracing the drug war with great enthusiasm. In August 1989, President Bush characterized drug use as "the most pressing problem facing the nation."[93] Shortly thereafter, a New York Times/CBS News Poll reported that 64 percent of those polled— the highest percentage ever recorded—now thought that drugs were the most significant problem in the United States.[94] This surge of public concern did not correspond to a dramatic shift in illegal drug activity, but instead was the product of a carefully orchestrated political campaign. The level of public concern about crime and drugs was only weakly correlated with actual crime rates, but highly correlated with political initiatives, campaigns, and partisan appeals.[95]

The shift to a general attitude of "toughness" toward problems associated with communities of color began in the 1960s, when the gains and goals of the Civil Rights Movement began to require real sacrifices on the part of white Americans, and conservative politicians found they could mobilize white racial resentment by vowing to crack down on crime. By the late 1980s, however, not only conservatives played leading roles in the get-tough movement, spouting the rhetoric once associated only with segregationists. Democratic politicians and policy makers were now attempting to wrest control of the crime and drug issues from Republicans by advocating stricter anticrime and antidrug laws—all in an effort to win back the so-called "swing voters" who were defecting to the Republican Party. Somewhat ironically, these "new Democrats" were joined by virulent racists, most notably the Ku Klux Klan, which announced in 1990 that it intended to "join the battle against illegal drugs" by becoming the "eyes and ears of the police."[96] Progressives concerned about racial justice in this period were mostly silent about the War on Drugs, preferring to channel their energy toward defense of affirmative action and other perceived gains of the Civil Rights Movement.

In the early 1990s, resistance to the emergence of a new system of racialized social control collapsed across the political spectrum. A century earlier, a similar political dynamic had resulted in the birth of Jim Crow. In the 1890s, Populists buckled under the political pressure created by the Redeemers, who had successfully appealed to poor and working-class whites by proposing overtly racist and increasingly absurd Jim Crow laws. Now, a new racial caste system—mass incarceration—was taking hold, as politicians of every stripe competed with each other to win the votes of poor and working-class whites, whose economic status was precarious, at best, and who felt threatened by racial reforms. As had happened before, former allies

of African Americans—as much as conservatives—adopted a political strategy that required them to prove how "tough" they could be on "them," the
dark-skinned pariahs.

The results were immediate. As law enforcement budgets exploded, so did
prison and jail populations. In 1991, the Sentencing Project reported that
the number of people behind bars in the United States was unprecedented in
world history, and that one fourth of young African American men were now
under the control of the criminal justice system. Despite the jaw-dropping
impact of the "get tough" movement on the African American community,
neither the Democrats nor the Republicans revealed any inclination to slow
the pace of incarceration.

To the contrary, in 1992, presidential candidate Bill Clinton vowed that
he would never permit any Republican to be perceived as tougher on crime
than he. True to his word, just weeks before the critical New Hampshire
primary, Clinton chose to fly home to Arkansas to oversee the execution of
Ricky Ray Rector, a mentally impaired black man who had so little conception of what was about to happen to him that he asked for the dessert from his
last meal to be saved for him until the morning. After the execution, Clinton
remarked, "I can be nicked a lot, but no one can say I'm soft on crime."[97]

Once elected, Clinton endorsed the idea of a federal "three strikes and
you're out" law, which he advocated in his 1994 State of the Union address
to enthusiastic applause on both sides of the aisle. The $30 billion crime
bill sent to President Clinton in August 1994 was hailed as a victory for
the Democrats, who "were able to wrest the crime issue from the Republicans and make it their own."[98] The bill created dozens of new federal capital
crimes, mandated life sentences for some three-time offenders, and authorized more than $16 billion for state prison grants and expansion of state
and local police forces. Far from resisting the emergence of the new caste
system, Clinton escalated the drug war beyond what conservatives had
imagined possible a decade earlier. As the Justice Policy Institute has observed, "the Clinton Administration's 'tough on crime' policies resulted in
the largest increases in federal and state prison inmates of any president in
American history."[99]

Clinton eventually moved beyond crime and capitulated to the conservative racial agenda on welfare. This move, like his "get tough" rhetoric and
policies, was part of a grand strategy articulated by the "new Democrats" to
appeal to the elusive white swing voters. In so doing, Clinton—more than

any other president—created the current racial undercaste. He signed the Personal Responsibility and Work Opportunity Reconciliation Act, which "ended welfare as we know it," replacing Aid to Families with Dependent Children (AFDC) with a block grant to states called Temporary Assistance to Needy Families (TANF). TANF imposed a five-year lifetime limit on welfare assistance, as well as a permanent, lifetime ban on eligibility for welfare and food stamps for anyone convicted of a felony drug offense—including simple possession of marijuana.

Despite claims that these radical policy changes were driven by fiscal conservatism—i.e., the desire to end big government and slash budget deficits—the reality is that government was *not* reducing the amount of money devoted to the management of the urban poor. It was radically altering what the funds would be used for. The dramatic shift toward punitiveness resulted in a massive reallocation of public resources. By 1996, the penal budget doubled the amount that had been allocated to AFDC or food stamps.[100] Similarly, funding that had once been used for public housing was being redirected to prison construction. During Clinton's tenure, Washington slashed funding for public housing by $17 billion (a reduction of 61 percent) and boosted corrections by $19 billion (an increase of 171 percent), "effectively making the construction of prisons the nation's main housing program for the urban poor."[101]

Clinton did not stop there. Determined to prove how "tough" he could be on "them," Clinton also made it easier for federally assisted public housing projects to exclude anyone with a criminal history—an extraordinarily harsh step in the midst of a drug war aimed at racial and ethnic minorities. In his announcement of the "One Strike and You're Out" Initiative, Clinton explained: "From now on, the rule for residents who commit crime and peddle drugs should be one strike and you're out."[102] The new rule promised to be "the toughest admission and eviction policy that HUD has implemented."[103] Thus, for countless poor people, particularly racial minorities targeted by the drug war, public housing was no longer available, leaving many of them homeless—locked out not only of mainstream society, but their own homes.

The law and order perspective, first introduced during the peak of the Civil Rights Movement by rabid segregationists, had become nearly hegemonic two decades later. By the mid-1990s, no serious alternatives to the War on Drugs and "get tough" movement were being entertained in mainstream

political discourse. Once again, in response to a major disruption in the prevailing racial order—this time the civil rights gains of the 1960s—a new system of racialized social control was created by exploiting the vulnerabilities
and racial resentments of poor and working-class whites. More than 2 million
people found themselves behind bars at the turn of the twenty-first century,
and millions more were relegated to the margins of mainstream society, ban-
ished to a political and social space not unlike Jim Crow, where discrimination in employment, housing, and access to education was perfectly legal,
and where they could be denied the right to vote. The system functioned
relatively automatically, and the prevailing system of racial meanings, identities, and ideologies already seemed natural. Ninety percent of those admitted to prison for drug offenses in many states were black or Latino, yet the
mass incarceration of communities of color was explained in race-neutral
terms, an adaptation to the needs and demands of the current political climate. The New Jim Crow was born.

2

The Lockdown

We may think we know how the criminal justice system works. Television is overloaded with fictional dramas about police, crime, and prosecutors— shows such as *Law & Order*. These fictional dramas, like the evening news, tend to focus on individual stories of crime, victimization, and punishment, and the stories are typically told from the point of view of law enforcement. A charismatic police officer, investigator, or prosecutor struggles with his own demons while heroically trying to solve a horrible crime. He ultimately achieves a personal and moral victory by finding the bad guy and throwing him in jail. That is the made-for-TV version of the criminal justice system. It perpetuates the myth that the primary function of the system is to keep our streets safe and our homes secure by rooting out dangerous criminals and punishing them. These television shows, especially those that romanticize drug-law enforcement, are the modern-day equivalent of the old movies portraying happy slaves, the fictional gloss placed on a brutal system of racialized oppression and control.

Those who have been swept within the criminal justice system know that the way the system actually works bears little resemblance to what happens on television or in movies. Full-blown trials of guilt or innocence rarely occur; many people never even meet with an attorney; witnesses are routinely paid and coerced by the government; police regularly stop and search people for no reason whatsoever; penalties for many crimes are so severe that innocent people plead guilty, accepting plea bargains to avoid harsh mandatory sentences; and children, even as young as fourteen, are sent to adult prisons.

Rules of law and procedure, such as "guilt beyond a reasonable doubt" or "probable cause" or "reasonable suspicion," can easily be found in court cases and law-school textbooks but are much harder to find in real life.

In this chapter, we shall see how the system of mass incarceration actually works. Our focus is the War on Drugs. The reason is simple: Convictions for drug offenses are the single most important cause of the explosion in incarceration rates in the United States. Drug offenses alone account for two-thirds of the rise in the federal inmate population and more than half of the rise in state prisoners between 1985 and 2000.[1] Approximately a half-million people are in prison or jail for a drug offense today, compared to an estimated 41,100 in 1980—an increase of 1,100 percent.[2] Drug arrests have tripled since 1980. As a result, more than 31 million people have been arrested for drug offenses since the drug war began.[3] To put the matter in perspective, consider this: there are more people in prisons and jails today just for drug offenses than were incarcerated for *all* reasons in 1980.[4] Nothing has contributed more to the systematic mass incarceration of people of color in the United States than the War on Drugs.

Before we begin our tour of the drug war, it is worthwhile to get a couple of myths out of the way. The first is that the war is aimed at ridding the nation of drug "kingpins" or big-time dealers. Nothing could be further from the truth. The vast majority of those arrested are *not* charged with serious offenses. In 2005, for example, four out of five drug arrests were for possession, and only one out of five was for sales. Moreover, most people in state prison for drug offenses have *no* history of violence or significant selling activity.[5]

The second myth is that the drug war is principally concerned with dangerous drugs. Quite to the contrary, arrests for marijuana possession—a drug less harmful than tobacco or alcohol—accounted for nearly 80 percent of the growth in drug arrests in the 1990s.[6] Despite the fact that most drug arrests are for nonviolent minor offenses, the War on Drugs has ushered in an era of unprecedented punitiveness.

The percentage of drug arrests that result in prison sentences (rather than dismissal, community service, or probation) has quadrupled, resulting in a prison-building boom the likes of which the world has never seen. In two short decades, between 1980 and 2000, the number of people incarcerated in our nation's prisons and jails soared from roughly 300,000 to more than 2 million. By the end of 2007, more than 7 million Americans—or one in every 31 adults—were behind bars, on probation, or on parole.[7]

We begin our exploration of the drug war at the point of entry—arrest by the police—and then consider how the system of mass incarceration is structured to reward mass drug arrests and facilitate the conviction and imprisonment of an unprecedented number of Americans, whether guilty or innocent. In subsequent chapters, we will consider how the system specifically targets people of color and then relegates them to a second-class status analogous to Jim Crow. At this point, we simply take stock of the means by which the War on Drugs facilitates the roundup and lockdown of an extraordinary percentage of the U.S. population.

Rules of the Game

Few legal rules meaningfully constrain the police in the War on Drugs. This may sound like an overstatement, but upon examination it proves accurate. The absence of significant constraints on the exercise of police discretion is a key feature of the drug war's design. It has made the roundup of millions of Americans for nonviolent drug offenses relatively easy.

With only a few exceptions, the Supreme Court has seized every opportunity to facilitate the drug war, primarily by eviscerating Fourth Amendment protections against unreasonable searches and seizures by the police. The rollback has been so pronounced that some commentators charge that a virtual "drug exception" now exists to the Bill of Rights. Shortly before his death, Justice Thurgood Marshall felt compelled to remind his colleagues that there is, in fact, "no drug exception" written into the text of the Constitution.[8]

Most Americans do not know what the Fourth Amendment of the U.S. Constitution actually says or what it requires of the police. It states, in its entirety:

> The right of the people to be secure in their persons, houses, papers, and effects, against unreasonable searches and seizures, shall not be violated, and no warrants shall issue, but upon probable cause, supported by oath or affirmation, and particularly describing the place to be searched, and the person or things to be seized.

Courts and scholars agree that the Fourth Amendment governs all searches and seizures by the police and that the amendment was adopted in response to the English practice of conducting arbitrary searches under general warrants to uncover seditious libels. The routine police harassment, arbitrary searches, and widespread police intimidation of those subject to English rule helped to inspire the American Revolution. Not surprisingly, then, preventing arbitrary searches and seizures by the police was deemed by the Founding Fathers an essential element of the U.S. Constitution. Until the War on Drugs, courts had been fairly stringent about enforcing the Fourth Amendment's requirements.

Within a few years after the drug war was declared, however, many legal scholars noted a sharp turn in the Supreme Court's Fourth Amendment jurisprudence. By the close of the Supreme Court's 1990–91 term, it had become clear that a major shift in the relationship between the citizens of this country and the police was under way. Justice Stevens noted the trend in a powerful dissent issued in *California v. Acevedo*, a case upholding the warrantless search of a bag locked in a motorist's trunk:

> In the years [from 1982 to 1991], the Court has heard argument in 30 Fourth Amendment cases involving narcotics. In all but one, the government was the petitioner. All save two involved a search or seizure without a warrant or with a defective warrant. And, in all except three, the Court upheld the constitutionality of the search or seizure. In the meantime, the flow of narcotics cases through the courts has steadily and dramatically increased. No impartial observer could criticize this Court for hindering the progress of the war on drugs. On the contrary, decisions like the one the Court makes today will support the conclusion that this Court has become a loyal foot soldier in the Executive's fight against crime.[9]

The Fourth Amendment is but one example. Virtually all constitutionally protected civil liberties have been undermined by the drug war. The Court has been busy in recent years approving mandatory drug testing of employees and students, upholding random searches and sweeps of public schools and students, permitting police to obtain search warrants based on an anonymous informant's tip, expanding the government's wiretapping authority, legitimating the use of paid, unidentified informants by police and prosecutors, approving the use of helicopter surveillance of homes without a warrant, and allowing the forfeiture of cash, homes, and other property based on unproven allegations of illegal drug activity.

For our purposes here, we limit our focus to the legal rules crafted by the Supreme Court that grant law enforcement a pecuniary interest in the drug war and make it relatively easy for the police to seize people virtually anywhere—on public streets and sidewalks, on buses, airplanes and trains, or any other public place—and usher them behind bars. These new legal rules have ensured that anyone, virtually anywhere, for any reason, can become a target of drug-law enforcement activity.

Unreasonable Suspicion

Once upon a time, it was generally understood that the police could not stop and search someone without a warrant unless there was probable cause to believe that the individual was engaged in criminal activity. That was a basic Fourth Amendment principle. In *Terry v. Ohio*, decided in 1968, the Supreme Court modified that understanding, but only modestly, by ruling that if and when a police officer observes unusual conduct by someone the officer reasonably believes to be dangerous and engaged in criminal activity, the officer "is entitled for the protection of himself and others in the area" to conduct a limited search "to discover weapons that might be used against the officer."[10] Known as the stop-and-frisk rule, the *Terry* decision stands for the proposition that, so long as a police officer has "reasonable articulable suspicion" that someone is engaged in criminal activity *and* dangerous, it is constitutionally permissible to stop, question, and frisk him or her—even in the absence of probable cause.

Justice Douglas dissented in *Terry* on the grounds that "grant[ing] police greater power than a magistrate [judge] is to take a long step down the totalitarian path."[11] He objected to the notion that police should be free to conduct warrantless searches whenever they suspect someone is a criminal, believing that dispensing with the Fourth Amendment's warrant requirement risked opening the door to the same abuses that gave rise to the American Revolution. His voice was a lonely one. Most commentators at the time agreed that affording police the power and discretion to protect themselves during an encounter with someone they believed to be a dangerous criminal is not "unreasonable" under the Fourth Amendment.

History suggests Justice Douglas had the better of the argument. In the years since *Terry*, stops, interrogations, and searches of ordinary people driving down the street, walking home from the bus stop, or riding the train, have become commonplace—at least for people of color. As Douglas suspected, the Court in *Terry* had begun its slide down a very slippery slope. Today it is no longer necessary for the police to have any reason to believe that people are engaged in criminal activity or actually dangerous to stop and search them. As long as you give "consent," the police can stop, interrogate, and search you for any reason or no reason at all.

Just Say No

The first major sign that the Supreme Court would not allow the Fourth Amendment to interfere with the prosecution of the War on Drugs came in *Florida v. Bostick*. In that case, Terrance Bostick, a twenty-eight-year-old African American, had been sleeping in the back seat of a Greyhound bus on his way from Miami to Atlanta. Two police officers, wearing bright green "raid" jackets and displaying their badges and a gun, woke him with a start. The bus was stopped for a brief layover in Fort Lauderdale, and the officers were "working the bus," looking for persons who might be carrying drugs. Bostick provided them with his identification and ticket, as requested. The officers then asked to search his bag. Bostick complied, even though he knew his bag contained a pound of cocaine. The officers had no basis for suspecting Bostick of any criminal activity, but they got lucky. They arrested Bostick, and he was charged and convicted of trafficking cocaine.

Bostick's search and seizure reflected what had become an increasingly common tactic in the War on Drugs: suspicionless police sweeps of buses in interstate or intrastate travel. The resulting "interviews" of passengers in these dragnet operations usually culminate in a request for "consent" to search the passenger's luggage.[12] Never do the officers inform passengers that they are free to remain silent or to refuse to answer questions. By proceeding systematically in this manner, the police are able to engage in an extremely high volume of searches. One officer was able to search over three thousand bags in a nine-month period employing these techniques.[13] By and large, however, the hit rates are low. For example, in one case, a sweep of one hundred buses resulted in only seven arrests.[14]

On appeal, the Florida Supreme Court ruled in Bostick's case that the police officer's conduct violated the Fourth Amendment's prohibition of unreasonable searches and seizures. The Fourth Amendment, the court reasoned, forbids the police from seizing people and searching them without some individualized suspicion that they have committed or are committing a crime. The court thus overturned Bostick's conviction, ruling that the cocaine, having been obtained illegally, was inadmissible. It also broadly condemned "bus sweeps" in the drug war, comparing them to methods employed by totalitarian regimes:

> The evidence in this case has evoked images of other days, under other flags, when no man traveled his nation's roads or railways without fear of unwarranted interruption, by individuals who had temporary power in Government. . . . This is not Hitler's Berlin, nor Stalin's Moscow, nor is it white supremacist South Africa. Yet in Broward County, Florida, these police officers approach every person on board buses and trains ("that time permits") and check identification, tickets, ask to search luggage—all in the name of "voluntary cooperation" with law enforcement.[15]

The U.S. Supreme Court reversed. The Court ruled that Bostick's encounter with the police was purely voluntary, and therefore he was not "seized" within the meaning of the Fourth Amendment. Even if Bostick did not feel free to leave when confronted by police at the back of the bus, the proper question, according to the Court, was whether "a reasonable person" in Bostick's shoes would have felt free to terminate the encounter. A reasonable person, the Court concluded, would have felt free to sit there and refuse to answer the police officer's questions, and would have felt free to tell the officer "No, you can't search my bag." Accordingly, Bostick was not really "seized" within the meaning of the Fourth Amendment, and the subsequent search was purely consensual. The Court made clear that its decision was to govern all future drug sweeps, no matter what the circumstances of the targeted individual. Given the blanket nature of the ruling, courts have found police encounters to be consensual in truly preposterous situations. For example, a few years after *Bostick*, the District of Columbia Court of Appeals applied the ruling to a case involving a fourteen-year-old girl interrogated by the police, concluding that she must be held to the same reasonable-person standard.[16]

Prior to the *Bostick* decision, a number of lower courts had found absurd the notion that "reasonable people" would feel empowered to refuse to answer

questions when confronted by the police. As federal judge Prentiss Marshall
explained, "The average person encountered will feel obliged to stop and respond. Few will feel that they can walk away or refuse to answer."[17] Professor Tracey Maclin put it this way: "Common sense teaches that most of us
do not have the chutzpah or stupidity to tell a police officer to 'get lost' after
he has stopped us and asked us for identification or questioned us about
possible criminal conduct."[18] Other courts emphasized that granting police
the freedom to stop, interrogate, and search anyone who consented would
likely lead to racial and ethnic discrimination. Young black men would be
the likely targets, rather than older white women. Justice Thurgood Marshall acknowledged as much in his dissent in *Bostick*, noting "the basis of
the decision to single out particular passengers during a suspicionless sweep
is less likely to be inarticulable than unspeakable."[19]

Studies have shown that Maclin's common sense is correct: the overwhelming majority of people who are confronted by police and asked questions respond, and when asked to be searched, they comply.[20] This is the
case even among those, like Bostick, who have every reason to resist these
tactics because they actually have something to hide. This is no secret to the
Supreme Court. The Court long ago acknowledged that effective use of
consent searches by the police depends on the ignorance (and powerless-
ness) of those who are targeted. In *Schneckloth v. Bustamonte*, decided in
1973, the Court admitted that if waiver of one's right to refuse consent were
truly "knowing, intelligent, and voluntary," it would "in practice create serious doubt whether consent searches would continue to be conducted."[21] In
other words, consent searches are valuable tools for the police only because
hardly anyone dares to say no.

Poor Excuse

So-called consent searches have made it possible for the police to stop and
search just about anybody walking down the street for drugs. All a police officer has to do in order to conduct a baseless drug investigation is ask to
speak with someone and then get their "consent" to be searched. So long as
orders are phrased as a question, compliance is interpreted as consent. "May
I speak to you?" thunders an officer. "Will you put your arms up and stand

against the wall for a search?" Because almost no one refuses, drug sweeps on the sidewalk (and on buses and trains) are easy. People are easily intimidated when the police confront them, hands on their revolvers, and most have no idea the question can be answered, "No." But what about all the people driving down the street? How do police extract consent from them? The answer: pretext stops.

Like consent searches, pretext stops are favorite tools of law enforcement in the War on Drugs. A classic pretext stop is a traffic stop motivated not by any desire to enforce traffic laws, but instead motivated by a desire to hunt for drugs in the absence of any evidence of illegal drug activity. In other words, police officers use minor traffic violations as an excuse—a pretext— to search for drugs, even though there is not a shred of evidence suggesting the motorist is violating drug laws. Pretext stops, like consent searches, have received the Supreme Court's unequivocal blessing. Just ask Michael Whren and James Brown.

Whren and Brown, both of whom are African American, were stopped by plainclothes officers in an unmarked vehicle in June 1993. The police admitted to stopping Whren and Brown because they wanted to investigate them for imagined drug crimes, even though they did not have probable cause or reasonable suspicion such crimes had actually been committed. Lacking actual evidence of criminal activity, the officers decided to stop them based on a pretext—a traffic violation. The officers testified that the driver failed to use his turn signal and accelerated abruptly from a stop sign. Although the officers weren't really interested in the traffic violation, they stopped the pair anyway because they had a "hunch" they might be drug criminals. It turned out they were right. According to the officers, the driver had a bag of cocaine in his lap—allegedly in plain view.

On appeal, Whren and Brown challenged their convictions on the ground that pretextual stops violate the Fourth Amendment. They argued that, because of the multitude of applicable traffic and equipment regulations, and the difficulty of obeying all traffic rules perfectly at all times, the police will nearly always have an excuse to stop someone and go fishing for drugs. Anyone driving more than a few blocks is likely to commit a traffic violation of some kind, such as failing to track properly between lanes, failing to stop at precisely the correct distance behind a crosswalk, failing to pause for precisely the right amount of time at a stop sign, or failing to use a turn signal

at the appropriate distance from an intersection. Allowing the police to use
minor traffic violations as a pretext for baseless drug investigations would
permit them to single out anyone for a drug investigation without any evidence of illegal drug activity whatsoever. That kind of arbitrary police conduct is precisely what the Fourth Amendment was intended to prohibit.

The Supreme Court rejected their argument, ruling that an officer's motivations are irrelevant when evaluating the reasonableness of police activity
under the Fourth Amendment. It does not matter, the Court declared, *why*
the police are stopping motorists under the Fourth Amendment, so long as
some kind of traffic violation gives them an excuse. The fact that the Fourth
Amendment was specifically adopted by the Founding Fathers to prevent
arbitrary stops and searches was deemed unpersuasive. The Court ruled
that the police are free to use minor traffic violations as a pretext to conduct
drug investigations, even when there is no evidence of illegal drug activity.

A few months later, in *Ohio v. Robinette*, the Court took its twisted logic
one step further. In that case, a police officer pulled over Robert Robinette,
allegedly for speeding. After checking Robinette's license and issuing a warn-
ing (but no ticket), the officer then ordered Robinette out of his vehicle,
turned on a video camera in the officer's car, and then asked Robinette
whether he was carrying any drugs and would "consent" to a search. He did.
The officer found a small amount of marijuana in Robinette's car, and a single pill, which turned out to be methamphetamine.

The Ohio Supreme Court, reviewing the case on appeal, was obviously
uncomfortable with the blatant fishing expedition for drugs. The court noted
that traffic stops were increasingly being used in the War on Drugs to extract
"consent" for searches, and that motorists may not believe they are free to
refuse consent and simply drive away. In an effort to provide some minimal
protection for motorists, the Ohio court adopted a bright-line rule, that is,
an unambiguous requirement that officers tell motorists they are free to
leave before asking for consent to search their vehicles. At the very least, the
justices reasoned, motorists should know they have the right to refuse consent and to leave, if they so choose.

The U.S. Supreme Court struck down this basic requirement as "unrealistic." In so doing, the Court made clear to all lower courts that, from now
on, the Fourth Amendment should place no meaningful constraints on the
police in the War on Drugs. No one needs to be informed of their rights dur-

ing a stop or search, and police may use minor traffic stops as well as the myth of "consent" to stop and search anyone they choose for imaginary drug crimes, whether or not any evidence of illegal drug activity actually exists.

One might imagine that the legal rules described thus far would provide more than enough latitude for the police to engage in an all-out, no-holds-barred war on drugs. But there's more. Even if motorists, after being detained and interrogated, have the nerve to refuse consent to a search, the police can arrest them anyway. In *Atwater v. City of Lago Vista*, the Supreme Court held that the police may arrest motorists for minor traffic violations and throw them in jail (even if the statutory penalty for the traffic violation is a mere fine, not jail time).

Another legal option for officers frustrated by a motorist's refusal to grant "consent" is to bring a drug-sniffing dog to the scene. This option is available to police in traffic stops, as well as to law enforcement officials confronted with resistant travelers in airports and in bus or train stations who refuse to give the police consent to search their luggage. The Supreme Court has ruled that walking a drug-sniffing dog around someone's vehicle (or someone's luggage) does not constitute a "search," and therefore does not trigger Fourth Amendment scrutiny.[22] If the dog alerts to drugs, then the officer has probable cause to search without the person's consent. Naturally, in most cases, when someone is told that a drug-sniffing dog will be called, the seized individual backs down and "consents" to the search, as it has become apparent that the police are determined to conduct the search one way or another.

Kissing Frogs

Court cases involving drug-law enforcement almost always involve guilty people. Police usually release the innocent on the street—often without a ticket, citation, or even an apology—so their stories are rarely heard in court. Hardly anyone files a complaint, because the last thing most people want to do after experiencing a frightening and intrusive encounter with the police is show up at the police station where the officer works and attract more attention to themselves. For good reason, many people—especially poor people of color—fear police harassment, retaliation, and abuse. After having your car torn apart by the police in a futile search for drugs, or being forced to lie spread-eagled on the pavement while the police search you and interrogate you for no reason at all, how much confidence do you have in law enforcement? Do you expect to get a fair hearing? Those who try to find an attorney to represent them in a lawsuit often learn that unless they have broken bones (and no criminal record), private attorneys are unlikely to be interested in their case. Many people are shocked to discover that what happened to them on the side of the road was not, in fact, against the law.

The inevitable result is that the people who wind up in front of a judge are usually guilty of some crime. The parade of guilty people through America's courtrooms gives the false impression to the public—as well as to judges—that when the police have a "hunch," it makes sense to let them act on it. Judges tend to imagine the police have a sixth sense—or some kind of special police training—that qualifies them to identify drug criminals in the absence of any evidence. After all, they seem to be right so much of the time, don't they?

The truth, however, is that most people stopped and searched in the War on Drugs are perfectly innocent of any crime. The police have received no training that enhances the likelihood they will spot the drug criminals as they drive by and leave everyone else alone. To the contrary, tens of thousands of law enforcement officers have received training that guarantees precisely the opposite. The Drug Enforcement Agency (DEA) trains police to conduct utterly unreasonable and discriminatory stops and searches throughout the United States.

Perhaps the best known of these training programs is Operation Pipeline. The DEA launched Operation Pipeline in 1984 as part of the Reagan administration's rollout of the War on Drugs. The federal program, administered by over three hundred state and local law enforcement agencies, trains state and local law enforcement officers to use pretextual traffic stops and consent searches on a large scale for drug interdiction. Officers learn, among other things, how to use a minor traffic violation as a pretext to stop someone, how to lengthen a routine traffic stop and leverage it into a search for drugs, how to obtain consent from a reluctant motorist, and how to use drug-sniffing dogs to obtain probable cause.[23] By 2000, the DEA had directly trained more than 25,000 officers in forty-eight states in Pipeline tactics and helped to develop training programs for countless municipal and state law enforcement agencies. In legal scholar Ricardo Bascuas's words, "Operation Pipeline is exactly what the Framers meant to prohibit: a federally-run general search program that targets people without cause for suspicion, particularly those who belong to disfavored groups."[24]

The program's success requires police to stop "staggering" numbers of people in shotgun fashion.[25] This "volume" approach to drug enforcement sweeps up extraordinary numbers of innocent people. As one California Highway Patrol Officer said, "It's sheer numbers.... You've got to kiss a lot of frogs before you find a prince."[26] Accordingly, every year, tens of thousands of motorists find themselves stopped on the side of the road, fielding questions about imaginary drug activity, and then succumbing to a request for their vehicle to be searched—sometimes torn apart—in the search for drugs. Most of these stops and searches are futile. It has been estimated that 95 percent of Pipeline stops yield no illegal drugs.[27] One study found that up to 99 percent of traffic stops made by federally funded narcotics task forces result in no citation and that 98 percent of task-force searches during traffic stops are discretionary searches in which the officer searches the car with the driver's verbal "consent" but has no other legal authority to do so.[28]

The "drug-courier profiles" utilized by the DEA and other law enforcement agencies for drug sweeps on highways, as well as in airports and train stations, are notoriously unreliable. In theory, a drug-courier profile reflects the collective wisdom and judgment of a law enforcement agency's officials. Instead of allowing each officer to rely on his or her own limited experience and biases in detecting suspicious behavior, a drug-courier profile affords every officer the advantage of the agency's collective experience and expertise. However, as legal scholar David Cole has observed, "in practice, the drug-courier profile is a scattershot hodgepodge of traits and characteristics so expansive that it potentially justifies stopping anybody and everybody."[29] The profile can include traveling with luggage, traveling without luggage, driving an expensive car, driving a car that needs repairs, driving with out-of-state license plates, driving a rental car, driving with "mismatched occupants," acting too calm, acting too nervous, dressing casually, wearing expensive clothing or jewelry, being one of the first to deplane, being one of the last to deplane, deplaning in the middle, paying for a ticket in cash, using large-denomination currency, using small-denomination currency, traveling alone, traveling with a companion, and so on. Even striving to obey the law fits the profile! The Florida Highway Patrol Drug Courier Profile cautioned troopers to be suspicious of "scrupulous obedience to traffic laws."[30] As Cole points out, "such profiles do not so much focus an investigation as provide law enforcement officials a ready-made excuse for stopping whomever they please."[31]

The Supreme Court has allowed use of drug-courier profiles as guides for the exercise of police discretion. Although it has indicated that the mere fact that someone fits a profile does not automatically constitute reasonable suspicion justifying a stop, courts routinely defer to these profiles, and the Court has yet to object. As one judge said after conducting a review of drug-courier profile decisions: "Many courts have accepted the profile, as well as the Drug Enforcement Agency's scattershot enforcement efforts, unquestioningly, mechanistically, and dispositively."[32]

It Pays to Play

Clearly, the rules of the game are designed to allow for the roundup of an unprecedented number of Americans for minor, nonviolent drug offenses. The number of annual drug arrests more than tripled between 1980 and 2005, as drug sweeps and suspicionless stops and searches proceeded in record numbers.[33]

Still, it is fair to wonder why the police would choose to arrest such an astonishing percentage of the American public for minor drug crimes. The fact that police are legally *allowed* to engage in a wholesale roundup of nonviolent drug offenders does not answer the question *why* they would choose to do so, particularly when most police departments have far more serious crimes to prevent and solve. Why would police prioritize drug-law enforcement? Drug use and abuse is nothing new; in fact, it was on the decline, not on the rise, when the War on Drugs began. So why make drug-law enforcement a priority now?

Once again, the answer lies in the system's design. Every system of control depends for its survival on the tangible and intangible benefits that are provided to those who are responsible for the system's maintenance and administration. This system is no exception.

At the time the drug war was declared, illegal drug use and abuse was not a pressing concern in most communities. The announcement of a War on Drugs was therefore met with some confusion and resistance within law enforcement, as well as among some conservative commentators.[34] The federalization of drug crime violated the conservative tenet of states' rights and local control, as street crime was typically the responsibility of local law enforcement. Many state and local law enforcement officials were less than pleased with the attempt by the federal government to assert itself in local crime fighting, viewing the new drug war as an unwelcome distraction. Participation in the drug war required a diversion of resources away from more serious crimes, such as murder, rape, grand theft, and violent assault— all of which were of far greater concern to most communities than illegal drug use.

The resistance within law enforcement to the drug war created something of a dilemma for the Reagan administration. In order for the war to actually work—that is, in order for it to succeed in achieving its political goals—it was necessary to build a consensus among state and local law enforcement agencies that the drug war should be a top priority in their hometowns. The solution: cash. Huge cash grants were made to those law enforcement agencies that were willing to make drug-law enforcement a top priority. The new system of control is traceable, to a significant degree, to a massive bribe offered to state and local law enforcement by the federal government.

In 1988, at the behest of the Reagan administration, Congress revised the program that provides federal aid to law enforcement, renaming it the Edward Byrne Memorial State and Local Law Enforcement Assistance Program after a New York City police officer who was shot to death while guarding the home of a drug-case witness. The Byrne program was designed to encourage every federal grant recipient to help fight the War on Drugs. Millions of dollars in federal aid have been offered to state and local law enforcement agencies willing to wage the war. This federal grant money has resulted in the proliferation of narcotics task forces, including those responsible for highway drug interdiction. Nationally, narcotics task forces make up about 40 percent of all Byrne grant funding, but in some states as much as 90 percent of all Byrne grant funds go toward specialized narcotics task forces.[35] In fact, it is questionable whether any specialized drug enforcement activity would exist in some states without the Byrne program.

Other forms of valuable aid have been offered as well. The DEA has offered free training, intelligence, and technical support to state highway patrol agencies that are willing to commit their officers to highway drug interdiction. The Pentagon, for its part, has given away military intelligence and millions of dollars in firepower to state and local agencies willing to make the rhetorical war a literal one.

Almost immediately after the federal dollars began to flow, law enforcement agencies across the country began to compete for funding, equipment, and training. By the late 1990s, the overwhelming majority of state and local police forces in the country had availed themselves of the newly available resources and added a significant military component to buttress their drug-war operations. According to the Cato Institute, in 1997 alone, the Pentagon handed over more than 1.2 million pieces of military equipment to local police departments.[36] Similarly, the *National Journal* reported that between January 1997 and October 1999, the agency handled 3.4 million orders of Pentagon equipment from over eleven thousand domestic police agencies in all fifty states. Included in the bounty were "253 aircraft (including six- and seven-passenger airplanes, UH-60 Blackhawk and UH-1 Huey helicopters, 7,856 M-16 rifles, 181 grenade launchers, 8,131 bulletproof helmets, and 1,161 pairs of night-vision goggles."[37] A retired police chief in New Haven, Connecticut, told the *New York Times*, "I was offered tanks, bazookas, anything I wanted."[38]

Waging War

In barely a decade, the War on Drugs went from being a political slogan to an actual war. Now that police departments were suddenly flush with cash and military equipment earmarked for the drug war, they needed to make use of their new resources. As described in a Cato Institute report, paramilitary units (most commonly called Special Weapons and Tactics, or SWAT, teams) were quickly formed in virtually every major city to fight the drug war.[39]

SWAT teams originated in the 1960s and gradually became more common in the 1970s, but until the drug war, they were used rarely, primarily for extraordinary emergency situations such as hostage takings, hijackings, or prison escapes. That changed in the 1980s, when local law enforcement agencies suddenly had access to cash and military equipment specifically for the purpose of conducting drug raids.

Today, the most common use of SWAT teams is to serve narcotics warrants, usually with forced, unannounced entry into the home. In fact, in some jurisdictions drug warrants are served *only* by SWAT teams—regardless of the nature of the alleged drug crime. As the *Miami Herald* reported in 2002, "Police say they want [SWAT teams] in case of a hostage situation or a Columbine-type incident, but in practice the teams are used mainly to serve search warrants on suspected drug dealers. Some of these searches yield as little as a few grams of cocaine or marijuana."[40]

The rate of increase in the use of SWAT teams has been astonishing. In 1972, there were just a few hundred paramilitary drug raids per year in the United States. By the early 1980s, there were three thousand annual SWAT deployments, by 1996 there were thirty thousand, and by 2001 there were forty thousand.[41] The escalation of military force was quite dramatic in cities throughout the United States. In the city of Minneapolis, Minnesota, for example, its SWAT team was deployed on no-knock warrants thirty-five times in 1986, but in 1996 that same team was deployed for drug raids more than seven hundred times.[42]

Drug raids conducted by SWAT teams are not polite encounters. In countless situations in which police could easily have arrested someone or conducted a search without a military-style raid, police blast into people's homes, typically in the middle of the night, throwing grenades, shouting, and pointing guns and rifles at anyone inside, often including young children. In recent years, dozens of people have been killed by police in the course of these raids, including elderly grandparents and those who are completely innocent of any crime. Criminologist Peter Kraska reports that between 1989 and 2001 at least 780 cases of flawed paramilitary raids reached the appellate level, a dramatic increase over the 1980s, when such cases were rare, or earlier, when they were nonexistent.[43] Many of these cases involve people killed in botched raids.

Alberta Spruill, a fifty-seven-year-old city worker from Harlem, is among the fallen. On May 16, 2003, a dozen New York City police officers stormed her apartment building on a no-knock warrant, acting on a tip from a confidential informant who told them a convicted felon was selling drugs on the sixth floor. The informant had actually been in jail at the time he said he'd bought drugs in the apartment, and the target of the raid had been arrested four days before, but the officers didn't check and didn't even interview the building superintendent. The only resident in the building was Alberta, described by friends as a "devout churchgoer." Before entering, police deployed a flash-bang grenade, resulting in a blinding, deafening explosion. Alberta went into cardiac arrest and died two hours later. The death was ruled a homicide but no one was indicted.

Those who survive SWAT raids are generally traumatized by the event. Not long after Spruill's death, Manhattan Borough President C. Virginia Fields held hearings on SWAT practices in New York City. According to the *Village Voice*, "Dozens of black and Latino victims—nurses, secretaries, and former officers—packed her chambers airing tales, one more horrifying than the next. Most were unable to hold back tears as they described police ransacking their homes, handcuffing children and grandparents, putting guns to their heads, and being verbally (and often physically) abusive. In many cases, victims had received no follow-up from the NYPD, even to fix busted doors or other physical damage."[44]

Even in small towns, such as those in Dodge County, Wisconsin, SWAT teams treat routine searches for narcotics as a major battlefront in the drug war. In Dodge County, police raided the mobile home of Scott Bryant in April 1995, after finding traces of marijuana in his garbage. Moments after busting into the mobile home, police shot Bryant—who was unarmed—killing him. Bryant's eight-year-old son was asleep in the next room and watched his father die while waiting for an ambulance. The district attorney theorized that the shooter's hand had clenched in "sympathetic physical reaction" as his other hand reached for handcuffs. A spokesman for the Beretta company called this unlikely because the gun's double-action trigger was designed to prevent unintentional firing. The Dodge County sheriff compared the shooting to a hunting accident.[45]

SWAT raids have not been limited to homes, apartment buildings, or public housing projects. Public high schools have been invaded by SWAT teams in search of drugs. In November 2003, for example, police raided Stratford High School in Goose Creek, South Carolina. The raid was recorded by the school's surveillance cameras as well as a police camera. The tapes show students as young as fourteen forced to the ground in handcuffs as officers in SWAT team uniforms and bulletproof vests aim guns at their heads and lead a drug-sniffing dog to tear through their book bags. The raid was initiated by the school's principal, who was suspicious that a single student might be dealing marijuana. No drugs or weapons were found during the raid and no charges were filed. Nearly all of the students searched and seized were students of color.

The transformation from "community policing" to "military policing," began in 1981, when President Reagan persuaded Congress to pass the Military Cooperation with Law Enforcement Act, which encouraged the military to give local, state, and federal police access to military bases, intelligence, research, weaponry, and other equipment for drug interdiction. That legislation carved a huge exception to the Posse Comitatus Act, the Civil War–era law prohibiting the use of the military for civilian policing. It was followed by Reagan's National Security Decision Directive, which declared drugs a threat to U.S. national security, and provided for yet more cooperation between local, state, and federal law enforcement. In the years that followed, Presidents George Bush and Bill Clinton enthusiastically embraced the drug war and increased the transfer of military equipment, technology, and training to local law enforcement, contingent, of course, on the willingness of agencies to prioritize drug-law enforcement and concentrate resources on arrests for illegal drugs.

The incentives program worked. Drug arrests skyrocketed, as SWAT teams swept through urban housing projects, highway patrol agencies organized drug interdiction units on the freeways, and stop-and-frisk programs were set loose on the streets. Generally, the financial incentives offered to local law enforcement to pump up their drug arrests have not been well publicized, leading the average person to conclude reasonably (but mistakenly) that when their local police departments report that drug arrests have doubled or tripled in a short period of time, the arrests reflect a surge in illegal drug activity, rather than an infusion of money and an intensified enforcement effort.

One exception is a 2001 report by the *Capital Times* in Madison, Wisconsin. The *Times* reported that as of 2001, sixty-five of the state's eighty-three local SWAT teams had come into being since 1980, and that the explosion of SWAT teams was traceable to the Pentagon's weaponry giveaway program, as well as to federal programs that provide money to local police departments for drug control. The paper explained that, in the 1990s, Wisconsin police departments were given nearly a hundred thousand pieces of military equipment. And although the paramilitary units were often justified to city councils and skeptical citizens as essential to fight terrorism or deal with hostage situations, they were rarely deployed for those reasons but instead were sent to serve routine search warrants for drugs and make drug arrests. In fact, the *Times* reported that police departments had an extraordinary incentive to use their new equipment for drug enforcement: the extra federal funding the local police departments received was tied to antidrug policing. The size of the disbursements was linked to the number of city or county drug arrests. Each arrest, in theory, would net a given city or county about $153 in state and federal funding. Non-drug-related policing brought no federal dollars, even for violent crime. As a result, when Jackson County, Wisconsin, quadrupled its drug arrests between 1999 and 2000, the county's federal subsidy quadrupled too.[46]

Finders Keepers

As if the free military equipment, training, and cash grants were not enough, the Reagan administration provided law enforcement with yet another financial incentive to devote extraordinary resources to drug law enforcement, rather than more serious crimes: state and local law enforcement agencies were granted the authority to keep, for their own use, the vast majority of cash and assets they seize when waging the drug war. This dramatic change in policy gave state and local police an enormous stake in the War on Drugs—not in its success, but in its perpetual existence. Law enforcement gained a pecuniary interest not only in the forfeited property, but in the profitability of the drug market itself.

Modern drug forfeiture laws date back to 1970, when Congress passed the Comprehensive Drug Abuse Prevention and Control Act. The Act included a civil forfeiture provision authorizing the government to seize and forfeit drugs, drug manufacturing and storage equipment, and conveyances used to transport drugs. As legal scholars Eric Blumenson and Eva Nilsen have explained, the provision was justified as an effort "to forestall the spread of drugs in a way criminal penalties could not—by striking at its economic roots."[47] When a drug dealer is sent to jail, there are many others ready and willing to take his place, but seizing the means of production, some legislators reasoned, may shut down the trafficking business for good. Over the years, the list of properties subject to forfeiture expanded greatly, and the required connection to illegal drug activity became increasingly remote, leading to many instances of abuse. But it was not until 1984, when Congress amended the federal law to allow federal law enforcement agencies to retain and use any and all proceeds from asset forfeitures, and to allow state and local police agencies to retain up to 80 percent of the assets' value, that a true revolution occurred.

Suddenly, police departments were capable of increasing the size of their budgets, quite substantially, simply by taking the cash, cars, and homes of people suspected of drug use or sales. At the time the new rules were adopted, the law governing civil forfeiture was so heavily weighted in favor of the government that fully 80 percent of forfeitures went uncontested. Property or cash could be seized based on mere suspicion of illegal drug activity, and the seizure could occur without notice or hearing, upon an ex parte showing of mere probable cause to believe that the property had somehow been "involved" in a crime. The probable cause showing could be based on nothing more than hearsay, innuendo, or even the paid, self-serving testimony of someone with interests clearly adverse to the property owner. Neither the owner of the property nor anyone else need be charged with a crime, much less found guilty of one. Indeed, a person could be found innocent of any criminal conduct and the property could still be subject to forfeiture. Once the property was seized, the owner had no right of counsel, and the burden was placed on him to prove the property's "innocence." Because those who were targeted were typically poor or of moderate means, they often lacked the resources to hire an attorney or pay the considerable court costs. As a result, most people who had their cash or property seized did not challenge the government's action, especially because the government could retaliate by filing criminal charges—baseless or not.

Not surprisingly, this drug forfeiture regime proved highly lucrative for law enforcement, offering more than enough incentive to wage the War on Drugs. According to a report commissioned by the Department of Justice, between 1988 and 1992 alone, Byrne-funded drug task forces seized over $1 billion in assets.[48] Remarkably, this figure does not include drug task forces funded by the DEA or other federal agencies.

The actual operation of drug forfeiture laws seriously undermines the usual rhetoric offered in support of the War on Drugs, namely that it is the big "kingpins" that are the target of the war. Drug-war forfeiture laws are frequently used to allow those with assets to buy their freedom, while drug users and small-time dealers with few assets to trade are subjected to lengthy prison terms. In Massachusetts, for example, an investigation by journalists found that on average a "payment of $50,000 in drug profits won a 6.3 year reduction in a sentence for dealers," while agreements of $10,000 or more bought elimination or reduction of trafficking charges in almost three-fourths of such cases.[49] Federal drug forfeiture laws are one reason, Blumenson and Nilsen note, "why state and federal prisons now confine large numbers of men and women who had relatively minor roles in drug distribution networks, but few of their bosses."[50]

The Shakedown

Quite predictably, the enormous economic rewards created by both the drug-war forfeiture and Byrne-grant laws has created an environment in which a very fine line exists between the lawful and the unlawful taking of other people's money and property—a line so thin that some officers disregard the formalities of search warrants, probable cause, and reasonable suspicion altogether. In *United States v. Reese*, for example, the Ninth Circuit Court of Appeals described a drug task force completely corrupted by its dependence on federal drug money. Operating as a separate unit within the Oakland Housing Authority, the task force behaved, in the words of one officer, "more or less like a wolfpack," driving up in police vehicles and taking "anything and everything we saw on the street corner."[51] The officers were under tremendous pressure from their commander to keep their arrest numbers up, and all of the officers were aware that their jobs depended on the renewal of a federal grant. The task force commander emphasized that they would need statistics to show that the grant money was well spent and sent the task force out to begin a shift with comments like, "Let's go out and kick ass," and "Everybody goes to jail tonight for everything, right?"[52]

Journalists and investigators have documented numerous other instances in which police departments have engaged in illegal shakedowns, searches, and threats in search of forfeitable property and cash. In Florida, reporters reviewed nearly one thousand videotapes of highway traffic stops and found that police had used traffic violations as an excuse—or pretext—to confiscate "tens of thousands of dollars from motorists against whom there [was] no evidence of wrongdoing," frequently taking the money without filing any criminal charges.[53] Similarly, in Louisiana, journalists reported that Louisiana police engaged in massive pretextual stops in an effort to seize cash, with the money diverted to police department ski trips and other unauthorized uses.[54] And in Southern California, a Los Angeles Sheriff's Department employee reported that deputies routinely planted drugs and falsified police reports to establish probable cause for cash seizures.[55]

Lots of small seizures can be nearly as profitable, and require the expenditure of fewer investigative resources, than a few large busts. The Western Area Narcotics Task Force (WANT) became the focus of a major investigation in 1996 when almost $66,000 was discovered hidden in its headquarters. The investigation revealed that the task force seized large amounts of money, but also small amounts, and then dispensed it freely, unconstrained by reporting requirements or the task force's mission. Some seizures were as small as eight cents. Another seizure of ninety-three cents prompted the local newspaper to observe that "once again the officers were taking whatever the suspects were carrying, even though by no stretch could pocket change be construed to be drug money."[56]

In 2000, Congress passed the Civil Asset Forfeiture Reform Act which was meant to address many of the egregious examples of abuse of civil forfeiture. Some of the most widely cited examples involved wealthy whites whose property was seized. One highly publicized case involved a reclusive millionaire, Donald Scott, who was shot and killed when a multiagency task force raided his two-hundred-acre Malibu ranch purportedly in search of marijuana plants. They never found a single marijuana plant in the course of the search. A subsequent investigation revealed that the primary motivation for the raid was the possibility of forfeiting Scott's property. If the forfeiture had been successful, it would have netted the law enforcement agencies about $5 million in assets.[57] In another case, William Munnerlynn had his Learjet seized by the DEA after he inadvertently used it to transport a drug dealer. Though charges were dropped against him within seventy-two hours, the DEA refused to return his Learjet. Only after five years of litigation and tens of thousands of dollars in legal fees was he able to secure return of his jet. When the jet was returned, it had sustained $100,000 worth of damage.[58] Such cases were atypical but got the attention of Congress.

The Reform Act resulted in a number of significant due-process changes, such as shifting the burden of proof onto the government, eliminating the requirement that an owner post a cost bond, and providing some minimal hardship protections for innocent parties who stand to lose their homes. These reforms, however, do not go nearly far enough.

Arguably the most significant reform is the creation of an "innocent owner" defense. Prior to the Reform Act, the Supreme Court had ruled that the guilt or innocence of the property's owner was irrelevant to the *property's* guilt—a ruling based on the archaic legal fiction that a piece of property could be "guilty" of a crime. The act remedied this insanity to some extent; it provides an "innocent owner" defense to those whose property has been seized. However, the defense is seriously undermined by the fact that the government's burden of proof is so low—the government need only establish by a "preponderance of the evidence" that the property was involved in the commission of a drug crime. This standard of proof is significantly lower than the "clear and convincing evidence" standard contained in an earlier version of the legislation, and it is far lower than the "proof beyond a reasonable doubt" standard for criminal convictions.

Once the government meets this minimal burden, the burden then shifts to the owner to prove that she "did not know of the conduct giving rise to the forfeiture" or that she did "all that reasonably could be expected under the circumstances to terminate such use of the property." This means, for example, that a woman who knew that her husband occasionally smoked pot could have her car forfeited to the government because she allowed him to use her car. Because the "car" was guilty of transporting someone who had broken a drug law at some time, she could legally lose her only form of transportation, even though she herself committed no crime. Indeed, women who are involved in some relationship with men accused of drug crimes, typically husbands or boyfriends, are among the most frequent claimants in forfeiture proceedings.[59] Courts have not been forgiving of women in these circumstances, frequently concluding that "the nature and circumstances of the marital relationship may give rise to an inference of knowledge by the spouse claiming innocent ownership."[60]

There are other problems with this framework, not the least of which being that the owner of the property is not entitled to the appointment of counsel in the forfeiture proceeding, unless he or she has been charged with a crime. The overwhelming majority of forfeiture cases do not involve any criminal charges, so the vast majority of people who have their cash, cars, or homes seized must represent themselves in court, against the federal government. Oddly, someone who has actually been charged with a crime is entitled to the appointment of counsel in civil forfeiture proceedings, but those whose property has been forfeited but whose conduct did not merit criminal charges are on their own. This helps to explain why up to 90 percent of forfeiture cases in some jurisdictions are not challenged. Most people simply cannot afford the considerable cost of hiring an attorney. Even if the cost is not an issue, the incentives are all wrong. If the police seized your car worth $5,000, or took $500 cash from your home, would you be willing to pay an attorney more than your assets are worth to get them back? If you haven't been charged with a crime, are you willing to risk the possibility that fighting the forfeiture might prompt the government to file criminal charges against you?

The greatest failure of the Reform Act, however, has nothing to do with one's due process rights once property has been seized in a drug investigation. Despite all of the new procedural rules and formal protections, the law does not address the single most serious problem associated with drug-war forfeiture laws: the profit motive in drug-law enforcement. Under the new law, drug busts motivated by the desire to seize cash, cars, homes, and other property are still perfectly legal. Law enforcement agencies are still allowed, through revenue-sharing agreements with the federal government, to keep seized assets for their own use. Clearly, so long as law enforcement is free to seize assets allegedly associated with illegal drug activity—without ever charging anyone with a crime—local police departments, as well as state and federal law enforcement agencies, will continue to have a direct pecuniary interest in the profitability and longevity of the drug war. The basic structure of the system remains intact.

None of this is to suggest that the financial rewards offered for police participation in the drug war are the only reason that law enforcement decided to embrace the war with zeal. Undoubtedly, the political and cultural context of the drug war—particularly in the early years—encouraged the roundup. When politicians declare a drug war, the police (our domestic warriors) undoubtedly feel some pressure to wage it. But it is doubtful that the drug war would have been launched with such intensity on the ground but for the bribes offered for law enforcement's cooperation.

Today the bribes may no longer be necessary. Now that the SWAT teams, the multiagency drug task forces, and the drug enforcement agenda have become a regular part of federal, state, and local law enforcement, it appears the drug war is here to stay. Funding for the Byrne-sponsored drug task forces had begun to dwindle during President Bush's tenure, but Barack Obama, as a presidential candidate, promised to revive the Byrne grant program, claiming that it is "critical to creating the anti-drug task forces our communities need."[61] Obama honored his word following the election, drastically increasing funding for the Byrne grant program despite its abysmal track record. The Economic Recovery Act of 2009 included more than $2 billion in new Byrne funding and an additional $600 million to increase state and local law enforcement across the country.[62] Relatively little organized opposition to the drug war currently exists, and any dramatic effort to scale back the war may be publicly condemned as "soft" on crime. The war has become institutionalized. It is no longer a special program or politicized project; it is simply the way things are done.

Legal Misrepresentation

So far, we have seen that the legal rules governing the drug war ensure that extraordinary numbers of people will be swept into the criminal justice system—arrested on drug charges, often for very minor offenses. But what happens after arrest? How does the design of the system help to ensure the creation of a massive undercaste?

Once arrested, one's chances of ever being truly free of the system of control are slim, often to the vanishing point. Defendants are typically denied meaningful legal representation, pressured by the threat of a lengthy sentence into a plea bargain, and then placed under formal control—in prison or jail, on probation or parole. Most Americans probably have no idea how common it is for people to be convicted without ever having the benefit of legal representation, or how many people plead guilty to crimes they did not commit because of fear of mandatory sentences.

Tens of thousands of poor people go to jail every year without ever talking to a lawyer, and those who do meet with a lawyer for a drug offense often spend only a few minutes discussing their case and options before making a decision that will profoundly affect the rest of their lives. As one public defender explained to the *Los Angeles Times*, "They are herded like cattle [into the courtroom lockup], up at 3 or 4 in the morning. Then they have to make decisions that affect the rest of their lives. You can imagine how stressful it is."[63]

More than forty years ago, in *Gideon v. Wainwright*, the Supreme Court ruled that poor people accused of serious crimes were entitled to counsel. Yet thousands of people are processed through America's courts annually either with no lawyer at all or with a lawyer who does not have the time, resources or, in some cases, the inclination to provide effective representation. In *Gideon*, the Supreme Court left it to state and local governments to decide how legal services should be funded. However, in the midst of a drug war, when politicians compete with each other to prove how "tough" they can be on crime and criminals, funding public defender offices and paying private attorneys to represent those accused of crimes has been a low priority.

Approximately 80 percent of criminal defendants are indigent and thus unable to hire a lawyer.[64] Yet our nation's public defender system is woefully inadequate. The most visible sign of the failed system is the astonishingly large caseloads public defenders routinely carry, making it impossible for them to provide meaningful representation to their clients. Sometimes defenders have well over one hundred clients at a time; many of these clients are facing decades behind bars or life imprisonment. Too often the quality of court-appointed counsel is poor because the miserable working conditions and low pay discourage good attorneys from participating in the system. And some states deny representation to impoverished defendants on the theory that somehow they should be able to pay for a lawyer, even though they are scarcely able to pay for food or rent. In Virginia, for example, fees paid to court-appointed attorneys for representing someone charged with a felony that carries a sentence of less than twenty years are capped at $428. And in Wisconsin, more than 11,000 poor people go to court without representation every year because anyone who earns more than $3,000 per year is considered able to afford a lawyer.[65] In Lake Charles, Louisiana, the public defender office has only two investigators for the 2,500 new felony cases and 4,000 new misdemeanor cases assigned to the office each year.[66] The NAACP Legal Defense Fund and the Southern Center for Human Rights in Atlanta sued the city of Gulfport, Mississippi, alleging that the city operated a "modern day debtor's prison" by jailing poor people who are unable to pay their fines and denying them the right to lawyers.

In 2004, the American Bar Association released a report on the status of indigent defense, concluding that, "All too often, defendants plead guilty, even if they are innocent, without really understanding their legal rights or what is occurring. Sometimes the proceedings reflect little or no recognition that the accused is mentally ill or does not adequately understand English. The fundamental right to a lawyer that Americans assume applies to everyone accused of criminal conduct effectively does not exist in practice for countless people across the United States."[67]

Even when people are charged with extremely serious crimes, such as murder, they may find themselves languishing in jail for years without meeting with an attorney, much less getting a trial. One extreme example is the experience of James Thomas, an impoverished day laborer in Baton Rouge, Louisiana, who was charged with murder in 1996, and waited eight and a half years for his case to go to trial. It never did. His mother finally succeeded in getting his case dismissed, after scraping together $500 to hire an attorney, who demonstrated to the court that, in the time Thomas spent waiting for his case to go to trial, his alibi witness had died of kidney disease. Another Louisiana man, Johnny Lee Ball, was convicted of second-degree murder and sentenced to life in prison without the possibility of parole after meeting with a public defender for just eleven minutes before trial. If indicted murderers have a hard time getting meaningful representation, what are the odds that small-time drug dealers find themselves represented by a zealous advocate? As David Carroll, the research director for the National Legal Aid & Defender Association explained to USA Today, "There's a real disconnect in this country between what people perceive is the state of indigent defense and what it is. I attribute that to shows like Law & Order, where the defendant says, 'I want a lawyer,' and all of a sudden Legal Aid appears in the cell. That's what people think."[68]

Children caught up in this system are the most vulnerable and yet are the least likely to be represented by counsel. In 1967, the U.S. Supreme Court ruled in In re Gault that children under the age of eighteen have the right to legal assistance with any criminal charges filed against them. In practice, however, children routinely "waive" their right to counsel in juvenile proceedings. In some states, such as Ohio, as many as 90 percent of children charged with criminal wrongdoing are not represented by a lawyer. As one public defender explained, "The kids come in with their parents, who want to get this dealt with as quickly as possible, and they say, 'You did it, admit it.' If people were informed about what could be done, they might actually ask for help."[69]

Bad Deal

Almost no one ever goes to trial. Nearly all criminal cases are resolved through plea bargaining—a guilty plea by the defendant in exchange for some form of leniency by the prosecutor. Though it is not widely known, the prosecutor is the most powerful law enforcement official in the criminal justice system. One might think that judges are the most powerful, or even the police, but in reality the prosecutor holds the cards. It is the prosecutor, far more than any other criminal justice official, who holds the keys to the jailhouse door.

After the police arrest someone, the prosecutor is in charge. Few rules constrain the exercise of his or her discretion. The prosecutor is free to dismiss a case for any reason or no reason at all. The prosecutor is also free to file more charges against a defendant than can realistically be proven in court, so long as probable cause arguably exists—a practice known as overcharging.

The practice of encouraging defendants to plead guilty to crimes, rather than affording them the benefit of a full trial, has always carried its risks and downsides. Never before in our history, though, have such an extraordinary number of people felt compelled to plead guilty, even if they are innocent, simply because the punishment for the minor, nonviolent offense with which they have been charged is so unbelievably severe. When prosecutors offer "only" three years in prison when the penalties defendants could receive if they took their case to trial would be five, ten, or twenty years—or life imprisonment—only extremely courageous (or foolish) defendants turn the offer down.

The pressure to plead guilty to crimes has increased exponentially since the advent of the War on Drugs. In 1986, Congress passed The Anti-Drug Abuse Act, which established extremely long mandatory minimum prison terms for low-level drug dealing and possession of crack cocaine. The typical mandatory sentence for a first-time drug offense in federal court is five or ten years. By contrast, in other developed countries around the world, a first-time drug offense would merit no more than six months in jail, if jail time is imposed at all.[70] State legislatures were eager to jump on the "get tough" bandwagon, passing harsh drug laws, as well as "three strikes" laws mandating a life sentence for those convicted of any third offense. These mandatory minimum statutory schemes have transferred an enormous amount of power from judges to prosecutors. Now, simply by charging someone with an offense carrying a mandatory sentence of ten to fifteen years or life, prosecutors are able to force people to plead guilty rather than risk a decade or more in prison. Prosecutors admit that they routinely charge people with crimes for which they technically have probable cause but which they seriously doubt they could ever win in court.[71] They "load up" defendants with charges that carry extremely harsh sentences in order to force them to plead guilty to lesser offenses and—here's the kicker—to obtain testimony for a related case. Harsh sentencing laws encourage people to snitch.

The number of snitches in drug cases has soared in recent years, partly because the government has tempted people to "cooperate" with law enforcement by offering cash, putting them "on payroll," and promising cuts of seized drug assets, but also because ratting out co-defendants, friends, family, or acquaintances is often the only way to avoid a lengthy mandatory minimum sentence.[72] In fact, under the federal sentencing guidelines, providing "substantial assistance" is often the only way defendants can hope to obtain a sentence below the mandatory minimum. The "assistance" provided by snitches is notoriously unreliable, as studies have documented countless informants who have fabricated stories about drug-related and other criminal activity in exchange for money or leniency in their pending criminal cases.[73] While such conduct is deplorable, it is not difficult to understand. Who among us would not be tempted to lie if it was the only way to avoid a forty-year sentence for a minor drug crime?

The pressure to plea-bargain and thereby "convict yourself" in exchange for some kind of leniency is not an accidental by-product of the mandatory-sentencing regime. The U.S. Sentencing Commission itself has noted that "the value of a mandatory minimum sentence lies not in its imposition, but in its value as a bargaining chip to be given away in return for the resource-saving plea from the defendant to a more leniently sanctioned charge." Describing severe mandatory sentences as a bargaining chip is a major understatement, given its potential for extracting guilty pleas from people who are innocent of any crime.

It is impossible to know for certain how many innocent drug defendants convict themselves every year by accepting a plea bargain out of fear of mandatory sentences, or how many are convicted due to lying informants and paid witnesses, but reliable estimates of the number of innocent people currently in prison tend to range from 2 percent to 5 percent.[74] While those numbers may sound small (and probably are underestimates), they translate into thousands of innocent people who are locked up, some of whom will die in prison. In fact, if only 1 percent of America's prisoners are actually innocent of the crimes for which they have been convicted, that would mean tens of thousands of innocent people are currently languishing behind bars in the United States.

The real point here, however, is not that innocent people are locked up. That has been true since penitentiaries first opened in America. The critical point is that thousands of people are swept into the criminal justice system every year pursuant to the drug war without much regard for their guilt or innocence. The police are allowed by the courts to conduct fishing expeditions for drugs on streets and freeways based on nothing more than a hunch. Homes may be searched for drugs based on a tip from an unreliable, confidential informant who is trading the information for money or to escape prison time. And once swept inside the system, people are often denied attorneys or meaningful representation and pressured into plea bargains by the threat of unbelievably harsh sentences—sentences for minor drug crimes that are higher than many countries impose on convicted murderers. This is the way the roundup works, and it works this way in virtually every major city in the United States.

Time Served

Once convicted of felony drug charges, one's chances of being released from the system in short order are slim, at best. The elimination of judicial discretion through mandatory sentencing laws has forced judges to impose sentences for drug crimes that are often longer than those violent criminals receive. When judges have discretion, they may consider a defendant's background and impose a lighter penalty if the defendant's personal circumstances—extreme poverty or experience of abuse, for example—warrant it. This flexibility—which is important in all criminal cases—is especially important in drug cases, as studies have indicated that many drug defendants are using or selling to support an addiction.[75] Referring a defendant to treatment, rather than sending him or her to prison, may well be the most prudent choice—saving government resources and potentially saving the defendant from a lifetime of addiction. Likewise, imposing a short prison sentence (or none at all) may increase the chances that the defendant will experience successful re-entry. A lengthy prison term may increase the odds that re-entry will be extremely difficult, leading to relapse, and re-imprisonment. Mandatory drug sentencing laws strip judges of their traditional role of considering all relevant circumstances in an effort to do justice in the individual case.

Nevertheless, harsh mandatory minimum sentences for drug offenders have been consistently upheld by the U.S. Supreme Court. In 1982, the Supreme Court upheld forty years of imprisonment for possession and an attempt to sell 9 ounces of marijuana.[76] Several years later, in *Harmelin v. Michigan*, the Court upheld a sentence of *life imprisonment* for a defendant with no prior convictions who attempted to sell 672 grams (approximately 23 ounces) of crack cocaine.[77] The Court found the sentences imposed in those cases "reasonably proportionate" to the offenses committed—and not "cruel and unusual" in violation of the Eighth Amendment. This ruling was remarkable given that, prior to the Drug Reform Act of 1986, the longest sentence Congress had ever imposed for possession of any drug in any amount was one year. A life sentence for a first-time drug offense is unheard of in the rest of the developed world. Even for high-end drug crimes, most countries impose sentences that are measured in months, rather than years. For example, a conviction for selling a kilogram of heroin yields a mandatory ten-year sentence in U.S. federal court, compared with six months in prison in England.[78] Remarkably, in the United States, a life sentence is deemed perfectly appropriate for a first-time drug offender.

The most famous Supreme Court decision upholding mandatory minimum sentences is *Lockyer v. Andrade*.[79] In that case, the Court rejected constitutional challenges to sentences of twenty-five years without parole for a man who stole three golf clubs from a pro shop, and fifty years without parole for another man for stealing children's videotapes from a Kmart store. These sentences were imposed pursuant to California's controversial three strikes law, which mandates a sentence of twenty-five years to life for recidivists convicted of a third felony, no matter how minor. Writing for the Court's majority, Justice Sandra Day O'Connor acknowledged that the sentences were severe but concluded that they are not grossly disproportionate to the offense, and therefore do not violate the Eighth Amendment's ban on "cruel and unusual" punishments. In dissent, Justice David H. Souter retorted, "If

Andrade's sentence [for stealing videotapes] is not grossly disproportionate, the principle has no meaning." Similarly, counsel for one of the defendants, University of Southern California law professor Erwin Chemerinsky, noted that the Court's reasoning makes it extremely difficult if not impossible to challenge any recidivist sentencing law: "If these sentences aren't cruel and unusual punishment, what would be?"[80]

Mandatory sentencing laws are frequently justified as necessary to keep "violent criminals" off the streets, yet those penalties are imposed most often against drug offenders and those who are guilty of nonviolent crimes. In fact, under the three-strikes regime in California, a "repeat offender" could be someone who had only a single prior case decades ago, and one arrest can result in multiple strikes. For example, imagine a young man, eighteen years old, who is arrested as part of an undercover operation and charged with two counts of dealing cocaine to minors. He had been selling to friends to earn extra money for shoes and basic things his mother could not afford. The prosecutor offers him probation if he agrees to plead guilty to both charges and to snitch on a bigger dealer. Terrified of doing prison time, he takes the deal. Several years later, he finds his punishment will never end. Branded a felon, he is struggling to survive and to support his children. One night he burglarizes a corner store and steals food, toothpaste, Pepsi, and diapers for his baby boy. He is arrested almost immediately a few blocks away. That's it for him. He now has three strikes. His burglary can be charged as a third strike because of his two prior felony convictions. He is eligible for life imprisonment. His children will be raised without a father.

Or imagine a woman struggling with drug addiction, unable to obtain treatment, and desperate for money so she can feed her habit. Together with her boyfriend, she burglarizes two homes, stealing televisions they hope to sell. After her arrest, she takes a plea deal, spends several years in prison, and is released with two strikes on her record, one for each burglary. Two decades later, she relapses—after being clean for fifteen years—and is arrested for selling crack. She made the sale to support her relapse. That's it for her. She can be locked up for the rest of her life.

These examples may sound extreme, but real life can be worse. Sentences for each charge can run consecutively, so a defendant can easily face a sentence of fifty, seventy-five, or one hundred years to life arising from a single case. It is not uncommon for people to receive prison sentences of more than fifty years for minor crimes. In fact, fifty years to life was the actual sentence given to Leandro Andrade for stealing videotapes, a sentence up-held by the Supreme Court.

The clear majority of those subject to harsh mandatory minimum sentences in the federal system are drug offenders. Most are low-level, minor drug dealers—not "drug kingpins." The stories are legion. Marcus Boyd was arrested after selling 3.9 grams of crack cocaine to a confidential informant working with a regional drug task force. At the time of his arrest, Marcus was twenty-four years old and had been addicted to drugs for six years, beginning shortly after his mother's death and escalating throughout his early twenties. He met the informant through a close family friend, someone he trusted. At sentencing, the judge based the drug quantity calculation on testimony from the informant and another witness, who both claimed they bought crack from Marcus on other occasions. As a result, Marcus was held accountable for 37.4 grams (the equivalent of 1.3 ounces) based on the statements made by the informant and the other witness. He was sentenced to more than fourteen years in prison. His two children were six and seven years old at the time of his sentencing. They will be adults when he is released.[81]

Weldon Angelos is another casualty of the drug war. He will spend the rest of his life in prison for three marijuana sales. Angelos, a twenty-four-year-old record producer, possessed a weapon—which he did not use or threaten to use—at the time of the sales. Under federal sentencing guidelines, however, the sentencing judge was obligated to impose a fifty-five-year mandatory minimum sentence. Upon doing so, the judge noted his reluctance to send the young man away for life for three marijuana sales. He said from the bench, "The Court believes that to sentence Mr. Angelos to prison for the rest of his life is unjust, cruel, and even irrational."[82]

Some federal judges, including conservative judges, have quit in protest of federal drug laws and sentencing guidelines. Face-to-face with those whose lives hang in the balance, they are far closer to the human tragedy occasioned by the drug war than the legislators who write the laws from afar. Judge Lawrence Irving, a Reagan appointee, noted upon his retirement: "If I remain on the bench, I have no choice but to follow the law. I just can't, in good conscience, continue to do this."[83] Other judges, such as Judge Jack Weinstein, publicly refused to take any more drug cases, describing "a sense of depression about much of the cruelty I have been a party to in connection with the 'war on drugs.'"[84] Another Reagan appointee, Judge Stanley Marshall, told a reporter, "I've always been considered a fairly harsh sentencer, but it's killing me that I'm sending so many low-level offenders away for all this time."[85] He made the statement after imposing a five-year sentence on a mother in Washington, D.C., who was convicted of "possession" of crack found by police in a locked box that her son had hidden in her attic. In California, reporters described a similar event:

> U.S. District Judge William W. Schwarzer, a Republican appointee, is not known as a light sentencer. Thus it was that everyone in his San Francisco courtroom watched in stunned silence as Schwarzer, known for his stoic demeanor, choked with tears as he anguished over sentencing Richard Anderson, a first offender Oakland longshoreman, to ten years in prison without parole for what appeared to be a minor mistake in judgment in having given a ride to a drug dealer for a meeting with an undercover agent.[86]

Even Supreme Court Justice Anthony Kennedy has condemned the harsh mandatory minimum sentences imposed on drug offenders. He told attorneys gathered for the American Bar Association's 2003 annual conference: "Our [prison] resources are misspent, our punishments too severe, our sentences too loaded." He then added, "I can accept neither the necessity nor the wisdom of federal mandatory minimum sentences. In all too many cases, mandatory minimum sentences are unjust."[87]

The Prison Label

Most people imagine that the explosion in the U.S. prison population during the past twenty-five years reflects changes in crime rates. Few would guess that our prison population leaped from approximately 350,000 to 2.3 million in such a short period of time due to changes in laws and policies, not changes in crime rates. Yet it has been changes in our laws—particularly the dramatic increases in the length of prison sentences—that have been responsible for the growth of our prison system, not increases in crime. One study suggests that the *entire* increase in the prison population from 1980 to 2001 can be explained by sentencing policy changes.[88]

Because harsh sentencing is a major cause of the prison explosion, one might reasonably assume that substantially reducing the length of prison sentences would effectively dismantle this new system of control. That view, however, is mistaken. This system depends on the prison label, not prison time.

Once a person is labeled a felon, he or she is ushered into a parallel universe in which discrimination, stigma, and exclusion are perfectly legal, and privileges of citizenship such as voting and jury service are off-limits. It does not matter whether you have actually spent time in prison; your second-class citizenship begins the moment you are branded a felon. Most people branded felons, in fact, are not sentenced to prison. As of 2008, there were approximately 2.3 million people in prisons and jails, and a staggering 5.1 million people under "community correctional supervision"—i.e., on probation or parole.[89] Merely reducing prison terms does not have a major impact on the majority of people in the system. It is the badge of inferiority—the felony record—that relegates people for their entire lives, to second-class status. As described in chapter 4, for drug felons, there is little hope of escape. Barred from public housing by law, discriminated against by private landlords, ineligible for food stamps, forced to "check the box" indicating a felony conviction on employment applications for nearly every job, and denied licenses for a wide range of professions, people whose only crime is drug addiction or possession of a small amount of drugs for recreational use find themselves locked out of the mainstream society and economy—permanently.

No wonder, then, that most people labeled felons find their way back into prison. According to a Bureau of Justice Statistics study, about 30 percent of released prisoners in its sample were rearrested within six months of release.[90] Within three years, nearly 68 percent were rearrested at least once for a new offense.[91] Only a small minority are rearrested for violent crimes; the vast majority are rearrested for property offenses, drug offenses, and offenses against the public order.[92]

For those released on probation or parole, the risks are especially high. They are subject to regular surveillance and monitoring by the police and may be stopped and searched (with or without their consent) for any reason or no reason at all. As a result, they are far more likely to be arrested (again) than those whose behavior is not subject to constant scrutiny by law enforcement. Probationers and parolees are at increased risk of arrest because their lives are governed by additional rules that do not apply to everyone else. Myriad restrictions on their travel and behavior (such as a prohibition on associating with other felons), as well as various requirements of probation and parole (such as paying fines and meeting with probation officers), create opportunities for arrest. Violation of these special rules can land someone right back in prison. In fact, that is what happens a good deal of the time.

The extraordinary increase in prison admissions due to parole and probation violations is due almost entirely to the War on Drugs. With respect to parole, in 1980, only 1 percent of all prison admissions were parole violators. Twenty years later, more than one third (35 percent) of prison admissions resulted from parole violations.[93] To put the matter more starkly: *About as many people were returned to prison for parole violations in 2000 as were admitted to prison in 1980 for all reasons.*[94] Of all parole violators returned to prison in 2000, only one-third were returned for a new conviction; two-thirds were returned for a technical violation such as missing appointments with a parole officer, failing to maintain employment, or failing a drug test.[95] In this system of control, failing to cope well with one's exile status is treated like a crime. If you fail, after being released from prison with a criminal record—your personal badge of inferiority—to remain drug free, or if you fail to get a job against all the odds, or if you get depressed and miss an appointment with your parole officer (or if you cannot afford the bus fare to take you there), you can be sent right back to prison—where society apparently thinks millions of Americans belong.

This disturbing phenomenon of people cycling in and out of prison, trapped by their second-class status, has been described by Loïc Wacquant as a "closed circuit of perpetual marginality."[96] Hundreds of thousands of people are released from prison every year, only to find themselves locked out of the mainstream society and economy. Most ultimately return to prison, sometimes for the rest of their lives. Others are released again, only to find themselves in precisely the circumstances they occupied before, unable to cope with the stigma of the prison label and their permanent pariah status.

Reducing the amount of time people spend behind bars—by eliminating harsh mandatory minimums—will alleviate some of the unnecessary suffering caused by this system, but it will not disturb the closed circuit. Those labeled felons will continue to cycle in and out of prison, subject to perpetual surveillance by the police, and unable to integrate into the mainstream society and economy. Unless the number of people who are labeled felons is dramatically reduced, and unless the laws and policies that keep ex-offenders marginalized from the mainstream society and economy are eliminated, the system will continue to create and maintain an enormous undercaste.

3

The Color of Justice

Imagine you are Erma Faye Stewart, a thirty-year-old, single African American mother of two who was arrested as part of a drug sweep in Hearne, Texas.[1] All but one of the people arrested were African American. You are innocent. After a week in jail, you have no one to care for your two small children and are eager to get home. Your court appointed attorney urges you to plead guilty to a drug distribution charge, saying the prosecutor has offered probation. You refuse, steadfastly proclaiming your innocence. Finally, after almost a month in jail, you decide to plead guilty so you can return home to your children. Unwilling to risk a trial and years of imprisonment, you are sentenced to ten years probation and ordered to pay $1,000 in fines, as well as court and probation costs. You are also now branded a drug felon. You are no longer eligible for food stamps; you may be discriminated against in employment; you cannot vote for at least twelve years; and you are about to be evicted from public housing. Once homeless, your children will be taken from you and put in foster care.

A judge eventually dismisses all cases against the defendants who did not plead guilty. At trial, the judge finds that the entire sweep was based on the testimony of a single informant who lied to the prosecution. You, however, are still a drug felon, homeless, and desperate to regain custody of your children.

Now place yourself in the shoes of Clifford Runoalds, another African American victim of the Hearne drug bust.[2] You returned home to Bryan, Texas, to attend the funeral of your eighteen-month-old daughter. Before the funeral services begin, the police show up and handcuff you. You beg the officers to let you take one last look at your daughter before she is buried. The police refuse. You are told by prosecutors that you are needed to testify against one of the defendants in a recent drug bust. You deny witnessing any drug transaction; you don't know what they are talking about. Because of your refusal to cooperate, you are indicted on felony charges. After a month of being held in jail, the charges against you are dropped. You are technically free, but as a result of your arrest and period of incarceration, you lose your job, your apartment, your furniture, and your car. Not to mention the chance to say good-bye to your baby girl.

This is the War on Drugs. The brutal stories described above are not isolated incidents, nor are the racial identities of Erma Faye Stewart and Clifford Runoalds random or accidental. In every state across our nation, African Americans—particularly in the poorest neighborhoods—are subjected to tactics and practices that would result in public outrage and scandal if committed in middle-class white neighborhoods. In the drug war, the enemy is racially defined. The law enforcement methods described in chapter 2 have been employed almost exclusively in poor communities of color, resulting in jaw-dropping numbers of African Americans and Latinos filling our nation's prisons and jails every year. We are told by drug warriors that the enemy in this war is a thing—drugs—not a group of people, but the facts prove otherwise.

Human Rights Watch reported in 2000 that, in seven states, African Americans constitute 80 to 90 percent of all drug offenders sent to prison.[3] In at least fifteen states, blacks are admitted to prison on drug charges at a rate from twenty to fifty-seven times greater than that of white men.[4] In fact, nationwide, the rate of incarceration for African American drug offenders dwarfs the rate of whites. When the War on Drugs gained full steam in the mid-1980s, prison admissions for African Americans skyrocketed, nearly quadrupling in three years, and then increasing steadily until it reached in 2000 a level *more than twenty-six times* the level in 1983.[5] The number of 2000 drug admissions for Latinos was twenty-two times the number of 1983 admissions.[6] Whites have been admitted to prison for drug offenses at increased rates as well—the number of whites admitted for drug offenses in 2000 was eight times the number admitted in 1983—but their relative numbers are small compared to blacks' and Latinos'.[7] Although the majority of illegal drug users and dealers nationwide are white, three-fourths of all people imprisoned for drug offenses have been black or Latino.[8] In recent years, rates of black imprisonment for drug offenses have dipped somewhat—declining approximately 25 percent from their zenith in the mid-1990s—but it remains the case that African Americans are incarcerated at grossly disproportionate rates throughout the United States.[9]

There is, of course, an official explanation for all of this: crime rates. This explanation has tremendous appeal—before you know the facts—for it is consistent with, and reinforces, dominant racial narratives about crime and criminality dating back to slavery. The truth, however, is that rates and patterns of drug crime do not explain the glaring racial disparities in our criminal justice system. People of all races use and sell illegal drugs at remarkably similar rates.[10] If there are significant differences in the surveys to be found, they frequently suggest that whites, particularly white youth, are more likely to engage in illegal drug dealing than people of color.[11] One study, for example, published in 2000 by the National Institute on Drug Abuse reported that white students use cocaine at seven times the rate of black students, use crack cocaine at eight times the rate of black students, and use heroin at seven times the rate of black students.[12] That same survey revealed that nearly identical percentages of white and black high school seniors use marijuana. The National Household Survey on Drug Abuse reported in 2000 that white youth aged 12–17 are more than a third more likely to have sold illegal drugs than African American youth.[13] Thus the very same year Human Rights Watch was reporting that African Americans were being arrested and imprisoned at unprecedented rates, government data revealed that blacks were no more likely to be guilty of drug crimes than whites and that white youth were actually the *most likely* of any racial or ethnic group to be guilty of illegal drug possession and sales. Any notion that drug use among blacks is more severe or dangerous is belied by the data; white youth have about three times the number of drug-related emergency room visits as their African American counterparts.[14]

The notion that whites comprise the vast majority of drug users and dealers—and may well be more likely than other racial groups to commit drug crimes—may seem implausible to some, given the media imagery we are fed on a daily basis and the racial composition of our prisons and jails. Upon reflection, however, the prevalence of white drug crime—including drug dealing—should not be surprising. After all, where do whites get their illegal drugs? Do they all drive to the ghetto to purchase them from somebody standing on a street corner? No. Studies consistently indicate that drug markets, like American society generally, reflect our nation's racial and socioeconomic boundaries. Whites tend to sell to whites; blacks to blacks.[15] University students tend to sell to each other.[16] Rural whites, for their part, don't make a special trip to the 'hood to purchase marijuana. They buy it from somebody down the road.[17] White high school students typically buy drugs from white classmates, friends, or older relatives. Even Barry McCaffrey, former director of the White House Office of National Drug Control Policy, once remarked, if your child bought drugs, "it was from a student of their own race generally."[18] The notion that most illegal drug use and sales happens in the ghetto is pure fiction. Drug trafficking occurs there, but it occurs everywhere else in America as well. Nevertheless, black men have been admitted to state prison on drug charges at a rate that is more than thirteen times higher than white men.[19] The racial bias inherent in the drug war is a major reason that 1 in every 14 black men was behind bars in 2006, compared with 1 in 106 white men.[20] For young black men, the statistics are even worse. One in 9 black men between the ages of twenty and thirty-five was behind bars in 2006, and far more were under some form of penal control—such as probation or parole.[21] These gross racial disparities simply cannot be explained by rates of illegal drug activity among African Americans.

What, then, does explain the extraordinary racial disparities in our criminal justice system? Old-fashioned racism seems out of the question. Politicians and law enforcement officials today rarely endorse racially biased practices, and most of them fiercely condemn racial discrimination of any kind. When accused of racial bias, police and prosecutors—like most Americans—express horror and outrage. Forms of race discrimination that were open and notorious for centuries were transformed in the 1960s and 1970s into something un-American—an affront to our newly conceived ethic of colorblindness. By the early 1980s, survey data indicated that 90 percent of whites thought black and white children should attend the same schools, 71 percent disagreed with the idea that whites have a right to keep blacks out of their neighborhoods, 80 percent indicated they would support a black candidate for president, and 66 percent opposed laws prohibiting intermarriage.[22] Although far fewer supported specific policies designed to achieve racial equality or integration (such as busing), the mere fact that large majorities of whites were, by the early 1980s, supporting the antidiscrimination principle reflected a profound shift in racial attitudes. The margin of support for colorblind norms has only increased since then.

This dramatically changed racial climate has led defenders of mass incarceration to insist that our criminal justice system, whatever its past sins, is now largely fair and nondiscriminatory. They point to violent crime rates in the African American community as a justification for the staggering number of black men who find themselves behind bars. Black men, they say, have much higher rates of violent crime; that's why so many of them are locked up.

Typically, this is where the discussion ends.

The problem with this abbreviated analysis is that violent crime is *not* responsible for mass incarceration. As numerous researchers have shown, violent crime rates have fluctuated over the years and bear little relationship to incarceration rates—which have soared during the past three decades regardless of whether violent crime was going up or down.[23] Today violent crime rates are at historically low levels, yet incarceration rates continue to climb.

Murder convictions tend to receive a tremendous amount of media attention, which feeds the public's sense that violent crime is rampant and forever on the rise. But like violent crime in general, the murder rate cannot explain the growth of the penal apparatus. Homicide convictions account for a tiny fraction of the growth in the prison population. In the federal system, for example, homicide offenders account for 0.4 percent of the past decade's growth in the federal prison population, while drug offenders account for nearly 61 percent of that expansion.[24] In the state system, less than 3 percent of new court commitments to state prison typically involve people convicted of homicide.[25] As much as half of state prisoners are violent offenders, but that statistic can easily be misinterpreted. Violent offenders tend to get longer prison sentences than nonviolent offenders, and therefore comprise a much larger share of the prison population than they would if they had earlier release dates. In addition, state prison data excludes federal prisoners, who are overwhelmingly incarcerated for nonviolent offenses. As of September 2009, only 7.9 percent of federal prisoners were convicted of violent crimes.[26]

The most important fact to keep in mind, however, is this: debates about prison statistics ignore the fact that most people who are under correctional control today are not in prison. As noted earlier, of the nearly 7.3 million people currently under correctional control, only 1.6 million are in prison.[27] This caste system extends far beyond prison walls and governs millions of people who are on probation and parole, primarily for nonviolent offenses. They have been swept into the system, branded criminals or felons, and ushered into a permanent second-class status—acquiring records that will follow them for life. Probationers are the clear majority of those who are under community supervision (84 percent), and only 19 percent of them were convicted of a violent offense.[28] The most common offense for which probationers are under supervision is a drug offense.[29] Even if the analysis is limited to people convicted of felonies—thus excluding extremely minor crimes and misdemeanors—nonviolent offenders still predominate. Only about a quarter of felony defendants in large urban counties were charged with a violent offense in 2006.[30] In cities such as Chicago, criminal courts are clogged with low-level drug cases. In one study, 72 percent of criminal cases in Cook County (Chicago) had a drug charge, and 70 percent of them were charged as class 4 felony possession (the lowest-level felony charge).[31]

None of this is to suggest that we ought not be concerned about violent crime in impoverished urban communities. We should care deeply, and as discussed in the final chapter, we must come to understand the ways in which mass imprisonment increases—not decreases—the likelihood of violence in urban communities. But at the same time, we ought not be misled by those who insist that violent crime has driven the rise of this unprecedented system of racial and social control. The uncomfortable reality is that arrests and convictions for drug offenses—not violent crime—have propelled mass incarceration. In many states, including Colorado and Maryland, drug offenders now constitute the single largest category of people admitted to prison.[32] People of color are convicted of drug offenses at rates out of all proportion to their drug crimes, a fact that has greatly contributed to the emergence of a vast new racial undercaste.

These facts may still leave some readers unsatisfied. The idea that the criminal justice system discriminates in such a terrific fashion when few people openly express or endorse racial discrimination may seem far-fetched, if not absurd. How could the War on Drugs operate in a discriminatory manner, on such a large scale, when hardly anyone advocates or engages in explicit race discrimination? That question is the subject of this chapter. As we shall see, despite the colorblind rhetoric and fanfare of recent years, the design of the drug war effectively guarantees that those who are swept into the nation's new undercaste are largely black and brown.

This sort of claim invites skepticism. Nonracial explanations and excuses for the systematic mass incarceration of people of color are plentiful. It is the genius of the new system of control that it can always be defended on nonracial grounds, given the rarity of a noose or a racial slur in connection with any particular criminal case. Moreover, because blacks and whites are almost never similarly situated (given extreme racial segregation in housing and disparate life experiences), trying to "control for race" in an effort to evaluate whether the mass incarceration of people of color is really about race or something else—anything else—is difficult. But it is not impossible.

A bit of common sense is overdue in public discussions about racial bias in the criminal justice system. The great debate over whether black men have been targeted by the criminal justice system or unfairly treated in the War on Drugs often overlooks the obvious. What is painfully obvious when one steps back from individual cases and specific policies is that the system of mass incarceration operates with stunning efficiency to sweep people of color off the streets, lock them in cages, and then release them into an inferior second-class status. Nowhere is this more true than in the War on Drugs.

The central question, then, is *how* exactly does a formally colorblind criminal justice system achieve such racially discriminatory results? Rather easily, it turns out. The process occurs in two stages. The first step is to grant law enforcement officials extraordinary discretion regarding whom to stop, search, arrest, and charge for drug offenses, thus ensuring that conscious and unconscious racial beliefs and stereotypes will be given free rein. Unbridled discretion inevitably creates huge racial disparities. Then, the damning step: Close the courthouse doors to all claims by defendants and private litigants that the criminal justice system operates in racially discriminatory fashion. Demand that anyone who wants to challenge racial bias in the system offer, in advance, clear proof that the racial disparities are the product of intentional racial discrimination—i.e., the work of a bigot. This evidence will almost never be available in the era of colorblindness, because everyone knows—but does not say—that the enemy in the War on Drugs can be identified by race. This simple design has helped to produce one of the most extraordinary systems of racialized social control the world has ever seen.

Picking and Choosing—The Role of Discretion

Chapter 2 described the first step in some detail, including the legal rules that grant police the discretion and authority to stop, interrogate, and search anyone, anywhere, provided they get "consent" from the targeted individual. It also examined the legal framework that affords prosecutors extraordinary discretion to charge or not charge, plea bargain or not, and load up defendants with charges carrying the threat of harsh mandatory sentences, in order to force guilty pleas, even in cases in which the defendants may well be innocent. These rules have made it possible for law enforcement agencies to boost dramatically their rates of drug arrests and convictions, even in communities where drug crime is stable or declining.[33] But that is not all. These rules have also guaranteed racially discriminatory results.

The reason is this: Drug-law enforcement is *unlike* most other types of law enforcement. When a violent crime or a robbery or a trespass occurs, someone usually calls the police. There is a clear victim and perpetrator. Someone is hurt or harmed in some way and wants the offender punished. But with drug crime, neither the purchaser of the drugs nor the seller has any incentive to contact law enforcement. It is consensual activity. Equally important, it is popular. The clear majority of Americans of all races have violated drug laws in their lifetime. In fact, in any given year, more than one in ten Americans violate drug laws. But due to resource constraints (and the politics of the drug war), only a small fraction are arrested, convicted, and incarcerated. In 2002, for example, there were 19.5 million illicit drug users, compared to 1.5 million drug arrests and 175,000 people admitted to prison for a drug offense.[34]

The ubiquity of illegal drug activity, combined with its consensual nature, requires a far more proactive approach by law enforcement than what is required to address ordinary street crime. It is impossible for law enforcement to identify and arrest every drug criminal. Strategic choices must be made about whom to target and what tactics to employ. Police and prosecutors did not declare the War on Drugs—and some initially opposed it—but once the financial incentives for waging the war became too attractive to ignore, law enforcement agencies had to ask themselves, if we're going to wage this war, where should it be fought and who should be taken prisoner?

That question was not difficult to answer, given the political and social context. As discussed in chapter 1, the Reagan administration launched a media campaign a few years after the drug war was announced in an effort to publicize horror stories involving black crack users and crack dealers in ghetto communities. Although crack cocaine had not yet hit the streets when the War on Drugs was declared in 1982, its appearance a few years later created the perfect opportunity for the Reagan administration to build support for its new war. Drug use, once considered a private, public-health matter, was reframed through political rhetoric and media imagery as a grave threat to the national order.

Jimmie Reeves and Richard Campbell show in their research how the media imagery surrounding cocaine changed as the practice of smoking cocaine came to be associated with poor blacks.[35] Early in the 1980s, the typical cocaine-related story focused on white recreational users who snorted the drug in its powder form. These stories generally relied on news sources associated with the drug treatment industry, such as rehabilitation clinics, and emphasized the possibility of recovery. By 1985, however, as the War on Drugs moved into high gear, this frame was supplanted by a new "siege paradigm," in which transgressors were poor, nonwhite users and dealers of crack cocaine. Law enforcement officials assumed the role of drug "experts," emphasizing the need for law and order responses—a crackdown on those associated with the drug. These findings are consistent with numerous other studies, including a study of network television news from 1990 and 1991, which found that a predictable "us against them" frame was used in the news stories, with "us" being white, suburban America, and "them" being black Americans and a few corrupted whites.[36]

The media bonanza inspired by the administration's campaign solidified in the public imagination the image of the black drug criminal. Although explicitly racial political appeals remained rare, the calls for "war" at a time when the media was saturated with images of black drug crime left little doubt about who the enemy was in the War on Drugs and exactly what he looked like. Jerome Miller, the former executive director of the National Center for Institutions and Alternatives, described the dynamic this way: "There are certain code words that allow you never to have to say 'race,' but everybody knows that's what you mean and 'crime' is one of those. . . . So when we talk about locking up more and more people, what we're really talking about is locking up more and more black men."[37] Another commentator noted, "It is unnecessary to speak directly of race [today] because speaking about crime is talking about race."[38] Indeed, not long after the drug war was ramped up in the media and political discourse, almost no one imagined that drug criminals could be anything other than black.

A survey was conducted in 1995 asking the following question: "Would you close your eyes for a second, envision a drug user, and describe that person to me?" The startling results were published in the *Journal of Alcohol and Drug Education*. Ninety-five percent of respondents pictured a black drug user, while only 5 percent imagined other racial groups.[39] These results contrast sharply with the reality of drug crime in America. African Americans constituted only 15 percent of current drug users in 1995, and they constitute roughly the same percentage today. Whites constituted the vast majority of drug users then (and now), but almost no one pictured a white person when asked to imagine what a drug user looks like. The same group of respondents also perceived the typical drug trafficker as black.

There is no reason to believe that the survey results would have been any different if police officers or prosecutors—rather than the general public—had been the respondents. Law enforcement officials, no less than the rest of us, have been exposed to the racially charged political rhetoric and media imagery associated with the drug war. In fact, for nearly three decades, news stories regarding virtually *all* street crime have disproportionately featured African American offenders. One study suggests that the standard crime news "script" is so prevalent and so thoroughly racialized that viewers imagine a black perpetrator even when none exists. In that study, 60 percent of viewers who saw a story with no image falsely recalled seeing one, and 70 percent of those viewers believed the perpetrator to be African American.[40]

Decades of cognitive bias research demonstrates that both unconscious and conscious biases lead to discriminatory actions, even when an individual does not want to discriminate.[41] The quotation commonly attributed to Nietzsche, that "there is no immaculate perception," perfectly captures how cognitive schemas—thought structures—influence what we notice and how the things we notice get interpreted.[42] Studies have shown that racial schemas operate not only as part of conscious, rational deliberations, but also automatically—without conscious awareness or intent.[43] One study, for example, involved a video game that placed photographs of white and black individuals holding either a gun or other object (such as a wallet, soda can, or cell phone) into various photographic backgrounds. Participants were told to decide as quickly as possible whether to shoot the target. Consistent with earlier studies, participants were more likely to mistake a black target as armed when he was not, and mistake a white target as unarmed, when in fact he was armed.[44] This pattern of discrimination reflected automatic, unconscious thought processes, not careful deliberations.

Most striking, perhaps, is the overwhelming evidence that implicit bias measures are disassociated from explicit bias measures.[45] In other words, the fact that you may honestly believe that you are not biased against African Americans, and that you may even have black friends or relatives, does not mean that you are free from unconscious bias. Implicit bias tests may still show that you hold negative attitudes and stereotypes about blacks, even though you do not believe you do and do not want to.[46] In the study described above, for example, black participants showed an amount of "shooter bias" similar to that shown by whites.[47] Not surprisingly, people who have the greatest explicit bias (as measured by self-reported answers to survey questions) against a racial group tend also to have the greatest implicit bias against them, and vice versa.[48] Yet there is often a weak correlation between degrees of explicit and implicit bias; many people who think they are not biased prove when tested to have relatively high levels of bias.[49] Unfortunately, a fairly consistent finding is that punitiveness and hostility almost always increase when people are primed—even subliminally—with images or verbal cues associated with African Americans. In fact, studies indicate that people become increasingly harsh when an alleged criminal is darker and more "stereotypically black"; they are more lenient when the accused is lighter and appears more stereotypically white. This is true of jurors as well as law enforcement officers.[50]

Viewed as a whole, the relevant research by cognitive and social psychologists to date suggests that racial bias in the drug war was *inevitable*, once a public consensus was constructed by political and media elites that drug crime is black and brown. Once blackness and crime, especially drug crime, became conflated in the public consciousness, the "criminalblackman," as termed by legal scholar Kathryn Russell, would inevitably become the primary target of law enforcement.[51] Some discrimination would be conscious and deliberate, as many honestly and consciously would believe that black men deserve extra scrutiny and harsher treatment. Much racial bias, though, would operate unconsciously and automatically—even among law enforcement officials genuinely committed to equal treatment under the law.

Whether or not one believes racial discrimination in the drug war was inevitable, it should have been glaringly obvious in the 1980s and 1990s that an extraordinarily high *risk* of racial bias in the administration of criminal justice was present, given the way in which all crime had been framed in the media and in political discourse. Awareness of this risk did not require intimate familiarity with cognitive bias research. Anyone possessing a television set during this period would likely have had some awareness of the extent to which black men had been demonized in the War on Drugs.

The risk that African Americans would be unfairly targeted should have been of special concern to the U.S. Supreme Court—the one branch of government charged with the responsibility of protecting "discrete and insular minorities" from the excesses of majoritarian democracy, and guaranteeing constitutional rights for groups deemed unpopular or subject to prejudice.[52] Yet when the time came for the Supreme Court to devise the legal rules that would govern the War on Drugs, the Court adopted rules that would *maximize*—not minimize—the amount of racial discrimination that would likely occur. It then closed the courthouse doors to claims of racial bias.

Whren v. United States is a case in point. As noted in chapter 2, the Court held in *Whren* that police officers are free to use minor traffic violations as an excuse to stop motorists for drug investigations—even when there is no evidence whatsoever that the motorist has engaged in drug crime. So long as a minor traffic violation—such as failing to use a turn signal, exceeding the speed limit by a mile or two, tracking improperly between the lines, or stopping on a pedestrian walkway—can be identified, police are free to stop motorists for the purpose of engaging in a fishing expedition for drugs. Such police conduct, the Court concluded, does not violate the Fourth Amendment's ban on "unreasonable searches and seizures."[53]

For good reason, the petitioners in *Whren* argued that granting police officers such broad discretion to investigate virtually anyone for drug crimes created a high risk that police would exercise their discretion in a racially discriminatory manner. With no requirement that any evidence of drug activity actually be present before launching a drug investigation, police officers' snap judgments regarding who seems like a drug criminal would likely be influenced by prevailing racial stereotypes and bias. They urged the Court to prohibit the police from stopping motorists for the purpose of drug investigations unless the officers actually had reason to believe a motorist was committing, or had committed, a drug crime. Failing to do so, they argued, was unreasonable under the Fourth Amendment and would expose African Americans to a high risk of discriminatory stops and searches.

Not only did the Court reject the petitioners' central claim—that using traffic stops as a pretext for drug investigations is unconstitutional—it ruled that claims of racial bias could not be brought under the Fourth Amendment. In other words, the Court barred any victim of race discrimination by the police *from even alleging a claim of racial bias* under the Fourth Amendment. According to the Court, whether or not police discriminate on the basis of race when making traffic stops is irrelevant to a consideration of whether their conduct is "reasonable" under the Fourth Amendment.

The Court did offer one caveat, however. It indicated that victims of race discrimination could still state a claim under the equal protection clause of the Fourteenth Amendment, which guarantees "equal treatment under the laws." This suggestion may have been reassuring to those unfamiliar with the Court's equal protection jurisprudence. But for those who have actually tried to prove race discrimination under the Fourteenth Amendment, the Court's remark amounted to cruel irony. As we shall see below, the Supreme Court has made it virtually impossible to challenge racial bias in the criminal justice system under the Fourteenth Amendment, and it has barred litigation of such claims under federal civil rights laws as well.

Closing the Courthouse Doors—*McCleskey v. Kemp*

First, consider sentencing. In 1987, when media hysteria regarding black drug crime was at fever pitch and the evening news was saturated with images of black criminals shackled in courtrooms, the Supreme Court ruled in *McCleskey v. Kemp* that racial bias in sentencing, even if shown through credible statistical evidence, could not be challenged under the Fourteenth Amendment in the absence of clear evidence of conscious, discriminatory intent. On its face, the case appeared to be a straightforward challenge to Georgia's death penalty scheme. Once the Court's opinion was released, however, it became clear the case was about much more than the death penalty. The real issue at hand was whether—and to what extent—the Supreme Court would tolerate racial bias in the criminal justice system as a whole. The Court's answer was that racial bias would be tolerated—virtually to any degree—so long as no one admitted it.

Warren McCleskey was a black man facing the death penalty for killing a white police officer during an armed robbery in Georgia. Represented by the

NAACP Legal Defense and Education Fund, McCleskey challenged his
death sentence on the grounds that Georgia's death penalty scheme was infected with racial bias and thus violated the Fourteenth and Eighth Amendments. In support of his claim, he offered an exhaustive study of more than
two thousand murder cases in Georgia. The study was known as the Baldus
study—named after Professor David Baldus, who was its lead author. The
study found that defendants charged with killing white victims received the
death penalty eleven times more often than defendants charged with killing
black victims. Georgia prosecutors seemed largely to blame for the disparity;
they sought the death penalty in 70 percent of cases involving black defendants and white victims, but only 19 percent of cases involving white defendants and black victims.[54]

Sensitive to the fact that numerous factors besides race can influence the
decision making of prosecutors, judges, and juries, Baldus and his colleagues
subjected the raw data to highly sophisticated statistical analysis to see if
nonracial factors might explain the disparities. Yet even after accounting for
thirty-five nonracial variables, the researchers found that defendants charged
with killing white victims were 4.3 times more likely to receive a death sentence than defendants charged with killing blacks. Black defendants, like
McCleskey, who killed white victims had the highest chance of being sentenced to death in Georgia.[55]

The case was closely watched by criminal lawyers and civil rights lawyers
nationwide. The statistical evidence of discrimination that Baldus had developed was the strongest ever presented to a court regarding race and criminal
sentencing. If McCleskey's evidence was not enough to prove discrimination in the absence of some kind of racist utterance, what would be?

By a one-vote margin, the Court rejected McCleskey's claims under the
Fourteenth Amendment, insisting that unless McCleskey could prove that
the prosecutor in his particular case had sought the death penalty because
of race or that the jury had imposed it for racial reasons, the statistical evidence of race discrimination in Georgia's death penalty system did not prove
unequal treatment under the law. The Court accepted the statistical evidence as valid but insisted that evidence of conscious, racial bias in Mc-
Cleskey's individual case was necessary to prove unlawful discrimination. In
the absence of such evidence, patterns of discrimination—even patterns as
shocking as demonstrated by the Baldus study—did not violate the Fourteenth Amendment.

In erecting this high standard, the Court knew full well that the standard could not be met absent an admission that a prosecutor or judge acted because of racial bias. The majority opinion openly acknowledged that long-standing rules generally bar litigants from obtaining discovery from the prosecution regarding charging patterns and motives, and that similar rules forbid introduction of evidence of jury deliberations even when a juror has chosen to make deliberations public.[56] The very evidence that the Court demanded in *McCleskey*—evidence of deliberate bias in his individual case—would almost always be unavailable and/or inadmissible due to procedural rules that shield jurors and prosecutors from scrutiny. This dilemma was of little concern to the Court. It closed the courthouse doors to claims of racial bias in sentencing.

There is good reason to believe that, despite appearances, the *McCleskey* decision was not really about the death penalty at all; rather, the Court's opinion was driven by a desire to immunize the entire criminal justice system from claims of racial bias. The best evidence in support of this view can be found at the end of the majority opinion where the Court states that discretion plays a necessary role in the implementation of the criminal justice system, and that discrimination is an inevitable by-product of discretion. Racial discrimination, the Court seemed to suggest, was something that simply must be tolerated in the criminal justice system, provided no one admits to racial bias.

The majority observed that significant racial disparities had been found in other criminal settings beyond the death penalty, and that McCleskey's case implicitly calls into question the integrity of the entire system. In the Court's words: "Taken to its logical conclusion, [Warren McCleskey's claim] throws into serious question the principles that underlie our criminal justice system. . . . [I]f we accepted McCleskey's claim that racial bias has impermissibly tainted the capital sentencing decision, we could soon be faced with similar claims as to other types of penalty."[57] The Court openly worried that other actors in the criminal justice system might also face scrutiny for allegedly biased decision-making if similar claims of racial bias in the system were allowed to proceed. Driven by these concerns, the Court rejected McCleskey's claim that Georgia's death penalty system violates the Eighth Amendment's ban on arbitrary punishment, framing the critical question as whether the Baldus study demonstrated a "constitutionally unacceptable risk" of discrimination. Its answer was no. The Court deemed the risk of racial bias in Georgia's capital sentencing scheme "constitutionally accept-able." Justice Brennan pointedly noted in his dissent that the Court's opinion "seems to suggest a fear of too much justice."[58]

Cracked Up—Discriminatory Sentencing in the War on Drugs

Anyone who doubts the devastating impact of *McCleskey v. Kemp* on African American defendants throughout the criminal justice system, including those ensnared by the War on Drugs, need only ask Edward Clary. Two months after his eighteenth birthday, Clary was stopped and searched in the St. Louis airport because he "looked like" a drug courier. At the time, he was returning home from visiting some friends in California. One of them persuaded him to take some drugs back home to St. Louis. Clary had never attempted to deal drugs before, and he had no criminal record.

During the search, the police found crack cocaine and promptly arrested him. He was convicted in federal court and sentenced under federal laws that punish crack offenses one hundred times more severely than offenses involving powder cocaine. A conviction for the sale of five hundred grams of powder cocaine triggers a five-year mandatory sentence, while only five grams of crack triggers the same sentence. Because Clary had been caught with more than fifty grams of crack (less than two ounces), the sentencing judge believed he had no choice but to sentence him—an eighteen-year-old, first-time offender—to a minimum of ten years in federal prison.

Clary, like defendants in other crack cases, challenged the constitutionality of the hundred-to-one ratio. His lawyers argued that the law is arbitrary and irrational, because it imposes such vastly different penalties on two forms of the same substance. They also argued that the law discriminates against African Americans, because the majority of those charged with crimes involving crack at that time were black (approximately 93 percent of convicted crack offenders were black, 5 percent were white), whereas powder cocaine offenders were predominantly white.

Every federal appellate court to have considered these claims had rejected them on the ground that Congress—rightly or wrongly—believed that crack was more dangerous to society, a view supported by the testimony of some drug-abuse "experts" and police officers. The fact that most of the evidence in support of *any* disparity had since been discredited was deemed irrelevant; what mattered was whether the law had seemed rational at the time it was adopted. Congress, the courts concluded, is free to amend the law if circumstances have changed.

Courts also had rejected claims that crack sentencing laws were racially discriminatory, largely on the grounds that the Supreme Court's decision in *McCleskey v. Kemp* precluded such a result. In the years following *McCleskey*, lower courts consistently rejected claims of race discrimination in the criminal justice system, finding that gross racial disparities do not merit strict scrutiny in the absence of evidence of explicit race discrimination—the very evidence unavailable in the era of colorblindness.

Judge Clyde Cahill of the Federal District of Missouri, an African American judge assigned Clary's case, boldly challenged the prevailing view that courts are powerless to address forms of race discrimination that are not overtly hostile. Cahill declared the hundred-to-one ratio racially discriminatory in violation of the Fourteenth Amendment, notwithstanding *McCleskey*.[59] Although no admissions of racial bias or racist intent could be found in the record, Judge Cahill believed race was undeniably a factor in the crack sentencing laws and policies. He traced the history of the get-tough movement and concluded that fear coupled with unconscious racism had led to a lynch-mob mentality and a desire to control crime—and those deemed responsible for it—at any cost. Cahill acknowledged that many people may not believe they are motivated by discriminatory attitudes but argued that we all have internalized fear of young black men, a fear reinforced by media imagery that has helped to create a national image of the young black male as a criminal. "The presumption of innocence is now a legal myth," he declared. "The 100-to-1 ratio, coupled with mandatory minimum sentencing provided by federal statute, has created a situation that reeks with inhumanity and injustice. . . . If young white males were being incarcerated at the same rate as young black males, the statute would have been amended long ago." Judge Cahill sentenced Clary as if the drug he had carried home had been powder cocaine. The sentence imposed was four years in prison. Clary served his term and was released.

The prosecution appealed Clary's case to the Eighth Circuit Court of Appeals, which reversed Judge Cahill in a unanimous opinion, finding that the case was not even close. In the court's view, there was no credible evidence that the crack penalties were motivated by any conscious racial bigotry, as required by *McCleskey v. Kemp*. The court remanded the case back to the

district court for resentencing. Clary—now married and a father—was ordered back to prison to complete his ten-year term.[60]

Few challenges to sentencing schemes, patterns, or results have been
brought since *McCleskey*, for the exercise is plainly futile. Yet in 1995, a few
brave souls challenged the implementation of Georgia's "two strikes and
you're out" sentencing scheme, which imposes life imprisonment for a second
drug offense. Georgia's district attorneys, who have unbridled discretion to
decide whether to seek this harsh penalty, had invoked it against only 1 percent
of white defendants facing a second drug conviction but against 16 percent of
black defendants. The result was that 98.4 percent of those serving life sentences under the provision were black. The Georgia Supreme Court ruled,
by a 4–3 vote, that the stark racial disparity presented a threshold case of
discrimination and required the prosecutors to offer a race-neutral explanation for the results. Rather than offer a justification, however, the Georgia
attorney general filed a petition for rehearing signed by every one of the
state's forty-six district attorneys, all of whom were white. The petition argued that the Court's decision was a dire mistake; if the decision were
allowed to stand and prosecutors were compelled to explain gross racial disparities such as the ones at issue, it would be a "substantial step toward
invalidating" the death penalty and would "paralyze the criminal justice
system"—apparently because severe and inexplicable racial disparities per-
vaded the system as a whole. Thirteen days later, the Georgia Supreme
Court reversed itself, holding that the fact that 98.4 percent of the defendants selected to receive life sentences for repeat drug offenses were black
required no justification. The court's new decision relied almost exclusively
on *McCleskey v. Kemp*. To date, not a single successful challenge has ever
been made to racial bias in sentencing under *McCleskey v. Kemp* anywhere
in the United States.

Charging Ahead—*Armstrong v. United States*

If sentencing were the only stage of the criminal justice process in which racial biases were allowed to flourish, it would be a tragedy of gargantuan proportions. Thousands of people have had years of their lives wasted in
prison—years they would have been free if they had been white. Some, like
McCleskey, have been killed because of the influence of race in the death

penalty. Sentencing, however, is not the end, but just the beginning. As we shall see, the legal rules governing prosecutions, like those that govern sentencing decisions, maximize rather than minimize racial bias in the drug war. The Supreme Court has gone to great lengths to ensure that prosecutors are free to exercise their discretion in any manner they choose, and it has closed the courthouse doors to claims of racial bias.

As discussed in chapter 2, no one has more power in the criminal justice system than prosecutors. Few rules constrain the exercise of prosecutorial discretion. The prosecutor is free to dismiss a case for any reason or no reason at all, regardless of the strength of the evidence. The prosecutor is also free to file more charges against a defendant than can realistically be proven in court, so long as probable cause arguably exists. Whether a good plea deal is offered to a defendant is entirely up to the prosecutor. And if the mood strikes, the prosecutor can transfer drug defendants to the federal system, where the penalties are far more severe. Juveniles, for their part, can be transferred to adult court, where they can be sent to adult prison. Angela J. Davis, in her authoritative study *Arbitrary Justice: The Power of the American Prosecutor*, observes that "the most remarkable feature of these important, sometimes life-and-death decisions is that they are totally discretionary and virtually unreviewable."[61] Most prosecutors' offices lack any manual or guidebook advising prosecutors how to make discretionary decisions. Even the American Bar Association's standards of practice for prosecutors are purely aspirational; no prosecutor is required to follow the standards or even consider them.

Christopher Lee Armstrong learned the hard way that the Supreme Court has little interest in ensuring that prosecutors exercise their extraordinary discretion in a manner that is fair and nondiscriminatory. He, along with four of his companions, was staying at a Los Angeles motel in April 1992 when federal and state agents on a joint drug crime task force raided their room and arrested them on federal drug charges—conspiracy to distribute more than fifty grams of crack cocaine. The federal public defenders assigned to Armstrong's case were disturbed by the fact that Armstrong and his friends had something in common with every other crack defendant their office had represented during the past year: they were all black. In fact, of the fifty-three crack cases their office had handled over the prior three years, forty-eight defendants were black, five were Hispanic, and not a single one was white. Armstrong's lawyers found it puzzling that no white crack offenders had been charged, given that most crack offenders are white. They suspected that whites were being diverted by federal prosecutors to the state system, where the penalties for crack offenses were far less severe. The only way to prove this, though, would be to gain access to the prosecutors' records and find out just how many white defendants were transferred to the state system and why. Armstrong's lawyers thus filed a motion asking the district court for discovery of the prosecutors' files to support their claim of selective prosecution under the Fourteenth Amendment.

Nearly one hundred years earlier, in a case called *Yick Wo v. Hopkins*, the Supreme Court had recognized that racially selective enforcement violates equal protection of the laws. In that case, decided in 1886, the Court unanimously overturned convictions of two Chinese men who were operating laundries without a license. San Francisco had denied licenses to all Chinese applicants, but granted licenses to all but one of the non-Chinese laundry operators who applied. Law enforcement arrested more than a hundred people for operating laundries without licenses, and every one of the arrestees was Chinese. Overturning Yick Wo's conviction, the Supreme Court declared in a widely quoted passage, "Though the law itself be fair on its face, and impartial in appearance, yet, if it is applied and administered by public authority with an evil eye and an unequal hand, so as practically to make unjust and illegal discriminations, between persons in similar circumstances . . . the denial of equal justice is still within the prohibition of the Constitution."[62] Armstrong's lawyers sought to prove that, like the law at issue in *Yick Wo*, federal crack laws were fair on their face and impartial in their appearance, but were selectively enforced in a racially discriminatory manner.

In support of their claim that Armstrong should, at the very least, be entitled to discovery, Armstrong's lawyers offered two sworn affidavits. One was from a halfway house intake coordinator who testified that, in his experience treating crack addicts, whites and blacks dealt and used the drugs in similar proportions. The other affidavit was from a defense attorney who had extensive experience in state prosecutions. He testified that nonblack defendants were routinely prosecuted in state, rather than federal, court. Arguably the best evidence in support of Armstrong's claims came from the government, which submitted a list of more than two thousand people charged with federal crack cocaine violations over a three-year period, all but eleven of whom were black. None were white.

The district court ruled that the evidence presented was sufficient to justify discovery for the purposes of determining whether the allegations of selective enforcement were valid. The prosecutors, however, refused to release any records and appealed the issue all the way to the U.S. Supreme Court. In May 1996, the Supreme Court reversed. As in *McCleskey*, the Court did not question the accuracy of the evidence submitted, but ruled that because Armstrong failed to identify any similarly situated white defendants who should have been charged in federal court but were not, he was not entitled even to discovery on his selective-prosecution claim. With no trace of irony, the Court demanded that Armstrong produce in advance the very thing he sought in discovery: information regarding white defendants who should have been charged in federal court. That information, of course, was in the prosecution's possession and control, which is why Armstrong filed a discovery motion in the first place.

As a result of the *Armstrong* decision, defendants who suspect racial bias on the part of prosecutors are trapped in a classic catch-22. In order to state a claim of selective prosecution, they are required to offer *in advance* the very evidence that generally can be obtained only through discovery of the prosecutor's files. The Court justified this insurmountable hurdle on the grounds that considerable deference is owed the exercise of prosecutorial discretion. Unless evidence of conscious, intentional bias on the part of the prosecutor could be produced, the Court would not allow any inquiry into the reasons for or causes of apparent racial disparities in prosecutorial decision making. Again the courthouse doors were closed, for all practical purposes, to claims of racial bias in the administration of the criminal justice system.

Immunizing prosecutors from claims of racial bias and failing to impose any meaningful check on the exercise of their discretion in charging, plea bargaining, transferring cases, and sentencing has created an environment in which conscious and unconscious biases are allowed to flourish. Numerous studies have shown that prosecutors interpret and respond to identical criminal activity differently based on the race of the offender.[63] One widely cited study was conducted by the *San Jose Mercury News*. The study reviewed 700,000 criminal cases that were matched by crime and criminal history of the defendant. The analysis revealed that similarly situated whites were far more successful than African Americans and Latinos in the plea bargaining process; in fact, "at virtually every stage of pretrial negotiation, whites are more successful than nonwhites."[64]

The most comprehensive studies of racial bias in the exercise of prosecutorial and judicial discretion involve the treatment of juveniles. These studies have shown that youth of color are more likely to be arrested, detained,
formally charged, transferred to adult court, and confined to secure residential facilities than their white counterparts.[65] A report in 2000 observed that
among youth who have never been sent to a juvenile prison before, African
Americans were more than six times as likely as whites to be sentenced to
prison for *identical* crimes.[66] A study sponsored by the U.S. Justice Department and several of the nation's leading foundations, published in 2007,
found that the impact of the biased treatment is magnified with each additional step into the criminal justice system. African American youth account
for 16 percent of all youth, 28 percent of all juvenile arrests, 35 percent of
the youth waived to adult criminal court, and 58 percent of youth admitted
to state adult prison.[67] A major reason for these disparities is unconscious
and conscious racial biases infecting decision making. In the state of Washington, for example, a review of juvenile sentencing reports found that prosecutors routinely described black and white offenders differently.[68] Blacks
committed crimes because of internal personality flaws such as disrespect.
Whites did so because of external conditions such as family conflict.

The risk that prosecutorial discretion will be racially biased is especially
acute in the drug enforcement context, where virtually identical behavior is
susceptible to a wide variety of interpretations and responses and the media
imagery and political discourse has been so thoroughly racialized. Whether
a kid is perceived as a dangerous drug-dealing thug or instead is viewed as a
good kid who was merely experimenting with drugs and selling to a few of
his friends has to do with the ways in which information about illegal drug
activity is processed and interpreted, in a social climate in which drug dealing is racially defined. As a former U.S. Attorney explained:

> I had an [assistant U.S. attorney who] wanted to drop the gun charge
> against the defendant [in a case in which] there were no extenuating
> circumstances. I asked, "Why do you want to drop the gun offense?"
> And he said, "'He's a rural guy and grew up on a farm. The gun he had
> with him was a rifle. He's a good ol' boy, and all good ol' boys have rifles,
> and it's not like he was a gun-toting drug dealer." But he was a gun-
> toting drug dealer, exactly.

The decision in *Armstrong* effectively shields this type of biased decision making from judicial scrutiny for racial bias. Prosecutors are well aware that the exercise of their discretion is unchecked, provided no explicitly racist remarks are made, as it is next to impossible for defendants to prove racial bias. It is difficult to imagine a system better designed to ensure that racial biases and stereotypes are given free rein—while at the same time appearing on the surface to be colorblind—than the one devised by the U.S. Supreme Court.

In Defense of the All-White Jury—*Purkett v. Elm*

The rules governing jury selection provide yet another illustration of the Court's complete abdication of its responsibility to guarantee racial minorities equal treatment under the law. In 1985, in *Batson v. Kentucky*, the Court held that the Fourteenth Amendment prohibits prosecutors from discriminating on the basis of race when selecting juries, a ruling hailed as an important safeguard against all-white juries locking up African Americans based on racial biases and stereotypes. Prior to *Batson*, prosecutors had been allowed to strike blacks from juries, provided they did not *always* strike black jurors. The Supreme Court had ruled in 1965, in *Swain v. Alabama*, that an equal-protection claim would arise only if a defendant could prove that a prosecutor struck African American jurors in every case, regardless of the crime involved or regardless of the races of the defendant or the victim.[69] Two decades later, in *Batson*, the Supreme Court reversed course, a nod to the newly minted public consensus that explicit race discrimination is an affront to American values. Almost immediately after *Batson* was decided, however, it became readily apparent that prosecutors had no difficulty circumventing the formal requirement of colorblindness in jury selection by means of a form of subterfuge the Court would come to accept, if not endorse.

The history of race discrimination in jury selection dates back to slavery. Until 1860, no black person had ever sat on a jury in the United States. During the Reconstruction era, African Americans began to serve on juries in the South for the first time. The all-white jury promptly returned, however, when Democratic conservatives sought to "redeem" the South by stripping blacks of their right to vote and their right to serve on juries. In 1880, the

Supreme Court intervened, striking down a West Virginia statute that expressly reserved jury service to white men. Citing the recently enacted Fourteenth Amendment, the Court declared that the exclusion of blacks from jury service was "practically a brand upon them, affixed by law, an assertion of their inferiority, and a stimulant to that race prejudice which is an impediment to . . . equal justice."[70] The Court asked, "How can it be maintained that compelling a colored man to submit to a trial for his life by a jury drawn from a panel from which the State has expressly excluded every man of his race, because of his color alone, however well qualified in other respects, is not a denial to him of equal protection?"[71]

For all its bluster, the Court offered no meaningful protection against jury discrimination in the years that followed. As legal scholar Benno Schmidt has observed, from the end of Reconstruction through the New Deal, "the systematic exclusion of black men from Southern juries was about as plain as any legal discrimination could be short of proclamation in state statutes or confession by state officials."[72] The Supreme Court repeatedly upheld convictions of black defendants by all-white juries in situations where exclusion of black jurors was obvious.[73] The only case in which the Court overturned a conviction on the grounds of discrimination in jury selection was *Neal v. Delaware*, a case decided in 1935. State law in Delaware once had explicitly restricted jury service to white men, and "no colored citizen had ever been summoned as a juror."[74] The Delaware Supreme Court had rejected Neal's equal protection claim on the grounds that "the great body of black men residing in this State are utterly unqualified [for jury service] by want of intelligence, experience, or moral integrity."[75] The Supreme Court reversed. Clearly, what offended the U.S. Supreme Court was not the exclusion of blacks from jury service per se, but rather doing so openly and explicitly. That orientation continues to hold today.

Notwithstanding *Batson*'s formal prohibition on race discrimination in jury selection, the Supreme Court and lower federal courts have tolerated all but the most egregious examples of racial bias in jury selection. *Miller El v. Cockrell* was such a case.[76] That case involved a jury-selection manual that sanctioned race-based selection. The Court noted that it was unclear whether the official policy of race-based exclusion was still in effect, but the prosecution did in fact exclude ten of eleven black jurors, in part by employing an unusual practice of "jury shuffling" that reduced the number of black jurors.[77] The prosecution also engaged in disparate questioning of jurors based on race—practices that seemed linked to the jury-selection manual. This was a highly unusual case. In typical cases, there are no official policies authorizing race discrimination in jury selection still lurking around, arguably in effect. Normally, the discrimination is obvious yet unstated, and the systematic exclusion of black jurors continues largely unabated through use of the peremptory strike.

Peremptory strikes have long been controversial. Both prosecutors and defense attorneys are permitted to strike "peremptorily" jurors they don't like—that is, people they believe will not respond favorably to the evidence or witnesses they intend to present at trial. In theory, peremptory strikes may increase the fairness of the proceeding by eliminating jurors who may be biased but whose biases cannot be demonstrated convincingly to a judge. In practice, however, peremptory challenges are notoriously discriminatory. Lawyers typically have little information about potential jurors, so their decisions to strike individual jurors tend to be based on nothing more than stereotypes, prejudices, and hunches. Achieving an all-white jury, or nearly all-white jury, is easy in most jurisdictions, because relatively few racial minorities are included in the jury pool. Potential jurors are typically called for service based on the list of registered voters or Department of Motor Vehicle lists—sources that contain disproportionately fewer people of color, because people of color are significantly less likely to own cars or register to vote. Making matters worse, thirty-one states and the federal government subscribe to the practice of lifetime felon exclusion from juries. *As a result, about 30 percent of black men are automatically banned from jury service for life.*[78] Accordingly, no more than a handful of strikes are necessary in many cases to eliminate all or nearly all black jurors. The practice of systematically excluding black jurors has not been halted by *Batson*; the only thing that has changed is that prosecutors must come up with a race-neutral excuse for the strikes—an exceedingly easy task.

In fact, one comprehensive study reviewed all published decisions involving *Batson* challenges from 1986 to 1992 and concluded that prosecutors almost never fail to successfully craft acceptable race-neutral explanations to justify striking black jurors.[79] Courts accept explanations that jurors are too young, too old, too conservative, too liberal, too comfortable, or too uncomfortable. Clothing is also a favorite reason; jurors have been stricken for wearing hats or sunglasses. Even explanations that might correlate with race, such as lack of education, unemployment, poverty, being single, living in the same neighborhood as the defendant, or prior involvement with the criminal justice system—have all been accepted as perfectly good, non-pretextual excuses for striking African Americans from juries. As professor Sheri Lynn Johnson once remarked, "If prosecutors exist who . . . cannot create a 'racially neutral' reason for discriminating on the basis of race, bar exams are too easy."[80]

Given how flagrantly prosecutors were violating *Batson's* ban on race discrimination in jury selection, it was reasonable to hope that, if presented with a particularly repugnant case, the Supreme Court might be willing to draw the line at practices that make a mockery of the antidiscrimination principle. Granted, the Court had been unwilling to accept statistical proof of race discrimination in sentencing in *McCleskey*, and it had brushed off concerns of racial bias in discretionary police stops in *Whren*, and it had granted virtual immunity to prosecutors in their charging decisions in *Armstrong*, but would it go so far as to allow prosecutors to offer blatantly absurd, downright laughable excuses for striking blacks from juries? It turns out the answer was yes.

In *Purkett v. Elm*, in 1995, the Supreme Court ruled that any race-neutral reason, no matter how silly, ridiculous, or superstitious, is enough to satisfy the prosecutor's burden of showing that a pattern of striking a particular racial group is not, in fact, based on race. In that case, the prosecutor offered the following explanation to justify his strikes of black jurors:

> I struck [juror] number twenty-two because of his long hair. He had long curly hair. He had the longest hair of anybody on the panel by far. He appeared not to be a good juror for that fact. . . . Also, he had a mustache and a goatee type beard. And juror number twenty-four also had a mustache and goatee type beard. . . . And I don't like the way they looked, with the way the hair is cut, both of them. And the mustaches and the beards look suspicious to me.[81]

The Court of Appeals for the Eighth Circuit ruled that the foregoing explanation for the prosecutor's strikes of black jurors was insufficient and should have been rejected by the trial court because long hair and facial hair are not plausibly related to a person's ability to perform as a juror. The appellate court explained: "Where the prosecution strikes a prospective juror who is a member of the defendant's racial group, solely on the basis of factors which are facially irrelevant to the question of whether that person is qualified to serve as a juror in the particular case, the prosecution must at least articulate some plausible race neutral reason for believing that those factors will somehow affect the person's ability to perform his or her duties as a juror."[82]

The U.S. Supreme Court reversed, holding that when a pattern of race-based strikes has been identified by the defense, the prosecutor need not provide "an explanation that is persuasive, or even plausible."[83] Once the reason is offered, a trial judge may choose to believe (or disbelieve) any "silly or superstitious" reason offered by prosecutors to explain a pattern of strikes that appear to be based on race.[84] The Court sent a clear message that appellate courts are largely free to accept the reasons offered by a prosecutor for excluding prospective black jurors—no matter how irrational or absurd the reasons may seem.

The Occupation—Policing the Enemy

The Court's blind eye to race discrimination in the criminal justice system has been especially problematic in policing. Racial bias is most acute at the point of entry into the system for two reasons: discretion and authorization. Although prosecutors, as a group, have the greatest power in the criminal justice system, police have the greatest discretion—discretion that is amplified in drug-law enforcement. And unbeknownst to the general public, the Supreme Court has actually authorized race discrimination in policing, rather than adopting legal rules banning it.

Racially biased police discretion is key to understanding how the overwhelming majority of people who get swept into the criminal justice system in the War on Drugs turn out to be black or brown, even though the police adamantly deny that they engage in racial profiling. In the drug war, police have discretion regarding whom to target (which individuals), as well as where to target (which neighborhoods or communities). As noted earlier, at least 10 percent of Americans violate drug laws every year, and people of all races engage in illegal drug activity at similar rates. With such an extraordinarily large population of offenders to choose from, decisions must be made regarding who should be targeted and where the drug war should be waged.

From the outset, the drug war could have been waged primarily in over-whelmingly white suburbs or on college campuses. SWAT teams could have rappelled from helicopters in gated suburban communities and raided the homes of high school lacrosse players known for hosting coke and ecstasy parties after their games. The police could have seized televisions, furniture, and cash from fraternity houses based on an anonymous tip that a few joints or a stash of cocaine could be found hidden in someone's dresser drawer. Suburban homemakers could have been placed under surveillance and sub-jected to undercover operations designed to catch them violating laws regulating the use and sale of prescription "uppers." All of this could have happened as a matter of routine in white communities, but it did not.

Instead, when police go looking for drugs, they look in the 'hood. Tactics that would be political suicide in an upscale white suburb are not even newswor-thy in poor black and brown communities. So long as mass drug arrests are con-centrated in impoverished urban areas, police chiefs have little reason to fear a political backlash, no matter how aggressive and warlike the efforts may be. And so long as the number of drug arrests increases or at least remains high, federal dollars continue to flow in and fill the department's coffers. As one for-mer prosecutor put it, "It's a lot easier to go out to the 'hood, so to speak, and pick somebody than to put your resources in an undercover [operation in a] community where there are potentially politically powerful people."[85]

The hypersegregation of the black poor in ghetto communities has made the roundup easy. Confined to ghetto areas and lacking political power, the black poor are convenient targets. Douglas Massey and Nancy Denton's book, *American Apartheid*, documents how racially segregated ghettos were deliberately created by federal policy, not impersonal market forces or pri-vate housing choices.[86] The enduring racial isolation of the ghetto poor has made them uniquely vulnerable in the War on Drugs. What happens to them does not directly affect—and is scarcely noticed by—the privileged beyond the ghetto's invisible walls. Thus it is here, in the poverty-stricken, racially segregated ghettos, where the War on Poverty has been abandoned and factories have disappeared, that the drug war has been waged with the greatest ferocity. SWAT teams are deployed here; buy-and-bust operations are concentrated here; drug raids of apartment buildings occur here; stop-and-frisk operations occur on the streets here. Black and brown youth are the primary targets. It is not uncommon for a young black teenager living in a ghetto community to be stopped, interrogated, and frisked numerous times in the course of a month, or even a single week, often by paramilitary units. Studies of racial profiling typically report the total number of people stopped and searched, disaggregated by race. These studies have led some policing experts to conclude that racial profiling is actually "worse" in white communities, because the racial disparities in stop and search rates are much greater there. What these studies do not reveal, however, is the frequency with which any given individual is likely to be stopped in specific, racially defined neighborhoods.

The militarized nature of law enforcement in ghetto communities has inspired rap artists and black youth to refer to the police presence in black communities as "The Occupation." In these occupied territories, many black youth automatically "assume the position" when a patrol car pulls up, knowing full well that they will be detained and frisked no matter what. This dynamic often comes as a surprise to those who have spent little time in ghettos. Craig Futterman, a law professor at the University of Chicago, reports that his students frequently express shock and dismay when they venture into those communities for the first time and witness the distance between abstract legal principles and actual practice. One student reported, following her ride along with Chicago police: "Each time we drove into a public housing project and stopped the car, every young black man in the area would almost reflexively place his hands up against the car and spread his legs to be searched. And the officers would search them. The officers would then get back in the car and stop in another project, and this would happen again. This repeated itself throughout the entire day. I couldn't believe it. This was nothing like we learned in law school. But it just seemed so normal—for the police and the young men."

Numerous scholars (and many law enforcement officials) attempt to justify the concentration of drug law enforcement resources in ghetto communities on the grounds that it is easier for the police to combat illegal drug activity there. The theory is that black and Latino drug users are more likely than white users to obtain illegal drugs in public spaces that are visible to the police, and therefore it is more efficient and convenient for the police to concentrate their efforts on open-air drug markets in ghetto communities. Sociologists have been major proponents of this line of reasoning, pointing out that differential access to private space influences the likelihood that criminal behavior will be detected. Because poor people lack access to private space (often sharing small apartments with numerous family members or relatives), their criminal activity is more likely to be conducted outdoors. Concentrating law enforcement efforts in locations where drug activity will be more easily detected is viewed as a race-neutral organizational necessity. This argument is often buttressed by claims that most citizen complaints about illegal drug activity come from ghetto areas, and that the violence associated with the drug trade occurs in inner cities. These facts, drug war defenders claim, make the decision to wage the drug war almost exclusively in poor communities of color an easy and logical choice.

This line of reasoning is weaker than it initially appears. Many law enforcement officials acknowledge that the demand for illegal drugs is so great—and the lack of alternative sources of income so few in ghetto communities—that "if you take one dealer off the street, he'll be replaced within an hour." Many also admit that a predictable consequence of breaking up one drug ring is a slew of violence as others fight for control of the previously stabilized market.[87] These realities suggest—if the past two decades of endless war somehow did not—that the drug war is doomed to fail. They also call into question the legitimacy of "convenience" as an excuse for the mass imprisonment of black and brown men in ghetto communities.

Even putting aside such concerns, though, recent research indicates that the basic assumptions upon which drug war defenses typically rest are simply wrong. The conventional wisdom—that "get tough" tactics are a regrettable necessity in poor communities of color and that efficiency requires the drug war to be waged in the most vulnerable neighborhoods—turns out to be, as many have long suspected, nothing more than wartime propaganda, not sound policy.

Unconventional Wisdom

In 2002, a team of researchers at the University of Washington decided to take the defenses of the drug war seriously, by subjecting the arguments to empirical testing in a major study of drug-law enforcement in a racially mixed city—Seattle.[88] The study found that, contrary to the prevailing "common sense," the high arrest rates of African Americans in drug-law enforcement could not be explained by rates of offending; nor could they be explained by other standard excuses, such as the ease and efficiency of policing open-air drug markets, citizen complaints, crime rates, or drug-related violence. The study also debunked the assumption that white drug dealers deal indoors, making their criminal activity more difficult to detect.

The authors found that it was untrue stereotypes about crack markets, crack dealers, and crack babies—not facts—that were driving discretionary decision making by the Seattle Police Department. The facts were as follows: Seattle residents were far more likely to report suspected narcotics activities in residences—not outdoors—but police devoted their resources to open-air drug markets and to the one precinct that was *least* likely to be identified as the site of suspected drug activity in citizen complaints. In fact, although hundreds of outdoor drug transactions were recorded in predominantly white areas of Seattle, police concentrated their drug enforcement efforts in one downtown drug market where the frequency of drug transactions was much lower. In racially mixed open-air drug markets, black dealers were far more likely to be arrested than whites, even though white dealers were present and visible. And the department focused overwhelmingly on crack—the one drug in Seattle more likely to be sold by African Americans—despite the fact that local hospital records indicated that overdose deaths involving heroin were more numerous than all overdose deaths for crack and powder cocaine combined. Local police acknowledged that no significant level of violence was associated with crack in Seattle and that other drugs were causing more hospitalizations, but steadfastly maintained that their deployment decisions were nondiscriminatory.

The study's authors concluded, based on their review and analysis of the empirical evidence, that the Seattle Police Department's decisions to focus so heavily on crack, to the near exclusion of other drugs, and to concentrate its efforts on outdoor drug markets in downtown areas rather than drug markets located indoors or in predominantly white communities, reflect "a racialized conception of the drug problem."[89] As the authors put it: "[The Seattle Police Department's] focus on black and Latino individuals and on the drug most strongly associated with 'blackness' suggest that law enforcement policies and practices are predicated on the assumption that the drug problem is, in fact, a black and Latino one, and that crack, the drug most strongly associated with urban blacks, is 'the worst.'"[90] This racialized cultural script about who and what constitutes the drug problem renders illegal drug activity by whites invisible. "White people," the study's authors observed, "are simply not perceived as drug offenders by Seattle police officers."[91]

Hollow Hope

One might imagine that the facts described above would provide grounds for a lawsuit challenging the Seattle Police Department's drug war tactics as a violation of the equal protection clause of the Fourteenth Amendment and demanding reform. After all, obtaining reform through the city council or state legislature may seem unlikely, for black "criminals" are perhaps the most despised minority in the U.S. population. Few politicians will leap at the opportunity to support black people labeled criminals. Accordingly, a lawsuit may seem like the best option. The purpose of our Constitution— especially the Fourteenth Amendment's equal-protection guarantee—is to protect minority rights even when, or especially when, they are unpopular. So shouldn't African American defendants be able to file a successful lawsuit demanding an end to these discriminatory practices or challenge their drug arrests on the grounds that these law enforcement practices are unlawfully tainted by race? The answer is yes, they should, but no, they probably can't.

As legal scholar David Cole has observed, "The Court has imposed nearly insurmountable barriers to persons challenging race discrimination at all stages of the criminal justice system."[92] The barriers are so high that few lawsuits are even filed, notwithstanding shocking and indefensible racial disparities. Procedural hurdles, such as the "standing requirement," have made it virtually impossible to seek reform of law enforcement agencies through the judicial process, even when the policies or practices at issue are illegal or plainly discriminatory.

Adolph Lyons's attempt to ban the use of lethal chokeholds by the Los Angeles Police Department (LAPD) is a good example. Lyons, a twenty-four-year-old black man, was driving his car in Los Angeles one morning when he was pulled over by four police officers for a burned-out taillight. With guns drawn, police ordered Lyons out of his car. He obeyed. The officers told him to face the car, spread his legs, and put his hands on his head. Again, Lyons did as he was told. After the officers completed a pat-down, Lyons dropped his hands, prompting an officer to slam Lyons's hands back on his head. When Lyons complained that the car keys he was holding were causing him pain, the officer forced Lyons into a chokehold. He lost consciousness and collapsed. When he awoke, "he was spitting up blood and dirt, had urinated and defecated, and had suffered permanent damage to his larynx."[93] The officers issued a traffic ticket for the burned-out taillight and released him.

Lyons sued the City of Los Angeles for violation of his constitutional rights and sought, as a remedy, a ban against future use of the chokeholds. By the time his case reached the Supreme Court, sixteen people had been killed by police use of the chokehold, twelve of them black men. The Supreme Court dismissed the case, however, ruling that Lyons lacked "standing" to seek an injunction against the deadly practice. In order to have standing, the Court reasoned, Lyons would have to show that he was highly likely to be subject to a chokehold again.

Lyons argued that, as a black man, he had good reason to fear he would be stopped by the police for a minor traffic violation and subjected to a chokehold again. He had done nothing to provoke the chokehold; to the contrary, he had obeyed instructions and cooperated fully. Why wouldn't he believe he was at risk of being stopped and choked again? The Court, however, ruled that in order to have standing

> Lyons would have had not only to allege that he would have another encounter with the police but also to make the incredible assertion either (1) that all police officers in Los Angeles always choke any citizen with whom they have an encounter, whether for the purpose of arrest, issuing a citation or for questioning, or (2) that the City ordered or authorized the police to act in such a manner.[94]

Lyons did not allege race discrimination, but if he had, that claim would almost certainly have been a loser too. The Court's ruling in *Lyons* makes it extremely difficult to challenge systemic race discrimination in law enforcement and obtain meaningful policy reform. For example, African Americans in Seattle who hope to end the Seattle police department's discriminatory tactics through litigation would be required to prove that they plan to violate drug laws and that they will almost certainly face race discrimination by Seattle police officers engaged in drug-law enforcement, in order to have standing to seek reform—i.e., just to get in the courthouse door.

It is worthy of note that the *Lyons* standard does not apply to suits for damages. But any suggestion that litigants need not worry about policy reform because they can always sue for damages would be disingenuous—particularly as applied to race discrimination cases. Why? Neither the state nor the state police can be sued for damages. In a series of cases, the Supreme Court has ruled that the state and its offices are immune from federal suits for damages under the Eleventh Amendment to the Constitution (unless they consent), and the state can't be sued for damages for constitutional violations in state court either.[95] City police departments, like the LAPD, are also typically off limits. The Court has ruled that a city police department cannot be sued for damages unless a specific city policy or custom can be identified authorizing the illegal practice.[96] Most cities, of course, do not have policies specifically authorizing illegal conduct (particularly race discrimination), and "custom" is notoriously difficult to prove. Accordingly, suing a city police department for damages is generally not an option. Yet even if all of those hurdles can somehow be overcome, there is still the matter of proving a claim of race discrimination. As we have seen, to establish an equal-protection violation, one must prove *intentional* discrimination— conscious racial bias. Law enforcement officials rarely admit to having acted for racial reasons, leaving most victims of discriminatory law enforcement without anyone to sue and without a claim that can be proven in a court of law. But even if a plaintiff managed to overcome all of the procedural hurdles and prove that a police officer deliberately exercised his or her discretion on the basis of race, that still might not be enough.

Race as a Factor

The dirty little secret of policing is that the Supreme Court has actually granted the police license to discriminate. This fact is not advertised by police departments, because law enforcement officials know that the public would not respond well to this fact in the era of colorblindness. It is the sort of thing that is better left unsaid. Civil rights lawyers—including those litigating racial profiling cases—have been complicit in this silence, fearing that any acknowledgment that race-based policing is authorized by law would legitimate in the public mind the very practice they are hoping to eradicate.

The truth, however, is this: At other stages of the criminal justice process, the Court has indicated that overt racial bias necessarily triggers strict scrutiny—a concession that has not been costly, as very few law enforcement officials today are foolish enough to admit bias openly. But the Supreme Court has indicated that in policing, race *can* be used as a factor in discretionary decision making. In *United States v. Brignoni-Ponce*, the Court concluded it was permissible under the equal protection clause of the Fourteenth Amendment for the police to use race as a factor in making decisions about which motorists to stop and search. In that case, the Court concluded that the police could take a person's Mexican appearance into account when developing reasonable suspicion that a vehicle may contain undocumented immigrants. The Court said that "the likelihood that any person of Mexican ancestry is an alien is high enough to make Mexican appearance a relevant factor."[97] Some commentators have argued that *Brignoni-Ponce* may be limited to the immigration context; the Court might not apply the same principle to drug-law enforcement. It is not obvious what the rational basis would be for limiting overt race discrimination by police to immigration. The likelihood that a person of Mexican ancestry is an "alien" could not be significantly higher than the likelihood that any random black person is a drug criminal.

The Court's quiet blessing of race-based traffic stops has led to something of an Orwellian public discourse regarding racial profiling. Police departments and highway patrol agencies frequently declare, "We do not engage in racial profiling," even though their officers routinely use race as a factor when making decisions regarding whom to stop and search. The justification for the implicit doublespeak—"we do not racial-profile; we just stop people based on race"—can be explained in part by the Supreme Court's jurisprudence. Because the Supreme Court has authorized the police to use race as a factor when making decisions regarding whom to stop and search, police departments believe that racial profiling exists only when race is the *sole* factor. Thus, if race is one factor but not the only factor, then it doesn't really count as a factor at all.

The absurdity of this logic is evidenced by the fact that police almost never stop anyone solely because of race. A young black male wearing baggy pants, standing in front of his high school surrounded by a group of similarly dressed black friends, may be stopped and searched because police believe he "looks like" a drug dealer. Clearly, race is not the only reason for that conclusion. Gender, age, attire, and location play a role. The police would likely ignore an eighty-five-year-old black man standing in the same spot surrounded by a group of elderly black women.

The problem is that although race is rarely the sole reason for a stop or search, it is frequently a *determinative* reason. A young white male wearing baggy pants, standing in front of his high school and surrounded by his friends, might well be ignored by police officers. It might never occur to them that a group of young white kids might be dealing dope in front of their high school. Similarly situated people inevitably are treated differently when police are granted permission to rely on racial stereotypes when making discretionary decisions.

Equally important, though, the sole-factor test ignores the ways in which seemingly race-neutral factors—such as location—operate in a highly discriminatory fashion. Some law enforcement officials claim that they would stop and search white kids wearing baggy jeans in the ghetto (that would be suspicious)—it just so happens they're rarely there. Subjecting people to stops and searches because they live in "high crime" ghettos cannot be said to be truly race-neutral, given that the ghetto itself was constructed to contain and control groups of people defined by race.[98] Even seemingly race-neutral factors such as "prior criminal history" are not truly race-neutral. A black kid arrested twice for possession of marijuana may be no more of a repeat offender than a white frat boy who regularly smokes pot in his dorm room. But because of his race and his confinement to a racially segregated ghetto, the black kid has a criminal record, while the white frat boy, because of his race and relative privilege, does not. Thus, when prosecutors throw the book at black repeat offenders or when police stalk ex-offenders and subject them to regular frisks and searches on the grounds that it makes sense to "watch criminals closely," they are often exacerbating racial disparities created by the discretionary decision to wage the War on Drugs almost exclusively in poor communities of color.

Defending against claims of racial bias in policing is easy. Because race is never the only reason for a stop or search, any police officer with a fifth-grade education will be able to cite multiple nonracial reasons for initiating an encounter, including any number of the so-called "indicators" of drug trafficking discussed in chapter 2, such as appearing too nervous or too calm. Police officers (like prosecutors) are highly adept at offering race-neutral reasons for actions that consistently disadvantage African Americans. Whereas prosecutors claim they strike black jurors not because of their race but because of their hairstyle, police officers have their own stock excuses— e.g., "Your honor, we didn't stop him because he's black; we stopped him because he failed to use his turn signal at the right time," or "It wasn't just because he was black; it was also because he seemed nervous when he saw the police car." Judges are just as reluctant to second-guess an officer's motives as they are to second-guess prosecutors'. So long as officers refrain from uttering racial epithets and so long as they show the good sense not to say "the only reason I stopped him was 'cause he's black," courts generally turn a blind eye to patterns of discrimination by the police.

Studies of racial profiling have shown that police do, in fact, exercise their discretion regarding whom to stop and search in the drug war in a highly discriminatory manner.[99] Not only do police discriminate in their determinations regarding where to wage the war, but they also discriminate in their judgments regarding whom to target outside of the ghetto's invisible walls.

The most famous of these studies were conducted in New Jersey and Maryland in the 1990s. Allegations of racial profiling in federally funded drug interdiction operations resulted in numerous investigations and comprehensive data demonstrating a dramatic pattern of racial bias in highway patrol stops and searches. These drug interdiction programs were the brainchild of the DEA, part of the federally funded program known as Operation Pipeline.

In New Jersey, the data showed that only 15 percent of all drivers on the New Jersey Turnpike were racial minorities, yet 42 percent of all stops and 73 percent of all arrests were of black motorists—despite the fact that blacks and whites violated traffic laws at almost exactly the same rate. While radar stops were relatively consistent with the percentage of minority violators, discretionary stops made by officers involved in drug interdiction resulted in double the number of stops of minorities.[100] A subsequent study conducted by the attorney general of New Jersey found that searches on the turnpike were even more discriminatory than the initial stops—77 percent of all consent searches were of minorities. The Maryland studies produced similar results: African Americans comprised only 17 percent of drivers along a stretch of I-95 outside of Baltimore, yet they were 70 percent of those who were stopped and searched. Only 21 percent of all drivers along that stretch of highway were racial minorities (Latinos, Asians, and African Americans), yet those groups comprised nearly 80 percent of those pulled over and searched.[101]

What most surprised many analysts was that, in both studies, whites were actually *more likely* than people of color to be carrying illegal drugs or contraband in their vehicles. In fact, in New Jersey, whites were almost twice as likely to be found with illegal drugs or contraband as African Americans, and five times as likely to be found with contraband as Latinos.[102] Although whites were more likely to be guilty of carrying drugs, they were far less likely to be viewed as suspicious, resulting in relatively few stops, searches, and arrests of whites. The former New Jersey attorney general dubbed this phenomenon the "circular illogic of racial profiling." Law enforcement officials, he explained, often point to the racial composition of our prisons and jails as a justification for targeting racial minorities, but the empirical evidence actually suggested the opposite conclusion was warranted. The disproportionate imprisonment of people of color was, in part, a product of racial profiling—not a justification for it.

In the years following the release of the New Jersey and Maryland data, dozens of other studies of racial profiling have been conducted. A brief sampling:

- In Volusia County, Florida, a reporter obtained 148 hours of video footage documenting more than 1,000 highway stops conducted by state troopers. Only 5 percent of the drivers on the road were African American or Latino, but more than 80 percent of the people stopped and searched were minorities.[103]
- In Illinois, the state police initiated a drug interdiction program known as Operation Valkyrie that targeted Latino motorists. While Latinos comprised less than 8 percent of the Illinois population and took fewer than 3 percent of the personal vehicle trips in Illinois, they comprised approximately 30 percent of the motorists stopped by drug interdiction officers for discretionary offenses, such as failure to signal a lane change.[104] Latinos, however, were significantly less likely than whites to have illegal contraband in their vehicles.
- A racial profiling study in Oakland, California, in 2001 showed that African Americans were approximately twice as likely as whites to be stopped, and three times as likely to be searched.[105]

Pedestrian stops, too, have been the subject of study and controversy. The New York Police Department released statistics in February 2007 showing that during the prior year its officers stopped an astounding 508,540 people—an average of 1,393 per day—who were walking down the street, perhaps on their way to the subway, grocery store, or bus stop. Often the stops included searches for illegal drugs or guns—searches that frequently required people to lie face down on the pavement or stand spread-eagled against a wall while police officers aggressively groped all over their bodies while bystanders watched or walked by. The vast majority of those stopped and searched were racial minorities, and more than half were African American.[106]

The NYPD began collecting data on pedestrian stops following the shooting of Amadou Diallo, an African immigrant who died in a hail of police bullets on the front steps of his own home in February 1999. Diallo was followed to his apartment building by four white police officers—members of the elite Street Crime Unit—who viewed him as suspicious and wanted to interrogate him. They ordered him to stop, but, according to the officers, Diallo did not respond immediately. He walked a bit farther to his apartment building, opened the door, and retrieved his wallet—probably to produce identification. The officers said they thought the wallet was a gun, and fired forty-one times. Amadou Diallo died at the age of twenty-two. He was unarmed and had no criminal record.

Diallo's murder sparked huge protests, resulting in a series of studies commissioned by the attorney general of New York. The first study found that African Americans were stopped six times more frequently than whites, and that stops of African Americans were less likely to result in arrests than stops of whites—presumably because blacks were less likely to be found with drugs or other contraband.[107] Although the NYPD attempted to justify the stops on the grounds that they were designed to get guns off the street, stops by the Street Crime Unit—the group of officers who supposedly are specially trained to identify gun-toting thugs—yielded a weapon in only 2.5 percent of all stops.[108]

Rather than reducing reliance on stop-and-frisk tactics following the Diallo shooting and the release of this disturbing data, the NYPD dramatically *increased* its number of pedestrian stops and continued to stop and frisk African Americans at grossly disproportionate rates. The NYPD stopped five times more people in 2005 than in 2002—the overwhelming majority of whom were African American or Latino.[109] By 2008, the NYPD was stopping 545,000 in a single year, and 80 percent of the people stopped were African Americans and Latinos. Whites comprised a mere 8 percent of people frisked by the NYPD, while African Americans accounted for 85 percent of all frisks.[110] A report by the *New York Times* found that the highest concentration of stops in the city was a roughly eight-block area of Brownsville, Brooklyn, that was predominately black. Residents there were stopped at a rate thirteen times the city average.[111]

Although the NYPD frequently attempts to justify stop-and-frisk operations in poor communities of color on the grounds that such tactics are necessary to get guns off the streets, less than 1 percent of stops (0.15 percent)
resulted in guns being found, and guns and other contraband were seized
less often in stops of African Americans and Latinos than of whites.[112] As
Darius Charney, a lawyer for the Center for Constitutional Rights, observed,
these studies "confirm what we have been saying for the last 10 or 11 years,
which is that with stop-and-frisk patterns—it is really race, not crime, that
is driving this."[113]

Ultimately, these stop-and-frisk operations amount to much more than
humiliating, demeaning rituals for young men of color, who must raise their
arms and spread their legs, always careful not to make a sudden move or
gesture that could provide an excuse for brutal—even lethal—force. Like
the days when black men were expected to step off the sidewalk and cast
their eyes downward when a white woman passed, young black men know the
drill when they see the police crossing the street toward them; it is a ritual
of dominance and submission played out hundreds of thousands of times
each year. But it is more than that. These routine encounters often serve
as the gateway into the criminal justice system. The NYPD made 50,300
marijuana arrests in 2010 alone, mostly of young men of color. As one report
noted, these marijuana arrests offer "training opportunities" for rookie police
who can practice on ghetto kids while earning overtime.[114] These arrests
serve another purpose as well: they "are the most effective way for the NYPD
to collect fingerprints, photographs and other information on young people
not yet entered into the criminal databases."[115] A simple arrest for marijuana
possession can show up on criminal databases as "a drug arrest" without
specifying the substance or the charge, and without clarifying even whether
the person was convicted. These databases are then used by police and prosecutors, as well as by employers and housing officials—an electronic record
that will haunt many for life. More than 353,000 people were arrested and
jailed by the NYPD between 1997 and 2006 for simple possession of small
amounts of marijuana, with blacks five times more likely to be arrested than
whites.[116]

In Los Angeles, mass stops of young African American men and boys resulted in the creation of a database containing the names, addresses, and other
biographical information of the overwhelming majority of young black men in
the entire city. The LAPD justified its database as a tool for tracking gang or

"gang-related" activity. However, the criterion for inclusion in the database is notoriously vague and discriminatory. Having a relative or friend in a gang and wearing baggy jeans is enough to put youth on what the ACLU calls a Black List. In Denver, displaying any two of a list of attributes—including slang, "clothing of a particular color," pagers, hairstyles, or jewelry—earns youth a spot in the Denver Police's gang database. In 1992, citizen activism led to an investigation, which revealed that eight out of every ten people of color in the entire city were on the list of suspected criminals.[117]

The End of an Era

The litigation that swept the nation in the 1990s challenging racial profiling practices has nearly vanished. The news stories about people being stopped and searched on their way to church or work or school have faded from the evening news. This is not because the problem has been solved or because the experience of being stopped, interrogated, and searched on the basis of race has become less humiliating, alienating, or demoralizing as time has gone by. The lawsuits have disappeared because, in a little noticed case called *Alexander v. Sandoval*, decided in 2001, the Supreme Court eliminated the last remaining avenue available for challenging racial bias in the criminal justice system.[118]

Sandoval was not, on its face, even about criminal justice. It was a case challenging the Alabama Department of Public Safety's decision to administer state driver's license examinations only in English. The plaintiffs argued that the department's policy violated Title VI of the Civil Rights Act of 1964 and its implementing regulations, because the policy had the effect of subjecting non-English speakers to discrimination based on their national origin. The Supreme Court did not reach the merits of the case, ruling instead that the plaintiffs lacked the legal right even to file the lawsuit. It concluded that Title VI does not provide a "private right of action" to ordinary citizens and civil rights groups; meaning that victims of discrimination can no longer sue under the law.

The *Sandoval* decision virtually wiped out racial profiling litigation nationwide. Nearly all of the cases alleging racial profiling in drug-law enforcement were brought pursuant to Title VI of the Civil Rights Act of 1964 and its implementing regulations. Title VI prohibits federally funded programs or activities from discriminating on the basis of race, and the regulations employ a "disparate impact test" for discrimination—meaning that plaintiffs could prevail in claims of race discrimination without proving discriminatory intent. Under the regulations, a federally funded law enforcement program or activity is unlawful if it has a racially discriminatory impact and if that impact cannot be justified by law enforcement necessity. Because nearly all law enforcement agencies receive federal funding in the drug war, and because drug war tactics—such as pretext stops and consent searches—have a grossly discriminatory impact and are largely ineffective, plaintiffs were able to argue persuasively that the tactics could not be justified by law enforcement necessity.

In 1999, for example, the ACLU of Northern California filed a class action lawsuit against the California Highway Patrol (CHP), alleging that its highway drug interdiction program violated Title VI of the Civil Rights Act because it relied heavily on discretionary pretext stops and consent searches that are employed overwhelmingly against African American and Latino motorists. During the course of the litigation, the CHP produced data that showed African Americans were twice as likely, and Latinos three times as likely, to be stopped and searched by its officers as were whites. The data further showed that consent searches were ineffective; only a tiny percentage of the discriminatory searches resulted in the discovery of drugs or other contraband, yet thousands of black and brown motorists were subjected to baseless interrogations, searches, and seizures as a result of having committed a minor traffic violation. The CHP entered into a consent decree that provided for a three-year moratorium on consent searches and pretext stops statewide and the collection of comprehensive data on the race and ethnicity of motorists stopped and searched by the police, so that it would be possible to determine whether discriminatory practices were continuing. Similar results were obtained in New Jersey, as a result of landmark litigation filed against the New Jersey State Police. After *Sandoval*, these cases can no longer be brought under Title VI by private litigants. Only the federal government can sue to enforce Title VI's antidiscrimination provisions—something it has neither the inclination nor the capacity to do in most racial profiling cases due to its limited resources and institutional reluctance to antagonize local law enforcement. Since the War on Drugs, private litigants represented by organizations such as the ACLU have been at the forefront of racial profiling litigation. Those days, however, have come to an end. The racial profiling cases that swept the nation in the 1990s may well be the last wave of litigation challenging racial bias in the criminal justice system that we see for a very long time.

The Supreme Court has now closed the courthouse doors to claims of racial bias at every stage of the criminal justice process, from stops and searches to plea bargaining and sentencing. The system of mass incarceration is now, for all practical purposes, thoroughly immunized from claims of racial bias. Staggering racial disparities in the drug war continue but rarely make the news. One recent development that did make news was President Obama's decision to sign legislation reducing the hundred-to-one disparity in sentencing for crack versus powder cocaine to eighteen to one, a small step in the right direction.[119] Under the new law, it takes 28 grams of crack cocaine to net a five-year mandatory minimum sentence, while it still takes selling 500 grams of powdered cocaine to net the same sentence. There should be no disparity—the ratio should be one-to-one. But that disparity is just the tip of the iceberg. As noted in chapter 2, this system depends primarily on the prison label, not prison time. What matters most is who gets swept into this system of control and then ushered into an undercaste. The legal rules adopted by the Supreme Court guarantee that those who find themselves locked up and permanently locked out due to the drug war are overwhelmingly black and brown.

4

The Cruel Hand

A heavy and cruel hand has been laid upon us. As a people, we feel ourselves to be not only deeply injured, but grossly misunderstood. Our white countrymen do not know us. They are strangers to our character, ignorant of our capacity, oblivious to our history and progress, and are misinformed as to the principles and ideas that control and guide us, as a people. The great mass of American citizens estimates us as being a characterless and purposeless people; and hence we hold up our heads, if at all, against the withering influence of a nation's scorn and contempt.[1]

—Frederick Douglass, in a statement on behalf of delegates to the National
Colored Convention held in Rochester, New York, in July 1853

When Frederick Douglass and the other delegates to the National Colored Convention converged in Rochester, New York, in the summer of 1853 to discuss the condition, status, and future of "coloreds" (as they were called then), they decried the stigma of race—the condemnation and scorn heaped upon them for no reason other than the color of their skin. Most of the delegates were freed slaves, though the younger ones may have been born free. Northern emancipation was complete, but freedom remained elusive. Blacks were finally free from the formal control of their owners, but they were not full citizens—they could not vote, they were subject to legal discrimination, and at any moment, Southern plantation owners could capture them on the street and whisk them back to slavery. Although Northern slavery had been abolished, every black person was still presumed a slave—by law—and could not testify or introduce evidence in court. Thus if a Southern plantation owner said you were a slave, you were—unless a white person interceded in a court of law on your behalf and testified that you were rightfully free. Slavery may have died, but for thousands of blacks, the badge of slavery lived on.

Today a criminal freed from prison has scarcely more rights, and arguably less respect, than a freed slave or a black person living "free" in Mississippi at the height of Jim Crow. Those released from prison on parole can be stopped and searched by the police for any reason—or no reason at all—and returned to prison for the most minor of infractions, such as failing to attend a meeting with a parole officer. Even when released from the system's formal control, the stigma of criminality lingers. Police supervision, monitoring, and harassment are facts of life not only for all those labeled criminals, but for all those who "look like" criminals. Lynch mobs may be long gone, but the threat of police violence is ever present. A wrong move or sudden gesture could mean massive retaliation by the police. A wallet could be mistaken for a gun. The "whites only" signs may be gone, but new signs have gone up— notices placed in job applications, rental agreements, loan applications, forms for welfare benefits, school applications, and petitions for licenses, informing the general public that "felons" are not wanted here. A criminal record today authorizes precisely the forms of discrimination we supposedly left behind—discrimination in employment, housing, education, public benefits, and jury service. Those labeled criminals can even be denied the right to vote.

Criminals, it turns out, are the one social group in America we have permission to hate. In "colorblind" America, criminals are the new whipping boys. They are entitled to no respect and little moral concern. Like the "coloreds" in the years following emancipation, criminals today are deemed a characterless and purposeless people, deserving of our collective scorn and contempt. When we say someone was "treated like a criminal," what we mean to say is that he or she was treated as less than human, like a shameful creature. Hundreds of years ago, our nation put those considered less than human in shackles; less than one hundred years ago, we relegated them to the other side of town; today we put them in cages. Once released, they find that a heavy and cruel hand has been laid upon them.

Brave New World

One might imagine that a criminal defendant, when brought before the judge—or when meeting with his attorney for the first time—would be told of the consequences of a guilty plea or conviction. He would be told that, if he pleads guilty to a felony, he will be deemed "unfit" for jury service and automatically excluded from juries for the rest of his life.[2] He would also be told that he could be denied the right to vote. In a country that preaches the virtues of democracy, one could reasonably assume that being stripped of basic political rights would be treated by judges and court personnel as a serious matter indeed. Not so. When a defendant pleads guilty to a minor drug offense, nobody will likely tell him that he may be permanently forfeiting his right to vote as well as his right to serve on a jury—two of the most fundamental rights in any modern democracy.

He will also be told little or nothing about the parallel universe he is about to enter, one that promises a form of punishment that is often more difficult to bear than prison time: a lifetime of shame, contempt, scorn, and exclusion. In this hidden world, discrimination is perfectly legal. As Jeremy Travis has observed, "In this brave new world, punishment for the original offense is no longer enough; one's debt to society is never paid."[3] Other commentators liken the prison label to "the mark of Cain" and characterize the perpetual nature of the sanction as "internal exile."[4] Myriad laws, rules, and regulations operate to discriminate against ex-offenders and effectively prevent their reintegration into the mainstream society and economy. These restrictions amount to a form of "civic death" and send the unequivocal message that "they" are no longer part of "us."

Once labeled a felon, the badge of inferiority remains with you for the rest of your life, relegating you to a permanent second-class status. Consider, for example, the harsh reality facing a first-time offender who pleads guilty to felony possession of marijuana. Even if the defendant manages to avoid prison time by accepting a "generous" plea deal, he may discover that the punishment that awaits him outside the courthouse doors is far more severe and debilitating than what he might have encountered in prison. A task force of the American Bar Association described the bleak reality facing a petty drug offender this way:

[The] offender may be sentenced to a term of probation, community service, and court costs. Unbeknownst to this offender, and perhaps any other actor in the sentencing process, as a result of his conviction he may be ineligible for many federally-funded health and welfare benefits, food stamps, public housing, and federal educational assistance. His driver's license may be automatically suspended, and he may no longer qualify for certain employment and professional licenses. If he is convicted of another crime he may be subject to imprisonment as a repeat offender. He will not be permitted to enlist in the military, or possess a firearm, or obtain a federal security clearance. If a citizen, he may lose the right to vote; if not, he becomes immediately deportable.[5]

Despite the brutal, debilitating impact of these "collateral consequences" on ex-offenders' lives, courts have generally declined to find that such sanctions are actually "punishment" for constitutional purposes. As a result, judges are not required to inform criminal defendants of some of the most important rights they are forfeiting when they plead guilty to a felony. In fact, judges, prosecutors, and defense attorneys may not even be aware of the full range of collateral consequences for a felony conviction. Yet these civil penalties, although not considered punishment by our courts, often make it virtually impossible for ex-offenders to integrate into the mainstream society and economy upon release. Far from collateral, these sanctions can be the most damaging and painful aspect of a criminal conviction. Collectively, these sanctions send the strong message that, now that you have been labeled, you are no longer wanted. You are no longer part of "us," the deserving. Unable to drive, get a job, find housing, or even qualify for public benefits, many ex-offenders lose their children, their dignity, and eventually their freedom—landing back in jail after failing to play by rules that seem hopelessly stacked against them.

The churning of African Americans in and out of prisons today is hardly surprising, given the strong message that is sent to them that they are not wanted in mainstream society. In Frederick Douglass's words, "Men are so constituted that they derive their conviction of their own possibilities largely from the estimate formed of them by others. If nothing is expected of a people, that people will find it difficult to contradict that expectation."[6] More than a hundred years later, a similar argument was made by a woman contemplating her eventual release into a society that had constructed a brand-new legal regime designed to keep her locked out, fifty years after the demise of Jim Crow. "Right now I'm in prison," she said. "Like society kicked me out. They're like, 'Okay, the criminal element, We don't want them in society, we're going to put them in prisons.' Okay, but once I get out, then what do you do? What do you do with all these millions of people that have been in prison and been released? I mean, do you accept them back? Or do you keep them as outcasts? And if you keep them as outcasts, how do you expect them to act?"[7]

Remarkably, the overwhelming majority of ex-offenders struggle mightily to play by the rules and to succeed in a society seemingly hell-bent on excluding them. Like their forbears, they do their best to survive, even thrive— against all odds.

No Place Like Home

The first question on the minds of many released prisoners as they take their first steps outside the prison gates is where will they sleep that night. Some prisoners have families eagerly awaiting them—families who are willing to let their newly released relative sleep on the couch, floor, or extra bed indefinitely. Most, however, desperately need to find a place to live—if not immediately, at least soon. After several days, weeks, or months of sleeping in your aunt's basement or on a friend's couch, a time comes when you are expected to fend for yourself. Figuring out how, exactly, to do that is no easy task, however, when your felony record operates to bar you from any public housing assistance. As one young man with a felony conviction explained in exasperation, "I asked for an application for Section 8. They asked me if I had a felony. I said, 'yes.' . . . They said, 'Well, then, this application isn't for you.'"[8]

This young man had just hit his first brick wall coming out of prison. Housing discrimination against people branded felons (as well as *suspected* "criminals") is perfectly legal. During Jim Crow, it was legal to deny housing on the basis of race, through restrictive covenants and other exclusionary practices. Today, discrimination against felons, criminal suspects, and their families is routine among public and private landlords alike. Rather than racially restrictive covenants, we have restrictive lease agreements, barring the new "undesirables."

The Anti-Drug Abuse Act of 1988, passed by Congress as part of the War on Drugs, called for strict lease enforcement and eviction of public housing tenants who engage in criminal activity. The act granted public housing agencies the authority to use leases to evict any tenant, household member, or guest engaged in any criminal activity on or near public housing premises. In 1996, President Clinton, in an effort to bolster his "tough on crime" credentials, declared that public housing agencies should exercise no discretion when a tenant or guest engages in criminal activity, particularly if it is drug-related. In his 1996 State of the Union address, he proposed "One Strike and You're Out" legislation, which strengthened eviction rules and strongly urged that drug offenders be automatically excluded from public housing based on their criminal records. He later declared, "If you break the law, you no longer have a home in public housing, one strike and you're out. That should be the law everywhere in America."[9] In its final form, the act, together with the Quality Housing and Work Responsibility Act of 1998, not only authorized public housing agencies to exclude automatically (and evict) drug offenders and other felons; it also allowed agencies to bar applicants *believed* to be using illegal drugs or abusing alcohol—whether or not they had been convicted of a crime. These decisions can be appealed, but appeals are rarely successful without an attorney—a luxury most public housing applicants cannot afford.

In response to the new legislation and prodding by President Clinton, the Housing and Urban Development Department (HUD) developed guidelines to press public housing agencies to "evict drug dealers and other criminals" and "screen tenants for criminal records."[10] HUD's "One Strike Guide" calls on housing agencies to "take full advantage of their authority to use stringent screening and eviction procedures." It also encourages housing authorities not only to screen all applicants' criminal records, but to develop their own exclusion criteria. The guide notes that agency ratings and funding are tied to whether they are "adopting and implementing effective applicant screening," a clear signal that agencies may be penalized for not cleaning house.[11]

Throughout the United States, public housing agencies have adopted exclusionary policies that deny eligibility to applicants even with the most minor criminal backgrounds. The crackdown inspired by the War on Drugs has resulted in unprecedented punitiveness, as housing officials began exercising their discretion to deny poor people access to public housing for virtually any crime. "Just about any offense will do, even if it bears scant relation to the likelihood the applicant will be a good tenant."[12]

The consequences for real families can be devastating. Without housing, people can lose their children. Take for example, the forty-two-year-old African American man who applied for public housing for himself and his three children who were living with him at the time.[13] He was denied because of an earlier drug possession charge for which he had pleaded guilty and served thirty days in jail. Of course, the odds that he would have been convicted of drug possession would have been extremely low if he were white. But as an African American, he was not only targeted by the drug war but then denied access to housing because of his conviction. Since being denied housing, he has lost custody of his children and is homeless. Many nights he sleeps outside on the streets. Stiff punishment, indeed, for a minor drug offense—especially for his children, who are innocent of any crime.

Remarkably, under current law, an actual conviction or finding of a formal violation is not necessary to trigger exclusion. Public housing officials are free to reject applicants simply on the basis of arrests, regardless of whether they result in convictions or fines. Because African Americans and Latinos are targeted by police in the War on Drugs, it is far more likely that they will be arrested for minor, nonviolent crimes. Accordingly, HUD policies excluding people from housing assistance based on arrests as well as convictions guarantee highly discriminatory results.

Perhaps no aspect of the HUD regulatory regime has been as controversial, however, as the "no-fault" clause contained in every public housing lease. Public housing tenants are required to do far more than simply pay their rent on time, keep the noise down, and make sure their homes are kept in good condition. The "One Strike and You're Out" policy requires every public housing lease to stipulate that if the tenant, or any member of the tenant's household, or any guest of the tenant, engages in any drug-related or other criminal activity on or off the premises, the tenancy will be terminated. Prior to the adoption of this policy, it was generally understood that a tenant could not be evicted unless he or she had some knowledge of or participation in alleged criminal activity. Accordingly, in *Rucker v. Davis*, the Ninth Circuit Court of Appeals struck down the "no-fault" clause, on the grounds that the eviction of innocent tenants—who were not accused or even aware of the alleged criminal activity—was inconsistent with the legislative scheme.[14]

The U.S. Supreme Court reversed.[15] The Court ruled in 2002 that, under federal law, public housing tenants can be evicted regardless of whether they had knowledge of or participated in alleged criminal activity. According to the Court, William Lee and Barbara Hill were rightfully evicted after their grandsons were charged with smoking marijuana in a parking lot near their apartments. Herman Walker was properly evicted as well, after police found cocaine on his caregiver. And Perlie Rucker was rightly evicted following the arrest of her daughter for possession of cocaine a few blocks from home. The Court ruled these tenants could be held civilly liable for the nonviolent behavior of their children and caregivers. They could be tossed out of public housing due to no fault of their own.

In the abstract, policies barring or evicting people who are somehow associated with criminal activity may seem like a reasonable approach to dealing with crime in public housing, particularly when crime has gotten out of control. Desperate times call for desperate measures, it is often said. The problem, however, is twofold: These vulnerable families have nowhere to go, and the impact is inevitably discriminatory. People who are not poor and who are not dependent upon public assistance for housing need not fear that, if their son, daughter, caregiver, or relative is caught with some marijuana at school or shoplifts from a drugstore, they will find themselves suddenly evicted—homeless. But for countless poor people—particularly racial minorities who disproportionately rely on public assistance—that possibility looms large. As a result, many families are reluctant to allow their relatives—particularly those who are recently released from prison—to stay with them, even temporarily.

No one knows exactly how many people are excluded from public housing because of criminal records, or even the number of people with criminal records who would be ineligible if they applied. There is no national data available. We do know, however, that roughly 65 million people have criminal records, including tens of millions of Americans who have been arrested but never convicted of any offense, or convicted only of minor misdemeanors, and they too are routinely excluded from public housing. What happens to these people denied housing assistance or evicted from their homes? Where do they go? Thousands of them become homeless. A study conducted by the McCormick Institute of Public Affairs found that nearly a quarter of guests in homeless shelters had been incarcerated within the previous year—people who were unable to find somewhere to live after release from prison walls.

Similarly, a California study reported that an estimated 30 to 50 percent of individuals under parole supervision in San Francisco and Los Angeles were homeless.[16] Access to decent, stable, and affordable housing is a basic human right, and it also increases substantially the likelihood a person with a past criminal record will obtain and retain employment and remain drug- and crime-free. Research conducted by the Corporation for Supportive Housing in New York State shows that the use of state prisons and city jails dropped by 74 percent and 40 percent respectively when people with past criminal records were provided with supportive housing.[17]

Prisoners returning "home" are typically the poorest of the poor, lacking the ability to pay for private housing and routinely denied public housing assistance—the type of assistance which could provide some much-needed stability in their lives. For them, "going home" is more a figure of speech than a realistic option. More than 650,000 people are released from prison each year, and for many, finding a new home appears next to impossible, not just in the short term, but for the rest of their lives. As a forty-one-year-old African American mother remarked after being denied housing because of a single arrest four years prior to her application, "I'm trying to do the right thing; I deserve a chance. Even if I was the worst criminal, I deserve a chance. Everybody deserves a chance."[18]

Boxed In

Aside from figuring out where to sleep, nothing is more worrisome for people leaving prison than figuring out where to work. In fact, a study by the Vera Institute found that during the first month after release from prison, people consistently were more preoccupied with finding work than anything else.[19] Some of the pressure to find work comes directly from the criminal justice system. According to one survey of state parole agencies, forty of the fifty-one jurisdictions surveyed (the fifty states and the District of Columbia) re-quired parolees to "maintain gainful employment."[20] Failure to do so could mean more prison time.

Even beyond the need to comply with the conditions of parole, employ-ment satisfies a more basic human need—the fundamental need to be self sufficient, to contribute, to support one's family, and to add value to society at large. Finding a job allows a person to establish a positive role in the community, develop a healthy self-image, and keep a distance from negative influences and opportunities for illegal behavior. Work is deemed so fundamental to human existence in many countries around the world that it is regarded as a basic human right. Deprivation of work, particularly among men, is strongly associated with depression and violence.

Landing a job after release from prison is no small feat. "I've watched the discrimination and experienced it firsthand when you have to check the box," says Susan Burton, a formerly incarcerated woman who has dedicated her life to providing women released from prison the support necessary to reestablish themselves in the workforce. The "box" she refers to is the question on job applications in which applicants are asked to check "yes" or "no" if they have ever been convicted of a crime. "It's not only [on] job [applications]," Burton explains. "It's on housing. It's on a school application. It's on welfare applications. It's everywhere you turn."[21]

Nearly every state allows private employers to discriminate on the basis of past criminal convictions. In fact, employers in most states can deny jobs to people who were arrested but never convicted of any crime. Only ten states prohibit all employers and licensing agencies from considering arrests, and three states prohibit some employers and occupational and licensing agencies from doing so.[22] Employers in a growing number of professions are barred by state licensing agencies from hiring people with a wide range of criminal convictions, even convictions unrelated to the job or license sought.[23]

The result of these discriminatory laws is that virtually every job application, whether for dog catcher, bus driver, Burger King cashier, or accountant, asks ex-offenders to "check the box." Most ex-offenders have difficulty even getting an interview after they have checked the box, because most employers are unwilling to consider hiring a self-identified criminal. One survey showed that although 90 percent of employers say they are willing to consider filling their most recent job vacancy with a welfare recipient, only 40 percent are willing to consider doing so with an ex-offender.[24] Similarly, a 2002 survey of 122 California employers revealed that although most employers would consider hiring someone convicted of a misdemeanor offense, the numbers dropped dramatically for those convicted of felonies. Less than a quarter of employers were willing to consider hiring someone convicted of a drug-related felony; the number plummeted to 7 percent for a property-related felony, and less than 1 percent for a violent felony.[25] Even those who hope to be self-employed—for example, as a barber, manicurist, gardener, or counselor—may discover that they are denied professional licenses on the grounds of past arrests or convictions, even if their offenses have nothing at all to do with their ability to perform well in their chosen profession.

For most people coming out of prison, a criminal conviction adds to their already problematic profile. About 70 percent of offenders and ex-offenders are high school dropouts, and according to at least one study, about half are functionally illiterate.[26] Many offenders are tracked for prison at early ages, labeled as criminals in their teen years, and then shuttled from their decrepit, underfunded inner city schools to brand-new, high-tech prisons. The communities and schools from which they came failed to prepare them for the workforce, and once they have been labeled criminals, their job prospects are forever bleak.

Adding to their troubles is the "spatial mismatch" between their residence and employment opportunities.[27] Willingness to hire ex-offenders is greatest in construction or manufacturing—industries that require little customer contact—and weakest in retail trade and other service sector businesses.[28] Manufacturing jobs, however, have all but disappeared from the urban core during the past thirty years. Not long ago, young, unskilled men could find decent, well-paying jobs at large factories in most major Northern cities. Today, due to globalization and deindustrialization, that is no longer the case. Jobs can be found in the suburbs—mostly service sector jobs—but employment for unskilled men with criminal convictions, while difficult to find anywhere, is especially hard to find close to home.

An ex-offender whose driver's license has been suspended or who does not have access to a car, often faces nearly insurmountable barriers to finding employment. Driving to the suburbs to pick up and drop off applications, attend interviews, and pursue employment leads may be perfectly feasible if you have a driver's license and access to a vehicle, but attempting to do so by bus is another matter entirely. An unemployed black male from Chicago's South Side explains: "Most of the time . . . the places be too far and you need transportation and I don't have none right now. If I had some I'd probably be able to get one [a job]. If I had a car and went way into the suburbs, 'cause there ain't none in the city."[29] Those who actually land jobs in the suburbs find it difficult to keep them without reliable, affordable transportation.

Murray McNair, a twenty-two-year-old African American, returned to Newark, New Jersey, after being locked up for drug offenses. He shares a small apartment with his pregnant girlfriend, his sister, and her two children.

Through a federally funded job training program operated by Goodwill Industries, McNair found a $9-an-hour job at a warehouse twenty miles—two buses and a taxi ride—away. "I know it's going to be tough," he told a *New York Times* reporter. "But I can't be thinking about myself anymore."[30]

The odds of McNair, or any ex-offender in a similar situation, succeeding under these circumstances are small. If you make $9 per hour, but spend $20 dollars or more getting to and from work every day, how do you manage to pay rent, buy food, and help to support yourself and a growing family? An unemployed thirty-six-year-old black man quit his suburban job because of the transportation problem. "I was spending more money getting to work than I earned working."[31]

The Black Box

Black ex-offenders are the most severely disadvantaged applicants in the modern job market. While all job applicants—regardless of race—are harmed by a criminal record, the harm is not equally felt. Not only are African Americans far more likely to be labeled criminals, they are also more strongly affected by the stigma of a criminal record. Black men convicted of felonies are the least likely to receive job offers of any demographic group, and suburban employers are the most unwilling to hire them.[32]

Sociologist Devah Pager explains that those sent to prison "are institutionally branded as a particular class of individuals" with major implications for their place and status in society.[33] The "negative credential" associated with a criminal record represents a unique mechanism of state-sponsored stratification. As Pager puts it, "it is the state that certifies particular individuals in ways that qualify them for discrimination or social exclusion." The "official status" of this negative credential differentiates it from other sources of social stigma, offering legitimacy to its use as a basis for discrimination. Four decades ago, employers were free to discriminate explicitly on the basis of race; today employers feel free to discriminate against those who bear the prison label—i.e., those labeled criminals by the state. The result is a system of stratification based on the "official certification of individual character and competence"—a form of branding by the government.[34]

Given the incredibly high level of discrimination suffered by black men in the job market and the structural barriers to employment in the new economy, it should come as no surprise that a huge percentage of African American men are unemployed. Nearly one-third of young black men in the United States today are out of work.[35] The jobless rate for young black male drop-outs, including those incarcerated, is a staggering 65 percent.[36]

In an effort to address the rampant joblessness among black men labeled criminals, a growing number of advocates in recent years have launched Ban the Box campaigns. These campaigns have been successful in cities like San Francisco, where All of Us or None, a nonprofit grassroots organization dedicated to eliminating discrimination against ex-offenders, persuaded the San Francisco Board of Supervisors to approve a resolution designed to eliminate hiring discrimination against people with criminal records. San Francisco's new policy (which took effect in June 2006) seeks to prevent discrimination on the basis of a criminal record by removing the criminal-history box from the initial application. An individual's past convictions will still be considered, but not until later in the hiring process, when the applicant has been identified as a serious candidate for the position. The only exception is for those jobs for which state or local laws expressly bar people with certain specific convictions from employment. These applicants will still be required to submit conviction-history information at the beginning of the hiring process. However, unlike a similar ordinance adopted in Boston, San Francisco's policy applies only to public employment, not to private vendors that do business with the city or county of San Francisco.

While these grassroots initiatives and policy proposals are major achievements, they raise questions about how best to address the complex and interlocking forms of discrimination experienced by black ex-offenders. Some scholars believe, based on the available data, that black males may suffer more discrimination—not less—when specific criminal history information is not available.[37] Because the association of race and criminality is so pervasive, employers may use less accurate and discriminatory methods to screen out those perceived to be likely criminals. Popular but misguided proxies for criminality—such as race, receipt of public assistance, low educational attainment, and gaps in work history—could be used by employers when no box is available on the application form to identify criminals. This concern is supported by ethnographic work suggesting that employers have fears of violence by black men relative to other groups of applicants and act on those fears when making hiring decisions. Without disconfirming information in the job application itself, employers may (consciously or unconsciously) treat all black men as though they have a criminal record, effectively putting all (or most) of them in the same position as black ex-offenders. This research suggests that banning the box is not enough. We must also get rid of the mind-set that puts black men "in the box." This is no small challenge.

A recent study by the National Employment Law Project (NELP) suggests that many employers refuse to consider people with criminal records for a wide range of jobs, despite the fact that the Equal Employment Opportunity Commission (EEOC) has advised employers that flat bans may be illegal. In 1987, the EEOC issued guidelines advising employers that discrimination against people with criminal histories is permissible if—and only if—employers consider the nature and gravity of the offense or offenses, the time that has passed since the conviction and/or completion of the sentence, and the nature of the job held or sought. According to the agency, an absolute bar to employment based on prior convictions—without consideration of these factors—violates Title VII of the Civil Rights Act if such a bar has a racially disparate impact.

EEOC guidelines do not have the force of law, but judges frequently turn to them when evaluating whether unlawful discrimination has occurred, and the EEOC has the power to sue employers that run afoul of Title VII. Apparently few employers are deterred. NELP's study of Craigslist.com, which operates in more than four hundred geographic areas, found that employers blatantly violate EEOC guidelines. Hundreds of ads precluded consideration of individuals with criminal conviction histories.[38] For example:

"No arrests or convictions of any kind for the past seven years. No Felony arrests or convictions of any kind for life." —Job ad for electrician contractor, September 29, 2010, OMNI Energy Services Corp

"We are looking for people with . . . spotless background/criminal history." —Job ad for warehouse worker or delivery drivers, September 2, 2010, CORT Furniture Rental

"ALL CANDIDATES WILL BE E-VERIFIED AND MUST CLEAR A BACKGROUND CHECK (NO PRIORS)." —Job ad for manufacturing jobs, October 5, 2010, Carlisle Staffing (staffing firm operating in Chicago area)

"IN ORDER TO QUALIFY AS A DRIVER FOR FEDEX, YOU MUST HAVE THE FOLLOWING: . . . Clean criminal record, no misdemeanors, no felonies." —Job ad for diesel mechanic/delivery driver, September 24, 2010, contractor for FedEx Ground

"DO NOT APPLY WITH ANY MISDEMEANORS / FELONIES" —Job ad for sewer-selling technician, February 10, 2010, Luskin-Clark Service Company

"Minimum requirements for Employment Consideration, No Exceptions!: No Misdemeanors and/or Felonies of any type ever in background." —Job ad for warehouse and manufacturing jobs, February 18, 2010, Perimeter Staffing (staffing firm operating in Atlanta)

Although each of these statements violates the EEOC prohibition against blanket hiring bans, employers and their recruitment/staffing agencies routinely limit the pool of qualified candidates to those with spotless records, thus excluding millions of people from having the opportunity even to interview for jobs. Millions find themselves locked out of the legal economy, and no one with a record has a more difficult time getting hired than black men.

Debtor's Prison

The lucky few who land a decent job—one that pays a living wage and is in reasonable proximity to their residence—often discover that the system is structured in such a way that they still cannot survive in the mainstream, legal economy. Upon release from prison, people are typically saddled with large debts—financial shackles that hobble them as they struggle to build a new life. In this system of control, like the one that prevailed during Jim Crow, one's "debt to society" often reflects the cost of imprisonment.

Throughout the United States, newly released prisoners are required to make payments to a host of agencies, including probation departments, courts, and child-support enforcement offices. In some jurisdictions, ex-offenders are billed for drug testing and even for the drug treatment they are supposed to receive as a condition of parole. These fees, costs, and fines are generally quite new—created by law within the past twenty years—and are associated with a wide range of offenses. Every state has its own rules and regulations governing their imposition. Florida, for example, has added more than twenty new categories of financial obligations for criminal defendants since 1996, while eliminating most exemptions for those who cannot pay.[39]

Examples of preconviction service fees imposed throughout the United States today include jail book-in fees levied at the time of arrest, jail per diems assessed to cover the cost of pretrial detention, public defender application fees charged when someone applies for court-appointed counsel, and the bail investigation fee imposed when the court determines the likelihood of the accused appearing at trial. Postconviction fees include presentence report fees, public defender recoupment fees, and fees levied on convicted persons placed in a residential or work-release program. Upon release, even more fees may attach, including parole or probation service fees. Such fees are typically charged on a monthly basis during the period of supervision.[40] In Ohio, for example, a court can order probationers to pay a $50 monthly supervision fee as a condition of probation. Failure to pay may warrant additional community control sanctions or a modification in the offender's sentence.[41]

Many states utilize "poverty penalties"—piling on additional late fees, payment plan fees, and interest when individuals are unable to pay all their debts at once, often enriching private debt collectors in the process. Some of the collection fees are exorbitant. Alabama charges a 30 percent collection fee, and Florida allows private debt collectors to tack on a 40 percent surcharge to the underlying debt.[42]

Two-thirds of people detained in jails report annual incomes under $12,000 prior to arrest. Predictably, most ex-offenders find themselves unable to pay the many fees, costs, and fines associated with their imprisonment, as well as their child-support debts (which continue to accumulate while a person is incarcerated). As a result, many ex-offenders have their paychecks garnished. Federal law provides that a child-support enforcement officer can garnish up to 65 percent of an individual's wages for child support. On top of that, probation officers in most states can require that an individual dedicate 35 percent of his or her income toward the payment of fines, fees, surcharges, and restitution charged by numerous agencies.[43] Accordingly, a former inmate living at or below the poverty level can be charged by four or five departments at once and can be required to surrender 100 percent of his or her earnings. As a *New York Times* editorial soberly observed, "People caught in this impossible predicament are less likely to seek regular employment, making them even more susceptible to criminal relapse."[44]

Whether or not ex-offenders make the rational choice to participate in the illegal economy (rather than have up to 100 percent of their wages garnisheed), they may still go back to prison for failure to meet the financial portion of their probation supervision requirements. Although "debtor's prison" is illegal in all states, many states use the threat of probation or parole revocation as a debt-collection tool. In fact, in some jurisdictions, individuals may "choose" to go to jail as a way to reduce their debt burdens, a practice that has been challenged as unconstitutional.[45] Adding to the insanity, many states suspend driving privileges for missed debt payments, a practice that often causes people to lose employment (if they had it) and creates yet another opportunity for jail time: driving with a suspended license.[46] In this regime, many people are thrown back in prison simply because they have been unable—with no place to live, and no decent job—to pay back thousands of dollars of prison-related fees, fines, and child support.

Some offenders, like Ora Lee Hurley, find themselves trapped by fees and fines in prison. Hurley was a prisoner held at the Gateway Diversion Center in Atlanta in 2006. She was imprisoned because she owed a $705 fine. As part of the diversion program, Hurley was permitted to work during the day and return to the center at night. "Five days a week she work[ed] fulltime at a restaurant earning $6.50 an hour and, after taxes, net about $700 a month."[47] Room and board at the diversion center was about $600, and her monthly transportation cost $52. Miscellaneous other expenses, including clothes, shoes, and personal items such as toothpaste, quickly exhausted what was left. Hurley's attorney decried the trap she was in: "This is a situation where if this woman was able to write a check for the amount of the fine, she would be out of there. And because she can't, she's still in custody. It's as simple as that."[48] Although she worked a full-time job while in custody, most of her income went to repay the diversion program, not the underlying fine that put her in custody in the first place.

This harsh reality harks back to the days after the Civil War, when former slaves and their descendents were arrested for minor violations, slapped with heavy fines, and then imprisoned until they could pay their debts. The only means to pay off their debts was through labor on plantations and farms—known as convict leasing—or in prisons that had been converted to work farms. Paid next to nothing, convicts were effectively enslaved in perpetuity, as they were unable to earn enough to pay off their debts.

Today, many inmates work in prison, typically earning far less than the minimum wage—often less than $3 per hour, sometimes as little as 25 cents. Their accounts are then "charged" for various expenses related to their incarceration, making it impossible for them to save the money that otherwise would allow them to pay off their debts or help them make a successful transition when released from prison. Prisoners are typically released with only the clothes on their backs and a pittance in gate money. Sometimes the money is barely enough to cover the cost of a bus ticket back home.

Let Them Eat Cake

So here you are—a newly released prisoner—homeless, unemployed, and carrying a mountain of debt. How do you feed yourself? Care for your children? There is no clear answer to that question, but one thing is for sure: do not count on the government for any help. Not only will you be denied housing, but you may well be denied food.

Welfare reform legislation signed by President Bill Clinton in 1996 ended individual entitlements to welfare and provided states with block grants. The Temporary Assistance for Needy Family Program (TANF) imposes a five-year lifetime limit on benefits and requires welfare recipients, including those who have young children and lack child care, to work in order to receive benefits. In the abstract, a five-year limit may sound reasonable. But consider this: When one is labeled a criminal, forced to "check the box" on applications for employment and housing, and burdened by thousands of dollars in debt, is it possible that one will live on the brink of severe poverty for more than five years and thus require food stamps for oneself and one's family? Until 1996, there was a basic understanding that poverty-stricken mothers raising children should be afforded some minimal level of assistance with food and shelter.

The five-year limit on benefits, however, is not the law's worst feature. The law also requires that states *permanently* bar individuals with drug-related felony convictions from receiving federally funded public assistance. The statute does contain an opt-out provision, but as of 2010 only thirteen states and the District of Columbia had opted out entirely. Most states have partially opted out, affording exceptions for people in drug treatment, for example.[49] It remains the case, however, that thousands of people with felony drug convictions in the United States are deemed ineligible for food stamps for the rest of their lives, including pregnant women, people in drug treatment or recovery, and people suffering from HIV/AIDS—simply because they were once caught with drugs.

The Silent Minority

If shackling former prisoners with a lifetime of debt and authorizing discrimination against them in employment, housing, education, and public benefits is not enough to send the message that they are not wanted and not even considered full citizens, then stripping voting rights from those labeled criminals surely gets the point across.

Forty-eight states and the District of Columbia prohibit inmates from voting while incarcerated for a felony offense. Only two states—Maine and Vermont—permit inmates to vote. The vast majority of states continue to withhold the right to vote when prisoners are released on parole. Even after the term of punishment expires, some states deny the right to vote for a period ranging from a number of years to the rest of one's life.[50]

This is far from the norm in other countries—like Germany, for instance, which allows (and even encourages) prisoners to vote. In fact, about half of European countries allow all incarcerated people to vote, while others disqualify only a small number of prisoners from the polls.[51] Prisoners vote either in their correctional facilities or by some version of absentee ballot in their town of previous residence. Almost all of the countries that place some restrictions on voting in prison are in Eastern Europe, part of the former Communist bloc.[52]

No other country in the world disenfranchises people who are released from prison in a manner even remotely resembling the United States. In fact, the United Nations Human Rights Committee has charged that U.S. disenfranchisement policies are discriminatory and violate international law. In those few European countries that permit limited postprison disqualification, the sanction is very narrowly tailored and the number of people disenfranchised is probably in the dozens or hundreds.[53] In the United States, by contrast, voting disqualification upon release from prison is automatic, with no legitimate purpose, and affects millions.

Even those former prisoners who are technically eligible to vote frequently remain disenfranchised for life. Every state has developed its own process for restoring voting rights to ex-offenders. Typically the restoration process is a bureaucratic maze that requires the payment of fines or court costs. The process is so cumbersome, confusing, and onerous that many ex-offenders who are theoretically eligible to vote never manage to get their voting rights back.[54] Throughout much of the United States, ex-offenders are expected to pay fines and court costs, and submit paperwork to multiple agencies in an effort to win back a right that should never have been taken away in a democracy. These bureaucratic minefields are the modern-day equivalent of poll taxes and literacy tests—"colorblind" rules designed to make voting a practical impossibility for a group defined largely by race.

The message communicated by felon disenfranchisement laws, policies, and bureaucratic procedures is not lost on those, such as Clinton Drake, who are effectively barred from voting for life.[55] Drake, a fifty-five-year-old African American man in Montgomery, Alabama, was arrested in 1988 for possession of marijuana. Five years later, he was arrested again, this time for having about $10 worth of the drug on him. Facing between ten and twenty years in prison as a repeat offender, Drake, a Vietnam veteran and, at the time, a cook on a local air force base, took his public defender's advice and accepted a plea bargain. Under the plea agreement, he would "only" have to spend five years behind bars. Five years for five joints.

Once released, Drake found he was forbidden by law from voting until he paid his $900 in court costs—an impossible task, given that he was unemployed and the low-wage jobs he might conceivably find would never allow him to accumulate hundreds of dollars in savings. For all practical purposes, he would never be able to vote again. Shortly before the 2004 presidential election, he said in despair:

I put my life on the line for this country. To me, not voting is not right; it led to a lot of frustration, a lot of anger. My son's in Iraq. In the army just like I was. My oldest son, he fought in the first Persian Gulf conflict. He was in the Marines. This is my baby son over there right now. But I'm not able to vote. They say I owe $900 in fines. To me, that's a poll tax. You've got to pay to vote. It's "restitution," they say. I came off parole on October 13, 1999, but I'm still not allowed to vote. Last time I voted was in '88. Bush versus Dukakis. Bush won. I voted for Dukakis. If it was up to me, I'd vote his son out this time too. I know a lot of friends got the same cases like I got, not able to vote. A lot of guys doing the same things like I was doing. Just marijuana. They treat marijuana in Alabama like you committed treason or something. I was on the 1965 voting rights march from Selma. I was fifteen years old. At eighteen, I was in Vietnam fighting for my country. And now? Unemployed and they won't allow me to vote.[56]

Drake's vote, along with the votes of millions of other people labeled felons, might have made a real difference in 2004. There is no doubt their votes would have changed things in 2000. Following the election, it was widely reported that, had the 600,000 former felons who had completed their sentence in Florida been allowed to vote, Al Gore would have been elected president of the United States rather than George W. Bush.[57]

Four years later, voter registration workers in the South encountered scores of ex-offenders who were reluctant to register to vote, even if they were technically eligible, because they were scared to have any contact with governmental authorities. Many on welfare were worried that any little thing they did to bring attention to themselves might put their food stamps at risk. Others had been told by parole and probation officers that they could not vote, and although it was not true, they believed it, and the news spread like wildfire. "How long you think it take if someone tells you you can't vote before it spreads?" asked one ex-offender. "It's been years and years people telling you you can't vote. You live in a slum, you're not counted."[58]

Even those who knew they were eligible to register worried that registering to vote would somehow attract attention to them—perhaps land them back in jail. While this might strike some as paranoia, many Southern blacks have vivid memories of the harsh consequences that befell their parents and grandparents who attempted to vote in defiance of poll taxes, literacy tests, and other devices adopted to suppress the black vote. Many were terrorized by the Klan. Today, ex-offenders live in constant fear of a different form of racial repression—racial profiling, police brutality, and revocation of parole. One investigative journalist described the situation this way: "Overwhelmingly, black people [in Mississippi] are scared of any form of contact with

authorities they saw as looking for excuses to reincarcerate them. In neighborhood after neighborhood, the grandchildren of the civil rights pioneers
from the 1950s were as scared to vote, because of prisons and the threat of
prisons, as their grandparents were half a century ago because of the threat
of the lynch mob."[59] Nshombi Lambright, of the Jackson ACLU, concurs.
"People aren't even trying to get their vote back," she said. "It's hard just getting them to attempt to register. They're terrorized. They're so scared of going back to jail that they won't even try it."[60]

Research indicates that a large number of close elections would have
come out differently if felons had been allowed to vote, including at least
seven senatorial races between 1980 and 2000.[61] The impact on those major
elections undoubtedly would be greater if all those deterred or prevented
from voting were taken into account. But as ex-offenders will hasten to em-
phasize, it is not just the "big" elections that matter. One ex-offender put it
this way: "I have no right to vote on the school referendums that . . . will affect my children. I have no right to vote on how my taxes is going to be spent
or used, which I have to pay whether I'm a felon or not, you know? So basically I've lost all voice or control over my government. . . . I get mad because
I can't say anything because I don't have a voice."[62]

Those who do have their voting rights restored often describe a feeling of
validation, even pride. "I got a voice now," said Willa Womack, a forty-four-
year-old African American woman who had been incarcerated on drug
charges. "I can decide now who will be my governor, who will be my president. I have a vote now. I feel like somebody. It's a feeling of relief from
where I came from—that I'm actually somebody."[63]

The Pariahs

For Americans who are *not* caught up in this system of control, it can be difficult to imagine what life would be like if discrimination against you were
perfectly legal—if you were not allowed to participate in the political system
and if you were not even eligible for food stamps or welfare and could be denied housing assistance. Yet as bad as these forms of discrimination are,
many ex-offenders will tell you that the formal mechanisms of exclusion are
not the worst of it. The shame and stigma that follows you for the rest of
your life—that is the worst. It is not just the job denial but the look that

flashes across the face of a potential employer when he notices that "the box" has been checked—the way he suddenly refuses to look you in the eye. It is not merely the denial of the housing application but the shame of being a grown man who has to beg his grandmother for a place to sleep at night. It is not simply the denial of the right to vote but the shame one feels when a co-worker innocently asks, "Who you gonna vote for on Tuesday?"

One need not be formally convicted in a court of law to be subject to this shame and stigma. As long as you "look like" or "seem like" a criminal, you are treated with the same suspicion and contempt, not just by police, security guards, or hall monitors at your school, but also by the woman who crosses the street to avoid you and by the store employees who follow you through the aisles, eager to catch you in the act of being the "criminalblackman"— the archetypal figure who justifies the New Jim Crow.[64]

Practically from cradle to grave, black males in urban ghettos are treated like current or future criminals. One may learn to cope with the stigma of criminality, but like the stigma of race, the prison label is not something that a black man in the ghetto can ever fully escape. For those newly released from prison, the pain is particularly acute. As Dorsey Nunn, an ex-offender and cofounder of All of Us or None, once put it, "The biggest hurdle you gotta get over when you walk out those prison gates is shame—that shame, that stigma, that label, that thing you wear around your neck saying 'I'm a criminal.' It's like a yoke around your neck, and it'll drag you down, even kill you if you let it." Many ex-offenders experience an existential angst associated with their permanent social exclusion. Henry, a young African American convicted of a felony, explains, "[It's like] you broke the law, you bad. You broke the law, bang—you're not part of us anymore."[65] That sentiment is shared by a woman, currently incarcerated, who described the experience this way:

> When I leave here it will be very difficult for me in the sense that I'm a felon. That I will always be a felon . . . for me to leave here, it will affect my job, it will affect my education . . . custody [of my children], it can affect child support, it can affect everywhere—family, friends, housing. . . . People that are convicted of drug crimes can't even get housing anymore. . . . Yes, I did my prison time. How long are you going to punish me as a result of it? And not only on paper, I'm only on paper for ten months when I leave here, that's all the parole I have. But, that parole isn't going to be anything. It's the housing, it's the credit re-

establishing. . . . I mean even to go into the school, to work with my child's class—and I'm not a sex offender—but all I need is one parent who says, "Isn't she a felon? I don't want her with my child."[66]

The permanence of one's social exile is often the hardest to swallow. For many it seems inconceivable that, for a minor offense, you can be subjected to discrimination, scorn, and exclusion for the rest of your life. Human Rights Watch, in its report documenting the experiences of America's under-caste, tells the story of a fifty-seven-year-old African American woman, denied rental housing by a federally funded landlord due to a minor conviction she did not even know was on her record. After being refused reconsideration, she asked her caseworker in pained exasperation, "Am I going to be a criminal for the rest of my life?"[67]

When someone is convicted of a crime today, their "debt to society" is never paid. The "cruel hand" that Frederick Douglass spoke of more than 150 years ago has appeared once again. In this new system of control, like the last, many black men "hold up [their] heads, if at all, against the withering influence of a nation's scorn and contempt." Willie Johnson, a forty-three-year-old African American man recently released from prison in Ohio, explained it this way:

My felony conviction has been like a mental punishment, because of all the obstacles. . . . Every time I go to put in a [job] application—I have had three companies hire me and tell me to come to work the next day. But then the day before they will call and tell me don't come in—because you have a felony. And that is what is devastating because you think you are about to go to work and they call you and say because of your felony we can't hire [you]. I have run into this at least a dozen times. Two times I got very depressed and sad because I couldn't take care of myself as a man. It was like I wanted to give up—because in society nobody wants to give us a helping hand. Right now I am considered homeless. I have never been homeless until I left the penitentiary, and now I know what it feels to be homeless. If it was not for my family I would be in the streets sleeping in the cold. . . . We [black men] have three strikes against us: 1) because we are black, and 2) because we are a black male, and the final strike is a felony. These are the greatest three strikes that a black man has against him in this country. I have friends who don't have a felony—and have a hard time getting a job. But if a black man can't find a job to take care of himself—he is ashamed that he can't take care of his children.[68]

Not surprisingly, for many black men, the hurt and depression gives way to anger. A black minister in Waterloo, Mississippi, explained his outrage at the fate that has befallen African Americans in the post–civil rights era. "It's a hustle," he said angrily. "'Felony' is the new N-word. They don't have to call you a nigger anymore. They just say you're a felon. In every ghetto you see alarming numbers of young men with felony convictions. Once you have that felony stamp, your hope for employment, for any kind of integration into society, it begins to fade out. Today's lynching is a felony charge. Today's lynching is incarceration. Today's lynch mobs are professionals. They have a badge; they have a law degree. A felony is a modern way of saying, 'I'm going to hang you up and burn you.' Once you get that F, you're on fire."[69]

Remarkably, it is not uncommon today to hear media pundits, politicians, social critics, and celebrities—most notably Bill Cosby—complain that the biggest problem black men have today is that they "have no shame." Many worry that prison time has become a badge of honor in some communities—"a rite of passage" is the term most often used in the press. Others claim that inner-city residents no longer share the same value system as mainstream society, and therefore are not stigmatized by criminality. Yet as Donald Braman, author of *Doing Time on the Outside*, states, "One can only assume that most participants in these discussions have had little direct contact with the families and communities they are discussing."[70]

Over a four-year period, Braman conducted a major ethnographic study of families affected by mass incarceration in Washington, D.C., a city where three out of every four young black men can expect to spend some time behind bars.[71] He found that, contrary to popular belief, the young men labeled criminals and their families are profoundly hurt and stigmatized by their status: "They are not shameless; they feel the stigma that accompanies not only incarceration but all the other stereotypes that accompany it—fatherlessness, poverty, and often, despite every intent to make it otherwise, diminished love." The results of Braman's study have been largely corroborated by similar studies elsewhere in the United States.[72]

These studies indicate that the biggest problem the black community may face today is not "shamelessness" but rather the severe isolation, distrust, and alienation created by mass incarceration. During Jim Crow, blacks were severely stigmatized and segregated on the basis of race, but in their own communities they could find support, solidarity, acceptance—love. Today, when those labeled criminals return to their communities, they are often met with scorn and contempt, not just by employers, welfare workers, and housing officials, but also by their own neighbors, teachers, and even members of their own families. This is so, even when they have been imprisoned for minor offenses, such as possession and sale of a small amount of drugs. Young black males in their teens are often told "you'll amount to nothing" or "you'll find yourself back in jail, just like your father"—a not-so-subtle suggestion that a shameful defect lies deep within them, an inherited trait perhaps—part of their genetic makeup. "You are a criminal, nothing but a criminal. You are a no good criminal."[73]

The anger and frustration directed at young black men returning home from prison is understandable, given that they are returning to communities that are hurt by joblessness and crime. These communities desperately need their young men to be holding down jobs and supporting their families, rather than wasting away in prison cells. While there is widespread recognition that the War on Drugs is racist and that politicians have refused to invest in jobs or schools in their communities, parents of offenders and ex-offenders still feel intense shame—shame that their children have turned to crime despite the lack of obvious alternatives. One mother of an incarcerated teen, Constance, described her angst this way: "Regardless of what you feel like you've done for your kid, it still comes back on you, and you feel like, 'Well, maybe I did something wrong. Maybe I messed up. You know, maybe if I had a did it this way, then it wouldn't a happened that way.'" After her son's arrest, she could not bring herself to tell friends and relatives and kept the family's suffering private. Constance is not alone.

Eerie Silence

David Braman's ethnographic research shows that mass incarceration, far from reducing the stigma associated with criminality, actually creates a deep silence in communities of color, one rooted in shame. Imprisonment is considered so shameful that many people avoid talking about it, even within their own families. Some, like Constance, are silent because they blame themselves for their children's fate and believe that others blame them as well. Others are silent because they believe hiding the truth will protect friends and family members—e.g., "I don't know what [his incarceration] would do to his aunt. She just thinks so highly of him." Others claim that a loved one's criminality is a private, family matter: "Somebody's business is nobody's business."[74]

Remarkably, even in communities devastated by mass incarceration, many people struggling to cope with the stigma of imprisonment have no idea that their neighbors are struggling with the same grief, shame, and isolation. Braman reported that "when I asked participants [in the study] if they knew of other people in the neighborhood, many did know of one or two out of the dozens of households on the block that had members incarcerated but did not feel comfortable talking with others."[75] This type of phenomenon has been described in the psychological literature as *pluralistic ignorance*, in which people misjudge the norm. One example is found in studies of college freshman who overestimate the drinking among other freshman.[76] When it comes to families of prisoners, however, their underestimation of the extent of incarceration in their communities exacerbates their sense of isolation by making the imprisonment of their family members seem more abnormal than it is.

Even in church, a place where many people seek solace in times of grief and sorrow, families of prisoners often keep secret the imprisonment of their children or relatives. As one woman responded when asked if she could turn to church members for support, "Church? I wouldn't dare tell anyone at church."[77] Far from being a place of comfort or refuge, churches can be a place where judgment, shame, and contempt are felt most acutely. Services in black churches frequently contain a strong mixture of concern for the less fortunate and a call to personal responsibility. As Cathy Cohen has observed, ministers and members of black congregations have helped to develop what she calls the "indigenous constructed image of 'good, black Christian folk.'"[78] Black churches, in this cultural narrative, are places where the "good" black people in the community can be found. To the extent that the imprisonment of one's son or relative (or one's own imprisonment) is experienced as a personal failure—a failure of personal responsibility—church can be a source of fresh pain rather than comfort.

Those who have had positive experiences of acceptance and sympathy after disclosing the status of a loved one (or their own status) report they are better able to cope. Notably, however, even after such positive experiences, most family members remain committed to maintaining tight control over who knows and who does not know about the status of their loved one. According to Braman, not one of the family members in his study "had 'come out' completely to their extended families at church and at work."[79]

Passing (Redux)

Lying about incarcerated family members is another common coping strategy—a form of passing. Whereas light-skinned blacks during the Jim Crow era sometimes cut off relations with friends and family in an effort to "pass" as white and enjoy the upward mobility and privilege associated with whiteness, today many family members of prisoners lie and try to hide the status of their relatives in an effort to mitigate the stigma of criminality. This is especially the case at work—employment settings where family members interact with people they believe could not possibly understand what they are going through.

One woman, Ruth, whose younger brother is incarcerated, says she would never discuss her brother with her co-workers or supervisor, though they have long shared information about their personal lives. "You know, I talk to [my supervisor] about stuff, but not this. This was too much, and it definitely made, well it was just harder to talk to him. He wants to know how my brother is. I just can't tell it to him. What does he know about prison?"[80] When asked to explain why her white co-workers and supervisors would have trouble understanding her brother's incarceration, Ruth explained that it was not just incarceration but "everything"—everything related to race. As an example, she mentioned nights when she works late: "I tell my boss all the time, I say, 'If you want me to take a taxi you go down there and flag one for me. I'm not going out there and stand twenty minutes for a cab when they'll run over me to get to you.' . . . He's white and, see, he don't know the difference because he's from Seattle, Washington. He looks at me real strange, like, 'What are you talking about?'"[81]

Many ex-offenders and families of prisoners are desperately attempting to be perceived as part of the modern upwardly mobile class, even if their income does not place them in it. Ex-offenders lie (by refusing to check the box on employment applications), and family members lie through omission or obfuscation because they are painfully aware of the historically intransigent stereotypes of criminal, dysfunctional families that pervade not only public discussions of inner cities but of the black community in general. This awareness can lead beyond shame to a place of self-hate.

One mother of an incarcerated teenager described the self-hate she perceives in the black community this way:

> All your life you been taught that you're not a worthy person, or something is wrong with you. So you don't have no respect for yourself. See, people of color have—not all of them, but a lot of them—have poor self-esteem, because we've been branded. We hate ourselves, you know. We have been programmed that it's something that's wrong with us. We hate ourselves.[82]

This self-hate, she explained, does not affect just the young boys who find themselves getting in trouble and fulfilling the negative expectations of those in the community and beyond. Self-hate is also part of the reason people in her neighborhood do not speak to each other about the impact of incarceration on their families and their lives. In her nearly all-black neighborhood, she worries about what the neighbors would think about her if she revealed that her son had been labeled a criminal: "It's hard, because, like I say . . . we've been labeled all our lives that we are the bad people."[83]

The silence this stigma engenders among family members, neighbors, friends, relatives, co-workers, and strangers is perhaps the most painful—yet least acknowledged—aspect of the new system of control. The historical anthropologist Gerald Sider once wrote, "We can have no significant understanding of any culture unless we also know the silences that were institutionally created and guaranteed along with it."[84] Nowhere is that observation more relevant in American society today than in an analysis of the culture of mass incarceration.

Descriptions of the silence that hovers over mass incarceration are rare because people—whether they are social scientists, judges, politicians, or reporters—are usually more interested in speech, acts, and events than in the negative field of silence and estrangement that lurks beneath the surface. But, as Braman rightly notes, those who live in the shadows of this silence are devalued as human beings:

> There is a repression of self experienced by these families in their silence. The retreat of a mother or wife from friendships in church and at work, the words not spoken between friends, the enduring silence of children who guard what for them is profound and powerful information—all are telling indicators of the social effects of incarceration. As relationships between family and friends become strained or false, not only are people's understandings of one another diminished, but, because people are social, they themselves are diminished as well.[85]

The harm done by this social silence is more than interpersonal. The silence—driven by stigma and fear of shame—results in a repression of public thought, a collective denial of lived experience. As Braman puts it, "By forcing out of public view the struggles that these families face in the most simple and fundamental acts—living together and caring for one another—this broader social silence makes it seem as though [ghetto families] simply are 'that way': broken, valueless, irreparable."[86] It also makes community healing and collective political action next to impossible.

Gangsta Love

For some, the notion that black communities are severely stigmatized and shamed by criminality is counterintuitive: if incarceration in many urban areas is the statistical norm, why isn't it socially normative as well? It is true that imprisonment has become "normal" in ghetto communities. In major cities across the United States, the majority of young black men are under the control of the criminal justice system or saddled with criminal records. But just because the prison label has become normal does not mean that it is generally viewed as acceptable. Poor people of color, like other Americans—indeed like nearly everyone around the world—want safe streets, peaceful communities, healthy families, good jobs, and meaningful opportunities to contribute to society. The notion that ghetto families do not, in fact, want those things, and instead are perfectly content to live in crime-ridden communities, feeling no shame or regret about the fate of their young men is, quite simply, racist. It is impossible to imagine that we would believe such a thing about whites.

The predictable response is: What about gangsta rap and the culture of violence that has been embraced by so many black youth? Is there not some truth to the notion that black culture has devolved in recent years, as reflected in youth standing on the street corners with pants sagging below their rears and rappers boasting about beating their "hos" and going to jail? Is there not some reason to wonder whether the black community, to some extent, has lost its moral compass?

The easy answer is to say yes and wag a finger at those who are behaving badly. That is the road most traveled, and it has not made a bit of difference. The media fawn over Bill Cosby and other figures when they give stern lectures to black audiences about black men failing to be good fathers and failing to lead respectable lives. They act as though this is a message black audiences have not heard many times before from their ministers, from their family members, and from politicians who talk about the need for more "personal responsibility." Many seem genuinely surprised that blacks in the audience applaud these messages; for them, it is apparently news that black people think men should be good fathers and help to support their families.

The more difficult answer—the more courageous one—is to say yes, yes we should be concerned about the behavior of men trapped in ghetto communities, but the deep failure of morality is our own. Economist Glenn Loury once posed the question: "are we willing to cast ourselves as a society that creates crimogenic conditions for some of its members, and then acts-out rituals of punishment against them as if engaged in some awful form of human sacrifice?" A similar question can be posed with respect to shaming those trapped in ghettos: are we willing to demonize a population, declare a war against them, and then stand back and heap shame and contempt upon them for failing to behave like model citizens while under attack?

In this regard, it is helpful to step back and put the behavior of young black men who appear to embrace "gangsta culture" in the proper perspective. There is absolutely nothing abnormal or surprising about a severely stigmatized group embracing their stigma. Psychologists have long observed that when people feel hopelessly stigmatized, a powerful coping strategy—often the only apparent route to self-esteem—is embracing one's stigmatized identity. Hence, "black is beautiful" and "gay pride"—slogans and anthems of political movements aimed at ending not only legal discrimination, but the stigma that justified it. Indeed, the act of embracing one's stigma is never merely a psychological maneuver; it is a political act—an act of resistance and defiance in a society that seeks to demean a group based on an inalterable trait. As a gay activist once put it, "Only by fully embracing the stigma itself can one neutralize the sting and make it laughable."[87]

For those black youth who are constantly followed by the police and shamed by teachers, relatives, and strangers, embracing the stigma of criminality is an act of rebellion—an attempt to carve out a positive identity in a society that offers them little more than scorn, contempt, and constant surveillance. Ronny, a sixteen-year-old African American on probation for a drug-related offense, explains it this way:

> My grandma keeps asking me about when I'm gonna get arrested again. She thinks just 'cause I went in before, I will go in again. . . . At my school my teachers talk about calling the cop[s] again to take me away. . . . [The] cop keeps checking up on me. He's always at the park making sure I don't get into trouble again. . . . My P.O. [probation officer] is always knocking on my door talking shit to me. . . . Even at the BYA [the local youth development organization] the staff treat me like I'm a fuck up. . . . Shit don't change. It doesn't matter where I go, I'm seen as a criminal. I just say, if you are going to treat me as a criminal then I'm gonna treat you like I am one, you feel me? I'm gonna make you shake so that you can say that there is a reason for calling me a criminal. . . . I grew up knowing that I had to show these fools [adults who criminalize youth] that I wasn't going to take their shit. I started to act like a thug even if I wasn't one. . . . Part of it was me trying to be hard, the other part was them treating me like a criminal.[88]

The problem, of course, is that embracing criminality—while a natural response to the stigma—is inherently self-defeating and destructive. While "black is beautiful" is a powerful antidote to the logic of Jim Crow, and "gay pride" is a liberating motto for those challenging homophobia, the natural corollary for young men trapped in the ghetto in the era of mass incarceration is something akin to "gangsta love." While race and sexual orientation are perfectly appropriate aspects of one's identity to embrace, criminality for its own sake most certainly is not. The War on Drugs has greatly exacerbated the problems associated with drug abuse, rather than solved them, but the fact remains that the violence associated with the illegal drug trade is nothing to be celebrated. Black crime cripples the black community and does no favors to the individual offender.

So herein lies the paradox and predicament of young black men labeled criminals. A war has been declared on them, and they have been rounded up for engaging in precisely the same crimes that go largely ignored in middle- and upper-class white communities—possession and sale of illegal drugs. For those residing in ghetto communities, employment is scarce—often nonexistent. Schools located in ghetto communities more closely resemble prisons than places of learning, creativity, or moral development. And because the drug war has been raging for decades now, the parents of children coming of age today were targets of the drug war as well. As a result, many fathers are in prison, and those who are "free" bear the prison label. They are often unable to provide for, or meaningfully contribute to, a family. Any wonder, then, that many youth embrace their stigmatized identity as a means of survival in this new caste system? Should we be shocked when they turn to gangs or fellow inmates for support when no viable family support structure exists? After all, in many respects, they are simply doing what black people did during the Jim Crow era—they are turning to each other for support and solace in a society that despises them.

Yet when these young people do what all severely stigmatized groups do—try to cope by turning to each other and embracing their stigma in a desperate effort to regain some measure of self esteem—we, as a society, heap more shame and contempt upon them. We tell them their friends are "no good," that they will "amount to nothing," that they are "wasting their lives," and that "they're nothing but criminals." We condemn their baggy pants (a fashion trend that mimics prison-issue pants) and the music that glorifies a life many feel they cannot avoid. When we are done shaming them, we throw up our hands and then turn our backs as they are carted off to jail.

The Minstrel Show

None of the foregoing should be interpreted as an excuse for the violence, decadence, or misogyny that pervades what has come to be known as gangsta culture. The images and messages are extremely damaging. On an average night, one need engage in only a few minutes of channel surfing during prime-time hours to stumble across images of gangsta culture on television. The images are so familiar no description is necessary here. Often these images emanate from BET or black-themed reality shows and thus are considered "authentic" expressions of black attitudes, culture, and mores.

Again, though, it is useful to put the commodification of gangsta culture in proper perspective. The worst of gangsta rap and other forms of blaxploitation (such as VH1's *Flavor of Love*) is best understood as a modern-day minstrel show, only this time televised around the clock for a worldwide audience. It is a for-profit display of the worst racial stereotypes and images associated with the era of mass incarceration—an era in which black people are criminalized and portrayed as out-of-control, shameless, violent, oversexed, and generally undeserving.

Like the minstrel shows of the slavery and Jim Crow eras, today's displays are generally designed for white audiences. The majority of consumers of gangsta rap are white, suburban teenagers. VH1 had its best ratings ever for the first season of *Flavor of Love*—ratings driven by large white audiences. MTV has expanded its offerings of black-themed reality shows in the hopes of attracting the same crowd. The profits to be made from racial stigma are considerable, and the fact that blacks—as well as whites—treat racial oppression as a commodity for consumption is not surprising. It is a familiar form of black complicity with racialized systems of control.

Many people are unaware that, although minstrel shows were plainly designed to pander to white racism and to make whites feel comfortable with—indeed, entertained by—racial oppression, African Americans formed a large part of the black minstrels' audience. In fact, their numbers were so great in some areas that theater owners had to relax rules segregating black patrons and restricting them to certain areas of the theater.[89]

Historians have long debated why blacks would attend minstrel shows when the images and content were so blatantly racist. Minstrels projected a greatly romanticized and exaggerated image of black life on plantations with cheerful, simple, grinning slaves always ready to sing, dance, and please their masters. Some have suggested that perhaps blacks felt in on the joke, laughing at the over-the-top characters from a sense of "in-group recognition."[90] It has also been argued that perhaps they felt some connection to elements of African culture that had been suppressed and condemned for so long but were suddenly visible on stage, albeit in racist, exaggerated form.[91] Undeniably, though, one major draw for black audiences was simply seeing fellow African Americans on stage. Black minstrels were largely viewed as celebrities, earning more money and achieving more fame than African Americans ever had before.[92] Black minstrelsy was the first large-scale opportunity for African Americans to enter show business. To some degree, then, black minstrelsy—as degrading as it was—represented success.

It seems likely that historians will one day look back on the images of black men in gangsta rap videos with a similar curiosity. Why would these young men, who are targets of a brutal drug war declared against them, put on a show—a spectacle—that romanticizes and glorifies their criminalization? Why would these young men openly endorse and perpetuate the very stereotypes that are invoked to justify their second-class status, their exclusion from mainstream society? The answers, historians may find, are not that different from the answers to the minstrelsy puzzle.

It is important to keep in mind, though, that many hip-hop artists today do not embrace and perpetuate the worst racial stereotypes associated with mass incarceration. Artists like Common, for example, articulate a sharp critique of American politics and culture and reject the misogyny and violence preached by gangsta rappers. And while rap is often associated with "gangsta life" in the mainstream press, the origins of rap and hip-hop culture are not rooted in outlaw ideology. When rap was born, the early rap stars were not rapping about gangsta life, but "My Adidas" and good times in the 'hood in tunes like "Rapper's Delight." Rap music changed after the War on Drugs shifted into high gear and thousands of young, black men were suddenly swept off the streets and into prisons. Violence in urban communities flared in those communities, not simply because of the new drug—crack—but because of the massive crackdown, which radically reshaped the traditional life course for young black men. As a tidal wave of punitiveness, stigma, and despair washed over poor communities of color, those who were demonized—not only in the mainstream press but often in their own communities—did what all stigmatized groups do: they struggled to preserve a positive identity by embracing their stigma. Gangsta rap—while it may amount to little more than a minstrel show when it appears on MTV today—has its roots in the struggle for a positive identity among outcasts.

The Antidote

It is difficult to look at pictures of black people performing in minstrel shows during the Jim Crow era. It is almost beyond belief that at one time black people actually covered their faces with pitch-black paint, covered their mouths with white paint drawn in an exaggerated, clownish smile, and pranced on stage for the entertainment and delight of white audiences, who were tickled by the sight of a black man happily portraying the worst racial stereotypes that justified slavery and later Jim Crow. The images are so painful they can cause a downright visceral reaction. The damage done by the minstrel's complicity in the Jim Crow regime was considerable. Even so, do we hate the minstrel? Do we despise him? Or do we understand him as an unfortunate expression of the times?

Most people of any race would probably condemn the minstrel show but stop short of condemning the minstrel as a man. Pity, more than contempt, seems the likely response. Why? With the benefit of hindsight, we can see the minstrel in his social context. By shuckin' and jivin' for white audiences, he was mirroring to white audiences the shame and contempt projected onto him. He might have made a decent living that way—may even have been treated as a celebrity—but from a distance, we can see the emptiness, the pain.

When the system of mass incarceration collapses (and if history is any guide, it will), historians will undoubtedly look back and marvel that such an extraordinarily comprehensive system of racialized social control existed in the United States. How fascinating, they will likely say, that a drug war was waged almost exclusively against poor people of color—people already trapped in ghettos that lacked jobs and decent schools. They were rounded up by the millions, packed away in prisons, and when released, they were stigmatized for life, denied the right to vote, and ushered into a world of discrimination. Legally barred from employment, housing, and welfare benefits—and saddled with thousands of dollars of debt—these people were shamed and condemned for failing to hold together their families. They were chastised for succumbing to depression and anger, and blamed for landing back in prison. Historians will likely wonder how we could describe the new caste system as a system of crime control, when it is difficult to imagine a system better designed to create—rather than prevent—crime.

None of this is to suggest that those who break the law bear no responsibility for their conduct or exist merely as "products of their environment." To deny the individual agency of those caught up in the system—their capacity to overcome seemingly impossible odds—would be to deny an essential element of their humanity. We, as human beings, are not simply organisms or animals responding to stimuli. We have a higher self, a capacity for transcendence.

Yet our ability to exercise free will and transcend the most extraordinary obstacles does not make the conditions of our life irrelevant. Most of us struggle and often fail to meet the biggest challenges of our lives. Even the smaller challenges—breaking a bad habit or sticking to a diet—often prove too difficult, even for those of us who are relatively privileged and comfortable in our daily lives.

In fact, what is most remarkable about the hundreds of thousands of people who return from prison to their communities each year is not how many fail, but how many somehow manage to survive and stay out of prison against all the odds. Considering the design of this new system of control, it is astonishing that so many people labeled criminals still manage to care for and feed their children, hold together marriages, obtain employment, and start businesses. Perhaps most heroic are those who, upon release, launch social justice organizations that challenge the discrimination ex-offenders face and provide desperately needed support for those newly released from prison. These heroes go largely unnoticed by politicians who prefer to blame those who fail, rather than praise with admiration and awe all those who somehow manage, despite seemingly insurmountable hurdles, to survive.

As a society, our decision to heap shame and contempt upon those who struggle and fail in a system designed to keep them locked up and locked out says far more about ourselves than it does about them.

There is another path. Rather than shaming and condemning an already deeply stigmatized group, we, collectively, can embrace them—not necessarily their behavior, but them—their humanness. As the saying goes, "You gotta hate the crime, but love the criminal." This is not a mere platitude; it is a prescription for liberation. If we had actually learned to show love, care, compassion, and concern across racial lines during the Civil Rights Movement—rather than go colorblind—mass incarceration would not exist today.

5

The New Jim Crow

It was no ordinary Sunday morning when presidential candidate Barack Obama stepped to the podium at the Apostolic Church of God in Chicago. It was Father's Day. Hundreds of enthusiastic congregants packed the pews at the overwhelmingly black church eager to hear what the first black Democratic nominee for president of the United States had to say.

The message was a familiar one: black men should be better fathers. Too many are absent from their homes. For those in the audience, Obama's speech was an old tune sung by an exciting new performer. His message of personal responsibility, particularly as it relates to fatherhood, was anything but new; it had been delivered countless times by black ministers in churches across America. The message had also been delivered on a national stage by celebrities such as Bill Cosby and Sidney Poitier. And the message had been delivered with great passion by Louis Farrakhan, who more than a decade earlier summoned one million black men to Washington, D.C., for a day of "atonement" and recommitment to their families and communities.

The mainstream media, however, treated the event as big news, and many pundits seemed surprised that the black congregants actually applauded the message. For them, it was remarkable that black people nodded in approval when Obama said: "If we are honest with ourselves, we'll admit that too many fathers are missing—missing from too many lives and too many homes. Too many fathers are MIA. Too many fathers are AWOL. They have abandoned their responsibilities. They're acting like boys instead of men. And the foundations of our families are weaker because of it. You and I know this is true everywhere, but nowhere is this more true than in the African American community."

The media did not ask—and Obama did not tell—where the missing fathers might be found.

The following day, social critic and sociologist Michael Eric Dyson published a critique of Obama's speech in *Time* magazine. He pointed out that the stereotype of black men being poor fathers may well be false. Research by Boston College social psychologist Rebekah Levine Coley found that black fathers not living at home are more likely to keep in contact with their children than fathers of any other ethnic or racial group. Dyson chided Obama for evoking a black stereotype for political gain, pointing out that "Obama's words may have been spoken to black folk, but they were aimed at those whites still on the fence about whom to send to the White House."[1] Dyson's critique was a fair one, but like other media commentators, he remained silent about where all the absent black fathers could be found. He identified numerous social problems plaguing black families, such as high levels of unemployment, discriminatory mortgage practices, and the gutting of early-childhood learning programs. Not a word was said about prisons.

The public discourse regarding "missing black fathers" closely parallels the debate about the lack of eligible black men for marriage. The majority of black women are unmarried today, including 70 percent of professional black women.[2] "Where have all the black men gone?" is a common refrain heard among black women frustrated in their efforts to find life partners.

The sense that black men have disappeared is rooted in reality. The U.S. Census Bureau reported in 2002 that there are nearly 3 million more black adult women than men in black communities across the United States, a gender gap of 26 percent.[3] In many urban areas, the gap is far worse, rising to more than 37 percent in places like New York City. The comparable disparity for whites in the United States is 8 percent.[4] Although a million black men can be found in prisons and jails, public acknowledgment of the role of the criminal justice system in "disappearing" black men is surprisingly rare. Even in the black media—which is generally more willing to raise and tackle issues related to criminal justice—an eerie silence can often be found.[5]

Ebony magazine, for example, ran an article in December 2006 entitled "Where Have the Black Men Gone?" The author posed the popular question but never answered it.[6] He suggested we will find our black men when we rediscover God, family, and self-respect. A more cynical approach was taken by Tyra Banks, the popular talk show host, who devoted a show in May 2008 to the recurring question, "Where Have All the Good Black Men Gone?" She wondered aloud whether black women are unable to find "good black men" because too many of them are gay or dating white women. No mention was made of the War on Drugs or mass incarceration.

The fact that Barack Obama can give a speech on Father's Day dedicated to the subject of fathers who are "AWOL" without ever acknowledging that the majority of young black men in many large urban areas are currently under the control of the criminal justice system is disturbing, to say the least. What is more problematic, though, is that hardly anyone in the mainstream media noticed the oversight. One might not expect serious analysis from Tyra Banks, but shouldn't we expect a bit more from the *New York Times* and CNN? Hundreds of thousands of black men are unable to be good fathers for their children, not because of a lack of commitment or desire but because they are warehoused in prisons, locked in cages. They did not walk out on their families voluntarily; they were taken away in handcuffs, often due to a massive federal program known as the War on Drugs.

More African American adults are under correctional control today—in prison or jail, on probation or parole—than were enslaved in 1850, a decade before the Civil War began.[7] The mass incarceration of people of color is a big part of the reason that a black child born today is less likely to be raised by both parents than a black child born during slavery.[8] The absence of black fathers from families across America is not simply a function of laziness, immaturity, or too much time watching Sports Center. Thousands of black men have disappeared into prisons and jails, locked away for drug crimes that are largely ignored when committed by whites.

The clock has been turned back on racial progress in America, though scarcely anyone seems to notice. All eyes are fixed on people like Barack Obama and Oprah Winfrey, who have defied the odds and risen to power, fame, and fortune. For those left behind, especially those within prison walls, the celebration of racial triumph in America must seem a tad premature. More black men are imprisoned today than at any other moment in our nation's history. More are disenfranchised today than in 1870, the year the Fifteenth Amendment was ratified prohibiting laws that explicitly deny the right to vote on the basis of race.[9] Young black men today may be just as likely to suffer discrimination in employment, housing, public benefits, and jury service as a black man in the Jim Crow era—discrimination that is perfectly legal, because it is based on one's criminal record.

This is the new normal, the new racial equilibrium.

The launching of the War on Drugs and the initial construction of the new system required the expenditure of tremendous political initiative and resources. Media campaigns were waged; politicians blasted "soft" judges and enacted harsh sentencing laws; poor people of color were vilified. The system now, however, requires very little maintenance or justification. In fact, if you are white and middle class, you might not even realize the drug war is still going on. Most high school and college students today have no recollection of the political and media frenzy surrounding the drug war in the early years. They were young children when the war was declared, or not even born yet. Crack is out; terrorism is in.

Today, the political fanfare and the vehement, racialized rhetoric regarding crime and drugs are no longer necessary. Mass incarceration has been normalized, and all of the racial stereotypes and assumptions that gave rise to the system are now embraced (or at least internalized) by people of all colors, from all walks of life, and in every major political party. We may wonder aloud "where have the black men gone?" but deep down we already know. It is simply taken for granted that, in cities like Baltimore and Chicago, the vast majority of young black men are currently under the control of the criminal justice system or branded criminals for life. This extraordinary circumstance—unheard of in the rest of the world—is treated here in America as a basic fact of life, as normal as separate water fountains were just a half century ago.

States of Denial

The claim that we really know where all the black men have gone may inspire considerable doubt. If we know, why do we feign ignorance? Could it be that most people really don't know? Is it possible that the roundup, lockdown, and exclusion of black men en masse from the body politic has occurred largely unnoticed? The answer is yes and no.

Much has been written about the ways in which people manage to deny, even to themselves, that extraordinary atrocities, racial oppression, and other forms of human suffering have occurred or are occurring. Criminologist

Stanley Cohen wrote perhaps the most important book on the subject, *States of Denial*. The book examines how individuals and institutions—victims, perpetrators, and bystanders—know about yet deny the occurrence of oppressive acts. They see only what they want to see and wear blinders to avoid seeing the rest. This has been true about slavery, genocide, torture, and every form of systemic oppression.

Cohen emphasizes that denial, though deplorable, is complicated. It is not simply a matter of refusing to acknowledge an obvious, though uncomfortable, truth. Many people "know" and "not-know" the truth about human suffering at the same time. In his words, "Denial may be neither a matter of telling the truth nor intentionally telling a lie. There seem to be states of mind, or even whole cultures, in which we know and don't know at the same time."[10]

Today, most Americans know and don't know the truth about mass incarceration. For more than three decades, images of black men in handcuffs have been a regular staple of the evening news. We know that large numbers of black men have been locked in cages. In fact, it is precisely because we know that black and brown people are far more likely to be imprisoned that we, as a nation, have not cared too much about it. We tell ourselves they "deserve" their fate, even though we know—and don't know—that whites are just as likely to commit many crimes, especially drug crimes. We know that people released from prison face a lifetime of discrimination, scorn, and exclusion, and yet we claim not to know that an undercaste exists. We know and we don't know at the same time.

Upon reflection, it is relatively easy to understand how Americans come to deny the evils of mass incarceration. Denial is facilitated by persistent racial segregation in housing and schools, by political demagoguery, by racialized media imagery, and by the ease of changing one's perception of reality simply by changing television channels. There is little reason to doubt the prevailing "common sense" that black and brown men have been locked up en masse merely in response to crime rates when one's sources of information are mainstream media outlets. In many respects, the reality of mass incarceration is easier to avoid knowing than the injustices and sufferings associated with slavery or Jim Crow. Those confined to prisons are out of sight and out of mind; once released, they are typically confined in ghettos. Most Americans only come to "know" about the people cycling in and out of prisons through fictional police dramas, music videos, gangsta rap, and "true" accounts of ghetto experience on the evening news. These racialized narratives tend to confirm and reinforce the prevailing public consensus that we need not care about "those people"; they deserve what they get.

Of all the reasons that we fail to know the truth about mass incarceration, though, one stands out: a profound misunderstanding regarding how racial oppression actually works. If someone were to visit the United States from another country (or another planet) and ask: Is the U.S. criminal justice system some kind of tool of racial control? Most Americans would swiftly deny it. Numerous reasons would leap to mind why that could not possibly be the case. The visitor would be told that crime rates, black culture, or bad schools were to blame. "The system is not run by a bunch of racists," the apologist would explain. "It's run by people who are trying to fight crime." That response is predictable because most people assume that racism, and racial systems generally, are fundamentally a function of attitudes. Because mass incarceration is officially colorblind, it seems inconceivable that the system could function much like a racial caste system. The widespread and mistaken belief that racial animus is necessary for the creation and maintenance of racialized systems of social control is the most important reason that we, as a nation, have remained in deep denial.

The misunderstanding is not surprising. As a society, our collective understanding of racism has been powerfully influenced by the shocking images of the Jim Crow era and the struggle for civil rights. When we think of racism we think of Governor Wallace of Alabama blocking the schoolhouse door; we think of water hoses, lynchings, racial epithets, and "whites only" signs. These images make it easy to forget that many wonderful, good-hearted white people who were generous to others, respectful of their neighbors, and even kind to their black maids, gardeners, or shoe shiners—and wished them well—nevertheless went to the polls and voted for racial segregation. Many whites who supported Jim Crow justified it on paternalist grounds, actually believing they were doing blacks a favor or believing the time was not yet "right" for equality. The disturbing images from the Jim Crow era also make it easy to forget that many African Americans were complicit in the Jim Crow system, profiting from it directly or indirectly or keeping their objections quiet out of fear of the repercussions. Our understanding of racism is therefore shaped by the most extreme expressions of individual bigotry, not by the way in which it functions naturally, almost invisibly (and sometimes with genuinely benign intent), when it is embedded in the structure of a social system.

The unfortunate reality we must face is that racism manifests itself not only in individual attitudes and stereotypes, but also in the basic structure of society. Academics have developed complicated theories and obscure jargon in an effort to describe what is now referred to as *structural racism*, yet the concept is fairly straightforward. One theorist, Iris Marion Young, relying on a famous "birdcage" metaphor, explains it this way: If one thinks about racism by examining only one wire of the cage, or one form of disadvantage, it is difficult to understand how and why the bird is trapped. Only a large number of wires arranged in a specific way, and connected to one another, serve to enclose the bird and to ensure that it cannot escape.[11]

What is particularly important to keep in mind is that any given wire of the cage may or may not be specifically developed for the purpose of trapping the bird, yet it still operates (together with the other wires) to restrict its freedom. By the same token, not every aspect of a racial caste system needs to be developed for the specific purpose of controlling black people in order for it to operate (together with other laws, institutions, and practices) to trap them at the bottom of a racial hierarchy. In the system of mass incarceration, a wide variety of laws, institutions, and practices—ranging from racial profiling to biased sentencing policies, political disenfranchisement, and legalized employment discrimination—trap African Americans in a virtual (and literal) cage.

Fortunately, as Marilyn Frye has noted, every birdcage has a door, and every birdcage can be broken and can corrode.[12] What is most concerning about the new racial caste system, however, is that it may prove to be more durable than its predecessors. Because this new system is not explicitly based on race, it is easier to defend on seemingly neutral grounds. And while all previous methods of control have blamed the victim in one way or another, the current system invites observers to imagine that those who are trapped in the system were free to avoid second-class status or permanent banishment from society simply by choosing not to commit crimes. It is far more convenient to imagine that a majority of young African American men in urban areas freely chose a life of crime than to accept the real possibility that their lives were structured in a way that virtually guaranteed their early admission into a system from which they can never escape. Most people are willing to acknowledge the existence of the cage but insist that a door has been left open.

One way of understanding our current system of mass incarceration is to think of it as a birdcage with a locked door. It is a set of structural arrangements that locks a racially distinct group into a subordinate political, social, and economic position, effectively creating a second-class citizenship. Those trapped within the system are not merely disadvantaged, in the sense that they are competing on an unequal playing field or face additional hurdles to political or economic success; rather, the system itself is structured to lock them into a subordinate position.

How It Works

Precisely how the system of mass incarceration works to trap African Americans in a virtual (and literal) cage can best be understood by viewing the system as a whole. In earlier chapters, we considered various wires of the cage in isolation; here, we put the pieces together, step back, and view the cage in its entirety. Only when we view the cage from a distance can we disengage from the maze of rationalizations that are offered for each wire and see how the entire apparatus operates to keep African Americans perpetually trapped.

This, in brief, is how the system works: The War on Drugs is the vehicle through which extraordinary numbers of black men are forced into the cage. The entrapment occurs in three distinct phases, each of which has been explored earlier, but a brief review is useful here. The first stage is the roundup. Vast numbers of people are swept into the criminal justice system by the police, who conduct drug operations primarily in poor communities of color. They are rewarded in cash—through drug forfeiture laws and federal grant programs—for rounding up as many people as possible, and they operate unconstrained by constitutional rules of procedure that once were considered inviolate. Police can stop, interrogate, and search anyone they choose for drug investigations, provided they get "consent." Because there is no meaningful check on the exercise of police discretion, racial biases are granted free rein. In fact, police are allowed to rely on race as a factor in selecting whom to stop and search (even though people of color are no more likely to be guilty of drug crimes than whites)—effectively guaranteeing that those who are swept into the system are primarily black and brown.

The conviction marks the beginning of the second phase: the period of formal control. Once arrested, defendants are generally denied meaningful legal representation and pressured to plead guilty whether they are or not. Prosecutors are free to "load up" defendants with extra charges, and their decisions cannot be challenged for racial bias. Once convicted, due to the drug war's harsh sentencing laws, drug offenders in the United States spend more time under the criminal justice system's formal control—in jail or prison, on probation or parole—than drug offenders anywhere else in the world. While under formal control, virtually every aspect of one's life is regulated and monitored by the system, and any form of resistance or disobedience is subject to swift sanction. This period of control may last a lifetime, even for those convicted of extremely minor, nonviolent offenses, but the vast majority of those swept into the system are eventually released. They are transferred from their prison cells to a much larger, invisible cage.

The final stage has been dubbed by some advocates as the period of invisible punishment.[13] This term, first coined by Jeremy Travis, is meant to describe the unique set of criminal sanctions that are imposed on individuals after they step outside the prison gates, a form of punishment that operates largely outside of public view and takes effect outside the traditional sentencing framework. These sanctions are imposed by operation of law rather than decisions of a sentencing judge, yet they often have a greater impact on one's life course than the months or years one actually spends behind bars. These laws operate collectively to ensure that the vast majority of convicted offenders will never integrate into mainstream, white society. They will be discriminated against, legally, for the rest of their lives—denied employment, housing, education, and public benefits. Unable to surmount these obstacles, most will eventually return to prison and then be released again, caught in a closed circuit of perpetual marginality.

In recent years, advocates and politicians have called for greater resources devoted to the problem of "prisoner re-entry," in view of the unprecedented numbers of people who are released from prison and returned to their communities every year. While the terminology is well intentioned, it utterly fails to convey the gravity of the situation facing prisoners upon their release. People who have been convicted of felonies almost never truly re-enter the society they inhabited prior to their conviction. Instead, they enter a separate society, a world hidden from public view, governed by a set of oppressive and discriminatory rules and laws that do not apply to everyone else. They become members of an undercaste—an enormous population of predominately black and brown people who, because of the drug war, are denied basic rights and privileges of American citizenship and are permanently relegated to an inferior status. This is the final phase, and there is no going back.

Nothing New?

Some might argue that as disturbing as this system appears to be, there is nothing particularly new about mass incarceration; it is merely a continuation of past drug wars and biased law enforcement practices. Racial bias in our criminal justice system is simply an old problem that has gotten worse, and the social excommunication of "criminals" has a long history; it is not a recent invention. There is some merit to this argument.

Race has always influenced the administration of justice in the United States. Since the day the first prison opened, people of color have been disproportionately represented behind bars. In fact, the very first person admitted to a U.S. penitentiary was a "light skinned Negro in excellent health," described by an observer as "one who was born of a degraded and depressed race, and had never experienced anything but indifference and harshness."[14] Biased police practices are also nothing new, a recurring theme of African American experience since blacks were targeted by the police as suspected runaway slaves. And every drug war that has ever been waged in the United States—including alcohol prohibition—has been tainted or driven by racial bias.[15] Even postconviction penalties have a long history. The American colonies passed laws barring criminal offenders from a wide variety of jobs and benefits, automatically dissolving their marriages and denying them the right to enter contracts. These legislatures were following a long tradition, dating back to ancient Greece, of treating criminals as less than full citizens. Although many collateral sanctions were repealed by the late 1970s, arguably the drug war simply revived and expanded a tradition that has ancient roots, a tradition independent of the legacy of American slavery.

In view of this history and considering the lack of originality in many of the tactics and practices employed in the era of mass incarceration, there is good reason to believe that the latest drug war is just another drug war corrupted by racial and ethnic bias. But this view is correct only to a point.

In the past, the criminal justice system, as punitive as it may have been during various wars on crime and drugs, affected only a relatively small percentage of the population. Because civil penalties and sanctions imposed on ex-offenders applied only to a few, they never operated as a comprehensive system of control over any racially or ethnically defined population. Racial minorities were always overrepresented among current and ex-offenders, but as sociologists have noted, until the mid-1980s, the criminal justice system was marginal to communities of color. While young minority men with little schooling have always had relatively high rates of incarceration, "before the 1980s the penal system was not a dominant presence in the disadvantaged neighborhoods."[16]

Today, the War on Drugs has given birth to a system of mass incarceration that governs not just a small fraction of a racial or ethnic minority but entire communities of color. In ghetto communities, nearly everyone is either directly or indirectly subject to the new caste system. The system serves to redefine the terms of the relationship of poor people of color and their communities to mainstream, white society, ensuring their subordinate and marginal status. The criminal and civil sanctions that were once reserved for a tiny minority are now used to control and oppress a racially defined majority in many communities, and the systematic manner in which the control is achieved reflects not just a difference in scale. The nature of the criminal justice system has changed. It is no longer concerned primarily with the prevention and punishment of crime, but rather with the management and control of the dispossessed. Prior drug wars were ancillary to the prevailing caste system. This time the drug war *is* the system of control.

If you doubt that this is the case, consider the effect of the war on the ground, in specific locales. Take Chicago, Illinois, for example. Chicago is widely considered to be one of America's most diverse and vibrant cities. It has boasted black mayors, black police chiefs, black legislators, and is home to the nation's first black president. It has a thriving economy, a growing Latino community, and a substantial black middle class. Yet as the Chicago Urban League reported in 2002, there is another story to be told.[17]

If Martin Luther King Jr. were to return miraculously to Chicago, some forty years after bringing his Freedom Movement to the city, he would be saddened to discover that the same issues on which he originally focused still produce stark patterns of racial inequality, segregation, and poverty. He would also be struck by the dramatically elevated significance of one particular institutional force in the perpetuation and deepening of those patterns: the criminal justice system. In the few short decades since King's death, a new regime of racially disparate mass incarceration has emerged in Chicago and become the primary mechanism for racial oppression and the denial of equal opportunity.

In Chicago, like the rest of the country, the War on Drugs is the engine of mass incarceration, as well as the primary cause of gross racial disparities in the criminal justice system and in the ex-offender population. About 90 percent of those sentenced to prison for a drug offense in Illinois are African American.[18] White drug offenders are rarely arrested, and when they are, they are treated more favorably at every stage of the criminal justice process, including plea bargaining and sentencing.[19] Whites are consistently more likely to avoid prison and felony charges, even when they are repeat offenders.[20] Black offenders, by contrast, are routinely labeled felons and released into a permanent racial undercaste.

The total population of black males in Chicago with a felony record (including both current and ex-felons) is equivalent to 55 percent of the black adult male population and an astonishing 80 percent of the adult black male workforce in the Chicago area.[21] This stunning development reflects the dramatic increase in the number and race of those sent to prison for drug crimes. From the Chicago region alone, the number of those annually sent to prison for drug crimes increased almost 2,000 percent, from 469 in 1985 to 8,755 in 2005.[22] That figure, of course, does not include the thousands who avoid prison but are arrested, convicted, and sentenced to jail or probation. They, too, have criminal records that will follow them for life. More than 70 percent of all criminal cases in the Chicago area involve a class D felony drug possession charge, the lowest-level felony charge.[23] Those who do go to prison find little freedom upon release.

When people are released from Illinois prisons, they are given as little as $10 in "gate money" and a bus ticket to anywhere in the United States. Most return to impoverished neighborhoods in the Chicago area, bringing few resources and bearing the stigma of their prison record.[24] In Chicago, as in most cities across the country, ex-offenders are banned or severely restricted from employment in a large number of professions, job categories, and fields by professional licensing statutes, rules, and practices that discriminate against potential employees with felony records. According to a study conducted by the DePaul University College of Law in 2000, of the then ninety-eight occupations requiring licenses in Illinois, fifty-seven placed stipulations and/or restrictions on applicants with a criminal record.[25] Even when not barred by law from holding specific jobs, ex-offenders in Chicago find it extraordinarily difficult to find employers who will hire them, regardless of the nature of their conviction. They are also routinely denied public housing and welfare benefits, and they find it increasingly difficult to obtain education, especially now that funding for public education has been hard hit, due to exploding prison budgets.

The impact of the new caste system is most tragically felt among the young. In Chicago (as in other cities across the United States), young black men are more likely to go to prison than to college.[26] As of June 2001, there were nearly 20,000 more black men in the Illinois state prison system than enrolled in the state's public universities.[27] In fact, there were more black men in the state's correctional facilities that year *just on drug charges* than the total number of black men enrolled in undergraduate degree programs in state universities.[28] To put the crisis in even sharper focus, consider this: just 992 black men received a bachelor's degree from Illinois state universities in 1999, while roughly 7,000 black men were released from the state prison system the following year just for drug offenses.[29] The young men who go to prison rather than college face a lifetime of closed doors, discrimination, and ostracism. Their plight is not what we hear about on the evening news, however. Sadly, like the racial caste systems that preceded it, the system of mass incarceration now seems normal and natural to most, a regrettable necessity.

Mapping the Parallels

Those cycling in and out of Illinois prisons today are members of America's new racial undercaste. The United States has almost always had a racial undercaste—a group defined wholly or largely by race that is permanently locked out of mainstream, white society by law, custom, and practice. The reasons and justifications change over time, as each new caste system reflects and adapts to changes in the social, political, and economic context. What is most striking about the design of the current caste system, though, is how closely it resembles its predecessor. There are important differences between mass incarceration and Jim Crow, to be sure—many of which will be discussed later—but when we step back and view the system as a whole, there is a profound sense of déjà vu. There is a familiar stigma and shame. There is an elaborate system of control, complete with political disenfranchisement and legalized discrimination in every major realm of economic and social life. And there is the production of racial meaning and racial boundaries.

Many of these parallels have been discussed at some length in earlier chapters; others have yet to be explored. Listed below are several of the most obvious similarities between Jim Crow and mass incarceration, followed by a discussion of a few parallels that have not been discussed so far. Let's begin with the historical parallels.

Historical parallels. Jim Crow and mass incarceration have similar political origins. As described in chapter 1, both caste systems were born, in part, due to a desire among white elites to exploit the resentments, vulnerabilities, and racial biases of poor and working-class whites for political or economic gain. Segregation laws were proposed as part of a deliberate and strategic effort to deflect anger and hostility that had been brewing against the white elite away from them and toward African Americans. The birth of mass incarceration can be traced to a similar political dynamic. Conservatives in the 1970s and 1980s sought to appeal to the racial biases and economic vulnerabilities of poor and working-class whites through racially coded rhetoric on crime and welfare. In both cases, the racial opportunists offered few, if any, economic reforms to address the legitimate economic anxieties of poor and working-class whites, proposing instead a crackdown on the racially defined "others." In the early years of Jim Crow, conservative white elites competed with each other by passing ever more stringent and oppressive Jim Crow legislation. A century later, politicians in the early years of the drug war competed with each other to prove who could be tougher on crime by passing ever harsher drug laws—a thinly veiled effort to appeal to poor and working-class whites who, once again, proved they were willing to forego economic and structural reform in exchange for an apparent effort to put blacks back "in their place."[30]

Legalized discrimination. The most obvious parallel between Jim Crow and mass incarceration is legalized discrimination. During Black History Month, Americans congratulate themselves for having put an end to discrimination against African Americans in employment, housing, public benefits, and public accommodations. Schoolchildren wonder out loud how discrimination could ever have been legal in this great land of ours. Rarely are they told that it is *still* legal. Many of the forms of discrimination that relegated African Americans to an inferior caste during Jim Crow continue to apply to huge segments of the black population today—provided they are first labeled felons. If they are branded felons by the time they reach the age of twenty-one (as many of them are), they are subject to legalized discrimination for their entire adult lives. The forms of discrimination that apply to ex–drug offenders, described in some detail in chapter 4, mean that, once prisoners are released, they enter a parallel social universe—much like Jim Crow—in which discrimination in nearly every aspect of social, political, and economic life is perfectly legal. Large majorities of black men in cities across the United States are once again subject to legalized discrimination effectively barring them from full integration into mainstream, white society. Mass incarceration has nullified many of the gains of the Civil Rights Movement, putting millions of black men back in a position reminiscent of Jim Crow.

Political disenfranchisement. During the Jim Crow era, African Americans were denied the right to vote through poll taxes, literacy tests, grandfather clauses, and felon disenfranchisement laws, even though the Fifteenth Amendment to the U.S. Constitution specifically provides that "the right of citizens of the United States to vote shall not be denied . . . on account of race, color, or previous condition of servitude." Formally race-neutral devices were adopted to achieve the goal of an all-white electorate without violating the terms of the Fifteenth Amendment. The devices worked quite well. Because African Americans were poor, they frequently could not pay poll taxes. And because they had been denied access to education, they could not pass literacy tests. Grandfather clauses allowed whites to vote even if they couldn't meet the requirements, as long as their ancestors had been able to vote. Finally, because blacks were disproportionately charged with felonies—in fact, some crimes were specifically defined as felonies with the goal of eliminating blacks from the electorate—felony disenfranchisement laws effectively suppressed the black vote as well.[31]

Following the collapse of Jim Crow, all of the race-neutral devices for excluding blacks from the electorate were eliminated through litigation or legislation, except felon disenfranchisement laws. Some courts have found that these laws have "lost their discriminatory taint" because they have been amended since the collapse of Jim Crow; other courts have allowed the laws to stand because overt racial bias is absent from the legislative record.[32] The failure of our legal system to eradicate all of the tactics adopted during the Jim Crow era to suppress the black vote has major implications today. Felon disenfranchisement laws have been more effective in eliminating black voters in the age of mass incarceration than they were during Jim Crow. Less than two decades after the War on Drugs began, one in seven black men nationally had lost the right to vote, and as many as one in four in those states with the highest African American disenfranchisement rate.[33] These figures may understate the impact of felony disenfranchisement, because they do not take into account the millions of ex-felons who cannot vote in states that require ex-felons to pay fines or fees before their voting rights can be restored—the new poll tax. As legal scholar Pamela Karlan has observed, "felony disenfranchisement has decimated the potential black electorate."[34]

It is worthy of note, however, that the exclusion of black voters from polling booths is not the only way in which black political power has been suppressed. Another dimension of disenfranchisement echoes not so much Jim Crow as slavery. Under the usual-residence rule, the Census Bureau counts imprisoned individuals as residents of the jurisdiction in which they are incarcerated. Because most new prison construction occurs in predominately white, rural areas, white communities benefit from inflated population totals at the expense of the urban, overwhelmingly minority communities from which the prisoners come.[35] This has enormous consequences for the redistricting process. White rural communities that house prisons wind up with more people in state legislatures representing them, while poor communities of color lose representatives because it appears their population has declined. This policy is disturbingly reminiscent of the three-fifths clause in the original Constitution, which enhanced the political clout of slaveholding states by including 60 percent of slaves in the population base for calculating Congressional seats and electoral votes, even though they could not vote.

Exclusion from juries. Another clear parallel between mass incarceration and Jim Crow is the systematic exclusion of blacks from juries. One hallmark of the Jim Crow era was all-white juries trying black defendants in the South. Although the exclusion of jurors on the basis of race has been illegal since 1880, as a practical matter, the removal of prospective black jurors through race-based peremptory strikes was sanctioned by the Supreme

Court until 1985, when the Court ruled in *Batson v. Kentucky* that racially biased strikes violate the equal protection clause of the Fourteenth Amendment.[36] Today defendants face a situation highly similar to the one they faced a century ago. As described in chapter 3, a formal prohibition against race-based peremptory strikes does exist; as a practical matter, however, the Court has tolerated the systematic exclusion of blacks from juries by allowing lower courts to accept "silly" and even "superstitious" reasons for striking black jurors.[37] To make matters worse, a large percentage of black men (about 30 percent) are automatically excluded from jury service because they have been labeled felons.[38] The combined effect of race-based peremptory strikes and the automatic exclusion of felons from juries has put black defendants in a familiar place—in a courtroom in shackles, facing an all-white jury.

   Closing the courthouse doors. The parallels between mass incarceration and Jim Crow extend all the way to the U.S. Supreme Court. Over the years, the Supreme Court has followed a fairly consistent pattern in responding to racial caste systems, first protecting them and then, after dramatic shifts in the political and social climate, dismantling these systems of control and some of their vestiges. In *Dred Scott v. Sanford*, the Supreme Court immunized the institution of slavery from legal challenge on the grounds that African Americans were not citizens, and in *Plessy v. Ferguson*, the Court established the doctrine of "separate but equal"—a legal fiction that protected the Jim Crow system from judicial scrutiny for racial bias.

   Currently, *McCleskey v. Kemp* and its progeny serve much the same function as *Dred Scott* and *Plessy*. In *McCleskey*, the Supreme Court demonstrated that it is once again in protection mode—firmly committed to the prevailing system of control. As chapter 3 demonstrated, the Court has closed the courthouse doors to claims of racial bias at every stage of the criminal justice process, from stops and searches to plea bargaining and sentencing. Mass incarceration is now off-limits to challenges on the grounds of racial bias, much as its predecessors were in their time. The new racial caste system operates unimpeded by the Fourteenth Amendment and federal civil rights legislation—laws designed to topple earlier systems of control. The Supreme Court's famous proclamation in 1857—"[the black man] has no rights which the white man is bound to respect"—remains true to a significant degree today, so long as the black man has been labeled a felon.[39]

Racial segregation. Although the parallels listed above should be enough to give anyone pause, there are a number of other, less obvious, similarities between mass incarceration and Jim Crow that have not been explored in earlier chapters. The creation and maintenance of racial segregation is one example. As we know, Jim Crow laws mandated residential segregation, and blacks were relegated to the worst parts of town. Roads literally stopped at the border of many black neighborhoods, shifting from pavement to dirt. Water, sewer systems, and other public services that supported the white areas of town frequently did not extend to the black areas. The extreme poverty that plagued blacks due to their legally sanctioned inferior status was largely invisible to whites—so long as whites remained in their own neighborhoods, which they were inclined to do. Racial segregation rendered black experience largely invisible to whites, making it easier for whites to maintain racial stereotypes about black values and culture. It also made it easier to deny or ignore their suffering.

Mass incarceration functions similarly. It achieves racial segregation by segregating prisoners—the majority of whom are black and brown—from mainstream society. Prisoners are kept behind bars, typically more than a hundred miles from home.[40] Even prisons—the actual buildings—are a rare sight for many Americans, as they are often located far from population centers. Although rural counties contain only 20 percent of the U.S. population, 60 percent of new prison construction occurs there.[41] Prisoners are thus hidden from public view—out of sight, out of mind. In a sense, incarceration is a far more extreme form of physical and residential segregation than Jim Crow segregation. Rather than merely shunting black people to the other side of town or corralling them in ghettos, mass incarceration locks them in cages. Bars and walls keep hundreds of thousands of black and brown people away from mainstream society—a form of apartheid unlike any the world has ever seen.

Prisons, however, are not the only vehicle for racial segregation. Segregation is also created and perpetuated by the flood of prisoners who return to ghetto communities each year. Because the drug war has been waged almost exclusively in poor communities of color, when drug offenders are released, they are generally returned to racially segregated ghetto communities—the places they call home. In many cities, the re-entry phenomenon is highly concentrated in a small number of neighborhoods. According to one study, during a twelve-year period, the number of prisoners returning home to "core counties"—those counties that contain the inner city of a metropolitan area—tripled.[42] The effects are felt throughout the United States. In interviews with one hundred residents of two Tallahassee, Florida, communities, researchers found that nearly every one of them had experienced or expected to experience the return of a family member from prison.[43] Similarly, a survey of families living in the Robert Taylor Homes in Chicago found that the majority of residents either had a family member in prison or expected one to return from prison within the next two years.[44] Fully 70 percent of men between the ages of eighteen and forty-five in the impoverished and overwhelmingly black North Lawndale neighborhood on Chicago's West Side are ex-offenders, saddled for life with a criminal record.[45] The majority (60 percent) were incarcerated for drug offenses.[46] These neighborhoods are a minefield for parolees, for a standard condition of parole is a promise not to associate with felons. As Paula Wolff, a senior executive at Chicago Metropolis 2020 observes, in these ghetto neighborhoods, "It is hard for a parolee to walk to the corner store to get a carton of milk without being subject to a parole violation."[47]

By contrast, whites—even poor whites—are far less likely to be imprisoned for drug offenses. And when they are released from prison, they rarely find themselves in the ghetto. The white poor have a vastly different experience in America than do poor people of color. Because whites do not suffer racial segregation, the white poor are not relegated to racially defined areas of intense poverty. In New York City, one study found that 70 percent of the city's poor black and Latino residents live in high-poverty neighborhoods, whereas 70 percent of the city's poor whites live in nonpoverty neighborhoods—communities that have significant resources, including jobs, schools, banks, and grocery stores.[48] Nationwide, nearly seven out of eight people living in high-poverty urban areas are members of a minority group.[49]

Mass incarceration thus perpetuates and deepens pre-existing patterns of racial segregation and isolation, not just by removing people of color from society and putting them in prisons, but by dumping them back into ghettos upon their release. Youth of color who might have escaped their ghetto communities—or helped to transform them—if they had been given a fair shot in life and not been labeled felons, instead find themselves trapped in a closed circuit of perpetual marginality, circulating between ghetto and prison.[50]

The racially segregated, poverty-stricken ghettos that exist in inner-city communities across America would not exist today but for racially biased government policies for which there has never been meaningful redress.[51] Yet every year, hundreds of thousands of poor people of color who have been targeted by the War on Drugs are forced to return to these racially segregated communities—neighborhoods still crippled by the legacy of an earlier system of control. As a practical matter, they have no other choice. In this way, mass incarceration, like its predecessor Jim Crow, creates and maintains racial segregation.

Symbolic production of race. Arguably the most important parallel between mass incarceration and Jim Crow is that both have served to define the meaning and significance of race in America. Indeed, a primary function of any racial caste system is to define the meaning of race in its time. Slavery defined what it meant to be black (a slave), and Jim Crow defined what it meant to be black (a second-class citizen). Today mass incarceration defines the meaning of blackness in America: black people, especially black men, are criminals. That is what it means to be black.

The temptation is to insist that black men "choose" to be criminals; the system does not make them criminals, at least not in the way that slavery made blacks slaves or Jim Crow made them second-class citizens. The myth of choice here is seductive, but it should be resisted. African Americans are not significantly more likely to use or sell prohibited drugs than whites, but they are *made* criminals at drastically higher rates for precisely the same conduct. In fact, studies suggest that white professionals may be the most likely of any group to have engaged in illegal drug activity in their lifetime, yet they are the least likely to be made criminals.[52] The prevalence of illegal drug activity among all racial and ethnic groups creates a situation in which, due to limited law enforcement resources and political constraints, some people are made criminals while others are not. Black people have been made criminals by the War on Drugs to a degree that dwarfs its effect on other racial and ethnic groups, especially whites. And the process of making them criminals has produced racial stigma.

Every racial caste system in the United States has produced racial stigma. Mass incarceration is no exception. Racial stigma is produced by defining negatively what it means to be black. The stigma of race was once the shame of the slave; then it was the shame of the second-class citizen; today the stigma of race is the shame of the criminal. As described in chapter 4, many ex-offenders describe an existential angst associated with their pariah status, an angst that casts a shadow over every aspect of their identity and social experience. The shame and stigma is not limited to the individual; it extends to family members and friends—even whole communities are stigmatized by the presence of those labeled criminals. Those stigmatized often adopt coping strategies African Americans once employed during the Jim Crow era, including lying about their own criminal history or the status of their family members in an attempt to "pass" as someone who will be welcomed by mainstream society.

The critical point here is that, for black men, the stigma of being a "criminal" in the era of mass incarceration is fundamentally a *racial* stigma. This is not to say stigma is absent for white criminals; it is present and powerful. Rather, the point is that the stigma of criminality for white offenders is different—it is a nonracial stigma.

An experiment may help to illustrate how and why this is the case. Say the following to nearly anyone and watch the reaction: "We really need to do something about the problem of white crime." Laughter is a likely response. The term *white crime* is nonsensical in the era of mass incarceration, unless one is really referring to white-collar crime, in which case the term is understood to mean the types of crimes that seemingly respectable white people commit in the comfort of fancy offices. Because the term *white crime* lacks social meaning, the term *white criminal* is also perplexing. In that formulation, *white* seems to qualify the term *criminal*—as if to say, "he's a criminal but not *that* kind of criminal." Or, he's not a *real* criminal—i.e., not what we mean by *criminal* today.

In the era of mass incarceration, what it means to be a criminal in our collective consciousness has become conflated with what it means to be black, so the term *white criminal* is confounding, while the term *black criminal* is nearly redundant. Recall the study discussed in chapter 3 that revealed that when survey respondents were asked to picture a drug criminal, nearly everyone pictured someone who was black. This phenomenon helps to explain why studies indicate that white ex-offenders may actually have an easier time gaining employment than African Americans *without* a criminal record.[53] To be a black man is to be thought of as a criminal, and to be a black criminal is to be despicable—a social pariah. To be a white criminal is not easy, by any means, but as a white criminal you are not a *racial* outcast, though you may face many forms of social and economic exclusion. Whiteness mitigates crime, whereas blackness defines the criminal.

As we have seen in earlier chapters, the conflation of blackness with crime did not happen organically; rather, it was constructed by political and media elites as part of the broad project known as the War on Drugs. This conflation served to provide a legitimate outlet to the expression of antiblack resentment and animus—a convenient release valve now that explicit forms of racial bias are strictly condemned. In the era of colorblindness, it is no longer permissible to hate blacks, but we can hate criminals. Indeed, we are encouraged to do so. As writer John Edgar Wideman points out, "It's respectable to tar and feather criminals, to advocate locking them up and throwing away the key. It's not racist to be against crime, even though the archetypal criminal in the media and the public imagination almost always wears Willie Horton's face."[54]

It is precisely because our criminal justice system provides a vehicle for the expression of conscious and unconscious antiblack sentiment that the prison label is experienced as a racial stigma. The stigma exists whether or not one has been formally branded a criminal, yet another parallel to Jim Crow. Just as African Americans in the North were stigmatized by the Jim Crow system even if they were not subject to its formal control, black men today are stigmatized by mass incarceration—and the social construction of the "criminalblackman"—whether they have ever been to prison or not. For those who have been branded, the branding serves to intensify and deepen the racial stigma, as they are constantly reminded in virtually every contact they have with public agencies, as well as with private employers and landlords, that they are the new "untouchables."

In this way, the stigma of race has become the stigma of criminality. Throughout the criminal justice system, as well as in our schools and public spaces, young + black + male is equated with reasonable suspicion, justifying the arrest, interrogation, search, and detention of thousands of African Americans every year, as well as their exclusion from employment and housing and the denial of educational opportunity. Because black youth are viewed as criminals, they face severe employment discrimination and are also "pushed out" of schools through racially biased school discipline policies.[55]

For black youth, the experience of being "made black" often begins with the first police stop, interrogation, search, or arrest. The experience carries social meaning—*this is what it means to be black*. The story of one's "first time" may be repeated to family or friends, but for ghetto youth, almost no one imagines that the first time will be the last. The experience is understood to define the terms of one's relationship not only to the state but to society at large. This reality can be frustrating for those who strive to help ghetto youth "turn their lives around." James Forman Jr., the cofounder of the See Forever charter school for juvenile offenders in Washington, D.C., made this point when describing how random and degrading stops and searches of ghetto youth "tell kids that they are pariahs, that no matter how hard they study, they will remain potential suspects." One student complained to him, "We can be perfect, perfect, doing everything right and still they treat us like dogs. No, worse than dogs, because criminals are treated worse than dogs." Another student asked him pointedly, "How can you tell us we can be anything when they treat us like we're nothing?"[56]

The process of marking black youth *as* black criminals is essential to the functioning of mass incarceration as a racial caste system. For the system to succeed—that is, for it to achieve the political goals described in chapter 1—black people must be labeled criminals before they are formally subject to control. The criminal label is essential, for forms of explicit racial exclusion are not only prohibited but widely condemned. Thus black youth must be made—labeled—criminals. This process of being made a criminal is, to a large extent, the process of "becoming" black. As Wideman explains, when "to be a man of color of a certain economic class and milieu is equivalent in the public eye to being a criminal," being processed by the criminal justice system is tantamount to being made black, and "doing time" behind bars is at the same time "marking race."[57] At its core, then, mass incarceration, like Jim Crow, is a "race-making institution." It serves to define the meaning and significance of race in America.

The Limits of the Analogy

Saying that mass incarceration is the New Jim Crow can leave a misimpression. The parallels between the two systems of control are striking, to say the least—in both, we find racial opportunism by politicians, legalized discrimination, political disenfranchisement, exclusion of blacks from juries, stigmatization, the closing of courthouse doors, racial segregation, and the symbolic production of race—yet there are important differences. Just as Jim Crow, as a system of racial control, was dramatically different from slavery, mass incarceration is different from its predecessor. In fact, if one were to draft a list of the differences between slavery and Jim Crow, the list might well be longer than the list of similarities. The same goes for Jim Crow and mass incarceration. Each system of control has been unique—well adapted to the circumstances of its time. If we fail to appreciate the differences, we will be hindered in our ability to meet the challenges created by the current moment. At the same time, though, we must be careful not to assume that differences exist when they do not, or to exaggerate the ones that do. Some differences may appear on the surface to be major, but on close analysis they prove less significant.

An example of a difference that is less significant than it may initially appear is the "fact" that Jim Crow was explicitly race-based, whereas mass incarceration is not. This statement initially appears self-evident, but it is partially mistaken. Although it is common to think of Jim Crow as an explicitly race-based system, in fact a number of the key policies were officially colorblind. As previously noted, poll taxes, literacy tests, and felon disenfranchisement laws were all formally race-neutral practices that were employed in order to avoid the prohibition on race discrimination in voting contained in the Fifteenth Amendment. These laws operated to create an all-white electorate because they excluded African Americans from the franchise but were not generally applied to whites. Poll workers had the discretion to charge a poll tax or administer a literacy test, or not, and they exercised their discretion in a racially discriminatory manner. Laws that said nothing about race operated to discriminate because those charged with enforcement were granted tremendous discretion, and they exercised that discretion in a highly discriminatory manner.

The same is true in the drug war. Laws prohibiting the use and sale of drugs are facially race neutral, but they are enforced in a highly discriminatory fashion. The decision to wage the drug war primarily in black and brown communities rather than white ones and to target African Americans but not whites on freeways and train stations has had precisely the same effect as the literacy and poll taxes of an earlier era. A facially race-neutral system of laws has operated to create a racial caste system.

Other differences between Jim Crow and mass incarceration are actually more significant than they may initially appear. An example relates to the role of racial stigma in our society. As discussed in chapter 4, during Jim Crow, racial stigma contributed to racial solidarity in the black community. Racial stigma today, however—that is, the stigma of black criminality—has turned the black community against itself, destroyed networks of mutual support, and created a silence about the new caste system among many of the people most affected by it.[58] The implications of this difference are profound. Racial stigma today makes collective action extremely difficult— sometimes impossible; whereas racial stigma during Jim Crow contained the seeds of revolt.

Described below are a number of the other important differences be tween Jim Crow and mass incarceration. Listing all of the differences here is impractical; so instead we will focus on a few of the major differences that are most frequently cited in defense of mass incarceration, including the absence of overt racial hostility, the inclusion of whites in the system of con trol, and African American support for some "get tough" policies and drug war tactics.

Absence of racial hostility. First, let's consider the absence of overt ra cial hostility among politicians who support harsh drug laws and the law en forcement officials charged with enforcing them. The absence of overt racial hostility is a significant difference from Jim Crow, but it can be exaggerated. Mass incarceration, like Jim Crow, was born of racial opportunism—an ef fort by white elites to exploit the racial hostilities, resentments, and insecu rities of poor and working-class whites. Moreover, racial hostility and racial violence have not altogether disappeared, given that complaints of racial slurs and brutality by the police and prison guards are fairly common. Some scholars and commentators have pointed out that the racial violence once associated with brutal slave masters or the Ku Klux Klan has been replaced, to some extent, by violence perpetrated by the state. Racial violence has been rationalized, legitimated, and channeled through our criminal justice system; it is expressed as police brutality, solitary confinement, and the dis criminatory and arbitrary imposition of the death penalty.[59]

But even granting that some African Americans may fear the police today as much as their grandparents feared the Klan (as a wallet can be mistaken for a gun) and that the penal system may be as brutal in many respects as Jim Crow (or slavery), the absence of racial hostility in the public discourse and the steep decline in vigilante racial violence is no small matter. It is also significant that the "whites only" signs are gone and that children of all colors can drink from the same water fountains, swim in the same pools, and play on the same playgrounds. Black children today can even dream of being president of the United States.

Those who claim that mass incarceration is "just like" Jim Crow make a serious mistake. Things have changed. The fact that a clear majority of Americans were telling pollsters in the early 1980s—when the drug war was kicking off—that they opposed race discrimination in nearly all its forms should not be dismissed lightly.[60] Arguably some respondents may have been telling pollsters what they thought was appropriate rather than what they actually believed, but there is no reason to believe that most of them were lying. It is more likely that most Americans by the early 1980s had come to reject segregationist thinking and values, and not only did not want to be thought of as racist but did not want to *be* racist.

This difference in public attitudes has important implications for reform efforts. Claims that mass incarceration is analogous to Jim Crow will fall on deaf ears and alienate potential allies if advocates fail to make clear that the claim is *not* meant to suggest or imply that supporters of the current system are racist in the way Americans have come to understand that term. Race plays a major role—indeed, a defining role—in the current system, but not because of what is commonly understood as old-fashioned, hostile bigotry. This system of control depends far more on *racial indifference* (defined as a lack of compassion and caring about race and racial groups) than racial hostility—a feature it actually shares with its predecessors.

All racial caste systems, not just mass incarceration, have been supported by racial indifference. As noted earlier, many whites during the Jim Crow era sincerely believed that African Americans were intellectually and morally inferior. They meant blacks no harm but believed segregation was a sensible system for managing a society comprised of fundamentally different and unequal people. The sincerity of many people's racial beliefs is what led Martin Luther King Jr. to declare, "Nothing in all the world is more dangerous than sincere ignorance and conscientious stupidity." The notion that racial caste systems are necessarily predicated on a desire to harm other racial groups, and that racial hostility is the essence of racism, is fundamentally misguided. Even slavery does not conform to this limited understanding of racism and racial caste. Most plantation owners supported the institution of black slavery not because of a sadistic desire to harm blacks but instead because they wanted to get rich, and black slavery was the most efficient means to that end. By and large, plantation owners were indifferent to the suffering caused by slavery; they were motivated by greed. Preoccupation with the role of racial hostility in earlier caste systems can blind us to the ways in which every caste system, including mass incarceration, has been supported by racial indifference—a lack of caring and compassion for people of other races.

White victims of racial caste. We now turn to another important difference between mass incarceration and Jim Crow: the direct harm to whites caused by the current caste system. Whites never had to sit at the back of the bus during Jim Crow, but today a white man may find himself in prison for a drug offense, sharing a cell with a black man. The direct harm caused to whites caused by mass incarceration seems to distinguish it from Jim Crow; yet, like many of the other differences, this one requires some qualification. Some whites were directly harmed by Jim Crow. For example, a white woman who fell in love with a black man and hoped to spend the rest of her life with him was directly harmed by anti-miscegenation laws. The laws were intended for her benefit—to protect her from the corrupting influence of the black man and the "tragedy" of mulatto children—but she was directly harmed nonetheless.

Still, it seems obvious that mass incarceration directly harms far more whites than Jim Crow ever did. For some, this fact alone may be reason enough to reject the analogy. An "interracial racial caste system" may seem like an oxymoron. What kind of racial caste system includes white people within its control? The answer: a racial caste system in the age of colorblindness.

If 100 percent of the people arrested and convicted for drug offenses were African American, the situation would provoke outrage among the majority of Americans who consider themselves nonracist and who know very well that Latinos, Asian Americans, and whites also commit drug crimes. We, as a nation, seem comfortable with 90 percent of the people arrested and convicted of drug offenses in some states being African American, but if the figure were 100 percent, the veil of colorblindness would be lost. We could no longer tell ourselves stories about why 90 percent might be a reasonable figure; nor could we continue to assume that good reasons exist for extreme racial disparities in the drug war, even if we are unable to think of such reasons ourselves. In short, the inclusion of some whites in the system of control is essential to preserving the image of a colorblind criminal justice system and maintaining our self-image as fair and unbiased people. Because most Americans, including those within law enforcement, want to believe they are non-racist, the suffering in the drug war crosses the color line.

Of course, the fact that white people are harmed by the drug war does not mean they are the real targets, the designated enemy. The harm white people suffer in the drug war is much like the harm Iraqi civilians suffer in U.S. military actions targeting presumed terrorists or insurgents. In any war, a tremendous amount of collateral damage is inevitable. Black and brown people are the principal targets in this war; white people are collateral damage.

Saying that white people are collateral damage may sound callous, but it reflects a particular reality. Mass incarceration as we know it would not exist today but for the racialization of crime in the media and political discourse. The War on Drugs was declared as part of a political ploy to capitalize on white racial resentment against African Americans, and the Reagan administration used the emergence of crack and its related violence as an opportunity to build a racialized public consensus in support of an all-out war—a consensus that almost certainly would not have been formed if the primary users and dealers of crack had been white.

Economist Glenn Loury made this observation in his book *The Anatomy of Racial Inequality*. He noted that it is nearly impossible to imagine anything remotely similar to mass incarceration happening to young white men. Can we envision a system that would enforce drug laws almost exclusively among young white men and largely ignore drug crime among young black men? Can we imagine large majorities of young white men being rounded up for minor drug offenses, placed under the control of the criminal justice system, labeled felons, and then subjected to a lifetime of discrimination, scorn, and exclusion? Can we imagine this happening while most black men landed decent jobs or trotted off to college? No, we cannot. If such a thing occurred, "it would occasion a most profound reflection about what had gone wrong, not only with THEM, but with US."[61] It would never be dismissed with the thought that white men were simply reaping what they have sown. The criminalization of white men would disturb us to the core. So the critical questions are: "What disturbs us? What is dissonant? What seems anomalous? What is contrary to expectation?"[62] Or more to the point: *Whom do we care about?*

An answer to the last question may be found by considering the drastically different manner that we, as a nation, responded to drunk driving in the mid-1980s, as compared to crack cocaine. During the 1980s, at the same time crack was making headlines, a broad-based, grassroots movement was under way to address the widespread and sometimes fatal problem of drunk driving. Unlike the drug war, which was initiated by political elites long before ordinary people identified it as an issue of extraordinary concern, the movement to crack down on drunk drivers was a bottom-up movement, led most notably by mothers whose families were shattered by deaths caused by drunk driving.

Media coverage of the movement peaked in 1988, when a drunk driver traveling the wrong way on Interstate 71 in Kentucky caused a head-on collision with a school bus. Twenty-seven people died and dozens more were injured in the ensuing fire. The tragic accident, known as the Carrollton bus disaster, was one of the worst in U.S. history. In the aftermath, several parents of the victims became actively involved in Mothers Against Drunk Driving (MADD), and one became its national president. Throughout the 1980s, drunk driving was a regular topic in the media, and the term *designated driver* became part of the American lexicon.

At the close of the decade, drunk drivers were responsible for approximately 22,000 deaths annually, while overall alcohol-related deaths were close to 100,000 a year. By contrast, during the same time period, there were no prevalence statistics at all on crack, much less crack-related deaths. In fact, the number of deaths related to *all illegal drugs combined* was tiny compared to the number of deaths caused by drunk drivers. The total of all drug-related deaths due to AIDS, drug overdose, or the violence associated with the illegal drug trade, was estimated at 21,000 annually—less than the number of deaths directly caused by drunk drivers, and a small fraction of the number of alcohol-related deaths that occur every year.[63]

In response to growing concern—fueled by advocacy groups such as MADD and by the media coverage of drunk-driving fatalities—most states adopted tougher laws to punish drunk driving. Numerous states now have some type of mandatory sentencing for this offense—typically two days in jail for a first offense and two to ten days for a second offense.[64] Possession of a tiny amount of crack cocaine, on the other hand, carries a mandatory minimum sentence of five years in federal prison.

The vastly different sentences afforded drunk drivers and drug offenders speaks volumes regarding who is viewed as disposable—someone to be purged from the body politic—and who is not. Drunk drivers are predominantly white and male. White men comprised 78 percent of the arrests for this offense in 1990 when new mandatory minimums governing drunk driving were being adopted.[65] They are generally charged with misdemeanors and typically receive sentences involving fines, license suspension, and community service. Although drunk driving carries a far greater risk of violent death than the use or sale of illegal drugs, the societal response to drunk drivers has generally emphasized keeping the person functional and in society, while attempting to respond to the dangerous behavior through treatment and counseling.[66] People charged with drug offenses, though, are disproportionately poor people of color. They are typically charged with felonies and sentenced to prison.

Another clue that mass incarceration, as we know it, would not exist but for the race of the imagined enemy can be found in the history of drug-law enforcement in the United States. Yale historian David Musto and other scholars have documented a disturbing, though unsurprising pattern: punishment becomes more severe when drug use is associated with people of color but softens when it is associated with whites.[67] The history of marijuana policy is a good example. In the early 1900s, marijuana was perceived— rightly or wrongly—as a drug used by blacks and Mexican Americans, leading to the Boggs Act of the 1950s, penalizing first-time possession of marijuana with a sentence of two to five years in prison.[68] In the 1960s, though, when marijuana became associated with the white middle class and college kids, commissions were promptly created to study whether marijuana was really as harmful as once thought. By 1970, the Comprehensive Drug Abuse Prevention and Control Act differentiated marijuana from other narcotics and lowered federal penalties.[69] The same drug that had been considered fearsome twenty years earlier, when associated with African Americans and Latinos, was refashioned as a relatively harmless drug when associated with whites.

In view of the nation's treatment of predominately white drunk drivers and drug offenders, it is extremely difficult to imagine that our nation would have declared all-out war on drug offenders if the enemy had been defined in the public imagination as white. It was the conflation of blackness and crime in the media and political discourse that made the drug war and the sudden, massive expansion of our prison system possible. White drug "criminals" are collateral damage in the War on Drugs because they have been harmed by a war declared with blacks in mind. While this circumstance is horribly unfortunate for them, it does create important opportunities for a multiracial, bottom-up resistance movement, one in which people of all races can claim a clear stake. For the first time in our nation's history, it may become readily apparent to whites how they, too, can be harmed by anti-black racism—a fact that, until now, has been difficult for many to grasp.

Black support for "get tough" policies. Yet another notable difference between Jim Crow and mass incarceration is that many African Americans seem to support the current system of control, while most believe the same could not be said of Jim Crow. It is frequently argued in defense of mass incarceration that African Americans want more police and more prisons because crime is so bad in some ghetto communities. It is wrong, these defenders claim, for the tactics of mass incarceration—such as the concentration of law enforcement in poor communities of color, the stop-and-frisk programs that have proliferated nationwide, the eviction of drug offenders and their families from public housing, and the drug sweeps of ghetto neighborhoods—to be characterized as racially discriminatory, because those programs and policies have been adopted for the benefit of African American communities and are supported by many ghetto residents.[70] Ignoring rampant crime in ghetto communities would be racially discriminatory, they say; responding forcefully to it is not.

This argument, on the surface, seems relatively straightforward, but there are actually many layers to it, some of which are quite problematic. To begin with, the argument implies that African Americans prefer harsh criminal justice policies to other forms of governmental intervention, such as job creation, economic development, educational reform, and restorative justice programs, as the long-term solution to problems associated with crime. There is no evidence to support such a claim. To the contrary, surveys consistently show that African Americans are generally less supportive of harsh criminal justice policies than whites, even though blacks are far more likely to be victims of crime.[71] This pattern is particularly remarkable in that less educated people tend to be more punitive and blacks on average are less educated than whites.[72]

The notion that African Americans support "get tough" approaches to crime is further complicated by the fact that "crime" is not a generic category.

There are many different types of crime, and violent crime tends to provoke the most visceral and punitive response. Yet as we have seen in chapter 2, the drug war has not been aimed at rooting out the most violent drug traffickers, or so-called kingpins. The vast majority of those arrested for drug crimes are *not* charged with serious offenses, and most of the people in state prison on drug charges have no history of violence or significant selling activity. Those who are "kingpins" are often able to buy their freedom by forfeiting their assets, snitching on other dealers, or becoming paid government informants. Thus, to the extent that some African Americans support harsh policies aimed at violent offenders, they cannot be said to support the War on Drugs, which has been waged primarily against nonviolent, low-level offenders in poor communities of color.

The one thing that is clear from the survey data and ethnographic research is that African Americans in ghetto communities experience an intense "dual frustration" regarding crime and law enforcement. As Glenn Loury explained more than a decade ago, when violent crime rates were making headlines, "The young black men wreaking havoc in the ghetto are still 'our youngsters' in the eyes of many of the decent poor and working-class black people who sometimes are their victims."[73] Throughout the black community, there is widespread awareness that black ghetto youth have few, if any, realistic options, and therefore dealing drugs can be an irresistible temptation. Suburban white youth may deal drugs to their friends and acquaintances as a form of recreation and extra cash, but for ghetto youth, drug sales—though rarely lucrative—are often a means of survival, a means of helping to feed and clothe themselves and their families. The fact that this "career" path leads almost inevitably to jail is often understood as an unfortunate fact of life, part of what it means to be poor and black in America.

Women, in particular, express complicated, conflicted views about crime, because they love their sons, husbands, and partners and understand their plight as current and future members of the racial undercaste. At the same time, though, they abhor gangs and the violence associated with inner-city life. One commentator explained, "African American women in poor neighborhoods are torn. They worry about their young sons getting involved in gang activity. They worry about their sons possibly selling or using drugs. They worry about their children getting caught in the crossfire of warring gangs. . . . These mothers want better crime and law enforcement. Yet, they understand that increased levels of law enforcement potentially saddle their children with a felony conviction—a mark that can ensure economic and social marginalization."[74]

Given the dilemma facing poor black communities, it is inaccurate to say that black people "support" mass incarceration or "get tough" policies. The fact that some black people endorse harsh responses to crime is best understood as a form of *complicity* with mass incarceration—not support for it. This complicity is perfectly understandable, for the threat posed by crime—particularly violent crime—is real, not imagined. Although African Americans do not engage in drug crime at significantly higher rates than whites, black men do have much higher rates of violent crime, and violent crime is concentrated in ghetto communities. Studies have shown that joblessness—not race or black culture—explains the high rates of violent crime in poor black communities. When researchers have controlled for joblessness, differences in violent crime rates between young black and white men disappear.[75] Regardless, the reality for poor blacks trapped in ghettos remains the same: they must live in a state of perpetual insecurity and fear. It is perfectly understandable, then, that some African Americans would be complicit with the system of mass incarceration, even if they oppose, as a matter of social policy, the creation of racially isolated ghettos and the subsequent transfer of black youth from underfunded, crumbling schools to brand-new, high-tech prisons. In the era of mass incarceration, poor African Americans are not given the option of great schools, community investment, and job training. Instead, they are offered police and prisons. If the only choice that is offered blacks is rampant crime or more prisons, the predictable (and understandable) answer will be "more prisons."

The predicament African Americans find themselves in today is not altogether different from the situation they faced during Jim Crow. Jim Crow, as oppressive as it was, offered a measure of security for blacks who were willing to play by its rules. Those who flouted the rules or resisted them risked the terror of the Klan. Cooperation with the Jim Crow system often seemed far more likely to increase or maintain one's security than any alternative. That reality helps to explain why African American leaders such as Booker T. Washington urged blacks to focus on improving themselves rather than on challenging racial discrimination. It is also why the Civil Rights Movement initially met significant resistance among some African Americans in the

South. Civil rights advocates strenuously argued that it was the mentality and ideology that gave rise to Jim Crow that was the real source of the danger experienced by blacks. Of course they were right. But it is understandable why some blacks believed their immediate safety and security could best be protected by cooperation with the prevailing caste system. The fact that black people during Jim Crow were often complicit with the system of control did not mean they supported racial oppression.

Disagreements within the African American community about how best to respond to systems of control—and even disagreements about what is, and is not, discriminatory—have a long history. The notion that black people have always been united in opposition to American caste systems is sheer myth. Following slavery, for example, there were some African Americans who supported disenfranchisement because they believed that black people were not yet "ready" for the vote. Former slaves, it was argued, were too illiterate to exercise the vote responsibly, and were ill-prepared for the duties of public office. This sentiment could even be found among black politicians such as Isaiah T. Montgomery, who argued in 1890 that voting rights should be denied to black people because enfranchisement should only be extended to literate men. In the same vein, a fierce debate raged between Booker T. Washington and W.E.B. Du Bois about whether—and to what extent—racial bias and discrimination were responsible for the plight of the Negro and ought to be challenged. Du Bois praised and embraced Washington's emphasis on "thrift, patience, and industrial training for the masses," but sharply disagreed with his public acceptance of segregation, disenfranchisement, and legalized discrimination. In Du Bois's view, Washington's public statements arguing that poor education and bad choices were responsible for the plight of former slaves ignored the damage wrought by caste and threatened to rationalize the entire system. In Du Bois's words:

> [T]he distinct impression left by Mr. Washington's propaganda is, first, that the South is justified in its present attitude toward the Negro because of the Negro's degradation; second, that the prime cause of the Negro's failure to rise more quickly is his wrong education in the past; and, thirdly, that his future rise depends primarily on his own efforts. Each of these propositions is a dangerous half-truth. . . . [Washington's] doctrine has tended to make the whites, North and South, shift the

burden of the Negro problem to the Negro's shoulders and stand aside as critical and rather pessimistic spectators; when in fact the burden belongs to the nation, and the hands of none of us are clean if we bend not our energies to righting these great wrongs.[76]

Today, a similar debate rages in black communities about the underlying causes of mass incarceration. While some argue that it is attributable primarily to racial bias and discrimination, others maintain that it is due to poor education, unraveling morals, and a lack of thrift and perseverance among the urban poor. Just as former slaves were viewed (even among some African Americans) as unworthy of full citizenship due to their lack of education and good morals, today similar arguments can be heard from black people across the political spectrum who believe that reform efforts should be focused on moral uplift and education for ghetto dwellers, rather than challenging the system of mass incarceration itself.

Scholars, activists, and community members who argue that moral uplift and education provide the best solution to black criminality and the phenomenon of mass incarceration have been influenced by what Evelyn Brooks Higginbotham has called the "politics of respectability"—a politics that was born in the nineteenth century and matured in the Jim Crow era.[77] This political strategy is predicated on the notion that the goal of racial equality can only be obtained if black people are able to successfully prove to whites that they are worthy of equal treatment, dignity, and respect. Supporters of the politics of respectability believe that African Americans, if they hope to be accepted by whites, must conduct themselves in a fashion that elicits respect and sympathy rather than fear and anger from other races. They must demonstrate through words and deeds their ability to live by and aspire to the same moral codes as the white middle class, even while they are being discriminated against wrongly.[78] The basic theory underlying this strategy is that white Americans will abandon discriminatory practices if and when it becomes apparent that black people aren't inferior after all.

The politics of respectability made sense to many black reformers during the Jim Crow era, since African Americans had no vote, could not change policy, and lived under the constant threat of the Klan. Back then, the only thing black people could control was their own behavior. Many believed they simply had no choice, no realistic option, but to cooperate with the caste system while conducting themselves in a such a dignified and respectable manner that it would eventually become obvious to whites that their bigotry was misplaced.

This strategy worked to some extent for a segment of the African American community, particularly those who had access to education and relative privilege. But a much larger segment—those who were uneducated and desperately poor—found themselves unable, as one historian put it, "to conform to the gender roles, public behavior, and economic activity deemed legitimate by bourgeois America but which the forces of Jim Crow sought to prevent black people from achieving."[79] In many cases, the relatively privileged black elite turned against the black urban poor, condemning them and distancing themselves, while at the same time presenting themselves as legitimate spokespeople for the disadvantaged. It was a pattern that would repeat itself in cities throughout the United States, as black communities found themselves embroiled in deep conflict over goals and strategies pursued by the black elite. What happened in Atlanta in the wake of the New Deal is a case in point.

During Jim Crow, all black people in Atlanta were bound together by the racial caste system, but there was a significant group of African Americans who were well educated and had influence in the halls of power. Numerous black colleges were located in Atlanta, and the city was home to the South's largest population of college-educated African Americans. Members of this relatively elite group believed they could prove their respectability to white Americans and often blamed less educated blacks for sabotaging their quest for racial equality, especially when they committed crimes or failed to conform to white, middle-class norms of dress, cleanliness, and behavior. In the view of these black elites, a "poverty complex" plagued the black poor, one that made them politically apathetic and content with broken-down, overcrowded, and dirty living conditions.[80] For decades, black elites engaged in private rescue efforts to make black communities tidy, clean, and respectable in a futile effort to gain white approval.[81]

Eventually, these rescue efforts gave way to black endorsement of harmful policies aimed at the urban poor. In the 1930s and early 1940s, President Franklin D. Roosevelt began to roll out the New Deal—a massive public works and investment program designed to lift the nation out of a severe depression. Almost immediately, black elites recognized the opportunity for the individual and collective advancement of Negroes who could present themselves favorably to whites. Some black Atlantans were brought from the margins into the sphere of opportunity by New Deal programs, but most were left behind. As historian Karen Ferguson observes, "when [black reformers] had the opportunity to determine the recipients of New Deal largesse, they did not choose the 'mudsills' of the black working class but rather the more prosperous elements who were more able to be respectable according to the reformers' vision."[82] Far from prioritizing the needs of the least advantaged, many black reformers began aggressively pursuing policy reforms that would benefit the black elite to the detriment of the poorest segments of the black community. Some of the most discriminatory federal programs of the New Deal era, including the slum-clearance program, received strong support from African American bureaucrats and reformers who presented themselves as speaking for the black community as a whole.[83]

Although many poor African Americans rejected the philosophies, tactics, and strategies of the black elite, ultimately moral uplift ideology became the new common sense. Not just in Atlanta but in cities nationwide, the tensions and debates between black reformers struggling to improve and uplift the "slum dwellers" and those committed to challenging discrimination and Jim Crow directly played out over and over again. Black elites found they had much to gain by positioning themselves as "race managers," and many poor African Americans became persuaded that perhaps their degraded status was, after all, their own fault.

Given this history, it should come as no surprise that today some black mayors, politicians, and lobbyists—as well as preachers, teachers, barbers, and ordinary folk—endorse "get tough" tactics and spend more time chastising the urban poor for their behavior than seeking meaningful policy solutions to the appalling conditions in which they are forced to live and raise their children. The fact that many African Americans endorse aspects of the current caste system and insist that the problems of the urban poor can be best explained by their behavior, culture, and attitude does not, in any meaningful way, distinguish mass incarceration from its predecessors. To the contrary, these attitudes and arguments have their roots in the struggles to end slavery and Jim Crow. Many African Americans today believe that uplift ideology worked in the past and ought to work again—forgetting that ultimately it took a major movement to end the last caste system, not simply good behavior. Many black people are confused—and the black community itself is divided—about how best to understand and respond to mass incarceration. A seemingly colorblind system has emerged that locks millions of African Americans into a permanent undercaste, and it appears that those who are trapped within it could have avoided it simply by not committing crimes. Isn't the answer not to challenge the system but to try to avoid it? Shouldn't the focus be on improving ourselves, rather than challenging a biased system? Familiar questions are asked decades after the end of the old Jim Crow.

Once again, complicity with the prevailing system of control may seem like the only option. Parents and schoolteachers counsel black children that, if they ever hope to escape this system and avoid prison time, they must be on their best behavior, raise their arms and spread their legs for the police without complaint, stay in failing schools, pull up their pants, and refuse all forms of illegal work and moneymaking activity, even if jobs in the legal economy are impossible to find. Girls are told not to have children until they are married to a "good" black man who can help provide for a family with a legal job. They are told to wait and wait for Mr. Right even if that means, in a jobless ghetto, never having children at all.

When black youth find it difficult or impossible to live up to these standards—or when they fail, stumble, and make mistakes, as all humans do—shame and blame is heaped upon them. If only they had made different choices, they're told sternly, they wouldn't be sitting in a jail cell; they'd be graduating from college. Never mind that white children on the other side of town who made precisely the same choices—often for less compelling reasons—are in fact going to college.

The genius of the current caste system, and what most distinguishes it from its predecessors, is that it appears voluntary. People choose to commit crimes, and that's why they are locked up or locked out, we are told. This feature makes the politics of responsibility particularly tempting, as it appears the system can be avoided with good behavior. But herein lies the trap. All people make mistakes. All of us are sinners. All of us are criminals. All of us violate the law at some point in our lives. In fact, if the worst thing you have ever done is speed ten miles over the speed limit on the freeway, you have put yourself and others at more risk of harm than someone smoking marijuana in the privacy of his or her living room. Yet there are people in the United States serving life sentences for first-time drug offenses, something virtually unheard of anywhere else in the world.

The notion that a vast gulf exists between "criminals" and those of us who have never served time in prison is a fiction created by the racial ideology that birthed mass incarceration, namely that there is something fundamentally wrong and morally inferior about "them." The reality, though, is that all of us have done wrong. As noted earlier, studies suggest that most Americans violate drug laws in their lifetime. Indeed, most of us break the law not once but repeatedly throughout our lives. Yet only some of us will be arrested, charged, convicted of a crime, branded a criminal or felon, and ushered into a permanent undercaste. Who becomes a social pariah and excommunicated from civil society and who trots off to college bears scant relationship to the morality of crimes committed. Who is more blameworthy: the young black kid who hustles on the street corner, selling weed to help his momma pay the rent? Or the college kid who deals drugs out of his dorm room so that he'll have cash to finance his spring break? Who should we fear? The kid in the 'hood who joined a gang and now carries a gun for security, because his neighborhood is frightening and unsafe? Or the suburban high school student who has a drinking problem but keeps getting behind the wheel? Our racially biased system of mass incarceration exploits the fact that all people break the law and make mistakes at various points in their lives and with varying degrees of justification. Screwing up— failing to live by one's highest ideals and values—is part of what makes us human.

Urging the urban poor—or anyone—to live up to their highest ideals and values is a good thing, as it demonstrates confidence in the ability of all people to stretch, grow, and evolve. Even in the most dire circumstances, we all have power and agency, the ability to choose what we think and how we respond to the circumstances of our lives. Moreover, we all have duties and responsibilities to each other, not the least of which is to do no harm. We ought never excuse violence or tolerate behavior that jeopardizes the safety and security of others. Just as all people—no matter who they are or what they have done—ought to be regarded as having basic human rights to work, housing, education, and food, residents of all communities have a basic human right to safety and security. The intuition underlying moral-uplift strategies is fundamentally sound: our communities will never thrive if we fail to respect ourselves and one another.

As a liberation strategy, however, the politics of responsibility is doomed to fail—not because there is something especially wrong with those locked in ghettos or prisons today, but because there is nothing special about them. They are merely human. They will continue to make mistakes and break the law for reasons that may or may not be justified; and as long as they do so, this system of mass incarceration will continue to function well. Generations of black men will continue to be lost—rounded up for crimes that go ignored on the other side of town and ushered into a permanent second-class status. It may seem at first blush that cooperating with the system while urging good behavior is the only option available, but in reality it is not a liberation strategy at all.

Fork in the Road

Du Bois got it right a century ago: "the burden belongs to the nation, and the hands of none of us are clean if we bend not our energies to righting these great wrongs." The reality is that, just a few decades after the collapse of one caste system, we constructed another. Our nation declared a war on people trapped in racially segregated ghettos   just at the moment their economics had collapsed—rather than providing community investment, quality education, and job training when work disappeared. Of course those communities are suffering from serious crime and dysfunction today. Did we expect otherwise? Did we think that, miraculously, they would thrive? And now, having waged this war for decades, we claim some blacks "support" mass incarceration, as though they would rather have their young men warehoused in prison than going off to college. As political theorist Tommie Shelby has observed, "Individuals are forced to make choices in an environment they did not choose. They would surely prefer to have a broader array of good opportunities. The question we should be asking—not instead of but in addition to questions about penal policy—is whether the denizens of the ghetto are entitled to a better set of options, and if so, whose responsibility it is to provide them."[84]

Clearly a much better set of options could be provided to African Americans—and poor people of all colors—today. As historian Lerone Bennett Jr. eloquently reminds us, "a nation is a choice." We could choose to be a nation that extends care, compassion, and concern to those who are locked up and locked out or headed for prison before they are old enough to vote. We could seek for them the same opportunities we seek for our own children; we could treat them like one of "us." We could do that. Or we can choose to be a nation that shames and blames its most vulnerable, affixes badges of dishonor upon them at young ages, and then relegates them to a permanent second-class status for life. That is the path we have chosen, and it leads to a familiar place.

We faced a fork in the road one decade after Martin Luther King Jr. and Malcolm X were laid to rest. As described in chapter 1, during the late 1970s, jobs had suddenly disappeared from urban areas across America, and unemployment rates had skyrocketed. In 1954, black and white youth unemployment rates in America were equal, with blacks actually having a slightly higher rate of employment in the age group sixteen to nineteen. By 1984, however, the black unemployment rate had nearly quadrupled, while the white rate had increased only marginally.[85] This was *not* due to a major change in black values, behavior, or culture; this dramatic shift was the result of deindustrialization, globalization, and technological advancement. Urban factories shut down as our nation transitioned to a service economy. Suddenly African Americans were trapped in jobless ghettos, desperate for work.

The economic collapse of inner-city black communities could have inspired a national outpouring of compassion and support. A new War on Poverty could have been launched. Economic stimulus packages could have sailed through Congress to bail out those trapped in jobless ghettos through no fault of their own. Education, job training, public transportation, and relocation assistance could have been provided, so that youth of color would have been able to survive the rough transition to a new global economy and secure jobs in distant suburbs. Constructive interventions would have been good not only for African Americans trapped in ghettos, but also for blue-collar workers of all colors, many of whom were suffering too, if less severely. A wave of compassion and concern could have flooded poor and working-class communities, in honor of the late Martin Luther King Jr. All of this could have happened, but it didn't. Instead we declared a War on Drugs.

The collapse of inner-city economies coincided with the conservative backlash against the Civil Rights Movement, resulting in the perfect storm.

Almost overnight, black men found themselves unnecessary to the American economy and demonized by mainstream society. No longer needed to pick cotton in the fields or labor in factories, lower-class black men were hauled off to prison in droves. They were vilified in the media and condemned for their condition as part of a well-orchestrated political campaign to build a new white, Republican majority in the South. Decades later, curious onlookers in the grips of denial would wonder aloud, "Where have all the black men gone?"

No one has made this point better than sociologist Loïc Wacquant. Wacquant has written extensively about the cyclical nature of racial caste in America. He emphasizes that the one thing that makes the current penal apparatus strikingly different from previous racial caste systems is that "it does not carry out the positive economic mission of recruitment and disciplining of the workforce."[86] Instead it serves only to warehouse poor black and brown people for increasingly lengthy periods of time, often until old age. The new system does not seek primarily to benefit unfairly from black labor, as earlier caste systems have, but instead views African Americans as largely irrelevant and unnecessary to the newly structured economy—an economy that is no longer driven by unskilled labor.

It is fair to say that we have witnessed an evolution in the United States from a racial caste system based entirely on exploitation (slavery), to one based largely on subordination (Jim Crow), to one defined by marginalization (mass incarceration). While marginalization may sound far preferable to exploitation, it may prove to be even more dangerous. Extreme marginalization, as we have seen throughout world history, poses the risk of extermination. Tragedies such as the Holocaust in Germany or ethnic cleansing in Bosnia are traceable to the extreme marginalization and stigmatization of racial and ethnic groups. As legal scholar john a. powell once commented, only half in jest, "It's actually better to be exploited than marginalized, in some respects, because if you're exploited presumably you're still needed."[87]

Viewed in this light, the frantic accusations of genocide by poor blacks in the early years of the War on Drugs seem less paranoid. The intuition of those residing in ghetto communities that they had suddenly become disposable was rooted in real changes in the economy—changes that have been devastating to poor black communities as factories have closed, low-skill jobs have disappeared, and all those who had the means to flee the ghetto did. The sense among those left behind that society no longer has use for them, and that the government now aims simply to get rid of them, reflects a reality that many of us who claim to care prefer to avoid simply by changing channels.

6

The Fire This Time

Shortly after sunrise on September 20, 2007, more than ten thousand protestors had already descended on Jena, Louisiana, a small town of about three thousand people. Because of the congestion on the roads to Jena, some protestors left their vehicles and walked into town on foot. Jesse Jackson, Al Sharpton, and Martin Luther King III were among those who traveled hundreds of miles to participate in what was heralded as "the beginnings of a new civil rights movement."[1]

Black youth turned out to protest in record numbers, joined by rappers Mos Def, Ice Cube, and Salt-n-Pepa. National news media swarmed the town; cameras rolled as thousands of protestors from all over the country poured into the rural community to condemn the attempted murder charges filed against six black teenagers who allegedly beat a white classmate at a local high school.

This was no ordinary schoolyard fight. Many believed the attack was related to a string of racially charged conflicts and controversies at the school, most notably the hanging of nooses from a tree in the school's main courtyard. Rev. Al Sharpton captured the spirit of the protest when he stated boldly, "We've gone from plantations to penitentiaries. . . . They have tried to create a criminal justice system that particularly targets our young black men. And now we sit and stand in a city that says it's a prank to hang a hangman's noose, but that it is attempted murder to have a fight. We cannot sit by silently. That's why we came, and that's why we intend to keep coming."[2]

For a moment, the nation's eyes were trained on the plight of the "Jena 6," and debates could be heard in barber shops, in cafés, and in lines at grocery stores about whether the criminal justice system was, in fact, biased against black men or whether the black teens got exactly what they deserved for a brutal attack on a defenseless young white teen. Grim statistics about the number of black men in prison were trotted out, and commentators argued over whether those numbers reflected crime rates or bias and whether white teens would ever be charged with attempted murder and tried as adults if they attacked a black kid in a schoolyard fight.

The uprising on behalf of the six black teens paid off. Although the prosecutor refused to back down from his decision to bring adult charges against the youths, an appellate court ultimately ruled the teens had to be tried as juveniles, and many of the charges were reduced or dropped. While this result undoubtedly cheered the thousands of Jena 6 supporters around the country, the spectacle may have been oddly unsettling to parents of children imprisoned for far less serious crimes, including those locked up for minor drug offenses. Where were the protestors and civil rights leaders when their children were tried as adults and carted off to adult prisons? Where was the national news media then? Their children were accused of no crimes of violence, no acts of cruelty, yet they faced adult criminal charges and the prospect of serving years, perhaps decades, behind bars for possessing or selling illegal drugs—crimes that go largely ignored when committed by white youth. Why the outpouring of support and the promises of a "new civil rights movement" on behalf of the Jena youth but not their children?

If there had been no nooses hanging from a schoolyard tree, there would have been no Jena 6—no mass protests, no live coverage on CNN. The decision to charge six black teens as adults with attempted murder in connection with a schoolyard fight was understood as possibly racist by the mainstream media and some protestors only because of the sensational fact that nooses were first hung from a tree. It was this relic—the noose—showing up so brazenly and leading to a series of racially charged conflicts and controversies that made it possible for the news media and the country as a whole to entertain the possibility that these six youths may well have been treated to Jim Crow justice. It was this evidence of old-fashioned racism that made it possible for a new generation of protestors to frame the attempted murder charges against six black teens in a manner that mainstream America would understand as racist.

Ironically, it was precisely this framing that ensured that the events in Jena would *not* actually launch a "new civil rights movement." A new civil rights movement cannot be organized around the relics of the earlier system of control if it is to address meaningfully the racial realities of our time. Any racial justice movement, to be successful, must vigorously challenge the public consensus that underlies the *prevailing* system of control. Nooses, racial slurs, and overt bigotry are widely condemned by people across the political spectrum; they are understood to be remnants of the past, no longer reflective of the prevailing public consensus about race. Challenging these forms of racism is certainly necessary, as we must always remain vigilant, but it will do little to shake the foundations of the current system of control. The new caste system, unlike its predecessors, is officially colorblind. We must deal with it on its own terms.

Rethinking Denial—Or, Where Are Civil Rights Advocates When You Need Them?

Dealing with this system on its own terms is complicated by the problem of denial. Few Americans today recognize mass incarceration for what it is: a new caste system thinly veiled by the cloak of colorblindness. Hundreds of thousands of people of color are swept into this system and released every year, yet we rationalize the systematic discrimination and exclusion and turn a blind eye to the suffering. Our collective denial is not merely an inconvenient fact; it is a major stumbling block to public understanding of the role of race in our society, and it sharply limits the opportunities for truly transformative collective action.

The general public's collective denial is fairly easy to forgive—if not excuse—for all the reasons discussed in chapter 5. The awkward silence of the civil rights community, however, is more problematic. If something akin to a racial caste system truly exists, why has the civil rights community been so slow to acknowledge it? Indeed, how could civil rights organizations, some of which are larger and better funded than at any point in American history, have allowed this human rights nightmare to occur on their watch?

The answer is not that civil rights advocates are indifferent to racial bias in the criminal justice system. To the contrary, we care quite a lot. Nor have we been entirely ignorant of the realities of the new caste system. In recent years, civil rights advocates have launched important reform efforts, most notably the campaigns challenging felon disenfranchisement laws, crack-sentencing policies, and racial profiling by law enforcement. Civil rights groups have also developed litigation and important coalitions related to the school-to-prison pipeline, inadequate indigent defense, and juvenile justice reform, to name a few.

Despite these important efforts, what is most striking about the civil rights community's response to the mass incarceration of people of color is the relative quiet. Given the magnitude—the sheer scale—of the New Jim Crow, one would expect that the War on Drugs would be the top priority of every civil rights organization in the country. Conferences, strategy sessions, and debates regarding how best to build a movement to dismantle the new caste system would be occurring on a regular basis. Major grassroots organizing efforts would be under way in nearly every state and city nationwide. Foundations would be lobbied to prioritize criminal justice reform. Media campaigns would be unleashed in an effort to overturn the punitive public consensus on race. The rhetoric associated with specific reform efforts would stress the need to end mass incarceration, not merely tinker with it, and efforts would be made to build multiracial coalitions based on the understanding that the racial politics that gave birth to the War on Drugs have harmed poor and working-class whites as well as people of color. All of that could have happened, but it didn't. Why not?

Part of the answer is that civil rights organizations—like all institutions—are comprised of fallible human beings. The prevailing public consensus affects everyone, including civil rights advocates. Those of us in the civil rights community are not immune to the racial stereotypes that pervade media imagery and political rhetoric; nor do we operate outside of the political context. Like most people, we tend to resist believing that we might be part of the problem.

One day, civil rights organizations may be embarrassed by how long it took them to move out of denial and do the hard work necessary to end mass incarceration. Rather than blaming civil rights groups, however, it is far more productive to understand the reasons why the response to mass incarceration has been so constrained. Again, it's not that civil rights advocates don't care; we do. And it's not just that we are afflicted by unconscious racial bias and stereotypes about those behind bars. Civil rights organizations have reasons for their constraint—reasons that no longer make good sense, even if they once did.

A bit of civil rights history may be helpful here. Civil rights advocacy has not always looked the way it does today. Throughout most of our nation's history—from the days of the abolitionist movement through the Civil Rights Movement—racial justice advocacy has generally revolved around grassroots organizing and the strategic mobilization of public opinion. In recent years, however, a bit of mythology has sprung up regarding the centrality of litigation to racial justice struggles. The success of the brilliant legal crusade that led to *Brown v. Board of Education* has created a widespread perception that civil rights lawyers are the most important players in racial justice advocacy. This image was enhanced following the passage of the Civil Rights Acts of 1965, when civil rights lawyers became embroiled in highly visible and controversial efforts to end hiring discrimination, create affirmative action plans, and enforce school desegregation orders. As public attention shifted from the streets to the courtroom, the extraordinary grassroots movement that made civil rights legislation possible faded from public view. The lawyers took over.

With all deliberate speed, civil rights organizations became "professionalized" and increasingly disconnected from the communities they claimed to represent. Legal scholar and former NAACP Legal Defense Fund lawyer Derrick Bell was among the first to critique this phenomenon, arguing in a 1976 *Yale Law Journal* article that civil rights lawyers were pursuing their own agendas in school desegregation cases even when they conflicted with their clients' expressed desires.[3] Two decades later, former NAACP Legal Defense Fund lawyer and current Harvard Law School professor Lani Guinier published a memoir in which she acknowledged that, "by the early 1990s, [civil rights] litigators like me had become like the Washington insiders we were so suspicious of. . . . We reflexively distanced ourselves from the very people on whose behalf we brought the cases in the first place."[4] This shift, she noted, had profound consequences for the future of racial justice advocacy; in fact, it was debilitating to the movement. Instead of a moral crusade, the movement became an almost purely legal crusade. Civil rights advocates pursued their own agendas as unelected representatives of communities defined by race and displayed considerable skill navigating courtrooms and halls of power across America. The law became what the lawyers and lobbyists said it was, with little or no input from the people whose fate hung in the balance. Guinier continued:

> In charge, we channeled a passion for change into legal negotiations and lawsuits. We defined the issues in terms of developing legal doctrine and establishing legal precedent; our clients became important, but secondary, players in a formal arena that required lawyers to translate lay claims into technical speech. We then disembodied plaintiffs' claims in judicially manageable or judicially enforceable terms, unenforceable without more lawyers. Simultaneously, the movement's center of gravity shifted to Washington, D.C. As lawyers and national pundits became more prominent than clients and citizens, we isolated ourselves from the people who were our anchor and on whose behalf we had labored. We not only left people behind; we also lost touch with the moral force at the heart of the movement itself.[5]

Not surprisingly, as civil rights advocates converted a grassroots movement into a legal campaign, and as civil rights leaders became political insiders, many civil rights organizations became top-heavy with lawyers. This development enhanced their ability to wage legal battles but impeded their ability to acknowledge or respond to the emergence of a new caste system. Lawyers have a tendency to identify and concentrate on problems they know how to solve—i.e., problems that can be solved through litigation. The mass incarceration of people of color is not that kind of problem.

Widespread preoccupation with litigation, however, is not the only—or even the main—reason civil rights groups have shied away from challenging the new caste system. Challenging mass incarceration requires something civil rights advocates have long been reluctant to do: advocacy on behalf of criminals. Even at the height of Jim Crow segregation—when black men were more likely to be lynched than to receive a fair trial in the South—NAACP lawyers were reluctant to advocate on behalf of blacks accused of crimes unless the lawyers were convinced of the men's innocence.[6] The major exception was anti–death penalty advocacy. Over the years, civil rights lawyers have made heroic efforts to save the lives of condemned criminals. But outside of the death penalty arena, civil rights advocates have long been reluctant to leap to the defense of accused criminals. The "politics of respectability" has influenced civil rights litigation and advocacy, leading even the most powerful civil rights organizations to distance themselves from the most stigmatized elements of the community, especially lawbreakers. Advocates have found they are most successful when they draw attention to certain types of black people (those who are easily understood by mainstream whites as "good" and "respectable") and tell certain types of stories about them. Since the days when abolitionists struggled to eradicate slavery, racial justice advocates have gone to great lengths to identify black people who defy racial stereotypes, and they have exercised considerable message discipline, telling only those stories of racial injustice that will evoke sympathy among whites.

A prime example is the Rosa Parks story. Rosa Parks was not the first person to refuse to give up her seat on a segregated bus in Montgomery, Alabama. Civil rights advocates considered and rejected two other black women as plaintiffs when planning a test case challenging segregation practices: Claudette Colvin and Mary Louise Smith. Both of them were arrested for refusing to give up their seats on Montgomery's segregated buses, just months before Rosa Parks refused to budge. Colvin was fifteen years old when she defied segregation laws. Her case attracted national attention, but civil rights advocates declined to use her as a plaintiff because she got pregnant by an older man shortly after her arrest. Advocates worried that her "immoral" conduct would detract from or undermine their efforts to show that blacks were entitled to (and worthy of) equal treatment. Likewise, they decided not to use Mary Louise Smith as a plaintiff because her father was rumored to be an alcoholic. It was understood that, in any effort to challenge racial discrimination, the litigant—and even the litigant's family—had to be above reproach and free from every negative trait that could be used as a justification for unequal treatment.

Rosa Parks, in this regard, was a dream come true. She was, in the words of Jo Ann Gibson Robinson (another key figure in the Montgomery Bus Boycott), a "medium-sized, cultured mulatto woman; a civic and religious worker; quiet, unassuming, and pleasant in manner and appearance; dignified and reserved; of high morals and strong character."[7] No one doubted that Parks was the perfect symbol for the movement to integrate public transportation in Montgomery. Martin Luther King Jr. recalled in his memoir that "Mrs. Parks was ideal for the role assigned to her by history," largely because "her character was impeccable" and she was "one of the most respected people in the Negro community."[8]

The time-tested strategy of using those who epitomize moral virtue as symbols in racial justice campaigns is far more difficult to employ in efforts to reform the criminal justice system. Most people who are caught up in the criminal justice system have less than flawless backgrounds. While many black people get stopped and searched for crimes they did not commit, it is not so easy these days to find young black men in urban areas who have never been convicted of a crime. The new caste system labels black and brown men as criminals early, often in their teens, making them "damaged goods" from the perspective of traditional civil rights advocates. With criminal records, the majority of young black men in urban areas are not seen as attractive plaintiffs for civil rights litigation or good "poster boys" for media advocacy.

The widespread aversion to advocacy on behalf of those labeled criminals reflects a certain political reality. Many would argue that expending scarce resources on criminal justice reform is a strategic mistake. After all, criminals are the one social group in America that nearly everyone—across political, racial, and class boundaries—feels free to hate. Why champion the cause of the despised when there are so many sympathetic stories about racial injustice one could tell? Why draw public attention to the "worst" of the black community, those labeled criminals? Shouldn't we direct scarce resources to battles that are more easily won, such as affirmative action? Shouldn't we focus the public's attention on the so-called root causes of mass incarceration, such as educational inequity?

We can continue along this road—it is a road well travelled—but we must admit the strategy has not made much of a difference. African Americans, as a group, are no better off than they were in 1968 in many respects.[9] In fact, to some extent, they are worse off. When the incarcerated population is counted in unemployment and poverty rates, the best of times for the rest of America have been among the worst of times for African Americans, particularly black men. As sociologist Bruce Western has shown, the notion that the 1990s—the Clinton years—were good times for African Americans, and that "a rising tide lifts all boats," is pure fiction. As unemployment rates sank to historically low levels in the late 1990s for the general population, jobless rates among noncollege black men in their twenties rose to their highest levels ever, propelled by skyrocketing incarceration rates.[10]

One reason so many people have a false impression of the economic well-being of African Americans, as a group, is that poverty and unemployment statistics do not include people who are behind bars. Prisoners are literally erased from the nation's economic picture, leading standard estimates to underestimate the true jobless rate by as much as 24 percentage points for less-educated black men.[11] Young African American men were the only group to experience a steep *increase* in joblessness between 1980 and 2000, a development directly traceable to the increase in the penal population. During the much heralded economic boom of the 1990s, the true jobless rate among noncollege black men was a staggering 42 percent (65 percent among black male dropouts).[12]

Despite these inconvenient truths, though, we can press on. We can continue to ignore those labeled criminals in our litigation and media advocacy and focus public attention on more attractive plaintiffs—like innocent doctors and lawyers stopped and searched on freeways, innocent black and brown schoolchildren attending abysmal schools, or innocent middle- and upper-middle-class black children who will be denied access to Harvard, Michigan, and Yale if affirmative action disappears. We can continue on this well-worn path. But if we do so, we should labor under no illusions that we will end mass incarceration or shake the foundations of the current racial order. We may improve some school districts, prolong affirmative action for another decade or two, or force some police departments to condemn racial profiling, but we will not put a dent in the prevailing caste system. We must face the realities of the new caste system and embrace those who are most oppressed by it if we hope to end the new Jim Crow.

That said, no effort is made here to describe, in any detail, what should or should not be done in the months and years ahead to challenge the new caste system. Such an undertaking is beyond the scope of this book. The aim of this chapter is simply to reflect on whether traditional approaches to racial justice advocacy are adequate to the task at hand. What follows is not a plan, but several questions and claims offered for serious consideration by those committed to racial justice and interested in dismantling mass incarceration. They are offered as conversation starters—food for thought, debate, and—I hope—collective action. Each is a challenge to conventional wisdom or traditional strategies. Far more should be said about each point made, but, as indicated, this is meant to be the beginning of a conversation, not an end.

Tinkering Is for Mechanics, Not Racial-Justice Advocates

The first and arguably most important point is that criminal justice reform efforts—standing alone—are futile. Gains can be made, yes, but the new caste system will not be overthrown by isolated victories in legislatures or courtrooms. If you doubt this is the case, consider the sheer scale of mass incarceration. If we hope to return to the rate of incarceration of the 1970s— a time when many civil rights activists believed rates of imprisonment were egregiously high—*we would need to release approximately four out of five people currently behind bars today.*[13] Prisons would have to be closed across America, an event that would likely inspire panic in rural communities that have become dependent on prisons for jobs and economic growth. Hundreds of thousands of people—many of them unionized—would lose their jobs. As Marc Mauer has observed, "The more than 700,000 prison and jail guards, administrators, service workers, and other personnel represent a potentially powerful political opposition to any scaling-down of the system. One need only recall the fierce opposition to the closing of military bases in recent years to see how these forces will function over time."[14]

Arguably, Mauer underestimates the scope of the challenge by focusing narrowly on the prison system, rather than counting all of the people employed in the criminal justice bureaucracy. According to a report released by the U.S. Department of Justice's Bureau of Statistics in 2006, the U.S. spent a record $185 billion for police protection, detention, judicial, and legal activities in 2003. Adjusting for inflation, these figures reflect a tripling of justice expenditures since 1982. The justice system employed almost 2.4 million people in 2003—58 percent of them at the local level and 31 percent at the state level. If four out of five people were released from prisons, far more than a million people could lose their jobs.

There is also the private-sector investment to consider. Prisons are big business and have become deeply entrenched in America's economic and political system. Rich and powerful people, including former vice president Dick Cheney, have invested millions in private prisons.[15] They are deeply interested in expanding the market—increasing the supply of prisoners— not eliminating the pool of people who can be held captive for a profit. The 2005 annual report for the Corrections Corporation of America explained the vested interests of private prisons matter-of-factly in a filing with the Securities and Exchange Commission:

Our growth is generally dependent upon our ability to obtain new contracts to develop and manage new correctional and detention facilities. This possible growth depends on a number of factors we cannot control, including crime rates and sentencing patterns in various jurisdictions and acceptance of privatization. The demand for our facilities and services could be adversely affected by the relaxation of enforcement efforts, leniency in conviction and sentencing practices or through the decriminalization of certain activities that are currently proscribed by our criminal laws. For instance, any changes with respect to drugs and controlled substances or illegal immigration could affect the number of persons arrested, convicted and sentenced, thereby potentially reducing demand for correctional facilities to house them.[16]

American Correctional Association President Gwendolyn Chunn put the matter more bluntly that same year when lamenting that the unprecedented prison expansion boom of the 1990s seemed to be leveling off. "We'll have a hard time holding on to what we have now," she lamented.[17] As it turns out, her fears were unfounded. Although prison growth appeared to be slowing in 2005, the market for prisoners has continued to expand. The nation's prison population broke new records in 2008, with no end in sight. The nonprofit PEW Charitable Trusts reports that inmate populations in at least ten states are expected to increase by 25 percent or more between 2006 and 2011. In short, the market for private prisons is as good as it has ever been. Damon Hininger, the president and chief operations officer of Corrections Corporation of America, the largest private-prison operator in the United States, is thoroughly optimistic. His company boosted net income by 14 percent in 2008, and he fully expects the growth to continue. "There is going to be a larger opportunity for us in the future," he said.[18]

   Even beyond private prison companies, a whole range of prison profiteers must be reckoned with if mass incarceration is to be undone, including phone companies that gouge families of prisoners by charging them exorbitant rates to communicate with their loved ones; gun manufacturers that sell Taser guns, rifles, and pistols to prison guards and police; private health care providers contracted by the state to provide (typically abysmal) health care to prisoners; the U.S. military, which relies on prison labor to provide military gear to soldiers in Iraq; corporations that use prison labor to avoid paying decent wages; and the politicians, lawyers, and bankers who structure deals to build new prisons often in predominately white rural communities—deals that often promise far more to local communities than they deliver.[19] All of these corporate and political interests have a stake in the expansion—not the elimination—of the system of mass incarceration.

Consider also the lengthy to-do list for reformers. If we become serious about dismantling the system of mass incarceration, we must end the War on Drugs. There is no way around it. The drug war is largely responsible for the prison boom and the creation of the new undercaste, and there is no path to liberation for communities of color that includes this ongoing war. So long as people of color in ghetto communities are being rounded up by the thousands for drug offenses, carted off to prisons, and then released into a permanent undercaste, mass incarceration as a system of control will continue to function well.

Ending the drug war is no simple task, however. It cannot be accomplished through a landmark court decision, an executive order, or single stroke of the presidential pen. Since 1982, the war has raged like a forest fire set with a few matches and a gallon of gasoline. What began as an audacious federal program, has spread to every state in the nation and nearly every city. It has infected law enforcement activities on roads, sidewalks, highways, train stations, airports, and the nation's border. The war has effectively shredded portions of the U.S. Constitution—eliminating Fourth Amendment protections once deemed inviolate—and it has militarized policing practices in inner cities across America. Racially targeted drug-law enforcement practices taken together with laws that specifically discriminate against drug offenders in employment, housing, and public benefits have relegated the majority of black men in urban areas across the United States to a permanent second-class status.

If we hope to end this system of control, we cannot be satisfied with a handful of reforms. All of the financial incentives granted to law enforcement to arrest poor black and brown people for drug offenses must be revoked. Federal grant money for drug enforcement must end; drug forfeiture laws must be stripped from the books; racial profiling must be eradicated; the concentration of drug busts in poor communities of color must cease;

and the transfer of military equipment and aid to local law enforcement agencies waging the drug war must come to a screeching halt. And that's just for starters.

Equally important, there must be a change within the culture of law enforcement. Black and brown people in ghetto communities must no longer be viewed as the designated enemy, and ghetto communities must no longer be treated like occupied zones. Law enforcement must adopt a compassionate, humane approach to the problems of the urban poor—an approach that goes beyond the rhetoric of "community policing" to a method of engagement that promotes trust, healing, and genuine partnership. Data collection for police and prosecutors should be mandated nationwide to ensure that selective enforcement is no longer taking place. Racial impact statements that assess the racial and ethnic impact of criminal justice legislation must be adopted.[20] Public defender offices should be funded at the same level as prosecutor's offices to eliminate the unfair advantage afforded the incarceration machine. The list goes on: Mandatory drug sentencing laws must be rescinded. Marijuana ought to be legalized (and perhaps other drugs as well). Meaningful re-entry programs must be adopted—programs that provide a pathway not just to dead-end, minimum-wage jobs, but also training and education so those labeled criminals can realistically reach for high-paying jobs and viable, rewarding career paths. Prison workers should be retrained for jobs and careers that do not involve caging human beings. Drug treatment on demand must be provided for all Americans, a far better investment of taxpayer money than prison cells for drug offenders. Barriers to re-entry, specifically the myriad laws that operate to discriminate against drug offenders for the rest of their lives in every aspect of their social, economic, and political life, must be eliminated.

The list could go on, of course, but the point has been made. The central question for racial justice advocates is this: are we serious about ending this system of control, or not? If we are, there is a tremendous amount of work to be done. The notion that all of these reforms can be accomplished piecemeal—one at a time, through disconnected advocacy strategies—seems deeply misguided. All of the needed reforms have less to do with failed policies than a deeply flawed public consensus, one that is indifferent, at best, to the experience of poor people of color. As Martin Luther King Jr. explained back in 1965, when describing why it was far more important to engage in mass mobilizations than file lawsuits, "We're trying to win the right to vote and we have to focus the attention of the world on that. We can't do that making legal cases. We have to make the case in the court of public opinion."[21] King certainly appreciated the contributions of civil rights lawyers (he relied on them to get him out of jail), but he opposed the tendency of civil rights lawyers to identify a handful of individuals who could make great plaintiffs in a court of law, then file isolated cases. He believed what was necessary was to mobilize thousands to make their case in the court of public opinion. In his view, it was a flawed public consensus—not merely flawed policy—that was at the root of racial oppression.

Today, no less than fifty years ago, a flawed public consensus lies at the core of the prevailing caste system. When people think about crime, especially drug crime, they do not think about suburban housewives violating laws regulating prescription drugs or white frat boys using ecstasy. Drug crime in this country is understood to be black and brown, and it is *because* drug crime is racially defined in the public consciousness that the electorate has not cared much what happens to drug criminals—at least not the way they would have cared if the criminals were understood to be white. It is this failure to care, really care across color lines, that lies at the core of this system of control and every racial caste system that has existed in the United States or anywhere else in the world.

Those who believe that advocacy challenging mass incarceration can be successful without overturning the public consensus that gave rise to it are engaging in fanciful thinking, a form of denial. Isolated victories can be won—even a string of victories—but in the absence of a fundamental shift in public consciousness, the system as a whole will remain intact. To the extent that major changes are achieved without a complete shift, the system will rebound. The caste system will reemerge in a *new form*, just as convict leasing replaced slavery, or it will be *reborn*, just as mass incarceration replaced Jim Crow.

Sociologists Michael Omi and Howard Winant make a similar point in their book *Racial Formation in the United States*. They attribute the cyclical nature of racial progress to the "unstable equilibrium" that characterizes the United States' racial order.[22] Under "normal" conditions, they argue, state institutions are able to normalize the organization and enforcement of the prevailing racial order, and the system functions relatively automatically. Challenges to the racial order during these periods are easily marginalized or suppressed, and the prevailing system of racial meanings, identity, and ideology seems "natural." These conditions clearly prevailed during slavery and Jim Crow. When the equilibrium is disrupted, however, as in Reconstruction and the Civil Rights Movement, the state initially resists, then attempts to absorb the challenge through a series of reforms "that are, if not entirely symbolic, at least not critical to the operation of the racial order." In the absence of a truly egalitarian racial consensus, these predictable cycles inevitably give rise to new, extraordinarily comprehensive systems of racialized social control.

One example of the way in which a well established racial order easily absorbs legal challenges is the infamous aftermath of the *Brown v. Board of Education* decision. After the Supreme Court declared separate schools inherently unequal in 1954, segregation persisted unabated. One commentator notes: "The statistics from the Southern states are truly amazing. For ten years, 1954–1964, virtually *nothing happened*."[23] Not a single black child attended an integrated public grade school in South Carolina, Alabama, or Mississippi as of the 1962–1963 school year. Across the South as a whole, a mere 1 percent of black school children were attending school with whites in 1964—a full decade after *Brown* was decided.[24] *Brown* did not end Jim Crow; a mass movement had to emerge first—one that aimed to create a new public consensus opposed to the evils of Jim Crow. This does not mean *Brown v. Board* was meaningless, as some commentators have claimed.[25] *Brown* gave critical legitimacy to the demands of civil rights activists who risked their lives to end Jim Crow, and it helped to inspire the movement (as well as a fierce backlash).[26] But standing alone, *Brown* accomplished for African Americans little more than Abraham Lincoln's Emancipation Proclamation. A civil war had to be waged to end slavery; a mass movement was necessary to bring a formal end to Jim Crow. Those who imagine that far less is required to dismantle mass incarceration and build a new, egalitarian racial consensus reflecting a compassionate rather than punitive impulse toward poor people of color fail to appreciate the distance between Martin Luther King Jr.'s dream and the ongoing racial nightmare for those locked up and locked out of American society.

The foregoing should not be read as a call for movement building to the exclusion of reform work. To the contrary, reform work *is* the work of movement building, provided that it is done consciously *as* movement-building work. If all the reforms mentioned above were actually adopted, a radical transformation in our society would have taken place. The relevant question is not whether to engage in reform work, but how. There is no shortage of worthy reform efforts and goals. Differences of opinion are inevitable about which reforms are most important and in what order of priority they should be pursued. These debates are worthwhile, but it is critical to keep in mind that the question of how we do reform work is even more important than the specific reforms we seek. If the way we pursue reforms does not contribute to the building of a movement to dismantle the system of mass incarceration, and if our advocacy does not upset the prevailing public consensus that supports the new caste system, none of the reforms, even if won, will successfully disrupt the nation's racial equilibrium. Challenges to the system will be easily absorbed or deflected, and the accommodations made will serve primarily to legitimate the system, not undermine it. We run the risk of winning isolated battles but losing the larger war.

Let's Talk About Race—
Resisting the Temptation of Colorblind Advocacy

So how should we go about building this movement to end mass incarceration? What should be the core philosophy, the guiding principles? Another book could be written on this subject, but a few key principles stand out that can be briefly explored here. These principles are rooted in an understanding that any movement to end mass incarceration must deal with mass incarceration as a racial caste system, not as a system of crime control. This is not to say crime is unimportant; it is very important. We *need* an effective system of crime prevention and control in our communities, but that is not what the current system is. This system is better designed to *create* crime, and a perpetual class of people labeled criminals, rather than to eliminate crime or reduce the number of criminals.

It is not uncommon, however, to hear people claim that the mere fact that we have the lowest crime rates, at the same time that we have the highest incarceration rates, is all the proof needed that this system works well to control crime. But if you believe this system effectively controls crime, consider this: standard estimates of the amount of crime reduction that can be attributable to mass incarceration range from 3 to 25 percent.[27] Some scholars believe we have long since passed a tipping point where the declining marginal return on imprisonment has dipped below zero. Imprisonment, they say, now creates far more crime than it prevents, by ripping apart fragile social networks, destroying families, and creating a permanent class of unemployables.[28] Although it is common to think of poverty and joblessness as leading to crime and imprisonment, this research suggests that the War on Drugs is a major *cause* of poverty, chronic unemployment, broken families, and crime today. Todd R. Clear's book *Imprisoning Communities: How Mass Incarceration Makes Disadvantaged Communities Worse* powerfully demonstrates that imprisonment has reached such extreme levels in many urban communities that a prison sentence and/or a felon label poses a much greater threat to urban families than crime itself. This is not to say that crime—especially violent crime—does not pose a serious threat in ghetto communities today; it does. In fact, although violent crime rates have been falling nationwide, among black men violent crime is actually on the rise, especially in cities such as Chicago, where the drug war has been waged with the greatest ferocity. What a growing number of sociologists have found ought to be common sense: by locking millions of people out of the mainstream legal economy, by making it difficult or impossible for people to find housing or feed themselves, and by destroying familial bonds by warehousing millions for minor crimes, we make crime more—not less—likely in the most vulnerable communities. The success of pilot programs like Operation Ceasefire and Oakland's Lifeline program—which reach out to gang members and offer them jobs and opportunities rather than prison time if they cease their criminal activities—in dramatically reducing violent crime rates should not be met with shock and amazement.[29] When given a choice, most people in the ghetto, like anywhere else, would prefer to be able to work, support their families, and live without fear of harm or violence, if given the chance.

But even assuming that our nation achieved as much as a 25 percent reduction in crime overall through mass incarceration, it still means that the overwhelming majority of incarceration—75 percent—has had absolutely no impact on crime, despite costing nearly $200 billion annually. As a crime reduction strategy, mass incarceration is an abysmal failure. It is largely ineffective and extraordinarily expensive.

Saying mass incarceration is an abysmal failure makes sense, though, only if one assumes that the criminal justice system is designed to prevent and control crime. But if mass incarceration is understood as a system of social control—specifically, racial control—then the system is a fantastic success.[30] In less than two decades, the prison population quadrupled, and large majorities of poor people of color in urban areas throughout the United States were placed under the control of the criminal justice system or saddled with criminal records for life. Almost overnight, huge segments of ghetto communities were permanently relegated to a second-class status, disenfranchised, and subjected to perpetual surveillance and monitoring by law enforcement agencies. One could argue this result is a tragic, unforeseeable mistake, and that the goal was always crime control, not the creation of a racial undercaste. But judging by the political rhetoric and the legal rules employed in the War on Drugs, this result is no freak accident.

In order to make this point, we need to talk about race openly and honestly. We must stop debating crime policy as though it were purely about crime. People must come to understand the racial history and origins of mass incarceration—the many ways our conscious and unconscious biases have distorted our judgments over the years about what is fair, appropriate, and constructive when responding to drug use and drug crime. We must come to see, too, how our economic insecurities and racial resentments have been exploited for political gain, and how this manipulation has caused suffering for people of all colors. Finally, we must admit, out loud, that it was *because of* race that we didn't care much what happened to "those people" and imagined the worst possible things about them. The fact that our lack of care and concern may have been, at times, unintentional or unconscious does not mitigate our crime—if we refuse, when given the chance, to make amends.

Admittedly, though, the temptation to ignore race in our advocacy may be overwhelming. Race makes people uncomfortable. One study found that some whites are so loath to talk about race and so fearful of violating racial etiquette that they indicate a preference for avoiding all contact with black people.[31] The striking reluctance of whites, in particular, to talk about or even acknowledge race has led many scholars and advocates to conclude that we would be better off not talking about race at all. This view is buttressed by the fact that white liberals, nearly as much as conservatives, seem to have lost patience with debates about racial equity. Barack Obama noted this phenomenon in his book, *The Audacity of Hope*: "Rightly or wrongly, white guilt has largely exhausted itself in America; even the most fair-minded of whites, those who would genuinely like to see racial inequality ended and poverty relieved, tend to push back against racial victimization—or race-specific claims based on the history of race discrimination in this country."

Adding to the temptation to avoid race is the fact that opportunities for challenging mass incarceration on purely race-neutral grounds have never been greater. With budgets busting, more than two dozen states have reduced or eliminated harsh mandatory minimum sentences, restored early-release programs, and offered treatment instead of incarceration for some drug offenders.[32] The financial crisis engulfing states large and small has led to a conversion among some legislators who once were "get tough" true believers. Declining crime rates, coupled with a decline in public concern about crime, have also helped to create a rare opening for a productive public conversation about the War on Drugs. A promising indicator of the public's receptivity to a change in course is California's Proposition 36, which mandated drug treatment rather than jail for first-time offenders, and was approved by more than 60 percent of the electorate in 2000.[33] Some states have decriminalized marijuana, including Massachusetts, where 65 percent of state voters approved the measure.[34] Taken together, these factors suggest that, if a major mobilization got under way, impressive changes in our nation's drug laws and policies would be not only possible, but likely, without ever saying a word about race.

This is tempting bait, to put it mildly, but racial justice advocates should not take it. The prevailing caste system cannot be successfully dismantled with a purely race-neutral approach. To begin with, it is extremely unlikely that a strategy based purely on costs, crime rates, and the wisdom of drug treatment will get us back even to the troubling incarceration rates of the 1970s. As indicated earlier, any effort to downsize dramatically our nation's prisons would inspire fierce resistance by those faced with losing jobs, investments, and other benefits provided by the current system. The emotion and high anxiety would likely express itself in the form of a racially charged debate about values, morals, and personal responsibility rather than a debate about the prison economy. Few would openly argue that we should lock up millions of poor people just so that other people can have jobs or get a good return on their private investments. Instead, familiar arguments would likely resurface about the need to be "tough" on criminals, not coddle them or give "free passes." The public debate would inevitably turn to race, even if no one was explicitly talking about it. As history has shown, the prevalence of powerful (unchallenged) racial stereotypes, together with widespread apprehension regarding major structural changes, would create a political environment in which implicit racial appeals could be employed, once again, with great success. Failure to anticipate and preempt such appeals would set the stage for the same divide-and-conquer tactics that have reliably preserved racial hierarchy in the United States for centuries.

Even if fairly dramatic changes were achieved while ignoring race, the results would be highly contingent and temporary. If and when the economy improves, the justification for a "softer" approach would no longer exist. States would likely gravitate back to their old ways if a new, more compassionate public consensus about race had not been forged. Similarly, if and when crime rates rise—which seems likely if the nation's economy continues to sour—nothing would deter politicians from making black and brown criminals, once again, their favorite whipping boys. Since the days of slavery, black men have been depicted and understood as criminals, and their criminal "nature" has been among the justifications for every caste system to date. The criminalization and demonization of black men is one habit America seems unlikely to break without addressing head-on the racial dynamics that have given rise to successive caste systems. Although colorblind approaches to addressing the problems of poor people of color often seem pragmatic in the short run, in the long run they are counterproductive. Colorblindness, though widely touted as the solution, is actually the problem.

Against Colorblindness

Saying that colorblindness is the problem may alarm some in the civil rights community, especially the pollsters and political consultants who have become increasingly influential in civil rights advocacy. For decades, civil rights leaders have been saying things like "we all want a colorblind society, we just disagree how to get there" in defense of race-conscious programs like affirmative action or racial data collection.[35] Affirmative action has been framed as a legitimate exception to the colorblindness principle—a principle now endorsed by the overwhelming majority of the American electorate. Civil rights leaders are quick to assure the public that when we reach a colorblind nirvana, race consciousness will no longer be necessary or appropriate.

Far from being a worthy goal, however, colorblindness has proved catastrophic for African Americans. It is not an overstatement to say the systematic mass incarceration of people of color in the United States would not have been possible in the post–civil rights era if the nation had not fallen under the spell of a callous colorblindness. The seemingly innocent phrase, "I don't care if he's black . . ." perfectly captures the perversion of Martin Luther King Jr.'s dream that we may, one day, be able to see beyond race to connect spiritually across racial lines. Saying that one does not care about race is offered as an exculpatory virtue, when in fact it can be a form of cruelty. It is precisely because we, as a nation, have not cared much about African Americans that we have allowed our criminal justice system to create a new racial undercaste.

The deeply flawed nature of colorblindness, as a governing principle, is evidenced by the fact that the public consensus supporting mass incarceration is officially colorblind. It purports to see black and brown men not as black and brown, but simply as men—raceless men—who have failed miserably to play by the rules the rest of us follow quite naturally. The fact that so many black and brown men are rounded up for drug crimes that go largely ignored when committed by whites is unseen. Our collective colorblindness prevents us from seeing this basic fact. Our blindness also prevents us from seeing the racial and structural divisions that persist in society: the segregated, unequal schools, the segregated, jobless ghettos, and the segregated public discourse—a public conversation that excludes the current pariah caste. Our commitment to colorblindness extends beyond individuals to institutions and social arrangements. We have become blind, not so much to race, but to the existence of racial caste in America.

More than forty-five years ago, Martin Luther King Jr. warned of this danger. He insisted that blindness and indifference to racial groups is actually more important than racial hostility to the creation and maintenance of racialized systems of control. Those who supported slavery and Jim Crow, he argued, typically were not bad or evil people; they were just blind. Even the Justices who decided the infamous *Dred Scott* case, which ruled "that the Negro has no rights which the white man is bound to respect," were not wicked men, he said. On the contrary, they were decent and dedicated men. But, he hastened to add, "They were victims of a spiritual and intellectual blindness. They knew not what they did. The whole system of slavery was largely perpetuated through spiritually ignorant persons." He continued:

This tragic blindness is also found in racial segregation, the not-too-distant cousin of slavery. Some of the most vigorous defenders of segregation are sincere in their beliefs and earnest in their motives. Although some men are segregationists merely for reasons of political expediency and political gain, not all of the resistance to integration is the rear-guard of professional bigots. Some people feel that their attempt to pre-serve segregation is best for themselves, their children, and their nation. Many are good church people, anchored in the religious faith of their mothers and fathers. . . . What a tragedy! Millions of Negroes have been crucified by conscientious blindness. . . . Jesus was right about those men who crucified him. They knew not what they did. They were inflicted by a terrible blindness.[36]

Could not the same speech be given about mass incarceration today? Again, African Americans have been "crucified by conscientious blindness." People of good will have been unwilling to see black and brown men, in their humanness, as entitled to the same care, compassion, and concern that would be extended to one's friends, neighbors, or loved ones. King recog-nized that it was this *indifference* to the plight of other races that supported the institutions of slavery and Jim Crow. In his words, "One of the great tragedies of man's long trek along the highway of history has been the limiting of neighborly concern to tribe, race, class or nation." The consequence of this narrow, insular attitude "is that one does not really mind what happens to the people outside his group."[37] Racial indifference and blindness—far more than racial hostility—form the sturdy foundation for all racial caste systems.

More than a little patience will be needed when explaining the complete about-face. Probably around the same number of people think the Earth is flat as think race consciousness should be the rule in perpetuity, rather than the exception. It would be a mistake, though, to assume that people are in-capable of embracing a permanent commitment to color consciousness. The shift may, in fact, come as something of a relief, as it moves our collective focus away from a wholly unrealistic goal to one that is within anyone's reach right now. After all, to aspire to colorblindness is to aspire to a state of being in which you are not capable of seeing racial difference—a practical impossibility for most of us. The shift also invites a more optimistic view of human capacity. The colorblindness ideal is premised on the notion that we, as a society, can never be trusted to see race and treat each other fairly or with genuine compassion. A commitment to color consciousness, by contrast, places faith in our capacity as humans to show care and concern for others, even as we are fully cognizant of race and possible racial differences.

If colorblindness is such a bad idea, though, why have people across the political spectrum become so attached to it? For conservatives, the ideal of colorblindness is linked to a commitment to individualism. In their view, society should be concerned with individuals, not groups. Gross racial disparities in health, wealth, education, and opportunity should be of no interest to our government, and racial identity should be a private matter, something best kept to ourselves. For liberals, the ideal of colorblindness is linked to the dream of racial equality. The hope is that one day we will no longer see race because race will lose all of its significance. In this fantasy, eventually race will no longer be a factor in mortality rates, the spread of disease, educational or economic opportunity, or the distribution of wealth. Race will correlate with nothing, it will mean nothing, we won't even notice it anymore. Those who are less idealistic embrace colorblindness simply because they find it difficult to imagine a society in which we see race and racial differences yet consistently act in a positive, constructive way. It is easier to imagine a world in which we tolerate racial differences by being blind to them.

The uncomfortable truth, however, is that racial differences will *always* exist among us. Even if the legacies of slavery, Jim Crow, and mass incarceration were completely overcome, we would remain a nation of immigrants (and indigenous people) in a larger world divided by race and ethnicity. It is a world in which there is extraordinary racial and ethnic inequality, and our nation has porous boundaries. For the foreseeable future, racial and ethnic inequality will be a feature of American life.

This reality is not cause for despair. The idea that we may never reach a state of perfect racial equality—a perfect racial equilibrium—is not cause for alarm. What is concerning is the real possibility that we, as a society, will choose not to care. We will choose to be blind to injustice and the suffering of others. We will look the other way and deny our public agencies the resources, data, and tools they need to solve problems. We will refuse to celebrate what is beautiful about our distinct cultures and histories, even as we blend and evolve. That is cause for despair.

Seeing race is not the problem. Refusing to care for the people we see is the problem. The fact that the meaning of race may evolve over time or lose much of its significance is hardly a reason to be struck blind. We should hope not for a colorblind society but instead for a world in which we can see each other fully, learn from each other, and do what we can to respond to each other with love. That was King's dream—a society that is capable of seeing each of us, as we are, with love. That is a goal worth fighting for.

The Racial Bribe—Let's Give It Back

The foregoing could be read as a ringing endorsement of affirmative action and other diversity initiatives. To a certain extent, it is. It is difficult to imagine a time, in the foreseeable future, when the free market and partisan politics could be trusted to produce equitable inclusion in all facets of American political, economic, and social life, without anyone giving any thought—caring at all—about race. It may always be necessary for us, as a society, to pay careful attention to the impact of our laws, policies, and practices on racial and ethnic groups and consciously strive to ensure that biases, stereotypes, and structural arrangements do not cause unnecessary harm or suffering to any individual or any group for reasons related to race.

There is, however, a major caveat. Racial justice advocates should consider, with a degree of candor that has not yet been evident, whether affirmative action—as it has been framed and defended during the past thirty years—has functioned more like a racial bribe than a tool of racial justice. One might wonder, what does affirmative action have to do with mass incarceration? Well, perhaps the two are linked more than we realize. We should ask ourselves whether efforts to achieve "cosmetic" racial diversity—that is, reform efforts that make institutions look good on the surface without the needed structural changes—have actually helped to facilitate the emergence of mass incarceration and interfered with the development of a more compassionate race consciousness. In earlier chapters, we have seen that throughout our nation's history, poor and working-class whites have been bought off by racial bribes. The question posed here is whether affirmative action has functioned similarly, offering relatively meager material advantages but significant psychological benefits to people of color, in exchange for the abandonment of a more radical movement that promised to alter the nation's economic and social structure.

To be clear: This is *not* an argument that affirmative action policies conflict with King's dream that we might one day be "judged by the content of our character, not the color of our skin." King himself would have almost certainly endorsed affirmative action as a remedy, at least under some circumstances. In fact, King specifically stated on numerous occasions that he believed special—even preferential—treatment for African Americans may be warranted in light of their unique circumstances.[38] And this is not an argument that affirmative action has made no difference in the lives of poor or working-class African Americans—as some have claimed. Fire departments, police departments, and other public agencies have been transformed, at least in part, due to affirmative action.[39] Finally, this is not an argument that affirmative action should be reconsidered simply on the grounds that it is "unfair" to white men as a group. The empirical evidence strongly supports the conclusion that declining wages, downsizing, deindustrialization, globalization, and cutbacks in government services represent much greater threats to the position of white men than so-called reverse discrimination.[40]

The argument made here is a less familiar one. It is not widely debated in the mainstream media or, for that matter, in civil rights organizations. The claim is that racial justice advocates should reconsider the traditional approach to affirmative action because (a) it has helped to render a new caste system largely invisible; (b) it has helped to perpetuate the myth that anyone can make it if they try; (c) it has encouraged the embrace of a "trickle down theory of racial justice"; (d) it has greatly facilitated the divide-and-conquer tactics that gave rise to mass incarceration; and (e) it has inspired such polarization and media attention that the general public now (wrongly) assumes that affirmative action is the main battlefront in U.S. race relations.

It may not be easy for the civil rights community to have a candid conversation about any of this. Civil rights organizations are populated with beneficiaries of affirmative action (like myself) and their friends and allies. Ending affirmative action arouses fears of annihilation. The reality that so many of us would disappear overnight from colleges and universities nationwide if affirmative action were banned, and that our children and grandchildren might not follow in our footsteps, creates a kind of panic that is difficult to describe. It may be analogous, in some respects, to the panic once

experienced by poor and working-class whites faced with desegregation—
the fear of a sudden demotion in the nation's racial hierarchy. Mari Matsuda
and Charles Lawrence's book *We Won't Go Back* captures the determination
of affirmative-action beneficiaries not to allow the clock to be turned back
on racial justice, back to days of racial caste in America. The problem, of
course, is that *we are already there*.

Affirmative action, particularly when it is justified on the grounds of diversity rather than equity (or remedy), masks the severity of racial inequality in
America, leading to greatly exaggerated claims of racial progress and overly
optimistic assessments of the future for African Americans. Seeing black
people graduate from Harvard and Yale and become CEOs or corporate
lawyers—not to mention president of the United States—causes us all to
marvel at what a long way we have come. As recent data shows, however,
much of black progress is a myth. Although some African Americans are doing very well—enrolling in universities and graduate schools at record rates
thanks to affirmative action—as a group, in many respects African Americans are doing no better than they were when Martin Luther King Jr. was
assassinated and riots swept inner cities across America. The child poverty
rate is actually higher today than it was in 1968.[41] Unemployment rates in
black communities rival those in Third World countries. And that is *with*
affirmative action!

When we pull back the curtain and take a look at what our so-called colorblind society creates without affirmative action, we see a familiar social,
political, and economic structure—the structure of racial caste. When those
behind bars are taken into account, America's institutions continue to create
nearly as much racial inequality as existed during Jim Crow.[42] Our elite universities, which now look a lot like America, would whiten overnight if affirmative action suddenly disappeared. One recent study indicates that the
elimination of race-based admissions policies would lead to a 63 percent decline in black matriculants at all law schools and a 90 percent decline at
elite law schools.[43] Sociologist Stephen Steinberg describes the bleak reality
this way: "Insofar as this black middle class is an artifact of affirmative action policy, it cannot be said to be the result of autonomous workings of
market forces. In other words, the black middle class does not reflect a low-
ering of racist barriers in occupations so much as the opposite: racism is so
entrenched that without government intervention there would be little
'progress' to boast about."[44]

In view of all this, we must ask, to what extent has affirmative action helped us remain blind to, and in denial about, the existence of a racial undercaste? And to what extent have the battles over affirmative action distracted us and diverted crucial resources and energy away from dismantling the structures of racial inequality?

The predictable response is that civil rights advocates are as committed to challenging mass incarceration and other forms of structural racism as they are to preserving affirmative action. But where is the evidence of this? Civil rights activists have created a national *movement* to save affirmative action, complete with the marches, organizing, and media campaigns, as well as incessant strategy meetings, conferences, and litigation. Where is the movement to end mass incarceration? For that matter, where is the movement for educational equity? Part of the answer is that it is far easier to create a movement when there is a sense of being under attack. It is also easier when a single policy is at issue, rather than something as enormous (and seemingly intractable) as educational inequity or mass incarceration. Those are decent explanations, but they are no excuse. Try telling a sixteen-year-old black youth in Louisiana who is facing a decade in adult prison and a lifetime of social, political, and economic exclusion that your civil rights organization is not doing much to end the War on Drugs—but would he like to hear about all the great things that are being done to save affirmative action? There is a fundamental disconnect today between the world of civil rights advocacy and the reality facing those trapped in the new racial undercaste.

There is another, more sinister consequence of affirmative action: the carefully engineered appearance of great racial progress strengthens the "color-blind" public consensus that personal and cultural traits, not structural arrangements, are largely responsible for the fact that the majority of young black men in urban areas across the United States are currently under the control of the criminal justice system or branded as felons for life. In other words, affirmative action helps to make the emergence of a new racial caste system seem implausible. It creates an environment in which it is reasonable to ask, how can something akin to a racial caste system exist when people like Condoleezza Rice, Colin Powell, and Barack Obama are capable of rising from next to nothing to the pinnacles of wealth and power? How could a caste system exist, in view of the black middle class?

There are answers to these questions, but they are difficult to swallow when millions of Americans have displayed a willingness to elect a black

man president of the United States. The truth, however, is this: far from undermining the current system of control, the new caste system depends, in
no small part, on black exceptionalism. The colorblind public consensus
that supports the new caste system insists that race no longer matters. Now
that America has officially embraced Martin Luther King Jr.'s dream (by reducing it to the platitude "that we should be judged by the content of our
character, not the color of our skin"), the mass incarceration of people of
color can be justified only to the extent that the plight of those locked up
and locked out is understood to be their choice, not their birthright.

In short, mass incarceration is predicated on the notion that an extraordinary number of African Americans (but not all) have freely chosen a life of
crime and thus belong behind bars. A belief that all blacks belong in jail
would be incompatible with the social consensus that we have "moved beyond" race and that race is no longer relevant. But a widespread belief that
a majority of black and brown men unfortunately belong in jail is compatible
with the new American creed, provided that their imprisonment can be interpreted as their own fault. If the prison label imposed on them can be
blamed on their culture, poor work ethic, or even their families, then society
is absolved of responsibility to do anything about their condition.

This is where black exceptionalism comes in. Highly visible examples of
black success are critical to the maintenance of a racial caste system in the
era of colorblindness. Black success stories lend credence to the notion that
anyone, no matter how poor or how black you may be, can make it to the
top, if only you try hard enough. These stories "prove" that race is no longer
relevant. Whereas black success stories undermined the logic of Jim Crow,
they actually reinforce the system of mass incarceration. Mass incarceration
depends for its legitimacy on the widespread belief that all those who appear
trapped at the bottom actually chose their fate.

Viewed from this perspective, affirmative action no longer appears entirely progressive. So long as some readily identifiable African Americans are
doing well, the system is largely immunized from racial critique. People like
Barack Obama who are truly exceptional by any standards, along with others
who have been granted exceptional opportunities, legitimate a system that
remains fraught with racial bias—especially when they fail to challenge, or
even acknowledge, the prevailing racial order. In the current era, white
Americans are often eager to embrace token or exceptional African Ameri-

cans, particularly when they go out of their way not to talk about race or racial inequality.

Affirmative action may be counterproductive in yet another sense: it lends credence to a trickle-down theory of racial justice. The notion that giving a relatively small number of people of color access to key positions or institutions will inevitably redound to the benefit of the larger group is belied by the evidence. It also seems to disregard Martin Luther King Jr.'s stern warnings that racial justice requires the complete transformation of social institutions and a dramatic restructuring of our economy, not superficial changes that can be purchased on the cheap. King argued in 1968, "The changes [that have occurred to date] are basically in the social and political areas; the problems we now face—providing jobs, better housing and better education for the poor throughout the country—will require money for their solution, a fact that makes those solutions all the more difficult."[45] He emphasized that "most of the gains of the past decade were obtained at bargain prices," for the desegregation of public facilities and the election and appointment of a few black officials cost close to nothing. "White America must recognize that justice for black people cannot be achieved without radical changes in the structure of our society. The comfortable, the entrenched, the privileged cannot continue to tremble at the prospect of change in the status quo."[46]

Against this backdrop, diversity-driven affirmative action programs seem to be the epitome of racial justice purchased on the cheap. They create the appearance of racial equity without the reality and do so at no great cost, without fundamentally altering any of the structures that create racial inequality in the first place. Perhaps the best illustration of this fact is that, thanks in part to affirmative action, police departments and law enforcement agencies nationwide have come to look more like America than ever, at precisely the moment that they have waged a war on the ghetto poor and played a leading role in the systematic mass incarceration of people of color. The color of police chiefs across the country has changed, but the role of the police in our society has not.

Gerald Torres and Lani Guinier offer a similar critique of affirmative action in *The Miner's Canary*. They point out that "conventional strategies for social change proceed as though a change in who administers power fundamentally affects the structure of power itself."[47] This narrow approach to social change is reflected in the justifications offered for affirmative action, most notably the claim that "previous outsiders, once given a chance, will exercise power *differently*."[48] The reality, however, is that the existing hierarchy disciplines newcomers, requiring them to exercise power in the same old ways and play by the same old rules in order to survive. The newcomers, Torres and Guinier explain, are easily co-opted, as they have much to lose but little to gain by challenging the rules of the game.

Their point is particularly relevant to the predicament of minority police officers charged with waging the drug war. Profound racial injustice occurs when minority police officers *follow the rules*. It is a scandal when the public learns they have broken the rules, but no rules need be broken for the systematic mass incarceration of people of color to proceed unabated. This uncomfortable fact creates strong incentives for minority officers to deny, to rationalize, or to be willingly blind to the role of law enforcement in creating a racial undercaste. Reports that minority officers may engage in nearly as much racial profiling as white officers have been met with some amazement, but the real surprise is that some minority police officers have been willing to speak out against the practice, given the ferocity of the drug war. A war has been declared against poor communities of color, and the police are expected to wage it. Do we expect minority officers, whose livelihood depends on the very departments charged with waging the war, to play the role of peacenik? That expectation seems unreasonable, yet the dilemma for racial justice advocates is a real one. The quiet complicity of minority officers in the War on Drugs serves to legitimate the system and insulate it from critique. In a nation still stuck in an old Jim Crow mind-set—which equates racism with white bigotry and views racial diversity as proof the problem has been solved—a racially diverse police department invites questions like: "How can you say the Oakland Police Department's drug raids are racist? There's a black police chief, and most of the officers involved in the drug raids are black." If the caste dimensions of mass incarceration were better understood and the limitations of cosmetic diversity were better appreciated, the existence of black police chiefs and black officers would be no more encouraging today than the presence of black slave drivers and black plantation owners hundreds of years ago.

When meaningful change fails to materialize following the achievement of superficial diversity, those who remain locked out can become extremely discouraged and demoralized, resulting in cynicism and resignation. Perhaps more concerning, though, is the fact that inclusion of people of color in power structures, particularly at the top, can paralyze reform efforts. People of color are often reluctant to challenge institutions led by people who look like them, as they feel a personal stake in the individual's success. After centuries of being denied access to leadership positions in key social institutions, people of color quite understandably are hesitant to create circumstances that could trigger the downfall of "one of their own." An incident of police brutality that would be understood as undeniably racist if the officers involved were white may be given a more charitable spin if the officers are black. Similarly, black community residents who might have been inspired to challenge aggressive stop-and-frisk policies of a largely white police department may worry about "hurting" a black police chief. People of color, because of the history of racial subjugation and exclusion, often experience success and failure vicariously through the few who achieve positions of power, fame, and fortune. As a result, cosmetic diversity, which focuses on providing opportunities to individual members of under-represented groups, both diminishes the possibility that unfair rules will be challenged and legitimates the entire system.

Obama the Promise and the Peril

This dynamic poses particular risks for racial justice advocacy during an Obama presidency. On the one hand, the election of Barack Obama to the presidency creates an extraordinary opportunity for those seeking to end the system of mass incarceration in America. Obama's stated positions on criminal justice reform suggest that he is opposed to the War on Drugs and the systematic targeting of African Americans for mass incarceration.[49] Shouldn't we trust him, now that he is holding the reins of power, to do the right thing?

Trust is tempting, especially because Obama himself violated our nation's drug laws and almost certainly knows that his life would not have unfolded as it did if he had been arrested on drug charges and treated like a common criminal. As he wrote in his memoir about his wayward youth, "Pot had helped, and booze; maybe a little blow when you could afford it." Unlike Bill Clinton, who famously admitted he experimented with marijuana on occasion "but didn't inhale," Obama has never minimized his illegal drug use. As he said in a 2006 speech to the American Society of Magazine Editors, "Look, you know, when I was a kid, I inhaled. Frequently. That was the point."[50] Those "bad decisions," Obama has acknowledged, could have led him to a personal dead end. "Junkie. Pothead. That's where I'd have been headed: the final, fatal role of the young would-be black man." No doubt if Obama had been arrested and treated like a common criminal, he could have served years in prison and been labeled a drug felon for life. What are the chances he would have gone to Harvard Law School, much less become president of the United States, if that had happened? It seems reasonable to assume that Obama, who knows a little something about poverty and the temptations of drugs, would have a "there but for the grace of God go I" attitude about the millions of African and Latino men imprisoned for drug offenses comparable to his own or saddled for life with felony records.

But before we kick back, relax, and wait for racial justice to trickle down, consider this: Obama chose Joe Biden, one of the Senate's most strident drug warriors, as his vice president. The man he picked to serve as his chief of staff in the White House, Rahm Emanuel, was a major proponent of the expansion of the drug war and the slashing of welfare rolls during President Clinton's administration. And the man he tapped to lead the U.S. Department of Justice—the agency that launched and continues to oversee the federal war on drugs—is an African American former U.S. attorney for the District of Columbia who sought to ratchet up the drug war in Washington, D.C., and fought the majority black D.C. City Council in an effort to impose harsh mandatory minimums for marijuana possession. Moreover, on the campaign trail, Obama took a dramatic step back from an earlier position opposing the death penalty, announcing that he now supports the death penalty for child rapists—even if the victim is not killed—even though the U.S. Supreme Court ruled the death penalty for nonhomicides unconstitutional and international law strongly disfavors the practice. The only countries that share Obama's view are countries like Saudi Arabia, Egypt, and China, which allow the death penalty for things like adultery and tax evasion. So why did Obama, on the campaign trail, go out of his way to announce disagreement with a Supreme Court decision ruling the death penalty for child rapists unconstitutional? Clearly he was attempting to immunize himself from any attempt to portray him as "soft" on crime—a tactic reminiscent of Bill Clinton's decision to fly back to Arkansas during the 1992 presidential campaign to oversee the execution of a mentally disabled black man.

Seasoned activists may respond that all of this is "just politics," but, as we have seen in earlier chapters, they are the same politics that gave rise to the

New Jim Crow. Obama has revived President Clinton's Community Oriented Policing Services (COPS) program and increased funding for the Byrne grant program—two of the worst federal drug programs of the Clinton era.[51] These programs, despite their benign names, are responsible for the militarization of policing, SWAT teams, Pipeline drug task forces, and the laundry list of drug-war horrors described in chapter 2.

Remarkably, the Obama administration chose to increase funding for Byrne programs twelvefold not in response to any sudden spike in crime rates or any new studies indicating the effectiveness of these programs, but instead because handing law enforcement billions of dollars in cash is an easy, efficient jobs program in the midst of an economic crisis.[52] The dramatically increased funding for Byrne grants was included as part of the Economic Reinvestment Act of 2009. While the channeling of stimulus dollars to law enforcement may help some police officers keep their jobs at a time when state and local budgets are being slashed, there is a cost. As *New York Times* columnist Charles Blow observed, "[it's] a callous political calculus. . . . The fact that they are ruining the lives of hundreds of thousands of black and Hispanic men and, by extension, the communities they belong to barely seems to register."[53]

Clinton once boasted that the COPS program, which put tens of thousands of officers on the streets, was responsible for the dramatic fifteen-year drop in violent crime that began in the 1990s. Recent studies, however, have shown that is not the case. A 2005 report by the Government Accountability Office concluded the program may have contributed to a 1 percent reduction in crime—at a cost of $8 billion.[54] A peer-reviewed study in the journal *Criminology* found that the COPS program, despite the hype, "had little or no effect on crime."[55] And while Obama's drug czar, former Seattle police chief Gil Kerlikowske, has said the War on Drugs should no longer be *called* a war, Obama's budget for law enforcement is actually worse than the Bush administration's in terms of the ratio of dollars devoted to prevention and drug treatment as opposed to law enforcement.[56] Obama, who is celebrated as evidence of America's triumph over race, is proposing nothing less than revving up the drug war through the same failed policies and programs that have systematically locked young men of color into a permanent racial undercaste.

The unique and concerning situation racial justice advocates now face is that the very people who are most oppressed by the current caste system—African Americans—may be the least likely to want to challenge it, now that a

black family is living in the White House. If Obama were white, there would
be no hesitation to remind him of his youthful drug use when arguing that
he should end the drug war and make good on his promises to end unjust
mandatory minimums. But do African Americans want the media to talk
about Obama's drug use? Do African Americans want to pressure Obama
on any issue, let alone issues of race? To go one step further, could it be
that many African Americans would actually prefer to ignore racial issues
during Obama's presidency, to help ensure him smooth sailing and a trium-
phant presidency, no matter how bad things are for African Americans in the
meantime?

The fact that the last question could plausibly be answered yes raises serious questions for the civil rights community. Have we unwittingly exaggerated the importance of individuals succeeding within pre-existing structures
of power, and thereby undermined King's call for a "complete restructuring"
of our society? Have we contributed to the disempowerment and passivity of
the black community, not only by letting the lawyers take over, but also by
communicating the message that the best path—perhaps the only path—to
the promised land is infiltrating elite institutions and seizing power at the
top, so racial justice can trickle down?

Torres and Guinier suggest the answer to these questions may be yes.
They observe that, "surprisingly, strategists on both the left and right, despite their differences, converge on the individual as the unit of power."[57]
Conservatives challenge the legitimacy of group rights or race consciousness
and argue that the best empowerment strategy is entrepreneurship and individual initiative. Civil rights advocates argue that individual group members
"represent" the race and that hierarchies of power that lack diversity are ille-
gitimate. The theory is, when black individuals achieve power for themselves, black people as a group benefit, as does society as a whole. "Here we
see both liberals and conservatives endorsing the same meta-narrative of
American individualism: When individuals get ahead, the group triumphs.
When individuals succeed, American democracy prevails."[58]

The absence of a thoroughgoing structural critique of the prevailing racial
order explains why so many civil rights advocates responded to Barack
Obama's election with glee, combined with hasty reminders that "we still
have a long way to go." The predictable response from the casual observer is:
well, how much further? A black man was just elected president. How much

further do black people want to go? If a black person can be elected president, can't a black person do just about anything now?

All of Us or None

At the same time that many civil rights advocates have been pursuing lawyer-
driven, trickle-down strategies for racial justice, a growing number of formerly incarcerated men and women have been organizing in major cities
across the United States, providing assistance to those newly released from
prison and engaging in grassroots political activism in pursuit of basic civil
rights. One such organization, based in Oakland, California, is named All of
Us or None. The name explicitly challenges a politics that affords inclusion
and acceptance for a few but guarantees exclusion for many. In spirit, it as-
serts solidarity with the "least of these among us."

Diversity-driven affirmative action, as described and implemented today,
sends a different message. The message is that "some of us" will gain inclusion. As a policy, it is blind to those who are beyond its reach, the colored
faces at the bottom of the well. One policy alone can't save the world, the
skeptic might respond. True enough. But what if affirmative action, as it has
been framed and debated, does more harm than good, viewed from the perspective of "all of us"?

This brings us to a critical question: who is the *us* that civil rights advocates
are fighting for? Judging from the plethora of groups that have embarked on
their own civil rights campaigns since Martin Luther King Jr.'s assassination—
women, gays, immigrants, Latinos, Asian Americans—the answer seems to be
that *us* includes everyone except white men.

This result is not illogical. When Malcolm X condemned "the white man"
and declared him the enemy, he was not, of course, speaking about any particular white man, but rather the white, patriarchal order that characterized
both slavery and Jim Crow. Malcolm X understood that the United States
was created by and for privileged white men. It was white men who dominated politics, controlled the nation's wealth, and wrote the rules by which
everyone else was forced to live. No group in the United States can be said
to have experienced more privilege, and gone to greater lengths to protect it,
than "the white man."

Yet the white man, it turns out, has suffered too. The fact that his suffering has been far less extreme, and has not been linked to a belief in his inherent inferiority, has not made his suffering less real. Civil rights advocates,
however, have treated the white man's suffering as largely irrelevant to the
pursuit of the promised land. As civil rights lawyers unveiled plans to desegregate public schools, it was poor and working-class whites who were expected to bear the burden of this profound social adjustment, even though
many of them were as desperate for upward social mobility and quality education as African Americans. According to the 1950 census, among Southerners in their late twenties, the state-by-state percentages of functional
illiterates (people with less than five years of schooling) for whites on farms
overlapped with those for blacks in the cities. The majority of Southern
whites were better off than Southern blacks, but they were not affluent or
well educated by any means; they were semiliterate (with less than twelve
years of schooling). Only a tiny minority of whites were affluent and well educated. They stood far apart from the rest of the whites and virtually all
blacks.[59]

What lower-class whites *did* have was what W.E.B. Du Bois described as
"the public and psychological wage" paid to white workers, who depended
on their status and privileges as whites to compensate for low pay and harsh
working conditions.[60] As described in chapter 1, time and time again, poor
and working-class whites were persuaded to choose their racial status interests over their common economic interests with blacks, resulting in the
emergence of new caste systems that only marginally benefited whites but
were devastating for African Americans.

In retrospect, it seems clear that nothing could have been more important
in the 1970s and 1980s than finding a way to create a durable, interracial,
bottom-up coalition for social and economic justice to ensure that another
caste system did not emerge from the ashes of Jim Crow. Priority should
have been given to figuring out some way for poor and working-class whites
to feel as though they had a stake—some tangible interest—in the nascent
integrated racial order. As Lani Guinier points out, however, the racial liberalism expressed in the *Brown v. Board of Education* decision and endorsed by
civil rights litigators "did not offer poor whites even an elementary framework for understanding what they might gain as a result of integration."[61]
Nothing in the opinion or in the subsequent legal strategy made clear that
segregation had afforded elites a crucial means of exercising social control

over poor and working-class whites as well as blacks. The Southern white elite, whether planters or industrialists, had successfully endeavored to make all whites think in racial rather than class terms, predictably leading whites to experience desegregation, as Derrick Bell put it, as a net "loss."[62]

Given that poor and working-class whites (not white elites) were the ones who had their world rocked by desegregation, it does not take a great leap of empathy to see why affirmative action could be experienced as salt in a wound. Du Bois once observed that the psychological wage of whiteness put "an indelible black face to failure."[63] Yet with the advent of affirmative action, suddenly African Americans were leapfrogging over poor and working-class whites on their way to Harvard and Yale and taking jobs in police departments and fire departments that had once been reserved for whites. Civil rights advocates offered no balm for the wound, publicly resisting calls for *class*-based affirmative action and dismissing claims of unfairness on the grounds that whites had been enjoying racial preferences for hundreds of years. Resentment, frustration, and anger expressed by poor and working-class whites was chalked up to racism, leading to a subterranean discourse about race and to implicitly racial political appeals, but little honest dialogue.

Perhaps the time has come to give up the racial bribes and begin an honest conversation about race in America. The topic of the conversation should be how *us* can come to include *all of us*. Accomplishing this degree of unity may mean giving up fierce defense of policies and strategies that exacerbate racial tensions and produce for racially defined groups primarily psychological or cosmetic racial benefits.

Of course, if meaningful progress is to be made, whites must give up their racial bribes too, and be willing to sacrifice their racial privilege. Some might argue that in this game of chicken, whites should make the first move. Whites should demonstrate that their silence in the drug war cannot be bought by tacit assurances that their sons and daughters will not be rounded up en masse and locked away. Whites should prove their commitment to dismantling not only mass incarceration, but all of the structures of racial inequality that guarantee for whites the resilience of white privilege. After all, why should "we" give up our racial bribes if whites have been unwilling to give up theirs? In light of our nation's racial history, that seems profoundly unfair. But if your strategy for racial justice involves waiting for whites to be fair, history suggests it will be a long wait. It's not that white people are more unjust than others. Rather it seems that an aspect of human nature is the tendency to cling tightly to one's advantages and privileges and to rationalize the suffering and exclusion of others. This tendency is what led Frederick Douglass to declare that "power concedes nothing without a demand; it never has and it never will."

So what is to be demanded in this moment in our nation's racial history? If the answer is more power, more top jobs, more slots in fancy schools for "us"—a narrow, racially defined *us* that excludes many—we will continue the same power struggles and can expect to achieve many of the same results. Yes, we may still manage to persuade mainstream voters in the midst of an economic crisis that we have relied too heavily on incarceration, that prisons are too expensive, and that drug use is a public health problem, not a crime. But if the movement that emerges to end mass incarceration does not meaningfully address the racial divisions and resentments that gave rise to mass incarceration, and if it fails to cultivate an ethic of genuine care, compassion, and concern for every human being—of every class, race, and nationality—within our nation's borders, including poor whites, who are often pitted against poor people of color, the collapse of mass incarceration will not mean the death of racial caste in America. Inevitably a new system of racialized social control will emerge—one that we cannot foresee, just as the current system of mass incarceration was not predicted by anyone thirty years ago. No task is more urgent for racial justice advocates today than ensuring that America's current racial caste system is its last.

Given what is at stake at this moment in history, bolder, more inspired action is required than we have seen to date. Piecemeal, top-down policy reform on criminal justice issues, combined with a racial justice discourse that revolves largely around the meaning of Barack Obama's election and "post-racialism," will not get us out of our nation's racial quagmire. We must flip the script. Taking our cue from the courageous civil rights advocates who brazenly refused to defend themselves, marching unarmed past white mobs that threatened to kill them, we, too, must be the change we hope to create. If we want to do more than just end mass incarceration—if we want to put an end to the history of racial caste in America—we must lay down our racial bribes, join hands with people of all colors who are not content to wait for change to trickle down, and say to those who would stand in our way: Accept all of us or none.

That is the basic message that Martin Luther King Jr. aimed to deliver through the Poor People's Movement back in 1968. He argued then that the time had come for racial justice advocates to shift from a civil rights to a human rights paradigm, and that the real work of movement building had only just begun.[64] A human rights approach, he believed, would offer far greater hope for those of us determined to create a thriving, multiracial, multiethnic democracy free from racial hierarchy than the civil rights model had provided to date. It would offer a positive vision of what we can strive *for*—a society in which all human beings of all races are treated with dignity, and have the right to food, shelter, health care, education, and security.[65] This expansive vision could open the door to meaningful alliances between poor and working-class people of all colors, who could begin to see their interests as aligned, rather than in conflict—no longer in competition for scarce resources in a zero-sum game.

A human rights movement, King believed, held revolutionary potential. Speaking at a Southern Christian Leadership Conference staff retreat in May 1967, he told SCLC staff, who were concerned that the Civil Rights Movement had lost its steam and its direction, "It is necessary for us to realize that we have moved from the era of civil rights to the era of human rights." Political reform efforts were no longer adequate to the task at hand, he said. "For the last 12 years, we have been in a reform movement. . . . [But] after Selma and the voting rights bill, we moved into a new era, which must be an era of revolution. We must see the great distinction between a reform movement and a revolutionary movement. We are called upon to raise certain basic questions about the whole society."[66]

More than forty years later, civil rights advocacy is stuck in a model of advocacy King was determined to leave behind. Rather than challenging the basic structure of society and doing the hard work of movement building— the work to which King was still committed at the end of his life—we have been tempted too often by the opportunity for people of color to be included within the political and economic structure as-is, even if it means alienating those who are necessary allies. We have allowed ourselves to be willfully blind to the emergence of a new caste system—a system of social excommunication that has denied millions of African Americans basic human dignity. The significance of this cannot be overstated, for the failure to acknowledge the humanity and dignity of all persons has lurked at the root of every racial caste system. This common thread explains why, in the 1780s, the British Society for the Abolition of Slavery adopted as its official seal a woodcut of a kneeling slave above a banner that read, "AM I NOT A MAN AND

A BROTHER?" That symbol was followed more than a hundred years later by signs worn around the necks of black sanitation workers during the Poor People's Campaign answering the slave's question with the simple statement, I AM A MAN.

The fact that black men could wear the same sign today in protest of the new caste system suggests that the model of civil rights advocacy that has been employed for the past several decades is, as King predicted, inadequate to the task at hand. If we can agree that what is needed now, at this critical juncture, is not more tinkering or tokenism, but as King insisted forty years ago, a "radical restructuring of our society," then perhaps we can also agree that a radical restructuring of our approach to racial justice advocacy is in order as well.

All of this is easier said than done, of course. Change in civil rights organizations, like change in society as a whole, will not come easy. Fully committing to a vision of racial justice that includes grassroots, bottom-up advocacy on behalf of "all of us" will require a major reconsideration of priorities, staffing, strategies, and messages. Egos, competing agendas, career goals, and inertia may get in the way. It may be that traditional civil rights organizations simply cannot, or will not, change. To this it can only be said, without a hint of disrespect: adapt or die.

If Martin Luther King Jr. is right that the arc of history is long, but it bends toward justice, a new movement will arise; and if civil rights organizations fail to keep up with the times, they will be pushed to the side as another generation of advocates comes to the fore. Hopefully the new generation will be led by those who know best the brutality of the new caste system—a group with greater vision, courage, and determination than the old guard can muster, trapped as they may be in an outdated paradigm. This new generation of activists should not disrespect their elders or disparage their contributions or achievements; to the contrary, they should bow their heads in respect, for their forerunners have expended untold hours and made great sacrifices in an elusive quest for justice. But once respects have been paid, they should march right past them, emboldened, as King once said, by the fierce urgency of now.

Those of us who hope to be their allies should not be surprised, if and when this day comes, that when those who have been locked up and locked out finally have the chance to speak and truly be heard, what we hear is rage. The rage may frighten us; it may remind us of riots, uprisings, and buildings aflame. We may be tempted to control it, or douse it with buckets of doubt, dismay, and disbelief. But we should do no such thing. Instead, when a young man who was born in the ghetto and who knows little of life beyond the walls of his prison cell and the invisible cage that has become his life, turns to us in bewilderment and rage, we should do nothing more than look him in the eye and tell him the truth. We should tell him the same truth the great African American writer James Baldwin told his nephew in a letter published in 1962, in one of the most extraordinary books ever written, *The Fire Next Time*. With great passion and searing conviction, Baldwin had this to say to his young nephew:

This is the crime of which I accuse my country and my countrymen, and for which neither I nor time nor history will ever forgive them, that they have destroyed and are destroying hundreds of thousands of lives and do not know it and do not want to know it. . . . It is their innocence which constitutes the crime. . . . This innocent country set you down in a ghetto in which, in fact, it intended that you should perish. The limits of your ambition were, thus, expected to be set forever. You were born into a society which spelled out with brutal clarity, and in as many ways as possible, that you were a worthless human being. You were not ex-pected to aspire to excellence: you were expected to make peace with mediocrity. . . . You have, and many of us have, defeated this intention; and, by a terrible law, a terrible paradox, those innocents who believed that your imprisonment made them safe are losing their grasp on reality. But these men are your brothers—your lost, younger brothers. And if the word integration means anything, this is what it means: that we, with love, shall force our brothers to see themselves as they are, to cease fleeing from reality and begin to change it. For this is your home, my friend, do not be driven from it; great men have done great things here, and will again, and we can make America what it must become. It will be hard, but you come from sturdy, peasant stock, men who picked cotton and dammed rivers and built railroads, and, in the teeth of the most terrifying odds, achieved an unassailable and monumental dignity. You come from a long line of great poets since Homer. One of them said, *The very time I thought I was lost, My dungeon shook and my chains fell off.* . . . We cannot be free until they are free. God bless you, and Godspeed.[67]

Notes

Introduction

1. Jarvious Cotton was a plaintiff in *Cotton v. Fordice*, 157 F.3d 388 (5th Cir. 1998), which held that Mississippi's felon disenfranchisement provision had lost its racially discriminatory taint. The information regarding Cotton's family tree was obtained by Emily Bolton on March 29, 1999, when she interviewed Cotton at Mississippi State Prison. Jarvious Cotton was released on parole in Mississippi, a state that denies voting rights to parolees.

2. The *New York Times* made the national media's first specific reference to crack in a story published in late 1985. Crack became known in a few impoverished neighborhoods in Los Angeles, New York, and Miami in early 1986. See Craig Reinarman and Harry Levine, "The Crack Attack: America's Latest Drug Scare, 1986–1992," in *Images of Issues: Typifying Contemporary Social Problems* (New York: Aldine De Gruyter, 1995), 152.

3. The Reagan administration's decision to publicize crack "horror stories" is discussed in more depth in chapter 1.

4. Clarence Page, "'The Plan': A Paranoid View of Black Problems," *Dover* (Delaware) *Herald*, Feb. 23, 1990. See also Manning Marable, *Race, Reform, and Rebellion: The Second Reconstruction in Black America, 1945–1990* (Jackson: University Press of Mississippi, 1991), 212–13.

5. See Alexander Cockburn and Jeffrey St. Clair, *Whiteout: The CIA, Drugs, and the Press* (New York: Verso, 1999). See also Nick Shou, "The Truth in 'Dark Alliance,'" *Los Angeles Times*, Aug. 18, 2006; Peter Kornbluh, "CIA's Challenge in South Central," *Los Angeles Times* (Washington edition), Nov. 15, 1996; and Alexander Cockburn, "Why They Hated Gary Webb," *The Nation*, Dec. 16, 2004.

6. Katherine Beckett and Theodore Sasson, *The Politics of Injustice: Crime and Punishment in America*, (Thousand Oaks, CA: Sage Publications, 2004), 163.

7. Marc Mauer, *Race to Incarcerate*, rev. ed. (New York: The New Press, 2006), 33.

8. PEW Center on the States, *One in 100: Behind Bars in America 2008* (Washington, DC: PEW Charitable Trusts, 2008), 5.

9. Donald Braman, *Doing Time on the Outside: Incarceration and Family Life in Urban America* (Ann Arbor: University of Michigan Press, 2004), 3, citing D.C. Department of Corrections data for 2000.

10. See, e.g., U.S. Department of Health and Human Services, Substance Abuse and Mental Health Services Administration, *Summary of Findings from the 2000 National Household Survey on Drug Abuse*, NHSDA series H-13, DHHS pub. no. SMA 01-3549 (Rockville, MD: 2001), reporting that 6.4 percent of whites, 6.4 percent of blacks, and 5.3 percent of Hispanics were current users of illegal drugs in 2000; *Results from the 2002 National Survey on Drug Use and Health: National Findings*, NHSDA series H-22, DHHS pub. no. SMA 03-3836 (2003), revealing nearly identical rates of illegal drug use among whites and blacks, only a single percentage point between them; and *Results from the 2007 National Survey on Drug Use and Health: National Findings*, NSDUH series H-34, DHHS pub. no. SMA 08-4343 (2007), showing essentially the same finding. See also Marc Mauer and Ryan S. King, *A 25-Year Quagmire: The "War on Drugs" and Its Impact on American Society* (Washington, DC: Sentencing Project, 2007), 19, citing a study suggesting that African Americans have slightly higher rates of illegal drug use than whites.

11. See, e.g., Howard N. Snyder and Melissa Sickman, *Juvenile Offenders and Victims: 2006 National Report*, U.S. Department of Justice, Office of Justice Programs, Office of Juvenile Justice and Delinquency Prevention (Washington, DC: U.S. Department of Justice, 2006), reporting that white youth are more likely than black youth to engage in illegal drug sales. See also Lloyd D. Johnson, Patrick M. O'Malley, Jerald G. Bachman, and John E. Schulenberg, *Monitoring the Future, National Survey Results on Drug Use, 1975–2006*, vol. 1, *Secondary School Students*, U.S. Department of Health and Human Services, National Institute on Drug Abuse, NIH pub. no. 07-6205 (Bethesda, MD: 2007), 32, "African American 12th graders have consistently shown lower usage rates than White 12th graders for most drugs, both licit and illicit"; and Lloyd D. Johnston, Patrick M. O'Malley, and Jerald G. Bachman, *Monitoring the Future: National Results on Adolescent Drug Use: Overview of Key Findings 2002*, U.S. Department of Health and Human Services, National Institute on Drug Abuse, NIH pub. no. 03-5374 (Bethesda, MD: 2003), presenting data showing that African American adolescents have slightly lower rates of illicit drug use than their white counterparts.

12. Human Rights Watch, *Punishment and Prejudice: Racial Disparities in the War on Drugs*, HRW Reports, vol. 12, no. 2 (New York, 2000).

13. See, e.g., Paul Street, *The Vicious Circle: Race, Prison, Jobs, and Community in Chicago, Illinois, and the Nation* (Chicago: Chicago Urban League, Department of Research and Planning, 2002).

14. Michael Tonry, *Thinking About Crime: Sense and Sensibility in American Penal Culture* (New York: Oxford University Press, 2004), 14.

15. Ibid.

16. Ibid., 20.

17. National Advisory Commission on Criminal Justice Standards and Goals, *Task Force Report on Corrections* (Washington, DC: Government Printing Office, 1973), 358.

18. Ibid., 597.

19. Mauer, *Race to Incarcerate*, 17–18.

20. The estimate that one in three black men will go to prison during their lifetime is drawn from Thomas P. Boncszar, "Prevalence of Imprisonment in the U.S. Population, 1974–2001," U.S. Department of Justice, Bureau of Justice Statistics, August 2003. In Baltimore, like many large urban areas, the majority of young African American men are currently under correctional supervision. See Eric Lotke and Jason Ziedenberg, "Tipping Point: Maryland's Overuse of Incarceration and the Impact on Community Safety," Justice Policy Institute, March 2005, 3.

1. The Rebirth of Caste

1. Reva Siegel, "Why Equal Protection No Longer Protects: The Evolving Forms of Status-Enforcing Action," *Stanford Law Review* 49 (1997): 1111; see also Michael Omi and Howard Winant, *Racial Formation in the United States: From the 1960s to the 1990s* (New York: Routledge, 1996), 84–91.

2. Loïc Wacquant, "America's New 'Peculiar Institution': On the Prison as Surrogate Ghetto," *Theoretical Criminology* 4, no. 3 (2000): 380.

3. Lerone Bennett Jr., *The Shaping of Black America* (Chicago: Johnson, 1975), 62.

4. For an excellent analysis of the development of race as a social construct in the United States and around the globe, see Howard Winant, *The World Is a Ghetto: Race and Democracy Since World War II* (New York: Basic Books, 2001).

5. Bennett, *Shaping of Black America*, 62.

6. Keith Kilty and Eric Swank, "Institutional Racism and Media Representations: Depictions of Violent Criminals and Welfare Recipients," *Sociological Imagination* 34, no. 2–3 (1997): 106.

7. Edmund Morgan, *American Slavery, American Freedom: The Ordeal of Colonial Virginia* (New York: Norton, 1975).

8. Ibid.; see also Leslie Carr, *Color-blind Racism* (Thousand Oaks, CA: Sage Publications, 1997), 14–16.

9. Gerald Fresia, *Toward an American Revolution: Exposing the Constitution and Other Illusions* (Boston: South End Press, 1998), 55.

10. Wacquant, "America's New 'Peculiar Institution,'" 380.

11. C. Vann Woodward, *The Strange Career of Jim Crow* (1955; reprint, New York: Oxford University Press, 2001).

12. William Cohen, *At Freedom's Edge: Black Mobility and the Southern White Quest for Racial Control* (Baton Rouge: Louisiana State University Press, 1991), 28.

13. Ibid., 33.

14. W.E.B. Du Bois, "Reconstruction and Its Benefits," *American Historical Review* 15, no. 4 (1910): 784.

15. James McPherson, "Comparing the Two Reconstructions," *Princeton Alumni Weekly*, Feb. 26, 1979, 17.

16. See Michael Klarman, *From Jim Crow to Civil Rights: The Supreme Court and the Struggle for Racial Equality* (New York: Oxford University Press, 2004), 49, 52–53.

17. John Hope Franklin and Alfred A. Moss, *From Slavery to Freedom: A History of African Americans*, 8th ed. (New York: Knopf, 2000), 82; and Eric Foner, *Reconstruction: America's Unfinished Revolution, 1863–1877* (New York: Harper & Row, 1988), 425.

18. Douglas Blackmon, *Slavery by Another Name: The Re-enslavement of Black People in America from the Civil War to World War II* (New York: Doubleday, 2008).

19. *Ruffin v. Commonwealth*, 62 Va. 790, 796 (1871).

20. David M. Oshinsky, *Worse Than Slavery: Parchman Farm and the Ordeal of Jim Crow Justice* (New York: Free Press Paperbacks, 1996), 63.

21. See Douglas Blackmon, "A Different Kind of Slavery," *Wall Street Journal Online*, Mar. 29, 2008.

22. Woodward, *Strange Career of Jim Crow*, 45–64.

23. Ibid., 61.

24. Tom Watson, "The Negro Question in the South," cited in Stokely Carmichael and Charles V. Hamilton, *Black Power: The Politics of Liberation in America* (New York: Random House, 1967).

25. Woodward, *Strange Career of Jim Crow*, 64.

26. William Julius Wilson, *The Declining Significance of Race: Blacks and Changing American Institutions* (Chicago: University of Chicago Press, 1978), 54.

27. Woodward, *Strange Career of Jim Crow*, 80.

28. Ibid., 81.

29. Ibid., 7.

30. Gunnar Myrdal, *An American Dilemma: The Negro Problem and Modern Democracy* (New York: Harper & Brothers, 1944).

31. Manning Marable, *Race, Reform and Rebellion: The Second Reconstruction in Black America, 1945–1990* (Jackson: University Press of Mississippi, 1991), 44; see also Michael Klarman, "*Brown*, Racial Change, and the Civil Rights Movement," *Virginia Law Review* 80 (1994): 7, 9.

32. Marable, *Race, Reform and Rebellion*, 69.

33. Stephen F. Lawson, *Black Ballots: Voting Rights in the South, 1944–1969* (New York: Columbia University Press, 1976), 300, 321, 329, 331.

34. Frances Fox Piven and Richard A. Cloward, *Poor People's Movements: Why They Succeed, How They Fail* (New York: Pantheon, 1977), 269.

35. John Donovan, *The Politics of Poverty* (Indianapolis: Pegasus, 1973), 23.

36. Gerald McKnight, *The Last Crusade: Martin Luther King, Jr., the FBI, and the Poor People's Campaign* (New York: Westview Press, 1998), 21–22.

37. Richard Nixon, "If Mob Rule Takes Hold in U.S.," *U.S. News and World Report*, Aug. 15, 1966, 64.

38. U.S. House, "Northern Congressmen Want Civil Rights but Their Constituents Do Not Want Negroes," *Congressional Record*, 86th Cong., 2d sess. (1960) 106, pt. 4: 5062–63.

39. Katherine Beckett, *Making Crime Pay: Law and Order in Contemporary American Politics* (New York: Oxford University Press, 1997), 32; Marc Mauer, "Two-Tiered Justice: Race, Class and Crime Policy," in *The Integration Debate: Competing Futures for American Cities*, ed. Chester Hartman and Gregory Squires (New York: Routledge, 2005), 171.

40. Vesla M. Weaver, "Frontlash: Race and the Development of Punitive Crime Policy," *Studies in American Political Development* 21 (Fall 2007): 242.

41. Barry Goldwater, "Peace Through Strength," in *Vital Speeches of the Day*, vol. 30 (New York: City News, 1964), 744.

42. "Poverty: Phony Excuse for Riots? Yes, Says a Key Senator," *U.S. News and World Report*, July 31, 1967, 14.

43. See Vanessa Barker, *The Politics of Imprisonment: How the Democratic Process Shapes the Way America Punishes Offenders* (New York: Oxford University Press, 2009), 151.

44. Joel Rosch, "Crime as an Issue in American Politics," in *The Politics of Crime and Criminal Justice* (Beverley Hills: Sage Publications, 1985).

45. Beckett, *Making Crime Pay*, 32.

46. Marc Mauer, *Race to Incarcerate* (New York: The New Press, 1999), 52.

47. Weaver, "Frontlash," 262.

48. Ibid.

49. Klarman, *From Jim Crow to Civil Rights*, 110.

50. See, e.g., Patrick Buchanan, *The New Majority: President Nixon at Mid-Passage* (Philadelphia: Girard Bank, 1973).

51. Willard M. Oliver, *The Law & Order Presidency* (Upper Saddle River, NJ: Prentice Hall, 2003), 127–28, citing Dan Baum, *Smoke and Mirrors: The War on Drugs and the Politics of Failure* (Boston: Little, Brown, 1996), 13; H.R. Haldeman, *The Haldeman Diaries* (New York: G.P. Putnam's Sons, 1994), 53 (emphasis in original).

52. John Ehrlichman, *Witness to Power: The Nixon Years* (New York: Simon & Schuster, 1970), 233.

53. Ibid.

54. See Kevin Phillips, *The Emerging Republican Majority* (New Rochelle, NY: Arlington House, 1969).

55. Warren Weaver, "The Emerging Republican Majority," *New York Times,* Sept. 21, 1969.

56. Beckett, *Making Crime Pay,* 34.

57. Lyndon Johnson, "Remarks on the City Hall Steps, Dayton, Ohio," in *Public Papers of the Presidents 1963–64,* vol. 2 (1965), 1371.

58. Thomas Byrne Edsall and Mary D. Edsall, *Chain Reaction: The Impact of Race, Rights, and Taxes on American Politics* (New York: Norton, 1992), 12–13.

59. Ibid., 38.

60. Ibid., 74.

61. Weaver, "Frontlash," 259.

62. See Philip A. Klinker and Rogers M. Smith, *The Unsteady March: The Rise and Decline of Racial Equality in America* (Chicago: University of Chicago Press, 1999), 292.

63. Edsall and Edsall, *Chain Reaction,* 4.

64. Ibid., 138; see also Jeremy Mayer, *Running on Race* (New York: Random House, 2002), 71.

65. Ibid.

66. Bob Herbert, "Righting Reagan's Wrongs?" *New York Times,* Nov. 13, 2007; see also Paul Krugman, "Republicans and Race," *New York Times,* Nov. 19, 2007.

67. Edsall and Edsall, *Chain Reaction,* 148, quoting *New York Times,* Feb. 15, 1976.

68. Ibid., quoting *Washington Post,* Jan. 28, 1976.

69. Dick Kirschten, "Jungle Warfare," *National Journal,* Oct. 3, 1981.

70. Edsall and Edsall, *Chain Reaction,* 164.

71. Beckett, *Making Crime Pay,* 47.

72. Ibid., 56; see also Julian Roberts, "Public Opinion, Crime and Criminal Justice," in *Crime and Justice: A Review of Research,* vol. 16, ed. Michael Tonry (Chicago: University of Chicago Press, 1992).

73. Beckett, *Making Crime Pay,* 53, citing Executive Office of the President, Budget of the U.S. Government (1990).

74. Ibid., citing U.S. Office of the National Drug Control Policy, National Drug Control Strategy (1992).

75. Ibid.

76. Ibid., 56.

77. See William Julius Wilson, *When Work Disappears: The World of the New Urban Poor* (New York: Vintage, 1997).

78. Ibid., 31 (citing John Kasarda, "Urban Industrial Transition and the Underclass," *Annals of the American Academy of Political and Social Science* 501, no. 1 (1990): 26–47.

79. Ibid., 30 (citing data from the Chicago Urban Poverty and Family Life Survey conducted in 1987 and 1988).

80. Ibid., 39.

81. Ibid., 27.

82. David M. Kennedy, *Don't Shoot: One Man, a Street Fellowship, and the End of Violence in Inner-City America* (New York: Bloomsbury, 2011), 10.

83. Ernesto Benavides, "Portugal Drug Law Show Results Ten Years On, Experts Say," AFP, July 1, 2010 (reporting that those who use hard drugs fell by half following decriminalization, along with a "spectacular" drop in HIV infections and a significant drop in drug-related crime), available at news.yahoo.com/portugal-drug-law -show-results-ten-years-experts-180013798.html; Barry Hatton and Martha Mendoza, "Portugal's Drug Policy Pays Off; US Eyes Lessons," Associated Press, Dec. 26, 2010; Glenn Greenwald, *Drug Decriminalization in Portugal: Lessons for Creating Fair and Successful Drug Policies* (Washington, DC: Cato Institute, 2009), www .cato.org/pubs/wtpapers/greenwald_whitepaper.pdf.

84. Robert Stutman, *Dead on Delivery: Inside the Drug Wars, Straight from the Street* (New York: Warner Books, 1992), 142.

85. See Craig Reinarman and Harry Levine, "The Crack Attack: America's Latest Drug Scare, 1986–1992," in *Images of Issues: Typifying Contemporary Social Problems*, ed. Joel Best (New York: Aldine De Gruyter, 1995).

86. Ibid., 154.

87. Ibid., 170–71.

88. Doris Marie Provine, *Unequal Under Law: Race in the War on Drugs* (Chicago: University of Chicago Press, 2007), 111, citing *Congressional Record* 132 (Sept. 24, 1986): S 13741.

89. Provine, *Unequal Under Law*, 117.

90. Mark Peffley, Jon Hurwitz, and Paul Sniderman, "Racial Stereotypes and Whites' Political Views of Blacks in the Context of Welfare and Crime," *American Journal of Political Science* 41, no. 1 (1997): 30–60; Martin Gilens, "Racial Attitudes and Opposition to Welfare," *Journal of Politics* 57, no. 4 (1995): 994–1014; Kathlyn Taylor Gaubatz, *Crime in the Public Mind* (Ann Arbor: University of Michigan Press, 1995); and John Hurwitz and Mark Peffley, "Public Perceptions of Race and Crime: The Role of Racial Stereotypes," *American Journal of Political Science* 41, no. 2 (1997): 375–401.

91. See Frank Furstenberg, "Public Reaction to Crime in the Streets," *American Scholar* 40 (1971): 601–10; Arthur Stinchcombe et al., *Crime and Punishment in America: Changing Attitudes in America* (San Francisco: Jossey-Bass, 1980); Michael Corbett, "Public Support for Law and Order: Interrelationships with System Affirmation and Attitudes Toward Minorities," *Criminology* 19 (1981): 337.

92. Stephen Earl Bennett and Alfred J. Tuchfarber, "The Social Structural Sources of Cleavage on Law and Order Policies," *American Journal of Political Science* 19 (1975): 419–38; Sandra Browning and Liqun Cao, "The Impact of Race on Criminal Justice Ideology," *Justice Quarterly* 9 (Dec. 1992): 685–99; and Steven F. Cohn, Steven E. Barkan, and William A. Halteman, "Punitive Attitudes Toward Criminals: Racial Consensus or Racial Conflict?" *Social Problems* 38 (1991): 287–96.

93. Beckett, *Making Crime Pay*, 44.

94. Ibid., citing New York Times/CBS News Poll, Aug. 1990, 2–4.

95. See Beckett, *Making Crime Pay*, 14–27.

96. "Ku Klux Klan Says It Will Fight Drugs," *Toledo Journal*, Jan. 3–9, 1990.

97. Michael Kramer, "Frying Them Isn't the Answer," *Time*, Mar. 14, 1994, 32.

98. David Masci, "$30 Billion Anti-Crime Bill Heads to Clinton's Desk," *Congressional Quarterly*, Aug. 27, 1994, 2488–93; and Beckett, *Making Crime Pay*, 61.

99. Justice Policy Institute, "Clinton Crime Agenda Ignores Proven Methods for Reducing Crime," Apr. 14, 2008, available online at www.justicepolicy.org/content-hmID=1817&smID=1571&ssmID=71.htm.

100. Loïc Wacquant, "Class, Race & Hyperincarceration in Revanchist America," *Dædalus*, Summer 2010, 77.

101. Ibid.

102. Address Before a Joint Session of Congress on the State of the Union, Jan. 23, 1996.

103. U.S. Department of Housing and Urban Development, *Meeting the Challenge: Public Housing Authorities Respond to the "One Strike and You're Out" Initiative*, Sept. 1997, v.

2. The Lockdown

1. See Marc Mauer, *Race to Incarcerate*, rev. ed. (New York: The New Press, 2006), 33.

2. Marc Mauer and Ryan King, *A 25-Year Quagmire: The "War on Drugs" and Its Impact on American Society* (Washington, DC: Sentencing Project, 2007), 2.

3. Ibid., 3.

4. Testimony of Marc Mauer, Executive Director of the Sentencing Project, Prepared for the House Judiciary Subcommittee on Crime, Terrorism, and Homeland Security, 111th Cong., *Hearing on Unfairness in Federal Cocaine Sentencing: Is It Time to Crack the 100 to 1 Disparity?* May 21, 2009, 2.

5. Mauer and King, *A 25-Year Quagmire*, 2–3.

6. Ibid.; and Ryan King and Marc Mauer, *The War on Marijuana: The Transformation of the War on Drugs in the 1990s* (New York: Sentencing Project, 2005), documenting the dramatic increase in marijuana arrests. Marijuana is a relatively harmless drug. The 1988 surgeon general's report lists tobacco as a more dangerous drug than marijuana, and Francis Young, an administrative law judge for the Drug Enforcement Administration found there are no credible medical reports to suggest that consuming marijuana, in any dose, has ever caused a single death. U.S. Department of Justice, Drug Enforcement Administration, Opinion and Recommended Ruling, Findings of Fact, Conclusions of Law and Decision of Administrative Law Judge Francis L. Young, in the *Matter of Marijuana Rescheduling Petition*, Docket no.

86-22, Sept. 6, 1988, 56–57. By comparison, tobacco kills roughly 390,000 Americns annually, and alcohol is responsible for some 150,000 U.S. deaths a year. See Doug Bandow, "War on Drugs or War on America?" *Stanford Law and Policy Review* 3: 242, 245 (1991).

7. Pew Center on the States, *One in 31: The Long Reach of American Corrections* (Washington, DC: Pew Charitable Trusts, 2009).

8. *Skinner v. Railway Labor Executive Association*, 489 U.S. 602, 641 (1980), Marshall, J., dissenting.

9. *California v. Acevedo*, 500 U.S. 565, 600 (1991), Stevens. J., dissenting.

10. *Terry v. Ohio*, 392 U.S. 1, 30 (1968).

11. Ibid., Douglas J., dissenting.

12. See generally *United States v. Lewis*, 921 F.2d 1294, 1296 (1990); *United States v. Flowers*, 912 F.2d 707, 708 (4th Cir. 1990); and *Florida v. Bostick*, 501 U.S. 429, 441 (1991).

13. See, e.g., *Florida v. Kerwick*, 512 So.2d 347, 349 (Fla. App. 4 Dist. 1987).

14. See *United States v. Flowers*, 912 F.2d 707, 710 (4th Cir. 1990).

15. *Bostick v. State*, 554 So. 2d 1153, 1158 (Fla. 1989), quoting *State v. Kerwick*, 512 So.2d 347, 348–49 (Fla. 4th DCA 1987).

16. *In re J.M.*, 619 A.2d 497, 501 (D.C. App. 1992).

17. *Illinois Migrant Council v. Pilliod*, 398 F. Supp. 882, 899 (N.D. Ill. 1975).

18. Tracy Maclin, "Black and Blue Encounters—Some Preliminary Thoughts About Fourth Amendment Seizures: Should Race Matter?" *Valparaiso University Law Review* 26 (1991): 249–50.

19. *Florida v. Bostick*, 501 U.S. 429, 441 n. 1 (1991), Marshall, J., dissenting.

20. Maclin, "Black and Blue Encounters."

21. *Schneckloth v. Bustamonte*, 412 U.S. 218, 229 (1973).

22. See *Illinois v. Caballes*, 543 U.S. 405 (2005) and *United States v. Place*, 462 U.S. 696 (1983).

23. See U.S. Department of Justice, Drug Enforcement Administration, *Operations Pipeline and Convoy* (Washington, DC, n.d.), www.usdoj.gov/dea/programs/pipecon.htm.

24. Ricardo J. Bascuas, "Fourth Amendment Lessons from the Highway and the Subway: A Principled Approach to Suspicionless Searches," *Rutgers Law Journal* 38 (2007): 719, 763.

25. *State v. Rutherford*, 93 Ohio App.3d 586, 593–95, 639 N.E. 2d 498, 503–4, n. 3 (Ohio Ct. App. 1994).

26. Gary Webb, "Driving While Black," *Esquire*, Apr. 1, 1999, 122.

27. Ibid.

28. Scott Henson, *Flawed Enforcement: Why Drug Task Force Highway Interdiction Violates Rights, Wastes Tax Dollars, and Fails to Limit the Availability of Drugs in Texas* (Austin: American Civil Liberties Union—Texas Chapter, 2004), 9, www.aclu.org/racialjustice/racialprofiling/15897pub20040519.html.

29. David Cole, *No Equal Justice: Race and Class in the American Criminal Justice System* (New York: The New Press, 1999), 47.

30. Florida Department of Highway Safety and Motor Vehicles, Office of General Counsel, *Common Characteristics of Drug Couriers* (1984), sec. I.A.4.

31. Cole, *No Equal Justice*, 49.

32. "Fluid Drug Courier Profiles See Everyone As Suspicious," *Criminal Practice Manual* 5 (Bureau of National Affairs: July 10, 1991): 334–35.

33. Mauer and King, *25-Year Quagmire*, 3.

34. Katherine Beckett, *Making Crime Pay: Law and Order in Contemporary American Politics* (New York: Oxford University Press, 1997), 45; and Mauer, *Race to Incarcerate,* 49.

35. U.S. Department of Justice, *Department of Justice Drug Demand Reduction Activities, Report No. 3-12* (Washington, DC: Office of the Inspector General, Feb. 2003), 35, www.usdoj.gov/oig/reports/plus/a0312.

36. Radley Balko, *Overkill: The Rise of Paramilitary Police Raids in America* (Washington, DC: Cato Institute, July 17, 2006), 8.

37. Megan Twohey, "SWATs Under Fire," *National Journal*, Jan. 1, 2000, 37; Balko, *Overkill*, 8.

38. Timothy Egan, "Soldiers of the Drug War Remain on Duty," *New York Times*, Mar. 1, 1999.

39. Ibid., 8–9.

40. Scott Andron, "SWAT: Coming to a Town Near You?" *Miami Herald*, May 20, 2002.

41. Balko, *Overkill*, 11, citing Peter Kraska, "Researching the Police-Military Blur: Lessons Learned," *Police Forum* 14, no. 3 (2005).

42. Balko, *Overkill*, 11, citing Britt Robson, "Friendly Fire," *Minneapolis City Pages*, Sept. 17, 1997.

43. Ibid., 43 (citing Kraska research).

44. Ibid., 49 (citing *Village Voice*).

45. Ibid., 50; "Not All Marijuana Law Victims Are Arrested: Police Officer Who Fatally Shot Suspected Marijuana User Cleared of Criminal Charges," NORML News, July 13, 1995, druglibrary.org/olsen/NORML/WEEKLY/95-07-13.html; Timothy Lynch, *After Prohibition* (Washington, DC: Cato Institute, 2000), 82; and various sources citing "Dodge County Detective Can't Remember Fatal Shot; Unarmed Man Killed in Drug Raid at His Home," *Milwaukee Journal-Sentinel*, Apr. 29, 1995, A1, and "The Week," *National Review*, June 12, 1995, 14.

46. Ibid., 10, citing Steven Elbow, "Hooked on SWAT: Fueled with Drug Enforcement Money, Military-Style Police Teams Are Exploding in the Backwoods of Wisconsin," *Madison Capitol Times*, Aug. 18, 2001.

47. Eric Blumenson and Eva Nilsen, "Policing for Profit: The Drug War's Hidden Economic Agenda," *University of Chicago Law Review* 65 (1998): 35, 45.

48. Ibid., 64.

49. Blumenson and Nilsen, "Policing for Profit," 72.

50. Ibid., 71.

51. Ibid., 82.

52. Ibid.

53. Ibid., 83.

54. Ibid.

55. Ibid.

56. Ibid., 98.

57. Michael Fessier Jr., "Trail's End Deep in a Wild Canyon West of Malibu, a Controversial Law Brought Together a Zealous Sheriff's Deputy and an Eccentric Recluse; a Few Seconds Later, Donald Scott Was Dead," *Los Angeles Times Magazine*, Aug. 1, 1993; and Office of the District Attorney of Ventura, California, "Report on the Death of Donald Scott," (Mar. 30, 1993), available at www.fear.org/chron/scott.txt.

58. Peter D. Lepsch, "Wanted: Civil Forfeiture Reform," *Drug Policy Letter*, Summer 1997, 12.

59. James Massey, Susan Miller, and Anna Wilhelmi, "Civil Forfeiture of Property: The Victimization of Women as Innocent Owners and Third Parties," in *Crime Control and Women*, ed. Susan Miller (Thousand Oaks, CA: Sage Publications, 1998), 17.

60. *United States v. One Parcel of Real Estate Located at 9818 S.W. 94 Terrace*, 788 F. Supp. 561, 565 (S.D. Fla. 1992).

61. David Hunt, "Obama Fields Questions on Jacksonville Crime," *Florida Times-Union*, Sept. 22, 2008.

62. See Phillip Smith, "Federal Budget: Economic Stimulus Bill Stimulates Drug War, Too," *Drug War Chronicle*, no. 573 (Feb. 20, 2009). See also Michelle Alexander, "Obama's Drug War," *The Nation*, Dec. 9, 2010 (noting that the 2009 economic stimulus package included a twelvefold increase in financing for Byrne programs).

63. John Balzar, "The System: Deals, Deadlines, Few Trials," *Los Angeles Times*, Sept. 4, 2006.

64. Marc Mauer and Ryan S. King, *Schools and Prisons: Fifty Years After Brown v. Board of Education* (Washington, DC: Sentencing Project, 2004), 4.

65. Laura Parker, "8 Years in a Louisiana Jail but He Never Went to Trial," *USA Today*, Aug. 29, 2005.

66. Mauer and King, *Schools and Prisons*, 4.

67. American Bar Association, Standing Committee on Legal Aid and Indigent Defendants, *Gideon's Broken Promise: America's Continuing Quest for Equal Justice* (Washington, DC: American Bar Association, Dec. 2004), Executive Summary IV; adopted by American Bar Association House of Delegates, Aug. 9, 2005, www.abanet.org/leadership/2005/annual/dailyjournal/107.doc.

68. Parker, "8 Years in a Louisiana Jail."

69. Kim Brooks and Darlene Kamine, eds., *Justice Cut Short: An Assessment of Access to Counsel and Quality of Representation in Delinquency Proceedings In Ohio* (Columbus: Ohio State Bar Foundation, 2003), 28.

70. Mauer, *Race to Incarcerate*, 35–37.

71. See Angela J. Davis, *Arbitrary Justice: The Power of the American Prosecutor* (New York: Oxford University Press, 2007), 31–33.

72. See Alexandra Natapoff, "Snitching: The Institutional and Communal Consequences," *University of Cincinnati Law Review* 645 (2004); and Emily Jane Dodds, "I'll Make You a Deal: How Repeat Informants Are Corrupting the Criminal Justice System and What to Do About It," *William and Mary Law Review* 50 (2008): 1063.

73. See "Riverside Drug Cases Under Review Over Use of Secret Informant," Associated Press, Aug. 20, 2004; Ruben Narvette Jr., "Blame Stretches Far and Wide in Drug Scandal," *Dallas Morning News*, Nov. 14, 2003; Rob Warden, *How Snitch Testimony Sent Randy Steidl and Other Innocent Americans to Death Row* (Chicago: Northwestern University School of Law, Center for Wrongful Convictions, 2004–5); "The Informant Trap," *National Law Journal*, Mar. 6, 1995; Steven Mills and Ken Armstrong, "The Jailhouse Informant," *Chicago Tribune*, Nov. 16, 1999; and Ted Rohrlich and Robert Stewart, "Jailhouse Snitches: Trading Lies for Freedom," *Los Angeles Times*, Apr. 16, 1989.

74. See Adam Liptak, "Consensus on Counting the Innocent: We Can't," *New York Times*, Mar. 25, 2008; and Adam Liptak, "Study Suspects Thousands of False Confessions," *New York Times*, Apr. 19, 2004.

75. Christopher J. Mumola and Jennifer C. Karberg, *Drug Use and Dependence, State and Federal Prisoners, 2004* (Washington, DC: U.S. Department of Justice, Bureau of Justice Statistics, 2006); and Ashley Nellis, Judy Greene, and Marc Mauer, *Reducing Racial Disparity in the Criminal Justice System: A Manual for Practitioners and Policymakers*, 2d ed. (Washington, DC: Sentencing Project, 2008), 8.

76. *Hutto v. Davis*, 454 U.S. 370 (1982).

77. *Harmelin v. Michigan*, 501 U.S. 967 (1991).

78. Marc Mauer, "The Hidden Problem of Time Served in Prison," *Social Research* 74, no. 2 (Summer 2007): 701, 703.

79. *Lockyer v. Andrade*, 538 U.S. 63 (2003).

80. Anne Gearam, "Supreme Court Upholds 'Three Strikes Law,'" Associated Press, Mar. 5, 2003.

81. See Families Against Mandatory Minimums, "Profiles of Injustice," at www.famm.org/ProfilesofInjustice/FederalProfiles/MarcusBoyd.aspx.

82. Marc Mauer, "Hidden Problem," 701–2.

83. Special to the *New York Times*, "Criticizing Sentencing Rules, US Judge Resigns," *New York Times*, Sept. 30, 1990.

84. Joseph Treaster, "Two Federal Judges, in Protest, Refuse to Accept Drug Cases," *New York Times*, Apr. 17, 1993.

85. Chris Carmody, "Revolt to Sentencing is Gaining Momentum," *National Law Journal,* May 17, 1993, 10.

86. Stuart Taylor Jr., "Ten Years for Two Ounces," *American Lawyer,* Mar. 1990, 65–66.

87. Michael Jacobson, *Downsizing Prisons: How to Reduce Crime and End Mass Incarceration* (New York: New York University Press, 2005), 215.

88. See Mauer, *Race to Incarcerate,* 33, 36–38, citing Warren Young and Mark Brown.

89. PEW Center for the States, *One in 31.*

90. Jeremy Travis, *But They All Come Back: Facing the Challenges of Prisoner Reentry* (Washington, DC: Urban Institute Press, 2002), 32, citing Bureau of Justice Statistics.

91. Ibid., 94, citing Bureau of Justice Statistics.

92. Ibid.

93. Ibid., 32.

94. Ibid.

95. Ibid., 49, citing Bureau of Justice Statistics.

96. Loïc Wacquant, "The New 'Peculiar Institution': On the Prison as Surrogate Ghetto," *Theoretical Criminology* 4, no. 3 (2000): 377–89.

3. The Color of Justice

1. Frontline, *The Plea,* www.pbs.org/wgbh/pages/frontline/shows/plea/four/stewart.html; and Angela Davis, *Arbitrary Justice: The Power of the American Prosecutor* (New York: Oxford University Press, 2007), 50–52.

2. American Civil Liberties Union, *Stories of ACLU Clients Swept Up in the Hearne Drug Bust of November 2000* (Washington, DC: American Civil Liberties Union, 2002), www.aclu.org/DrugPolicy/DrugPolicy.cfm?ID=11160&c=80.

3. Human Rights Watch, *Punishment and Prejudice: Racial Disparities in the War on Drugs,* HRW Reports, vol. 12, no. 2 (May 2000).

4. Ibid.

5. Jeremy Travis, *But They All Come Back: Facing the Challenges of Prisoner Reentry* (Washington, DC: Urban Institute Press, 2002), 28.

6. Ibid.

7. Ibid.

8. Marc Mauer and Ryan S. King, *Schools and Prisons: Fifty Years After Brown v. Board of Education* (Washington, DC: Sentencing Project, 2004), 3.

9. Marc Mauer, *The Changing Racial Dynamics of the War on Drugs* (Washington, DC: Sentencing Project, Apr. 2009).

10. See, e.g., U.S. Department of Health and Human Services, Substance Abuse and Mental Health Services Administration, *Summary of Findings from the 2000 National Household Survey on Drug Abuse,* NHSDA series H-13, DHHS pub. no.

SMA 01-3549 (Rockville, MD: 2001), reporting that 6.4 percent of whites, 6.4 percent of blacks, and 5.3 percent of Hispanics were current illegal drug users in 2000; *Results from the 2002 National Survey on Drug Use and Health: National Findings*, NSDUH series H-22, DHHS pub. no. SMA 03-3836 (2003), revealing nearly identical rates of illegal drug use among whites and blacks, only a single percentage point between them; *Results from the 2007 National Survey on Drug Use and Health: National Findings*, NSDUH series H-34, DHHS pub. no. SMA 08-4343 (2007) showing essentially the same findings; and Marc Mauer and Ryan S. King, *A 25-Year Quagmire: The War on Drugs and Its Impact on American Society* (Washington, DC: Sentencing Project, Sept. 2007), 19, citing a study suggesting that African Americans have slightly higher rates of illegal drug use than whites.

11. See, e.g., Howard N. Snyder and Melissa Sickman, *Juvenile Offenders and Victims: 2006 National Report*, U.S. Department of Justice, Office of Justice Programs, Office of Juvenile Justice and Delinquency Prevention (Washington, DC: 2006), reporting that white youth are more likely than black youth to engage in illegal drug sales; Lloyd D. Johnson, Patrick M. O'Malley, Jerald G. Bachman, and John E. Schulenberg, *Monitoring the Future, National Survey Results on Drug Use, 1975–2006, vol. 1, Secondary School Students*, U.S. Department of Health and Human Services, National Institute on Drug Abuse, NIH pub. no. 07-6205 (Bethesda, MD: 2007), 32, stating "African American 12th graders have consistently shown lower usage rates than White 12th graders for most drugs, both licit and illicit"; and Lloyd D. Johnston, Patrick M. O'Malley, and Jerald G. Bachman, *Monitoring the Future: National Results on Adolescent Drug Use: Overview of Key Findings 2002*, U.S. Department of Health and Human Services, National Institute on Drug Abuse, NIH pub. no. 03-5374 (Bethesda, MD: 2003), presenting data showing that African American adolescents have slightly lower rates of illicit drug use than their white counterparts.

12. National Institute on Drug Abuse, *Monitoring the Future, National Survey Results on Drug Use, 1975–1999*, vol. 1, *Secondary School Students* (Washington, DC: National Institute on Drug Abuse, 2000).

13. U.S. Department of Health, *National Household Survey on Drug Abuse, 1999* (Washington, DC: Substance Abuse and Mental Health Services Administration, Office of Applied Studies, 2000), table G, p. 71, www.samhsa.gov/statistics/statistics.html.

14. Bruce Western, *Punishment and Inequality* (New York: Russell Sage Foundation, 2006), 47.

15. Researchers have found that drug users are most likely to report using as a main source for drugs someone who is of their own racial or ethnic background. See, e.g., K. Jack Riley, *Crack, Powder Cocaine and Heroin: Drug Purchase and Use Patterns in Six U.S. Cities* (Washington, DC: National Institute of Justice, 1997), 1; see also George Rengert and James LeBeau, "The Impact of Ethnic Boundaries on the Spatial Choice of Illegal Drug Dealers," paper presented at the annual meeting of

the American Society of Criminology, Atlanta, Georgia, Nov. 13, 2007 (unpublished manuscript), finding that most illegal drug dealers sell in their own neighborhood and that a variety of factors influence whether dealers are willing to travel outside their home community.

16. See Rafik Mohamed and Erik Fritsvold, "Damn, It Feels Good to Be a Gangsta: The Social Organization of the Illicit Drug Trade Servicing a Private College Campus," *Deviant Behavior* 27 (2006): 97–125.

17. See Ralph Weisheit, *Domestic Marijuana: A Neglected Industry* (Westport, CT: Greenwood, 1992); and Ralph Weisheit, David Falcone, and L. Edward Wells, *Crime and Policing in Rural and Small-Town America* (Prospect Heights, IL: Waveland, 1996).

18. Patricia Davis and Pierre Thomas, "In Affluent Suburbs, Young Users and Sellers Abound," *Washington Post*, Dec. 14, 1997.

19. Human Rights Watch, *Punishment and Prejudice*.

20. PEW Center on the States, *One in 100: Behind Bars in America 2008* (Washington, DC: Pew Charitable Trusts, 2008)—data analysis is based on statistics for midyear 2006 published by the U.S. Department of Justice in June 2007.

21. Ibid.; Pew Center on the States, *One in 31: The Long Reach of American Corrections* (Washington, DC: Pew Charitable Trusts, 2009).

22. Howard Schuman, Charlotte Steeh, Lawrence Bobo, and Maria Krysan, *Racial Attitudes in America: Trends and Interpretations* (Cambridge, MA: Harvard University Press, 1985).

23. See, e.g., Marc Mauer, *Race to Incarcerate* (New York: The New Press, 1999), 28–35, 92–112.

24. Ibid.

25. Katherine Beckett and Theodore Sasson, *The Politics of Injustice: Crime and Punishment in America* (Thousand Oaks, CA: Sage Publications, 2004), 22.

26. Heather West and William Sobol, "Prisoners in 2009," Bureau of Justice Statistics, Dec. 2010.

27. Lauren Glaze, "Correctional Populations in the United States, 2009," Bureau of Justice Statistics, Dec. 2010.

28. Ibid.

29. Ibid.

30. Thomas Cohen and Tracey Kyckelhahn, "Felony Defendants in Large Urban Counties, 2006," Bureau of Justice Statistics Bulletin, May 2010.

31. Report of the Illinois Disproportionate Justice Impact Study Commission, Dec. 2010, available at www.centerforhealthandjustice.org/DJIS_ExecSumm _FINAL.pdf.

32. Mike Drause, "The Case for Further Sentencing Reform in Colorado," Independence Institute, Jan. 2011, 3. In 1982, drug offenders made up only 6 percent of total prison admissions in Colorado; today they comprise 23 percent of total admissions. Ibid. See also Eric Lotke and Jason Ziedenberg, "Tipping Point: Maryland's

Overuse of Incarceration and the Impact on Community Safety," Justice Policy Institute, Mar. 2005 (noting that the size of Maryland's prison system has tripled in recent years, and that "this expansion was driven mainly by drug imprisonment and drug addiction").

33. Cities with similar demographic profiles often have vastly different drug arrest and conviction rates—not because of disparities in drug crime but rather because of differences in the amount of resources dedicated to drug law enforcement. Ryan S. King, *Disparity by Geography: The War on Drugs in America's Cities* (Washington, DC: Sentencing Project, 2008).

34. Substance Abuse and Mental Health Services Administration, *Results from the 2002 National Survey on Drug Use and Health: Detailed Tables, Prevalence Estimates, Standard Errors and Sample Sizes* (Washington, DC: Office of National Drug Control Policy, 2003), table 34.

35. Jimmie Reeves and Richard Campbell, *Cracked Coverage: Television News, the Anti-Cocaine Crusade and the Reagan Legacy* (Durham, NC: Duke University Press, 1994).

36. David Jernigan and Lori Dorfman, "Visualizing America's Drug Problems: An Ethnographic Content Analysis of Illegal Drug Stories on the Nightly News," *Contemporary Drug Problems* 23 (1996): 169, 188.

37. Rick Szykowny, "No Justice, No Peace: An Interview with Jerome Miller," *Humanist*, Jan.–Feb. 1994, 9–19.

38. Melissa Hickman Barlow, "Race and the Problem of Crime in *Time* and *Newsweek* Cover Stories, 1946 to 1995," *Social Justice* 25 (1989): 149–83.

39. Betty Watson Burston, Dionne Jones, and Pat Robertson-Saunders, "Drug Use and African Americans: Myth Versus Reality," *Journal of Alcohol and Drug Abuse* 40 (Winter 1995): 19.

40. Franklin D. Gilliam and Shanto Iyengar, "Prime Suspects: The Influence of Local Television News on the Viewing Public," *American Journal of Political Science* 44 (2000): 560–73.

41. See, e.g., Nilanjana Dasgupta, "Implicit Ingroup Favoritism, Outgroup Favoritism, and Their Behavioral Manifestations," *Social Justice Research* 17 (2004): 143. For a review of the social science literature on this point and its relevance to critical race theory and antidiscrimination law, see Jerry Kang, "Trojan Horses of Race," *Harvard Law Review* 118 (2005): 1489.

42. There is some dispute whether Nietzsche actually said this. He did use the term "immaculate perception" in *Thus Spoke Zarathustra* to disparage traditional views of knowledge, but apparently did not say the precise quote attributed to him. See Friedrich Nietzsche, *Thus Spoke Zarathustra*, reprinted in *The Portable Nietzsche*, ed. and trans. Walter Kaufmann (New York: Viking Penguin, 1954), 100, 233–36.

43. See, e.g., John F. Dovidio et al., "On the Nature of Prejudice: Automatic and Controlled Processes," *Journal of Experimental Social Psychology* 33 (1997): 510, 516–17, 534.

44. Joshua Correll et al., "The Police Officer's Dilemma: Using Ethnicity to Disambiguate Potentially Threatening Individuals, *Journal of Personality and Social Psychology* 83 (2001): 1314; see also Keith Payne, "Prejudice and Perception: The Role of Automatic and Controlled Processes in Misperceiving a Weapon," *Journal of Personality and Social Psychology* 81 (2001): 181.

45. See, e.g., Dovidio et al., "On the Nature of Prejudice"; and Dasgupta, "Implicit Ingroup Favoritism."

46. Ibid.; see also Brian Nosek, Mahzarin Banaji, and Anthony Greenwald, "Harvesting Implicit Group Attitudes and Beliefs from a Demonstration Web Site," *Group Dynamics* 6 (2002): 101.

47. Correll, "Police Officer's Dilemma."

48. Nosek et al., "Harvesting Implicit Group Attitudes."

49. Ibid.

50. John A. Bargh et al., "Automaticity of Social Behavior: Direct Effects of Trait Construct and Stereotype Activation on Action," *Journal of Personality and Social Psychology* 71 (1996): 230; Gilliam and Iyengar, "Prime Suspects"; Jennifer L. Eberhardt et al., "Looking Deathworthy," *Psychological Science* 17, no. 5 (2006): 383–86 ("[J]urors are influenced not simply by the knowledge that the defendant is Black, but also by the extent to which the defendant appears to be stereotypically Black. In fact for the Blacks with [the most stereotypical faces], the chance of receiving a death sentence more than doubled"); Jennifer L. Eberhardt et al., "Seeing Black: Race, Crime, and Visual Processing," *Journal of Personality and Social Psychology* 87, no. 6 (2004): 876–93 (not only were black faces considered more criminal by law enforcement, but the more stereotypical black faces were considered to be the most criminal of all); and Irene V. Blair, "The Influence of Afrocentric Facial Features in Criminal Sentencing," *Psychological Science* 15, no. 10 (2004): 674–79 (finding that inmates with more Afrocentric features received harsher sentences than individuals with less Afrocentric features).

51. See Kathryn Russell, *The Color of Crime* (New York: New York University Press, 1988), coining the term *criminalblackman*.

52. The notion that the Supreme Court must apply a higher standard of review and show special concern for the treatment of "discrete and insular minorities"— who may not fare well through the majoritarian political process—was first recognized by the Court in the famous footnote 4 of *United States v. Caroline Products Co.*, 301 U.S. 144, n. 4 (1938).

53. *Whren v. United States*, 517 U.S. 806 (1996).

54. *McCleskey v. Kemp*, 481 U.S. 279, 327 (1989), Brennan, J., dissenting.

55. Ibid., 321.

56. Ibid., 296. Ironically, the Court expressed concern that these rules would make it difficult for *prosecutors* to disprove racial bias. Apparently, the Court was unconcerned that defendants, due to its ruling in the case, would not be able to prove racial bias because of the same rules.

57. Ibid., 314–16.

58. Ibid., 339.

59. *United States v. Clary*, 846 F.Supp. 768, 796–97 (E.D.Mo. 1994).

60. Doris Marie Provine, *Unequal Under Law: Race in the War on Drugs* (Chicago: University of Chicago Press, 2007), 26.

61. Davis, *Arbitrary Justice*, 5.

62. *Yick Wo v. Hopkins*, 118 U.S. 356, 373–74 (1886).

63. See, e.g., Sandra Graham and Brian Lowery, "Priming Unconscious Racial Stereotypes About Adolescent Offenders," *Law and Human Behavior* 28, no. 5 (2004): 483–504.

64. Christopher Schmitt, "Plea Bargaining Favors Whites, as Blacks, Hispanics Pay Price," *San Jose Mercury News*, Dec. 8, 1991.

65. See, e.g., Carl E. Pope and William Feyerherm, "Minority Status and Juvenile Justice Processing: An Assessment of the Research Literature," *Criminal Justice Abstracts* 22 (1990): 527–42; Carl E. Pope, Rick Lovell, and Heidi M. Hsia, U.S. Department of Justice, *Disproportionate Minority Confinement: A Review of the Research Literature from 1989 Through 2001* (Washington, DC: U.S. Department of Justice, 2002); Eleanor Hinton Hoytt, Vincent Schiraldi, Brenda V. Smith, and Jason Ziedenberg, *Reducing Racial Disparities in Juvenile Detention* (Baltimore: Annie E. Casey Foundation, 2002), 20–21.

66. Eileen Poe-Yamagata and Michael A. Jones, *And Justice for Some: Differential Treatment of Youth of Color in the Justice System* (Washington, DC: Building Blocks for Youth, 2000).

67. Christopher Hartney and Fabiana Silva, *And Justice for Some: Differential Treatment of Youth of Color in the Justice System* (Washington, DC: National Council on Crime and Delinquency, 2007).

68. See George Bridges and Sara Steen, "Racial Disparities in Official Assessments of Juvenile Offenders: Attributional Stereotypes as Mediating Mechanisms," *American Sociological Review* 63, no. 4 (1998): 554–70.

69. *Swain v. Alabama*, 380 U.S. 202 (1965), overruled by *Batson v. Kentucky*, 476 U.S. 79 (1986).

70. *Strauder v. West Virginia*, 100 U.S. 303, 308 (1880).

71. Ibid., 309.

72. Benno C. Schmidt Jr., "Juries, Jurisdiction, and Race Discrimination: The Lost Promise of *Strauder v. West Virginia*," *Texas Law Review* 61 (1983): 1401.

73. See, e.g., *Smith v. Mississippi*, 162 U.S. 592 (1896); *Gibson v. Mississippi*, 162 U.S. 565 (1896); and *Brownfield v. South Carolina*, 189 U.S. 426 (1903).

74. *Neal v. Delaware*, 103 U.S. 370, 397 (1880).

75. Ibid., 402–3 (quoting Delaware Supreme Court).

76. *Miller-El v. Cockrell*, 537 U.S. 322, 333–34 (2003).

77. Ibid., 334–35.

78. Brian Kalt, "The Exclusion of Felons from Jury Service," *American University Law Review* 53 (2003): 65, 67.

79. Michael J. Raphael and Edward J. Ungvarsky, "Excuses, Excuses: Neutral Explanations Under *Batson v. Kentucky*," *University of Michigan Journal of Law Reform* 27 (1993): 229, 236.

80. Sheri Lynn Johnson, "The Language and Culture (Not to Say Race) of Peremptory Challenges," *William and Mary Law Review* 35 (1993): 21, 59.

81. *Purkett v. Elm*, 514 U.S. 765, 771 n. 4 (1995), Stevens, J., dissenting and quoting prosecutor.

82. Ibid., 767.

83. Ibid., 768.

84. Ibid.

85. See Lynn Lu, "Prosecutorial Discretion and Racial Disparities in Sentencing: Some Views of Former U.S. Attorneys," *Federal Sentencing Reporter* 19 (Feb. 2007): 192.

86. Douglas S. Massey and Nancy A. Denton, *American Apartheid: Segregation and the Making of the Underclass* (Cambridge, MA: Harvard University Press, 1993), 2.

87. For a discussion of possible replacement effects, see Robert MacCoun and Peter Reuter, *Drug War Heresies: Learning from Other Vices, Times, and Places* (New York: Cambridge University Press, 2001).

88. See Katherine Beckett, Kris Nyrop, Lori Pfingst, and Melissa Bowen, "Drug Use, Drug Possession Arrests, and the Question of Race: Lessons from Seattle," *Social Problems* 52, no. 3 (2005): 419–41; and Katherine Beckett, Kris Nyrop, and Lori Pfingst, "Race, Drugs and Policing: Understanding Disparities in Drug Delivery Arrests," *Criminology* 44, no. 1 (2006): 105.

89. Beckett, "Drug Use," 436.

90. Ibid.

91. Ibid.

92. David Cole, *No Equal Justice: Race and Class in the American Criminal Justice System* (New York: The New Press, 1999), 161.

93. Ibid., 162.

94. *City of Los Angeles v. Lyons*, 461 U.S. 95, 105 (1983).

95. *Quern v. Jordan*, 440 U.S. 332 (1979); and *Will v. Mich. Dept. of State Police*, 491 U.S. 58 (1989).

96. *Monell v. Dept. of Social Services*, 436 U.S. 658 (1978).

97. See *United States v. Brignoni-Ponce*, 422 U.S. 873 (1975); and *United States v. Martinez-Fuerte*, 428 U.S. 543 (1976).

98. See Massey, *American Apartheid*.

99. For a thoughtful overview of these studies, see David Harris, *Profiles in Injustice: Why Racial Profiling Cannot Work* (New York: The New Press, 2002).

100. *State v. Soto*, 324 N.J.Super. 66, 69–77, 83–85, 734 A.2d 350, 352–56, 360 (N.J. Super. Ct. Law Div. 1996).

101. Harris, *Profiles in Injustice*, 80.

102. Ibid.

103. Jeff Brazil and Steve Berry, "Color of Drivers Is Key to Stops on I-95 Videos," *Orlando Sentinel*, Aug. 23, 1992; and David Harris, "Driving While Black and All Other Traffic Offenses: The Supreme Court and Pretextual Traffic Stops," *Journal of Criminal Law and Criminology* 87 (1997): 544, 561–62.

104. ACLU, *Driving While Black: Racial Profiling on our Nation's Highways* (New York: American Civil Liberties Union, 1999) 3, 27–28.

105. ACLU of Northern California, "Oakland Police Department Announces Results of Racial Profiling Data Collection Program Praised by ACLU," press release, May 11, 2001, www.aclunc.org/news/press_releases/oakland_police_department_an nouces_results_of_racial_profiling_data_collection_program_praised_by_aclu.shtml.

106. Al Baker and Emily Vasquez, "Number of People Stopped by Police Soars in New York," *New York Times*, Feb. 3, 2007.

107. Office of the Attorney General of New York State, *Report on the New York City Police Department's "Stop & Frisk" Practices* (New York: Office of the Attorney General of New York State, 1999), 95, 111, 121, 126.

108. Ibid., 117 n. 23

109. Baker and Vasquez, "Number of People Stopped by Police Soars."

110. Center for Constitutional Rights, "Racial Disparity in NYPD Stops-and-Frisks: Preliminary Report on UF-250 Data from June 2005 through June 2008," Jan. 15, 2009, ccrjustice.org/files/Report_CCR_NYPD_Stop_and_Frisk_0 .pdf.

111. Al Baker and Ray Rivera, "Study Finds Tens of Thousands of Street Stops by N.Y. Police Unjustified," *New York Times*, Oct. 26, 2010.

112. Ibid.

113. Ibid.

114. Harry G. Levine and Loren Siegel, "$75 Million a Year: The Cost of New York City's Marijuana Possession Arrests," and the appendix "Human Costs of Marijuana Possession Arrests," Drug Policy Alliance, Mar. 15, 2011, www.drugpolicy.org/ sites/default/files/%2475%20Million%20A%20Year.pdf.

115. Ibid.

116. See Harry G. Levine and Deborah Peterson Small, *Marijuana Arrest Crusade: Racial Bias and Police Policy in New York City, 1997–2007* (New York: New York Civil Liberties Union, 2008), 4.

117. Ryan Pintado-Vertner and Jeff Chang. "The War on Youth," *Colorlines* 2, no. 4 (Winter 1999–2000): 36.

118. *Alexander v. Sandoval*, 532 U.S. 275 (2001).

119. The Fair Sentencing Act was signed by President Obama on August 3, 2010. As originally introduced in the Senate, the bill would have completely eliminated

the discriminatory disparity between crack and powder cocaine sentencing under federal law. But during the bill's markup in the Senate, a deal was struck with Republican Senate Judiciary Committee members to simply reduce the disparity to an 18:1 ratio. See Peter Baker, "Obama Signs Law Narrowing Cocaine Sentencing Disparities," *New York Times*, Aug. 3, 2010, thecaucus.blogs.nytimes.com/2010/08/03/obama-signs-law-narrowing-cocaine-sentencing-disparities/. See also Nicole Porter and Valerie Wright, "Cracked Justice," Sentencing Project, Mar. 2011 (documenting the persistence of crack vs. powder sentencing disparities in numerous states).

4. The Cruel Hand

1. Proceedings of the Colored National Convention, held in Rochester, July 6–8, 1853 (Rochester: Printed at the office of *Frederick Douglass's Papers*, 1853), 16.

2. Approximately 30 percent of African American men are banned for life from jury service because they are felons. See Brian Kalt, "The Exclusion of Felons from Jury Service," *American University Law Review* 53 (2003): 65.

3. Jeremy Travis, *But They All Come Back: Facing the Challenges of Prisoner Reentry* (Washington, DC: Urban Institute Press, 2002), 73.

4. Webb Hubbell, "The Mark of Cain," *San Francisco Chronicle*, June 10, 2001; Nora Demleitner, "Preventing Internal Exile: The Need for Restrictions on Collateral Sentencing and Consequences," *Stanford Law and Policy Review* 11, no. 1 (1999): 153–63.

5. Marc Mauer and Meda Chesney-Lind, eds., *Invisible Punishment: The Collateral Consequences of Mass Imprisonment* (New York: The New Press, 2002), 5, citing American Bar Association, Task Force on Collateral Sanctions, *Introduction, Proposed Standards on Collateral Sanctions and Administrative Disqualification of Convicted Persons*, draft, Jan. 18, 2002.

6. Frederick Douglass, "What Negroes Want," in *The Life and Writings of Frederick Douglass*, vol. 4, ed. Philip S. Foner (New York: International, 1955), 159–60.

7. Jeff Manza and Christopher Uggen, *Locked Out: Felon Disenfranchisement and American Democracy* (New York: Oxford University Press, 2006), 152.

8. Human Rights Watch, *No Second Chance: People with Criminal Records Denied Access to Housing* (New York: Human Rights Watch, 2006), ix.

9. President Bill Clinton, "Remarks by the President at One Strike Symposium," White House, Office of the Press Secretary, Mar. 28, 1996, clinton6.nara.gov/1996/03/1996-03-28-president-remarks-at-one-strike-symposium.html.

10. Memorandum from President Clinton to HUD Secretary on "One Strike and You're Out" Guidelines, Mar. 28, 1996, clinton6.nara.gov/1996/03/1996-03-28-memo-on-one-strike-and-you're-out-guidelines.html; and President Bill Clinton, "Remarks by the President at One Strike Symposium."

11. U.S. Department of Housing and Urban Development, notice PIH 96-16 (HA), Apr. 29, 1996, and attached "one strike" guidelines, HUD, "'One Strike and

You're Out' Screening and Eviction Guidelines for Public Housing Authorities," Apr. 12, 1996.

12. Human Rights Watch, *No Second Chance*.

13. Ibid., vi.

14. *Rucker v. Davis*, 237 F.3d 1113 (9th Cir. 2001).

15. *Department of Housing and Urban Development v. Rucker*, 535 U.S. 125 (2002).

16. California Department of Corrections, *Preventing Parolee Failure Program: An Evaluation* (Sacramento: California Department of Corrections, 1997), available at www.ncjrs.gov/App/publications/Abstract.aspx?id=180542.

17. Dennis Culhane et al., *The New York/New York Agreement Cost Study: The Impact of Supportive Housing on Services Use for Homeless Mentally Ill Individuals* (New York: Corporation for Supportive Housing, 2001), 4.

18. Human Rights Watch, *No Second Chance,* i.

19. Martha Nelson, Perry Dees, and Charlotte Allen, *The First Month Out: Post-Incarceration Experiences in New York City* (New York: Vera Institute of Justice, 1999).

20. Edward Rhine, William Smith, and Ronald Jackson, *Paroling Authorities: Recent History and Current Practice* (Laurel, MD: American Correctional Association, 1991).

21. Gene Johnson, "'Ban the Box' Movement Gains Steam," *Wave Newspapers*, New America Media, Aug. 15, 2006.

22. Legal Action Center, *After Prison: Roadblocks to Reentry, a Report on State Legal Barriers Facing People with Criminal Records* (New York: Legal Action Center, 2004), 10.

23. Ibid.

24. Harry Holzer, Steven Raphael, and Michael Stoll, "Will Employers Hire Ex-Offenders? Employer Preferences, Background Checks and Their Determinants," in *The Impact of Incarceration on Families and Communities*, ed. Mary Pattillo, David Weiman, and Bruce Western (New York: Russell Sage Foundation, 2002).

25. Employers Group Research Services, "Employment of Ex-Offenders: A Survey of Employers' Policies and Practices," San Francisco: SF Works, Apr. 12, 2002.

26. Jeremy Travis, Amy Solomon, and Michelle Waul, *From Prison to Home: The Dimensions and Consequences of Prisoner Reentry* (Washington, DC: Urban Institute, 2001); and Amy Hirsch et al., *Every Door Closed: Barriers Facing Parents with Criminal Records* (Washington, DC: Center for Law and Social Policy and Community Legal Services, 2002).

27. Keith Ihlanfeldt and David Sjoquist, "The Spatial Mismatch Hypothesis: A Review of Recent Studies and Their Implications for Welfare Reform," *Housing Policy Debate* 9, no. 4 (1998): 849; and Michael Stoll, Harry Holzer, and Keith Ihlanfeldt, "Within Cities and Suburbs: Employment Decentralization, Neighborhood Composition, and Employment Opportunities for White and Minority Workers," *Journal of Policy Analysis and Management*, Spring 2000.

28. Harry Holzer et al., "Employer Demand for Ex-Offenders: Recent Evidence from Los Angeles," Mar. 2003, unpublished manuscript.

29. Wilson, *When Work Disappears*, 40.

30. Andrew Jacobs, "Crime-Ridden Newark Tries Getting Jobs for Ex-Convicts, but finds Success Elusive," *New York Times*, Apr. 27, 2008.

31. Wilson, *When Work Disappears*, 41.

32. Harry Holzer and Robert LaLonde, "Job Stability and Job Change Among Young Unskilled Workers," in *Finding Jobs: Work and Welfare Reform*, ed. David Card and Rebecca Blank (New York: Russell Sage Foundation, 2000); see also Joleen Kirshenman and Kathryn Neckerman, "We'd Love to Hire Them But . . ." in *The Urban Underclass*, ed. Christopher Jencks and Paul Peterson (Washington, DC: Brookings Institution Press, 1991).

33. Ibid., 942.

34. Ibid., 962.

35. Bruce Western, *Punishment and Inequality in America* (New York: Russell Sage Foundation, 2006), 90.

36. Ibid., 91.

37. See Devah Pager, *Marked: Race, Crime and Finding Work in an Era of Mass Incarceration* (University of Chicago Press, 2007), 157; Steven Raphael, "Should Criminal History Records Be Universally Available?" (reaction essay) in Greg Pogarsky, "Criminal Records, Employment and Recidivism," *Criminology & Public Policy* 5, no. 3 (Aug. 2006): 479–521; and Shawn Bushway, "Labor Market Effects of Permitting Employer Access to Criminal History Records," *Journal of Contemporary Criminal Justice* 20 (2004): 276–91.

38. Michelle Natividad Rodriguez and Maurice Emsellem, *65 Million "Need Not Apply": The Case for Reforming Criminal Background Checks for Employment* (New York: National Employment Law Project, 2011), www.nelp.org/page/-/65_Million_Need_Not_Apply.pdf?nocdn=1.

39. Rebekah Diller, *The Hidden Costs of Florida's Criminal Justice Fees* (New York: Brennan Center for Justice, 2010).

40. Kirsten Livingston, "Making the Bad Guy Pay: Growing Use of Cost Shifting as Economic Sanction," in *Prison Profiteers: Who Makes Money from Mass Incarceration*, ed. Tara Herivel and Paul Wright (New York: The New Press, 2007), 61.

41. Ibid., 69, citing Ohio Rev. Code Ann. Sec. 2951.021 and Ohio Rev. Code Sec. 2951.021.

42. Alicia Bannon, Mitali Nagrecha, and Rebekah Diller, *Criminal Justice Debt: A Barrier to Reentry* (New York: Brennan Center for Justice, 2010).

43. Rachel L. McLean and Michael D. Thompson, *Repaying Debts* (New York: Council of State Governments Justice Center, 2007).

44. "Out of Prison and Deep in Debt," editorial, *New York Times*, Oct. 6, 2007.

45. Bannon, Nagrecha, and Diller, *Criminal Justice Debt*.

46. Ibid.

47. Livingston, "Making the Bad Guy Pay," 55.

48. Ibid.

49. See Legal Action Center, "Opting Out of Federal Ban on Food Stamps and TANF: Summary of State Laws," www.lac.org/toolkits/TANF/TANF.htm.

50. Ryan S. King, *Felony Disenfranchisement Laws in the United States* (Washington, DC: Sentencing Project, 2008).

51. Laleh Ispahani, *Out of Step with the World: An Analysis of Felony Disenfranchisement in the U.S. and Other Democracies* (New York: American Civil Liberties Union, 2006), 4.

52. Ibid.

53. Ibid., 6.

54. See Laleh Ispahani and Nick Williams, *Purged!* (New York: American Civil Liberties Union, 2004); and Alec Ewald, *A Crazy Quilt of Tiny Pieces: State and Local Administration of American Criminal Disenfranchisement Law* (Washington, DC: Sentencing Project, 2005).

55. Sasha Abramsky, *Conned: How Millions Went to Prison, Lost the Vote, and Helped Send George W. Bush to the White House* (New York: The New Press, 2006), 224.

56. Ibid.

57. Gail Russell Chaddock, "U.S. Notches World's Highest Incarceration Rate," *Christian Science Monitor*, Aug. 18, 2003.

58. Abramsky, *Conned*, 207.

59. Ibid., 207–8.

60. Ibid.

61. Christopher Uggen and Jeff Manza, "Democratic Contraction? Political Consequences of Felon Disenfranchisement in the United States," *American Sociological Review* 67 (2002): 777.

62. Manza and Uggen, *Locked Out*, 137.

63. Abramsky, *Conned*, 206–7.

64. See Kathryn Russell-Brown, *The Color of Crime: Racial Hoaxes, White Fear, Black Protectionism, Police Harassment, and Other Macroaggressions* (New York: New York University Press, 1998), coining the term *criminalblackman*.

65. Manza and Uggen, *Locked Out*, 154.

66. Ibid., 152.

67. Human Rights Watch, *No Second Chance*, 79.

68. Willie Thompson, interviewed by Guylando A.M. Moreno, Mar. 2008, Cincinnati, OH.

69. Abramsky, *Conned*, 140.

70. Donald Braman, *Doing Time on the Outside: Incarceration and Family Life in Urban America* (Ann Arbor: University of Michigan Press, 2004), 219.

71. Ibid., 3, citing data from D.C. Department of Corrections (2000).

72. See Todd R. Clear, *Imprisoning Communities: How Mass Incarceration Makes Disadvantaged Neighborhoods Worse* (New York: Oxford University Press, 2007), 121–48.

73. See, e.g., Steve Liss, *No Place for Children: Voices from Juvenile Detention* (Austin: University of Texas Press, 2005). Stories include youth describing the verbal abuse they receive from their parents.

74. Braman, *Doing Time on the Outside*, 171.

75. Ibid., 219, fn. 2.

76. See Deborah A. Prentice and Dale T. Miller, "Pluralistic Ignorance and Alcohol Use on Campus: Some Consequences of Misperceiving the Social Norm," *Journal of Personality and Social Psychology* 64, no. 2 (1993): 243–56.

77. Braman, *Doing Time on the Outside*, 216.

78. Cathy Cohen, *The Boundaries of Blackness: AIDS and the Breakdown of Black Politics* (Chicago: University of Chicago Press, 1999), 287.

79. Braman, *Doing Time on the Outside*, 174.

80. Ibid., 184.

81. Ibid., 185.

82. Ibid., 186.

83. Ibid.

84. Gerald Sider, "Against Experience: The Struggles for History, Tradition, and Hope Among a Native American People," in *Between History and Histories*, ed. Gerald Sider and Gavin Smith (Toronto: University of Toronto Press, 1997), 74–75.

85. Braman, *Doing Time on the Outside*, 220.

86. Ibid.

87. James Thomas Sears, *Growing Up Gay in the South: Race, Gender, and Journeys of the Spirit* (New York: Routledge, 1991), 257.

88. Victor M. Rios, "The Hyper-Criminalization of Black and Latino Male Youth in the Era of Mass Incarceration," unpublished manuscript on file with author.

89. Robert Toll, *Blacking Up: The Minstrel Show in Nineteenth-Century America* (New York: Oxford University Press, 1974), 227.

90. Ibid., 258.

91. Mel Watkins, *On the Real Side: Laughing, Lying and Signifying: The Underground Tradition of African-American Humor That Transformed American Culture, from Slavery to Richard Pryor* (New York: Simon & Schuster, 1994), 124–29.

92. Ibid.; see also Toll, *Blacking Up*, 226.

5. The New Jim Crow

1. Michael Eric Dyson, "Obama's Rebuke of Absentee Black Fathers," *Time*, June 19, 2008.

2. Sam Roberts, "51% of Women Now Living with a Spouse, *New York Times*, Jan. 16, 2007.

3. See Jonathan Tilove, "Where Have All the Men Gone? Black Gender Gap Is Widening," *Seattle Times*, May 5, 2005; and Jonathan Tilove, "Where Have All the Black Men Gone?" *Star-Ledger* (Newark), May 8, 2005.

4. Ibid.

5. Cf. Salim Muwakkil, "Black Men: Missing," *In These Times*, June 16, 2005.

6. G. Garvin, "Where Have the Black Men Gone?" *Ebony*, Dec. 2006.

7. One in eleven black adults was under correctional supervision at year end 2007, or approximately 2.4 million people. See Pew Center on the States, *One in 31: The Long Reach of American Corrections* (Washington, DC: Pew Charitable Trusts, 2009). According to the 1850 Census, approximately 1.7 million adults (ages 15 and older) were slaves.

8. See Andrew J. Cherlin, *Marriage, Divorce, Remarriage*, rev. ed. (Cambridge, MA: Harvard University Press, 1992), 110.

9. See Glenn C. Loury, *Race, Incarceration, and American Values* (Cambridge, MA: MIT Press, 2008), commentary by Pam Karlan.

10. Stanley Cohen, *States of Denial: Knowing About Atrocities and Suffering* (Cambridge, UK: Polity, 2001), 4–5.

11. Iris Marilyn Young, *Inclusion and Democracy* (New York: Oxford University Press, 2000), 92–99.

12. Marilyn Frye, "Oppression," in *The Politics of Reality* (Trumansburg, NY: Crossing Press, 1983).

13. See Marc Mauer and Meda Chesney-Lind, eds., *Invisible Punishment: The Collateral Consequences of Mass Imprisonment* (New York: The New Press, 2002); and Jeremy Travis, *But They All Come Back: Facing the Challenges of Prisoner Reentry* (Washington, DC: Urban Institute Press, 2005).

14. Negley K. Teeters and John D. Shearer, *The Prison at Philadelphia, Cherry Hill: The Separate System of Prison Discipline, 1829–1913* (New York: Columbia University Press, 1957), 84.

15. See David Musto, *The American Disease: Origins of Narcotics Control*, 3rd ed. (New York: Oxford University Press, 1999), 4, 7, 43–44, 219–20, describing the role of racial bias in earlier drug wars; and Doris Marie Provine, *Unequal Under Law: Race in the War on Drugs* (Chicago: University of Chicago Press, 2007), 37–90, describing racial bias in alcohol prohibition, as well as other drug wars.

16. Mary Pattillo, David F. Weiman, and Bruce Western, *Imprisoning America: The Social Effect of Mass Incarceration* (New York: Russell Sage Foundation, 2004), 2.

17. Paul Street, *The Vicious Circle: Race, Prison, Jobs, and Community in Chicago, Illinois, and the Nation* (Chicago: Chicago Urban League, Department of Research and Planning, 2002).

18. Street, *Vicious Circle*, 3.

19. Alden Loury, "Black Offenders Face Stiffest Drug Sentences," *Chicago Reporter*, Sept. 12, 2007.

20. Ibid.

21. Street, *Vicious Circle*, 15.

22. Donald G. Lubin et al., *Chicago Metropolis 2020: 2006 Crime and Justice Index*, (Washington, DC: Pew Center on the States, 2006), 5, www.pewcenteronthestates .org/report_detail.aspx?id=33022.

23. Report of the Illinois Disproportionate Justice Impact Study Commission, Dec. 2010, available at www.centerforhealthandjustice.org/DJIS_ExecSumm _FINAL.pdf.

24. Lubin et al., *Chicago Metropolis 2020*, 37.

25. Ibid., 35.

26. Ibid., 3; see also Bruce Western, *Punishment and Inequality in America* (New York: Russell Sage Foundation, 2006), 12.

27. Street, *Vicious Circle*, 3.

28. Ibid.

29. Ibid.

30. See chapter 1, p. 61, which describes the view that President Ronald Reagan's appeal derived primarily from the "emotional distress of those who fear or resent the Negro, and who expect Reagan somehow to keep him 'in his place' or at least echo their own anger and frustration."

31. For an excellent discussion of the history of felon disenfranchisement laws, as well as their modern day impact, see Jeff Manza and Christopher Uggen, *Locked Out: Felon Disenfranchisement and American Democracy* (New York: Oxford University Press, 2006).

32. *Cotton v. Fordice*, 157 F.3d 388, 391 (5th Cir. 1998); see also Martine J. Price, Note and Comment: Addressing Ex-Felon Disenfranchisement: Legislation v. Litigation, *Brooklyn Journal of Law and Policy* 11 (2002): 369, 382–83.

33. See Jamie Fellner and Marc Mauer, *Losing the Vote: The Impact of Felony Disenfranchisement Laws in the United States* (Washington, DC: Sentencing Project, 1998).

34. Loury, *Race, Incarceration, and American Values*, 48

35. See Eric Lotke and Peter Wagner, "Prisoners of the Census: Electoral and Financial Consequences of Counting Prisoners Where They Go, Not Where They Come From," *Pace Law Review* 24 (2004): 587, available at www.prisonpolicy .org/pace.pdf.

36. See *Batson v. Kentucky* 476 U.S. 79 (1986), discussed in chapter 3, p. 146.

37. See *Purkett v. Elm*, 514 U.S. 765 discussed in chapter 3, p. 150.

38. Brian Kalt, "The Exclusion of Felons from Jury Service," *American University Law Review* 53 (2003): 65.

39. See *Dred Scott v. Sandford*, 60 U.S. (How. 19) 393 (1857).

40. Travis, *But They All Come Back*, 132.

41. Peter Wagner, "Prisoners of the Census"; for more information, see www .prisonersofthecensus.org.

42. Travis, *But They All Come Back*, 281, citing James Lynch and William Sabol, *Prisoner Reentry in Perspective*, Crime Policy Report, vol. 3 (Washington, DC: Urban Institute, 2001).

43. Dina R. Rose, Todd R. Clear, and Judith A. Ryder, *Drugs, Incarcerations, and Neighborhood Life: The Impact of Reintegrating Offenders into the Community* (Washington, DC: U.S. Department of Justice, National Institute of Justice, 2002).

44. Sudhir Alladi Venkatesh, *The Robert Taylor Homes Relocation Study* (New York: Center for Urban Research and Policy, Columbia University, 2002).

45. Street, *Vicious Circle*, 16.

46. Ibid., 17.

47. Keynote address by Paula Wolff at Annual Luncheon for Appleseed Fund for Justice and Chicago Council of Lawyers, Oct. 7, 2008, www.chicagometropolis2020 .org/10_25.htm.

48. Katherine Beckett and Theodore Sasson, *The Politics of Injustice: Crime and Punishment in America* (Thousand Oaks, CA: Sage Publications, 2004), 36, citing Mercer Sullivan, *Getting Paid: Youth Crime and Work in the Inner City* (New York: Cornell University Press, 1989).

49. Ibid.

50. Loïc Wacquant, "The New 'Peculiar Institution': On the Prison as Surrogate Ghetto," *Theoretical Criminology* 4, no. 3 (2000): 377–89.

51. See, e.g., Douglas Massey and Nancy Denton, *American Apartheid: Segregation and the Making of the Underclass* (Cambridge, MA: Harvard University Press, 1993).

52. Whites are far more likely than African Americans to complete college, and college graduates are more likely to have tried illicit drugs in their lifetime when compared to adults who have not completed high school. See U.S. Department of Health and Human Services, Substance Abuse and Mental Health Services Administration, *Findings from the 2000 National Household Survey on Drug Abuse* (Rockville, MD: 2001). Adults who have not completed high school are disproportionately African American.

53. Devah Pager, *Marked: Race, Crime, and Finding Work in an Era of Mass Incarceration* (Chicago: University of Chicago Press, 2007), 90–91, 146–47.

54. John Edgar Wideman, "Doing Time, Marking Race," *The Nation*, Oct. 30, 1995.

55. See Julia Cass and Connie Curry, *America's Cradle to Prison Pipeline* (New York: Children's Defense Fund, 2007).

56. James Forman Jr., "Children, Cops and Citizenship: Why Conservatives Should Oppose Racial Profiling," in *Invisible Punishment*, ed. Mauer and Lind, 159.

57. Wideman, "Doing Time, Marking Race."

58. See discussion of stigma in chapter 4.

59. See, e.g., Charles Ogletree and Austin Sarat, eds., *From Lynch Mobs to the Killing State: Race and the Death Penalty in America* (New York: New York University

Press, 2006); and Joy James, *The New Abolitionists: (Neo) Slave Narratives and Contemporary Prison Writings* (New York: State University of New York Press, 2005).

60. See discussion of polling data in chapter 3.

61. Glenn C. Loury, *The Anatomy of Racial Inequality* (Cambridge, MA: Harvard University Press, 2003), 82.

62. Ibid., 82–83.

63. Craig Reinarman, "The Crack Attack: America's Latest Drug Scare, 1986–1992" in *Images of Issues: Typifying Contemporary Social Problems* (New York: Aldine De Gruyter, 1995), 162.

64. Marc Mauer, *Race to Incarcerate*, rev. ed. (New York: The New Press, 2006), 150.

65. Ibid., 151

66. Ibid.

67. See Musto, *American Disease*, 4, 7, 43–44, 219–20; and Doris Marie Provine, *Unequal Under Law*, 37–90

68. Eric Schlosser, "Reefer Madness," *Atlantic Monthly*, Aug. 1994, 49.

69. Mauer, *Race to Incarcerate*, 149.

70. The most compelling version of this argument has been made by Randall Kennedy in *Race, Crime and the Law* (New York: Vintage Books, 1997).

71. Tracy Meares, "Charting Race and Class Differences in Attitudes Toward Drug Legalization and Law Enforcement: Lessons for Federal Criminal Law," *Buffalo Criminal Law Review* 1 (1997). 137, Stephen Bennett and Alfred Tuchfarber, "The Social Structural Sources of Cleavage on Law and Order Policies," *American Journal of Political Science* 19 (1975): 419–38; and Sandra Browning and Ligun Cao, "The Impact of Race on Criminal Justice Ideology," *Justice Quarterly* 9 (Dec. 1992): 685–99.

72. Meares, "Charting Race and Class Differences," 157.

73. Glenn Loury, "Listen to the Black Community," *Public Interest*, Sept. 22, 1994, 35.

74. Meares, "Charting Race and Class Differences," 160–61.

75. See William Julius Wilson, *When Work Disappears: The World of the New Urban Poor* (New York: Vintage Books, 1997), 22, citing Delbert Elliott study.

76. W.E.B. Du Bois, *The Souls of Black Folk* (1903; New York: Bantam, 1989), TK.

77. See Evelyn Brooks Higginbotham, *Righteous Discontent: The Women's Movement in the Black Baptist Church, 1880–1920* (Cambridge, MA: Harvard University Press, 1994), 188.

78. Ibid. See also Karen Ferguson, *Black Politics in New Deal Atlanta* (Chapel Hill: University of North Carolina Press, 2002), 5–11; and Randall Kennedy, *Race, Crime and the Law* (New York: Vintage Books, 1997), 17.

79. Ferguson, *Black Politics in New Deal Atlanta*, 5.

80. Ibid., 192.

81. Ibid.

82. Ibid., 9.

83. Ibid., 13.

84. Glenn C. Loury, *Race, Incarceration and American Values* (Cambridge, MA: MIT Press, 2008), 81, commentary by Tommie Shelby.

85. See Troy Duster, "Pattern, Purpose, and Race in the Drug War: The Crisis of Credibility in Criminal Justice," in *Crack in America: Demon Drugs and Social Justice*, ed. Craig Reinarman and Harry G. Levine (Berkeley: University of California Press, 1997).

86. Loïc Wacquant, "From Slavery to Mass Incarceration: Rethinking the Race Question," *New Left Review*, Jan.–Feb. 2002, 53.

87. john a. powell, Executive Director of the Kirwan Institute for the Study of Race and Ethnicity, personal communication, Jan. 2007.

6. The Fire This Time

1. Salim Muwakkil, "Jena and the Post–Civil Rights Fallacy," *In These Times*, Oct. 16, 2007.

2. *Democracy Now*, "Rev. Al Sharpton: Jena Marks 'Beginning of a 21st Century Rights Movement,'" Sept. 21, 2007, www.democracynow.org/shows/2007/9/21.

3. See Derrick Bell, "Serving Two Masters: Integration Ideals and Client Interests in School Desegregation Litigation," *Yale Law Journal* 85 (1976): 470.

4. Lani Guinier, *Lift Every Voice* (New York: Simon & Schuster, 1998), 220–21.

5. Ibid., 222.

6. See Michael Klarman, "The Racial Origins of Modern Criminal Procedure," *Michigan Law Review* 99 (2000): 48, 86; Dan Carter, *Scottsboro: A Tragedy of the American South*, 2d ed. (Baton Rouge: Louisiana State University Press, 1979), 52–53; and Mark Tushnet, *Making Civil Rights Law: Thurgood Marshall and the Supreme Court, 1936–1969* (New York: Oxford University Press, 1994), 28–29.

7. Jo Ann Gibson Robinson, *The Montgomery Bus Boycott and the Women Who Started It* (Knoxville: University of Tennessee Press, 1987), 43.

8. Martin Luther King Jr. and Claybourne Carson, *The Autobiography of Martin Luther King, Jr.* (New York: Grand Central, 2001), 44.

9. See Abby Rapoport, "The Work That Remains: A Forty-Year Update of the Kerner Commission Report," Economic Policy Institute, Nov. 19, 2008.

10. Bruce Western, *Punishment and Inequality in America* (New York: Russell Sage Foundation, 2006), 97.

11. Ibid., 90.

12. Ibid., 91.

13. In 1972, the total rate of incarceration (prison and jail) was approximately 160 per 100,000. Today, it is about 760 per 100,000. A reduction of 79 percent would be needed to get back to the 160 figure—itself a fairly high number when judged by international standards.

14. Marc Mauer, *Race to Incarcerate* (New York: The New Press, 1999), 11.

15. Christopher Sherman, "Cheney, Gonzales, Indicted Over Prisons," *Washington Times*, Nov. 19, 2008.

16. U.S. Securities and Exchange Commission, Corrections Corporation of America, Form 10K for the fiscal year ended Dec. 31, 2005.

17. Silja J.A. Talvi, "On the Inside with the American Correctional Association," in *Prison Profiteers: Who Makes Money from Mass Incarceration*, ed. Tara Herivel and Paul Wright (New York: The New Press, 2007).

18. Stephanie Chen, "Larger Inmate Population Is Boon to Private Prisons," *Wall Street Journal*, Nov. 28, 2008.

19. See generally Herivel and Wright, *Prison Profiteers*. For an excellent discussion of how surplus capital, labor, and land helped to birth the prison industry in rural America, see Ruth Wilson Gilmore, *Golden Gulag* (Berkeley: University of California Press, 2007).

20. For more information on racial impact statements, see Marc Mauer, "Racial Impact Statements as a Means of Reducing Unwarranted Sentencing Disparities," *Ohio State Journal of Criminal Law* 5 (2007): 19.

21. Guinier, *Lift Every Voice*, 223.

22. Michael Omi and Howard Winant, *Racial Formation in the United States from the 1960s to the 1990s* (New York: Routledge, 1994), 84–88.

23. Gerald Rosenberg, *The Hollow Hope: Can Courts Bring About Social Change?* (Chicago: University of Chicago Press, 1991), 52.

24. Michael Klarman, "*Brown*, Racial Change, and the Civil Rights Movement," *Virginia Law Review* 80 (1994): 7, 9.

25. See ibid., arguing that *Brown* was "merely a ripple" with only a "negligible effect" on the South and civil rights advocacy.

26. See David Garrow, "Hopelessly Hollow History: Revisionist Devaluing of *Brown v. Board of Education*," *Virginia Law Review* 80 (1994): 151, persuasively making the case that *Brown* was a major inspiration to civil rights activists and provoked a fierce white backlash.

27. Western, *Punishment and Inequality in America*, 5, 187; William Spelman, "The Limited Importance of Prison Expansion," in *The Crime Drop in America*, ed. Alfred Blumstein and Joel Wallman (New York: Cambridge University Press, 2000), 97–129; and Todd R. Clear, *Imprisoning Communities: How Mass Incarceration Makes Disadvantaged Neighborhoods Worse* (New York: Oxford University Press, 2007), 41–48.

28. See, e.g., Clear, *Imprisoning Communities*, 3.

29. See, e.g., Chris Smith, "On the Block," *American Prospect*, Jan.–Feb. 2011, 6–8.

30. Jeffrey Reiman makes a similar argument in *The Rich Get Richer and the Poor Get Prison*, 8th ed. (New York: Allyn & Bacon, 2006), although he mostly ignores the distinctive role of race in structuring the criminal justice system.

31. See "Study Finds Whites Anxious About Race," *Bryant Park Project*, National Public Radio, Dec. 3, 2007.

32. Fox Butterfield, "With Cash Tight, States Reassess Long Jail Terms," *New York Times*, Nov. 10, 2003.

33. Marc Mauer, "State Sentencing Reforms: Is the 'Get Tough' Era Coming to a Close?" *Federal Sentencing Reporter* 15, no. 1 (Oct. 2002).

34. Abby Goodnough, "Relaxing Marijuana Law Has Some Nervous," *New York Times*, Dec. 18, 2008, noting that eleven states have decriminalized first-time possession of marijuana.

35. For example, the ballot argument drafted by civil rights groups opposed to Proposition 54, a 2003 California ballot initiative that would have banned the collection of racial data by the state government, read: "We all want a colorblind society. But we won't get there by banning information."

36. Martin Luther King Jr., *Strength to Love* (Philadelphia: Fortress Press, 1963), 45–48.

37. Ibid., 31–32.

38. See Mary Frances Berry, "Vindicating Martin Luther King, Jr.: The Road to a Color-Blind Society," *Journal of Negro History* 81, no. 1–4 (Winter–Autumn 1996): 137, 140.

39. Stephen Steinberg, *Turning Back: The Retreat from Racial Justice in American Thought and Policy* (Boston: Beacon Press, 1995), 167.

40. Fred L. Pincus, *Reverse Discrimination: Dismantling the Myth* (Boulder, CO: Lynne Rienner, 2003).

41. Eisenhower Foundation, *What Together We Can Do: A Forty Year Update of the National Advisory Commission on Civil Disorder: Executive Summary, Preliminary Findings and Recommendations* (Washington, DC: Eisenhower Foundation, 2008).

42. For an analysis of the impact of incarceration on unemployment, poverty, and education, see Western, *Punishment and Inequality in America*, 83–131.

43. Jesse Rothstein and Albert Yoon, "Affirmative Action in Law School Admissions: What Do Racial Preferences Do?" National Bureau of Economic Research, Cambridge, MA, Aug. 2008, www.nber.org/papers/w14276.

44. Steinberg, *Turning Back*, 195–96.

45. Martin Luther King Jr., "A Testament of Hope," in *A Testament of Hope: The Essential Writings and Speeches of Martin Luther King, Jr.* (New York: HarperCollins, 1986), 321.

46. Ibid., 315.

47. Lani Guinier and Gerald Torres, *The Miner's Canary: Enlisting Race, Resisting Power, Transforming Democracy* (Cambridge, MA: Harvard University Press, 2002), 114.

48. Ibid.

49. Sentencing Project, "2008 Leading Presidential Candidates' Platforms on Criminal Justice Policy," Mar. 24, 2008, www.sentencingproject.org/doc/publications/publi

cations/Presidential%20Candidates%27%20Platforms%20-%20Spreadsheet%207%2018%2008.pdf.

50. Drew Harwell, "Obama's Drug Use Debated," CBS News, UWIRE.com, Feb. 12, 2008.

51. Obama promised to increase Byrne funds when running for president. See David Hunt, "Obama Fields Questions on Jacksonville Crime," *Florida-Times Union*, Sept. 22, 2008. Once elected, he made good on his promise, drastically increasing funding for the drug war. See "Federal Budget: Economic Stimulus Bill Stimulates Drug War, Too," *Drug War Chronicle*, no. 573 (Feb. 20, 2009); Michelle Alexander, "Obama's Drug War," *The Nation*, Dec. 9, 2010 (noting that the 2009 economic stimulus package included a twelvefold increase in financing for Byrne programs).

52. See Charles Blow, "Smoke and Horrors," *New York Times*, Oct. 22, 2010, www.nytimes.com/2010/10/23/opinion/23blow.html.

53. Ibid.

54. United States Government Accountability Office, Report to the Chairman, Committee on the Judiciary, House of Representatives, *Community Policing Grants: COPS Grants Were a Modest Contribution to Decline in Crime in 1990s*, GAO-06-104, Oct. 2005, www.gao.gov/new/items/d06104.pdf.

55. John L. Worrall and Tomislav V. Kovandzic, "COPS Grants and Crime Revisited," *Criminology* 45, no. 1 (Feb. 2007): 159–90.

56. Gary Fields, "White House Czar Calls for End of 'War on Drugs,'" *Wall Street Journal*, May 24, 2009; see also Office of National Drug Control Policy, *White House Drug Control Budget, FY2010 Funding Highlights* (May 2009).

57. Guinier and Torres, *Miner's Canary*, 118.

58. Ibid.

59. See Lani Guinier, "From Racial Liberalism to Racial Literacy: *Brown v. Board of Education* and the Interest-Divergence Dilemma," *Journal of American History* 92 (June 2004): 103, citing C. Arnold Anderson, "Social Class Differentials in the Schooling of Youth Within the Regions and Community-Size Groups of the United States," *Social Forces* 25 (May 1947): 440, 436; and C. Arnold Anderson, "Inequalities in Schooling in the South," *American Journal of Sociology* 60 (May 1955): 549, 553, 557.

60. W.E.B. Du Bois, *Black Reconstruction in America, 1860–1880* (New York: Free Press, 1935), 700.

61. Guinier, "Racial Liberalism," 102. See also Beth Roy, *Bitters in the Honey: Tales of Hope and Disappointment Across Divides of Race and Time* (Fayetteville: University of Arkansas Press, 1999), 318; and Pete Daniel, *Lost Revolutions: The South in the 1950s* (Chapel Hill: University of North Carolina Press, 2000), 270.

62. See Derrick Bell, "*Brown v. Board of Education* and the Interest-Convergence Dilemma," *Harvard Law Review* 93 (1980): 518, 525; David J. Armor, *Forced Justice: School Desegregation and the Law* (New York: Oxford University Press, 1996), 174–93, 206–7; and Robert J. Norrell, "Labor at the Ballot Box: Alabama Politics from the

New Deal to the Dixiecrat Movement," *Journal of Southern History* 57 (May 1991): 201, 227, 233, 234.

63. W.E.B. Du Bois, *The Souls of Black Folk* (1903; New York: Bantam, 1989).

64. For a more detailed exploration of Martin Luther King Jr.'s journey from civil rights to human rights, see Thomas F. Jackson, *From Civil Rights to Human Rights: Martin Luther King, Jr. and the Struggle for Economic Justice* (Philadelphia: University of Pennsylvania Press, 2006); and Stewart Burns, *To the Mountaintop: Martin Luther King Jr.'s Sacred Mission to Save America* (New York: Harper One, 2005).

65. For background on the nature, structure, and history of human rights, see Cynthia Soohoo et al., eds., *Bringing Human Rights Home*, vol. 1 (New York: Praeger, 2007).

66. Stewart Burns, "America, You Must Be Born Again," *Sojourners* 33, no. 1, (Jan. 2004): 14.

67. James Baldwin, *The Fire Next Time* (New York: Vintage, 1962, 1993), 5–10.

Index